LIBERALISM ANCIENT AND MODERN

LIBERALISM ANCIENT AND MODERN

Leo Strauss

BASIC BOOKS, INC., PUBLISHERS
New York / London

© 1968 by Leo Strauss
Library of Congress Catalog Card Number: 68–54139
Manufactured in the United States of America
Designed by Loretta Li

Preface

Liberalism is understood here and now in contradistinction to conservativism. This distinction is sufficient for most present practical purposes. To admit this is tantamount to admitting that the distinction is not free from theoretical difficulties which need not be barren of practical consequences. Of one difficulty one can dispose easily. Most people are liberal in some respects and conservative in others; a very moderate liberal may not be distinguishable from a very moderate conservative. This very observation implies, indeed, the existence at least of the liberal and the conservative as ideal types. Yet in this case, at any rate, the ideal types are quite real. Here and now a man who is in favor of the war on poverty and opposed to the war in Vietnam is generally regarded as doubtlessly a liberal, and a man who is in favor of the war in Vietnam and opposed to the war on poverty is generally regarded as doubtlessly a conservative.

A somewhat more serious difficulty comes to sight once one considers the fact that here and now liberalism and conservativism have a common basis; for both are based here and now on liberal democracy, and therefore both are antagonistic to Communism. Hence the opposition does not seem to be fundamental. Still, they differ profoundly in their opposition to Communism. At first glance liberalism seems to agree with Communism as regards the ultimate goal, while it radically disagrees with it as regards the way to the goal. The goal may be said to be the universal and classless society or, to use the correction proposed by Kojève, the universal and homogeneous state of which every adult human being is a full member; more precisely, the necessary and sufficient title to full membership is supplied by one's being an adult nonmoronic human being for all those times when he is not locked up in an insane asylum or a penitentiary. The way toward that goal, according to liberalism in contradistinction to Communism, is preferably democratic or peaceful, surely not war, that is, foreign war; for revolutions backed by the sympathy, or at least the interests, of the majority of the people concerned are not necessarily rejected by liberals. There remains, however, one important difference between liberalism and Communism regarding the goal itself. Liberals regard as sacred the right of everyone, however humble, odd, or inarticulate, to criticize the government, including the man at the top.

Someone might say that many liberals are much too pragmatic to aim at the universal and homogeneous state: they would be fully satisfied with a federation of all now existing or soon emerging states, with a truly universal and greatly strengthened United Nations organization—an organization that would include Communist China, the Federal Republic of Germany, and Communist East Germany, although not necessarily Nationalist China. Still, this would mean that liberals aim at the greatest possible approximation to the universal and homogeneous state or that they are guided by the ideal of the universal and homogeneous state. Some of them will object to the term "ideal" on the ground that the universal and homogeneous state (or the greatest possible approximation to it) is a requirement of hardheaded politics: that state has been rendered necessary by economic and technological progress, which includes the necessity of making thermonuclear war impossible for all the future, and by ever increasing wealth of the advanced countries which are compelled by sheer self-interest to develop the underdeveloped countries. As regards the still existing tension between the liberal-democratic and the Communist countries, liberals believe that this tension will be relaxed and will eventually disappear as a consequence of the ever increasing welfarism of the former and the ever increasing liberalism, due to the overwhelming demand for consumer goods of all kinds, of the latter.

Conservatives regard the universal and homogeneous state as either undesirable, though possible, or as both undesirable and impossible. They do not deny the necessity or desirability of larger political units than what one may call the typical nation-state. For good or ill, they can indeed no longer be imperialists. But there is no reason whatever why they should be opposed to a United Free Europe, for instance. Yet they are likely to understand such units differently from the liberals. An outstanding European conservative has spoken of *l'Europe des patries*. Conservatives look with greater sympathy than liberals on the particular or particularist and the heterogeneous; at least they are more willing than liberals to respect and perpetuate a more fundamental diversity than the one ordinarily respected or taken for granted by liberals and even by Communists, that is, the diversity regarding language, folk songs, pottery, and the like. Inasmuch as the universalism in politics is founded on the universalism proceeding from reason, conservativism is frequently characterized by distrust of reason or by trust in tradition which as such is necessarily this or that tradition and hence particular. Conservativism is therefore exposed to criticism that is guided by the notion of the unity of truth. Liberals, on the other hand, especially those who know that their aspirations have their roots in the Western tradition, are not sufficiently concerned with the fact that that tradition is ever more being eroded by the very changes in the direction of One World which they demand or applaud.

We remain closer to the surface by saying that the conservatives' distrust of the universal and homogeneous state is rooted in their distrust of change, in what is polemically called their "stand-patism," whereas liberals are more inclined than conservatives to be sanguine regarding change. Liberals are inclined to believe that on the whole change is change for the better, or progress. As a matter of fact, liberals frequently call themselves progressives. Progressivism is indeed a better term than liberalism for the opposite to conservativism. For if conservativism is, as its name indicates, aversion to change or distrust of change, its opposite should be identified with the opposite posture toward change, and not with something substantive like liberty or liberality.

The difficulty of defining the difference between liberalism and conservativism with the necessary universality is particularly great in the United States, since this country came into being through a revolution, a violent change or break with the past. One of the most conservative groups here calls itself Daughters of the American Revolution. The opposition between conservativism and liberalism had a clear meaning at the time at which and in the places in which it arose in these terms. Then and there the conservatives stood for "throne and altar," and the liberals stood for popular sovereignty and the strictly nonpublic (private) character of religion. Yet conservativism in this sense is no longer politically important. The conservativism of our age is identical with what originally was liberalism, more or less modified by changes in the direction of present-day liberalism. One could go further and say that much of what goes now by the name of conservativism has in the last analysis a common root with present-day liberalism and even with Communism. That this is the case would appear most clearly if one were to go back to the origin of modernity, to the break with the premodern tradition that took place in the seventeenth century, or to the quarrel between the ancients and the moderns.

We are reminded of that quarrel immediately by the fact that the term "liberal" is still used in its premodern sense, especially in the expression "liberal education." Liberal education is not the opposite of conservative education, but of illiberal education. To be liberal in the original sense means to practice the virtue of liberality. If it is true that all virtues in their perfection are inseparable from one another, the genuinely liberal man is identical with the genuinely virtuous man. According to the now prevailing usage, however, to be liberal means not to be conservative. Hence it is no longer assumed that being liberal is the same as being virtuous or even that being liberal has anything to do with being virtuous. Being liberal in the original sense is so little incompatible with being conservative that generally speaking it goes together with a conservative posture.

Premodern political philosophy, and in particular classical political philosophy, is liberal in the original sense of the term. It cannot be simply conservative since it is guided by the awareness that all man seek by nature, not the ancestral or traditional, but the good. On the other hand, classical political philosophy opposes to the universal and homogeneous state a substantive principle. It asserts that the society natural to man is the city, that is, a closed society that can well be taken in in one view or that corresponds to man's natural (macroscopic, not microscopic or telescopic) power of perception. Less literally and more importantly, it asserts that every political society that ever has been or ever will be rests on a particular fundamental opinion which cannot be replaced by knowledge and hence is of necessity a particular or particularist society. This state of things imposes duties on the philosopher's public speech or writing which would not be duties if a rational society were actual or emerging; it thus gives rise to a specific art of writing.

In earlier publications I have tried to lay bare the fundamental difference between classical and modern political philosophy. In the present volume I adumbrate that difference in the following manners. First I discuss liberal education and then the question as to the sense in which classical political philosophy can be called liberal. I next illustrate the liberalism of premodern thinkers by elucidating some examples of their art of writing. The most extensive discussion is devoted to Lucretius' poem. In that poem, not to say in Epicureanism generally, premodern thought seems to come closer to modern thought than anywhere else. No premodern writer seems to have been as deeply moved as Lucretius was by the thought that nothing lovable is eternal or sempiternal or deathless, or that the eternal is not lovable. Apart from this, it may suffice here to refer to Kant's presentation of Epicureanism as identical with the spirit of modern natural science prior to the subjection of that science to the critique of pure reason.

Every observer of present-day liberalism must be struck by the very frequent "personal union" of liberalism and value-free social science. One is thus led to wonder whether this union is merely accidental or whether there is not a necessary connection between value-free social science and liberalism, although liberalism is not, as goes without saying, value-free. At any rate, the critical study of present-day social science is no mean part of the critical study of liberalism. The essay entitled "An Epilogue" deals with this subject.

Not much familiarity with political life is needed in order to see that it is particularly difficult for a nonorthodox Jew to adopt a critical posture toward liberalism. Even Jews who are politically conservative can be observed to defer to contemporary Jewish "opinion leaders" who can in no sense be described as politically conservative. This state of things induces one to raise questions such as these: In what sense or to what extent is Judaism one of the roots of liberalism? Are Jews compelled by their heritage or their self-interest to be liberals? Is liberalism necessarily friendly to Jews and Judaism? Can the liberal state claim to have solved the Jewish problem? Can any state claim to have solved it? To these questions I address myself in the two statements that conclude this volume.

Leo Strauss

Claremont, California

Contents

LIBERALISM ANCIENT AND MODERN

1/ What Is Liberal Education?

Liberal education is education in culture or toward culture. The finished product of a liberal education is a cultured human being. "Culture" (*cultura*) means primarily agriculture: the cultivation of the soil and its products, taking care of the soil, improving the soil in accordance with its nature. "Culture" means derivatively and today chiefly the cultivation of the mind, the taking care and improving of the native faculties of the mind in accordance with the nature of the mind. Just as the soil needs cultivators of the soil, the mind needs teachers. But teachers are not as easy to come by as farmers. The teachers themselves are pupils and must be pupils. But there cannot be an infinite regress: ultimately there must be teachers who are not in turn pupils. Those teachers who are not in turn pupils are the great minds or, in order to avoid any ambiguity in a matter of such importance, the greatest minds. Such men are extremely rare. We are not likely to meet any of them in any classroom. We are not likely to meet any of them anywhere. It is a piece of good luck if there is a single one alive in one's time. For all practical purposes, pupils, of whatever degree of proficiency, have access to the teachers who are not in turn pupils, to the greatest minds, only through the great books. Liberal education will then consist in studying with the proper care the great books which the greatest minds have left behind—a study in which the more experienced pupils assist the less experienced pupils, including the beginners.

This is not an easy task, as would appear if we were to consider the formula which I have just mentioned. That formula requires a long commentary. Many lives have been spent and may still be spent in writing such commentaries. For instance, what is meant by the remark that the great books should be studied "with the proper care"? At present I mention only one difficulty which is obvious to everyone among you: the greatest minds do not all tell us the same things regarding the most important themes; the

3

community of the greatest minds is rent by discord and even by various kinds of discord. Whatever further consequences this may entail, it certainly entails the consequence that liberal education cannot be simply indoctrination. I mention yet another difficulty. "Liberal education is education in culture." In what culture? Our answer is: culture in the sense of the Western tradition. Yet Western culture is only one among many cultures. By limiting ourselves to Western culture, do we not condemn liberal education to a kind of parochialism, and is not parochialism incompatible with the liberalism, the generosity, the openmindedness, of liberal education? Our notion of liberal education does not seem to fit an age which is aware of the fact that there is not *the* culture of *the* human mind, but a variety of cultures. Obviously, culture if susceptible of being used in the plural is not quite the same thing as culture which is a *singulare tantum*, which can be used only in the singular. Culture is now no longer, as people say, an absolute, but has become relative. It is not easy to say what culture susceptible of being used in the plural means. As a consequence of this obscurity people have suggested, explicitly or implicitly, that culture is any pattern of conduct common to any human group. Hence we do not hesitate to speak of the culture of suburbia or of the cultures of juvenile gangs, both nondelinquent and delinquent. In other words, every human being outside of lunatic asylums is a cultured human being, for he participates in a culture. At the frontiers of research there arises the question as to whether there are not cultures also of inmates of lunatic asylums. If we contrast the present-day usage of "culture" with the original meaning, it is as if someone would say that the cultivation of a garden may consist of the garden's being littered with empty tin cans and whisky bottles and used papers of various descriptions thrown around the garden at random. Having arrived at this point, we realize that we have lost our way somehow. Let us then make a fresh start by raising the question: what can liberal education mean here and now?

Liberal education is literate education of a certain kind: some sort of education in letters or through letters. There is no need to make a case for literacy; every voter knows that modern democracy stands or falls by literacy. In order to understand this need we must reflect on modern democracy. What is modern democracy? It was once said that democracy is the regime that stands or falls by virtue: a democracy is a regime in which all or most adults are men of virtue, and since virtue seems to require wisdom, a regime in which all or most adults are virtuous and wise, or the society in which all or most adults have developed their reason to a high degree, or *the* rational society. Democracy, in a word, is meant to be an aristocracy which has broadened into a universal aristocracy. Prior to the emergence of modern democracy some doubts were felt whether democracy thus understood is possible. As one of the two greatest minds among the theorists of democracy put it, "If there were a people consisting of gods, it would rule itself democratically. A government of such perfection is not suitable for human beings." This still and small voice has by now become a high-powered loud-speaker.

There exists a whole science—the science which I among thousands profess to teach, political science—which so to speak has no other theme than the contrast between the original conception of democracy, or what one may call the ideal of democracy, and democracy as it is. According to an extreme view, which is the predominant view in the profession, the ideal of democracy was a sheer delusion, and the only thing which matters is the behavior of democracies and the behavior of men in democracies. Modern democracy, so far from being universal aristocracy, would be mass rule were it not for the fact that the mass cannot rule, but is ruled by elites, that is, groupings of men who for whatever reason are on top or have a fair chance to arrive at the top; one of the most important virtues required for the smooth working of democracy, as far as the mass is concerned, is said to be electoral apathy, viz., lack of public spirit; not indeed the salt of the earth, but the salt of modern democracy are those citizens who read nothing except the sports page and the comic section. Democracy is then not indeed mass rule, but mass culture. A mass culture is a culture which can be appropriated by the meanest capacities without any intellectual and moral effort whatsoever and at a very low monetary price. But even a mass culture and precisely a mass culture requires a constant supply of what are called new ideas, which are the products of what are called creative minds: even singing commercials lose their appeal if they are not varied from time to time. But democracy, even if it is only regarded as the hard shell which protects the soft mass culture, requires in the long run qualities of an entirely different kind: qualities of dedication, of concentration, of breadth, and of depth. Thus we understand most easily what liberal education means here and now. Liberal education is the counterpoison to mass culture, to the corroding effects of mass culture, to its inherent tendency to produce nothing but "specialists without spirit or vision and voluptuaries without heart." Liberal education is the ladder by which we try to ascend from mass democracy to democracy as originally meant. Liberal education is the necessary endeavor to found an aristocracy within democratic mass society. Liberal education reminds those members of a mass democracy who have ears to hear, of human greatness.

Someone might say that this notion of liberal education is merely political, that it dogmatically assumes the goodness of modern democracy. Can we not turn our backs on modern society? Can we not return to nature, to the life of preliterate tribes? Are we not crushed, nauseated, degraded by the mass of printed material, the graveyards of so many beautiful and majestic forests? It is not sufficient to say that this is mere romanticism, that we today cannot return to nature: may not coming generations, after a man-wrought cataclysm, be compelled to live in illiterate tribes? Will our thoughts concerning thermonuclear wars not be affected by such prospects? Certain it is that the horrors of mass culture (which include guided tours to integer nature) render intelligible the longing for a return to nature. An illiterate society at its best is a society ruled by age-old ancestral custom which it traces to original founders, gods, or sons of gods or pupils of gods; since there are no letters in such a society, the late heirs cannot be in direct contact with the original founders; they cannot know whether the fathers or grandfathers have not deviated from what the original founders meant, or have not defaced the divine message by merely human additions or subtractions; hence an illiterate society cannot consistently act on its principle that the best is the oldest. Only letters which have come down from the founders can make it possible for the founders to speak directly to the latest heirs. It is then self-contradictory to wish to return to illiteracy. We are compelled to live with books. But life is too short to live with any but the greatest books. In this respect as well as in some others, we do well to take as our model that one among the greatest minds who because of his common sense is *the* mediator between us and the greatest minds. Socrates never wrote a book, but he read books. Let me quote a statement of Socrates which says almost everything that has to be said on our subject, with the noble simplicity and quiet greatness of the ancients. "Just as others are pleased by a good horse or dog or bird, I myself am pleased to an even higher degree by good friends. . . . And the treasures of the wise men of old which they left behind by writing them in books, I unfold and go through them together with my friends, and if we see something good, we pick it out and regard it as a great gain if we thus become useful to one another." The man who reports this utterance adds the remark: "When I heard this, it seemed to me both that Socrates was blessed and that he was leading those listening to him toward perfect gentlemanship." This report is defective since it does not tell us anything as to what Socrates did regarding those passages in the books of the wise men of old of which he did not know whether they were good. From another report we learn that Euripides once gave Socrates the writing of Heraclitus and then asked him for his opinion about that writing. Socrates said: "What I have understood is great and noble; I believe this is also true of what I have not understood; but one surely needs for understanding that writing some special sort of a diver."

Education to perfect gentlemanship, to human excellence, liberal education consists in reminding oneself of human excellence, of human greatness. In what way, by what means does liberal education remind us of human greatness? We cannot think highly enough of what liberal education is meant to be. We have heard Plato's suggestion that education in the highest sense is philosophy. Philosophy is quest for wisdom or quest for knowledge regarding the most important, the highest, or the most comprehensive things; such knowledge, he suggested, is virtue and is happiness.

But wisdom is inaccessible to man, and hence virtue and happiness will always be imperfect. In spite of this, the philosopher, who, as such, is not simply wise, is declared to be the only true king; he is declared to possess all the excellences of which man's mind is capable, to the highest degree. From this we must draw the conclusion that we cannot be philosophers— that we cannot acquire the highest form of education. We must not be deceived by the fact that we meet many people who say that they are philosophers. For those people employ a loose expression which is perhaps necessitated by administrative convenience. Often they mean merely that they are members of philosophy departments. And it is as absurd to expect members of philosophy departments to be philosophers as it is to expect members of art departments to be artists. We cannot be philosophers, but we can love philosophy; we can try to philosophize. This philosophizing consists at any rate primarily and in a way chiefly in listening to the conversation between the great philosophers or, more generally and more cautiously, between the greatest minds, and therefore in studying the great books. The greatest minds to whom we ought to listen are by no means exclusively the greatest minds of the West. It is merely an unfortunate necessity which prevents us from listening to the greatest minds of India and of China: we do not understand their languages, and we cannot learn all languages.

To repeat: liberal education consists in listening to the conversation among the greatest minds. But here we are confronted with the overwhelming difficulty that this conversation does not take place without our help—that in fact we must bring about that conversation. The greatest minds utter monologues. We must transform their monologues into a dialogue, their "side by side" into a "together." The greatest minds utter monologues even when they write dialogues. When we look at the Platonic dialogues, we observe that there is never a dialogue among minds of the highest order: all Platonic dialogues are dialogues between a superior man and men inferior to him. Plato apparently felt that one could not write a dialogue between two men of the highest order. We must then do something which the greatest minds were unable to do. Let us face this difficulty—a difficulty so great that it seems to condemn liberal education as an absurdity. Since the greatest minds contradict one another regarding the most important matters, they compel us to judge of their monologues; we cannot take on trust what any one of them says. On the other hand, we cannot but notice that we are not competent to be judges.

This state of things is concealed from us by a number of facile delusions. We somehow believe that our point of view is superior, higher than those of the greatest minds—either because our point of view is that of our time, and our time, being later than the time of the greatest minds, can be presumed to be superior to their times; or else because we believe that each of the greatest minds was right from his point of view but not, as he claims, simply right: we know that there cannot be *the* simply true substantive view, but only a simply true formal view; that formal view consists in the insight that every comprehensive view is relative to a specific perspective, or that all comprehensive views are mutually exclusive and none can be simply true. The facile delusions which conceal from us our true situation all amount to this: that we are, or can be, wiser than the wisest men of the past. We are thus induced to play the part, not of attentive and docile listeners, but of impresarios or lion-tamers. Yet we must face our awesome situation, created by the necessity that we try to be more than attentive and docile listeners, namely, judges, and yet we are not competent to be judges. As it seems to me, the cause of this situation is that we have lost all simply authoritative traditions in which we could trust, the *nomos* which gave us authoritative guidance, because our immediate teachers and teachers' teachers believed in the possibility of a simply rational society. Each of us here is compelled to find his bearings by his own powers, however defective they may be.

We have no comfort other than that inherent in this activity. Philosophy, we have learned, must be on its guard against the wish to be edifying —philosophy can only be intrinsically edifying. We cannot exert our understanding without from time to time understanding something of importance; and this act of understanding may be accompanied by the awareness of our understanding, by the understanding of understanding, by *noesis noeseos*, and this is so high, so pure, so noble an experience that Aristotle could ascribe it to his God. This experience is entirely independent of whether what we understand primarily is pleasing or displeasing, fair or ugly. It leads us to realize that all evils are in a sense necessary if there is to be understanding. It enables us to accept all evils which befall us and which may well break our hearts in the spirit of good citizens of the city of God. By becoming aware of the dignity of the mind, we realize the true ground of the dignity of man and therewith the goodness of the world, whether we understand it as created or as uncreated, which is the home of man because it is the home of the human mind.

Liberal education, which consists in the constant intercourse with the greatest minds, is a training in the highest form of modesty, not to say of humility. It is at the same time a training in boldness: it demands from us the complete break with the noise, the rush, the thoughtlessness, the cheapness of the Vanity Fair of the intellectuals as well as of their enemies. It demands from us the boldness implied in the resolve to regard the accepted views as mere opinions, or to regard the average opinions as extreme opinions which are at least as likely to be wrong as the most strange or the least popular opinions. Liberal education is liberation from vulgarity. The Greeks had a beautiful word for "vulgarity"; they called it *apeirokalia*, lack of experience in things beautiful. Liberal education supplies us with experience in things beautiful.

2/ Liberal Education
and Responsibility

When I was approached by The Fund for Adult Education with the suggestion that I prepare an essay on liberal education and responsibility, my first reaction was not one of delight. While I am in many ways dependent on the administration of education and hence on the organizations serving education, I looked at these things, if I looked at them, with that awe which arises from both gratitude and apprehension mixed with ignorance. I thought that it was my job, my responsibility, to do my best in the class-room, in conversations with students wholly regardless of whether they are registered or not, and last but not least in my study at home. I own that education is in a sense the subject matter of my teaching and my research. But I am almost solely concerned with the goal or end of education at its best or highest—of the education of the perfect prince, as it were—and very little with its conditions and its how. The most important conditions, it seems to me, are the qualities of the educator and of the human being who is to be educated; in the case of the highest form of education those conditions are very rarely fulfilled, and one cannot do anything to produce them; the only things we can do regarding them are not to interfere with their interplay and to prevent such interference. As for the how, one knows it once one knows what education is meant to do to a human being or once one knows the end of education. Certainly, there are some rules of thumb. Almost every year I meet once with the older students of my department in order to discuss with them how to teach political theory in college. Once on such an occasion a student asked me whether I could not give him a general rule regarding teaching. I replied: "Always assume that there is one silent student in your class who is by far superior to you in head and in heart." I meant by this: do not have too high an opinion of your importance, and have the highest opinion of your duty, your responsibility.

There was another reason why I was somewhat bewildered when I first

9

began to prepare this essay. That reason has to do with the word "responsibility." For clearly, liberal education and responsibility are not identical. They may not be separable from each other. Before one could discuss their relation, one would have to know what each of them is. As for the word "responsibility," it is now in common use, and I myself have used it from time to time, for instance a very short while ago. In the sense in which it is now frequently used, it is a neologism. It is, I believe, the fashionable substitute for such words as "duty," "conscience," or "virtue." We frequently say of a man that he is a responsible man, where people of former generations would have said that he is a just man or a conscientious man or a virtuous man. Primarily, a man is responsible if he can be held accountable for what he does—for example, for a murder; being responsible is so far from being the same as being virtuous that it is merely the condition for being either virtuous or vicious. By substituting responsibility for virtue, we prove to be much more easily satisfied than our forefathers, or, more precisely perhaps, we assume that by being responsible one is already virtuous or that no vicious man is responsible for his viciousness. There is a kinship between "responsibility" thus understood and "decency" as sometimes used by the British: if a man ruins himself in order to save a complete stranger, the stranger, if British, is supposed to thank him by saying, "It was rather decent of you." We seem to loathe the grand old words and perhaps also the things which they indicate and to prefer more subdued expressions out of delicacy or because they are more businesslike. However this may be, my misgivings were caused by my awareness of my ignorance as to what the substitution of responsibility for duty and for virtue means.

I certainly felt that I was particularly ill-prepared to address professional educators on the subject "Education and Responsibility." But then I learnt to my relief that I was merely expected to explain two sentences occurring in my speech "What is Liberal Education?" The sentences run as follows: "Liberal education is the ladder by which we try to ascend from mass democracy to democracy as originally meant. Liberal education is the necessary endeavor to found an aristocracy within democratic mass society."

To begin at the beginning, the word "liberal" had at the beginning, just as it has now, a political meaning, but its original political meaning is almost the opposite of its present political meaning. Originally a liberal man was a man who behaved in a manner becoming a free man, as distinguished from a slave. "Liberality" referred then to slavery and presupposed it. A slave is a human being who lives for another human being, his master; he has in a sense no life of his own: he has no time for himself. The master, on the other hand, has all his time for himself, that is, for the pursuits becoming him: politics and philosophy. Yet there are very many free men who are almost like slaves since they have very little time for themselves, because they have to work for their livelihood and to rest so that they can work the next day. Those free men without leisure are the poor, the majority of citizens. The truly free man who can live in a manner becoming a free man is the man of leisure, the gentleman who must possess some wealth—but wealth of a certain kind: a kind of wealth the administration of which, to say nothing of its acquisition, does not take up much of his time, but can be taken care of through his supervising of properly trained supervisors; the gentleman will be a gentleman farmer and not a merchant or entrepreneur. Yet if he spends much of his time in the country he will not be available sufficiently for the pursuits becoming him; he must therefore live in town. His way of life will be at the mercy of those of his fellow citizens who are not gentlemen, if he and his like do not rule: the way of life of the gentlemen is not secure if they are not the unquestioned rulers of their city, if the regime of their city is not aristocratic.

One becomes a gentleman by education, by liberal education. The Greek word for education is derived from the Greek word for child: education in general, and therefore liberal education in particular, is, then, to say the least, primarily not adult education. The Greek word for education is akin to the Greek word for play, and the activity of the gentlemen is emphatically earnest; in fact, the gentlemen are "the earnest ones." They are earnest because they are concerned with the most weighty matters, with the only things which deserve to be taken seriously for their own sake, with the good order of the soul and of the city. The education of the potential gentlemen is the playful anticipation of the life of gentlemen. It consists above all in the formation of character and of taste. The fountains of that education are the poets. It is hardly necessary to say that the gentleman is in need of skills. To say nothing of reading, writing, counting, reckoning, wrestling, throwing of spears, and horsemanship, he must possess the skill of administering well and nobly the affairs of his household and the affairs of his city by deed and by speech. He acquires that skill by his familiar intercourse with older or more experienced gentlemen, preferably with elder statesmen, by receiving instruction from paid teachers in the art of speaking, by reading histories and books of travel, by meditating on the works of the poets, and, of course, by taking part in political life. All this requires leisure on the part of the youths as well as on the part of their elders; it is the preserve of a certain kind of wealthy people.

This fact gives rise to the question of the justice of a society which in the best case would be ruled by gentlemen ruling in their own right. Just government is government which rules in the interest of the whole society, and not merely of a part. The gentlemen are therefore under an obligation to show to themselves and to others that their rule is best for everyone in the city or for the city as a whole. But justice requires that equal men be treated equally, and there is no good reason for thinking that the gentlemen are by nature superior to the vulgar. The gentlemen are indeed superior to the vulgar by their breeding, but the large majority of men are by nature capable of the same breeding if they are caught young, in their cradles; only the accident of birth decides whether a given individual has a chance of becoming a gentleman or will necessarily become a villain; hence aristocracy is unjust. The gentlemen replied as follows: the city as a whole is much too poor to enable everyone to bring up his sons so that they can become gentlemen; if you insist that the social order should correspond with tolerable strictness to the natural order—that is, that men who are more or less equal by nature should also be equal socially or by convention —you will merely bring about a state of universal drabness. But only on the ground of a narrow conception of justice, owing its evidence to the power of the ignoble passion of envy, must one prefer a flat building which is everywhere equally drab to a structure which from a broad base of drabness rises to a narrow plateau of distinction and of grace and therefore gives some grace and some distinction to its very base. There must then be a few who are wealthy and well born and many who are poor and of obscure origin. Yet there seems to be no good reason why this family is elected to gentility and that family is condemned to indistinctness; that selection seems to be arbitrary, to say the least. It would indeed be foolish to deny that old wealth sometimes has its forgotten origins in crime. But it is more noble to believe, and probably also truer, that the old families are the descendants from the first settlers and from leaders in war or counsel; and it is certainly just that one be grateful.

Gentlemen may rule without being rulers in their own right; they may rule on the basis of popular election. This arrangement was regarded as unsatisfactory for the following reason. It would mean that the gentlemen are, strictly speaking, responsible to the common people—that the higher is responsible to the lower—and this would appear to be against nature. The gentlemen regard virtue as choiceworthy for its own sake, whereas the others praise virtue as a means for acquiring wealth and honor. The gentlemen and the others disagree, then, as regards the end of man or the highest good; they disagree regarding first principles. Hence they cannot have genuinely common deliberations.[1] The gentlemen cannot possibly give a sufficient or intelligible account of their way of life to the others. While being responsible to themselves for the well-being of the vulgar, they cannot be responsible to the vulgar.

But even if one rests satisfied with a less exacting notion of the rule of gentlemen, the principle indicated necessarily leads one to reject democracy. Roughly speaking, democracy is the regime in which the majority of adult free males living in a city rules, but only a minority of them are educated. The principle of democracy is therefore not virtue, but freedom as the right of every citizen to live as he likes. Democracy is rejected because it is as such the rule of the uneducated. One illustration must here suffice. The sophist Protagoras came to the democratic city of Athens in order to educate human beings, or to teach for pay the art of administering well the affairs of one's household and of the city by deed and by speech—the political art. Since in a democracy everyone is supposed to possess the political art somehow, yet the majority, lacking equipment, cannot have acquired that art through education, Protagoras must assume that the citizens received that art through something like a divine gift, albeit a gift which becomes effective only through human punishments and rewards: the true political art, the art which enables a man not only to obey the laws but to frame laws, is acquired by education, by the highest form of education, which is necessarily the preserve of those who can pay for it.

To sum up, liberal education in the original sense not only fosters civic responsibility: it is even required for the exercise of civic responsibility. By being what they are, the gentlemen are meant to set the tone of society in the most direct, the least ambiguous, and the most unquestionable way: by ruling it in broad daylight.

It is necessary to take a further step away from our opinions in order to understand our opinions. The pursuits becoming the gentleman are said to be politics and philosophy. Philosophy can be understood loosely or strictly. If understood loosely, it is the same as what is now called intellectual interests. If understood strictly, it means quest for the truth about the most weighty matters or for the comprehensive truth or for the truth about the whole or for the science of the whole. When comparing politics to philosophy strictly understood, one realizes that philosophy is of higher rank than politics. Politics is the pursuit of certain ends; decent politics is the decent pursuit of decent ends. The responsible and clear distinction between ends which are decent and ends which are not is in a way presupposed by politics. It surely transcends politics. For everything which comes into being through human action and is therefore perishable or corruptible presupposes incorruptible and unchangeable things—for instance, the natural order of the human soul—with a view to which we can distinguish between right and wrong actions.

In the light of philosophy, liberal education takes on a new meaning: liberal education, especially education in the liberal arts, comes to sight as a preparation for philosophy. This means that philosophy transcends gentlemanship. The gentleman as gentleman accepts on trust certain most weighty things which for the philosopher are the themes of investigation and of questioning. Hence the gentleman's virtue is not entirely the same as the philosopher's virtue. A sign of this difference is the fact that whereas the gentleman must be wealthy in order to do his proper work, the philosopher may be poor. Socrates lived in tenthousandfold poverty. Once he saw many people following a horse and looking at it, and he heard some of them conversing much about it. In his surprise he approached the groom with the question whether the horse was rich. The groom looked at him as if he were not only grossly ignorant but not even sane: "How can a horse have any property?" At that Socrates understandably recovered, for he thus learned that it is lawful for a horse which is a pauper to become good provided it possesses a naturally good soul: it may then be lawful for Socrates to become a good man in spite of his poverty. Since it is not necessary for the philosopher to be wealthy, he does not need the entirely lawful arts by which one defends one's property, for example, forensically; nor does he have to develop the habit of self-assertion in this or other respects—a habit which necessarily enters into the gentleman's virtue. Despite these differences, the gentleman's virtue is a reflection of the philosopher's virtue; one may say it is its political reflection.

This is the ultimate justification of the rule of gentlemen. The rule of the gentlemen is only a reflection of the rule of the philosophers, who are understood to be the men best by nature and best by education. Given the fact that philosophy is more evidently quest for wisdom than possession of wisdom, the education of the philosopher never ceases as long as he lives; it is the adult education par excellence. For, to say nothing of other things, the highest kind of knowledge which a man may have acquired can never be simply at his disposal as other kinds of knowledge can; it is in constant need of being acquired again from the start. This leads to the following consequence. In the case of the gentleman, one can make a simple distinction between the playful education of the potential gentleman and the earnest work of the gentleman proper. In the case of the philosopher this simple distinction between the playful and the serious no longer holds, not in spite of the fact that his sole concern is with the weightiest matters, but because of it. For this reason alone, to say nothing of others, the rule of philosophers proves to be impossible. This leads to the difficulty that the philosophers will be ruled by the gentlemen, that is, by their inferiors.

One can solve this difficulty by assuming that the philosophers are not as such a constituent part of the city. In other words, the only teachers who are as such a constituent part of the city are the priests. The end of the city is then not the same as the end of philosophy. If the gentlemen represent the city at its best, one must say that the end of the gentleman is not the same as the end of the philosopher. What was observed regarding the gentleman in his relation to the vulgar applies even more to the philosopher in his relation to the gentlemen and a fortiori to all other nonphilosophers: the philosopher and the nonphilosophers cannot have genuinely common deliberations. There is a fundamental disproportion between philosophy and the city. In political things it is a sound rule to let sleeping dogs lie or to prefer the established to the nonestablished or to recognize the right of the first occupier. Philosophy stands or falls by its intransigent disregard of this rule and of anything which reminds of it. Philosophy can then live only side by side with the city. As Plato put it in the *Republic*, only in a city in which the philosophers rule and in which they therefore owe their training in philosophy to the city is it just that the philosopher be compelled to engage in political activity; in all other cities—that is, in all actual cities—the philosopher does not owe his highest gift of human origin to the city and therefore is not under an obligation to do the work of the city. In entire agreement with this, Plato suggests in his *Crito*, where he avoids the very term "philosophy," that the philosopher owes indeed very much to the city and therefore he is obliged to obey at least passively even the unjust laws of the city and to die at the behest of the city. Yet he is not obliged to engage in political activity. The philosopher as philosopher is responsible to the city only to the extent that by doing his own work, by his own well-being, he contributes to the well-being of the city: philosophy has necessarily a humanizing or civilizing effect. The city needs philosophy, but only mediately or indirectly, not to say in a diluted form. Plato has presented this state of things by comparing the city to a cave from which only a rough and steep ascent leads to the light of the sun: the city as city is more closed to philosophy than open to it.

The classics had no delusions regarding the probability of a genuine aristocracy's ever becoming actual. For all practical purposes they were satisfied with a regime in which the gentlemen share power with the people in such a way that the people elect the magistrates and the council from among the gentlemen and demand an account of them at the end of their term of office. A variation of this thought is the notion of the mixed regime, in which the gentlemen form the senate and the senate occupies the key position between the popular assembly and an elected or hereditary monarch as head of the armed forces of society. There is a direct connection between the notion of the mixed regime and modern republicanism. Lest this be misunderstood, one must immediately stress the important differences between the modern doctrine and its classic original. The modern doctrine starts from the natural equality of all men, and it leads therefore to the assertion that sovereignty belongs to the people; yet it understands that sovereignty in such a way as to guarantee the natural rights of each; it achieves this result by distinguishing between the sovereign and the government and by demanding that the fundamental governmental powers be separated from one another. The spring of this regime was held to be the desire of each to improve his material conditions. Accordingly the commercial and industrial elite, rather than the landed gentry, predominated.

The fully developed doctrine required that one man have one vote, that the voting be secret, and that the right to vote be not abridged on account of poverty, religion, or race. Governmental actions, on the other hand, are to be open to public inspection to the highest degree possible, for government is only the representative of the people and responsible to the people. The responsibility of the people, of the electors, does not permit of legal definition and is therefore the most obvious crux of modern republicanism. In the earlier stages the solution was sought in the religious education of the people, in the education, based on the Bible, of everyone to regard himself as responsible for his actions and for his thoughts to a God who would judge him, for, in the words of Locke, rational ethics proper is as much beyond the capacities of "day laborers and tradesmen, and spinsters and dairy maids" as is mathematics. On the other hand, the same authority advises the gentlemen of England to set their sons upon Puffendorf's *Natural Right* "wherein (they) will be instructed in the natural rights of men, and the origin and foundation of society, and the duties resulting from thence." Locke's *Some Thoughts Concerning Education* is addressed to the gentlemen, rather than to "those of the meaner sort," for if the gentlemen "are by their education once set right, they will quickly bring all the rest into order." For, we may suppose, the gentlemen are those called upon to act as representatives of the people, and they are to be prepared for this calling by a liberal education which is, above all, an education in "good breeding." Locke takes his models from the ancient Romans and Greeks, and the liberal education which he recommends consists to some extent in acquiring an easy familiarity with classical literature: "Latin I look upon as absolutely necessary to a gentleman." [2]

Not a few points which Locke meant are brought out clearly in the *Federalist Papers*. These writings reveal their connection with the classics simply enough by presenting themselves as the work of one Publius. This eminently sober work considers chiefly that diversity and inequality in the faculties of men which shows itself in the acquisition of property, but it is very far from being blind to the difference between business and government. According to Alexander Hamilton, the mechanics and manufacturers "know that the merchant is their natural patron and friend," their natural representative, for the merchant possesses "those acquired endowments without which, in a deliberative assembly, the greatest natural abilities are for the most part useless." Similarly, the wealthier landlords are the natural representatives of the landed interest. The natural arbiter between the landed and the moneyed interests will be "the man of the learned professions," for "the learned professions . . . truly form no distinct interest in society" and therefore are more likely than others to think of "the general interests of the society." It is true that in order to become a representative of the people, it sometimes suffices that one practice "with success the vicious arts by which elections are too often carried," but these deplorable cases are the exception, the rule being that the representatives will be respectable landlords, merchants, and members of the learned professions. If the electorate is not depraved, there is a fair chance that it will elect as its representatives for deliberation as well as for execution those among the three groups of men "who possess most wisdom to discern, and most virtue to pursue, the common good of the society," or those who are most outstanding by "merits and talents," by "ability and virtue." [3]

Under the most favorable conditions, the men who will hold the balance of power will then be the men of the learned professions. In the best case,

Hamilton's republic will be ruled by the men of the learned professions. This reminds one of the rule of the philosophers, but only reminds one of it. Will the men of the learned professions at least be men of liberal education? It is probable that the men of the learned professions will chiefly be lawyers. No one ever had a greater respect for law and hence for lawyers than Edmund Burke: "God forbid I should insinuate anything derogatory to that profession, which is another priesthood, administrating the rites of sacred justice." Yet he felt compelled to describe the preponderance of lawyers in the national counsels as "mischievous." "Law . . . is, in my opinion, one of the first and noblest of human sciences; a science which does more to quicken and invigorate the understanding, than all the other kinds of learning put together; but it is not apt, except in persons very happily born, to open and to liberalize the mind exactly in the same proportion." For to speak "legally and constitutionally" is not the same as to speak "prudently." "Legislators ought to do what lawyers cannot; for they have no other rules to bind them, but the great principles of reason and equity, and the general sense of mankind." [4] The liberalization of the mind obviously requires understanding of "the great principles of reason and equity," which for Burke are the same thing as the natural law.

But it is not necessary to dwell on this particular shortcoming from which representative government might suffer. Two generations after Burke, John Stuart Mill took up the question concerning the relation of representative government and liberal education. One does not exaggerate too much by saying that he took up these two subjects in entire separation from each other. His *Inaugural Address at St. Andrews* deals with liberal education as "the education of all who are not obliged by their circumstances to discontinue their scholastic studies at a very early age," not to say the education of "the favorites of nature and fortune." That speech contains a number of observations which will require our consideration and reconsideration. Mill traces the "superiority" of classical literature "for purposes of education" to the fact that that literature transmits to us "the wisdom of life": "In cultivating . . . the ancient languages as our best literary education, we are all the while laying an admirable foundation for ethical and philosophical culture." Even more admirable than "the substance" is "the form" of treatment: "It must be remembered that they had more time and that they wrote chiefly for a select class possessed of leisure," whereas we "write in a hurry for people who read in a hurry." The classics used "the right words in the right places" or, which means the same thing, they were not "prolix." [5] But liberal education has very little effect on the "miscellaneous assembly" which is the legal sovereign and which is frequently ruled by men who have no qualification for legislation except "a fluent tongue, and a faculty of getting elected by a constituency." To secure "the intellectual qualifications desirable in representatives," Mill thought, there is no other mode than proportional representation as devised by Hare and Fawcett, a scheme which in his opinion is of "perfect feasibility" and possesses "transcendent advantages."

> The natural tendency of representative government, as of modern civilization, is toward collective mediocrity: and this tendency is increased by all reductions and extensions of the franchise, their effect being to place the principal power in the hands of classes more and more below the highest level of instruction in the community. . . . It is an admitted fact that in the American democracy, which is constructed on this faulty model, the highly-cultivated members of the community, except such of them as are willing to sacrifice their own opinions and modes of judgment, and become the servile mouthpieces of their inferiors in knowledge, do not ever offer themselves for Congress or State legislatures, so certain is it that they would have no chance of being returned. Had a plan like Mr. Hare's by good fortune suggested itself to the enlightened and patriotic founders of the American Republic, the Federal and State Assemblies would have contained many of those distinguished men, and democracy would have been spared its greatest reproach and one of its most formidable evils.

Only proportional representation which guarantees or at least does not exclude the proper representation of the best part of society in the government will transform "the falsely called democracies which now prevail, and from which the current idea of democracy is exclusively derived" into "the only true type of democracy," into democracy as originally meant.

For reasons which are not all bad, Mill's remedy has come to be regarded as insufficient, not to say worthless. Perhaps it was a certain awareness of this which induced him to look for relief in another part of the body politic. From the fact that the representative assemblies are not necessarily "a selection of the greatest political minds of the country," he drew the conclusion that for "the skilled legislation and administration" one must secure "under strict responsibility to the nation, the acquired knowledge and practiced intelligence of a specially trained and experienced Few." [6] Mill appears to suggest that with the growth and maturity of democracy, the institutional seat of public-spirited intelligence could and should be sought in the high and middle echelons of the appointed officials. This hope presupposes that the bureaucracy can be transformed into a civil service properly so called, the specific difference between the bureaucrat and the civil servant being that the civil servant is a liberally educated man whose liberal education affects him decisively in the performance of his duties.

Permit me to summarize the preceding argument. In the light of the original conception of modern republicanism, our present predicament appears to be caused by the decay of religious education of the people and by the decay of liberal education of the representatives of the people. By the decay of religious education I mean more than the fact that a very large part of the people no longer receive any religious education, although it is not necessary on the present occasion to think beyond that fact. The question as to whether religious education can be restored to its pristine power by the means at our disposal is beyond the scope of this year's Arden House Institute. Still, I cannot help stating to you these questions: Is our present concern with liberal education of adults, our present expectation from such liberal education, not due to the void created by the decay of religious education? Is such liberal education meant to perform the function formerly performed by religious education? Can liberal education perform that function? It is certainly easier to discuss the other side of our predicament—the predicament caused by the decay of liberal education of the governors. Following Mill's suggestion, we would have to consider whether and to what extent the education of the future civil servants can and should be improved, or in other words whether the present form of their education is liberal education in a tolerably strict sense. If it is not, one would have to raise the broader question whether the present colleges and universities supply such a liberal education and whether they can be reformed. It is more modest, more pertinent, and more practical to give thought to some necessary reforms of the teaching in the Departments of Political Science and perhaps also in the Law Schools. The changes I have in mind are less in the subjects taught than in the emphasis and in the approach: whatever broadens and deepens the understanding should be more encouraged than what in the best case cannot as such produce more than narrow and unprincipled efficiency.

No one, I trust, will misunderstand the preceding remarks so as to impute to me the ridiculous assertion that education has ceased to be a public or political power. One must say, however, that a new type of education or a new orientation of education has come to predominate. Just as liberal education in its original sense was supported by classical philosophy, so the new education derives its support, if not its being, from modern philosophy. According to classical philosophy the end of the philosophers is radically different from the end or ends actually pursued by the nonphilosophers. Modern philosophy comes into being when the end of philosophy is identified with the end which is capable of being actually pursued by all men. More precisely, philosophy is now asserted to be essentially subservient to the end which is capable of being actually pursued by all men. We have suggested that the ultimate justification for the distinction between gentlemen and nongentlemen is the distinction between philosophers and nonphilosophers. If this is true, it follows that by causing the purpose of the philosophers, or more generally the purpose which essentially transcends society, to collapse into the purpose of the nonphilosophers, one causes the purpose of the gentlemen to collapse into the purpose of the nongentlemen. In this respect, the modern conception of philosophy is fundamentally democratic. The end of philosophy is now no longer what one may call disinterested contemplation of the eternal, but the relief of man's estate. Philosophy thus understood could be presented with some plausibility as inspired by biblical charity, and accordingly philosophy in the classic sense could be disparaged as pagan and as sustained by sinful pride. One may doubt whether the claim to biblical inspiration was justified and even whether it was always raised in entire sincerity. However this may be, it is conducive to greater clarity, and at the same time in agreement with the spirit of the modern conception, to say that the moderns opposed a "realistic," earthly, not to say pedestrian conception to the "idealistic," heavenly, not to say visionary conception of the classics. Philosophy or science was no longer an end in itself, but in the service of human power, of a power to be used for making human life longer, healthier, and more abundant. The economy of scarcity, which is the tacit presupposition of all earlier social thought, was to be replaced by an economy of plenty. The radical distinction between science and manual labor was to be replaced by the smooth co-operation of the scientist and the engineer. According to the original conception, the men in control of this stupendous enterprise were the philosopher-scientists. Everything was to be done by them for the people, but, as it were, nothing by the people. For the people were, to begin with, rather distrustful of the new gifts from the new sort of sorcerers, for they remembered the commandment, "Thou shalt not suffer a sorcerer to live." In order to become the willing recipients of the new gifts, the people had to be enlightened. This enlightenment is the core of the new education. It is the same as the diffusion or popularization of the new science. The addressees of the popularized science were in the first stage countesses and duchesses, rather than spinsters and dairymaids, and popularized science often surpassed science proper in elegance and charm of diction. But the first step entailed all the further steps which were taken in due order. The enlightenment was destined to become universal enlightenment. It appeared that the difference of natural gifts did not have the importance which the tradition had ascribed to it; method proved to be the great equalizer of naturally unequal minds. While invention or discovery continued to remain the preserve of the few, the results could be transmitted to all. The leaders in this great enterprise did not rely entirely on the effects of formal education for weaning men away from concern with the bliss of the next world to work for happiness in this. What study did not do, and perhaps could not do, trade did: immensely facilitated and encouraged by the new inventions and discoveries, trade which unites all peoples, took precedence over religion, which divides the peoples.

But what was to be done to moral education? The identification of the end of the gentlemen with the end of the nongentlemen meant that the understanding of virtue as choiceworthy for its own sake gave way to an instrumental understanding of virtue: honesty is nothing but the best policy, the policy most conducive to commodious living or comfortable self-preservation. Virtue took on a narrow meaning, with the final result that the word "virtue" fell into desuetude. There was no longer a need for a genuine conversion from the premoral if not immoral concern with worldly goods to the concern with the goodness of the soul, but only for the calculating transition from unenlightened to enlightened self-interest. Yet even this was not entirely necessary. It was thought that at least the majority of men will act sensibly and well if the alternative will be made unprofitable by the right kind of institution, political and economic. The devising of the right kind of institutions and their implementation came to be regarded as more important than the formation of character by liberal education.

Yet let us not for one moment forget the other side of the picture. It is a demand of justice that there should be a reasonable correspondence between the social hierarchy and the natural hierarchy. The lack of such a correspondence in the old scheme was defended by the fundamental fact of scarcity. With the increasing abundance it became increasingly possible to see and to admit the element of hypocrisy which had entered into the traditional notion of aristocracy; the existing aristocracies proved to be oligarchies, rather than aristocracies. In other words it became increasingly easy to argue from the premise that natural inequality has very little to do with social inequality, that practically or politically speaking one may safely assume that all men are by nature equal, that all men have the same natural rights, provided one uses this rule of thumb as the major premise for reaching the conclusion that everyone should be given the same opportunity as everyone else: natural inequality has its rightful place in the use, nonuse, or abuse of opportunity in the race as distinguished from at the start. Thus it became possible to abolish many injustices or at least many things which had become injustices. Thus was ushered in the age of tolerance. Humanity, which was formerly rather the virtue appropriate in one's dealings with one's inferiors—with the underdog—became the crowning virtue. Goodness became identical with compassion.

Originally the philosopher-scientist was thought to be in control of the progressive enterprise. Since he had no power, he had to work through the princes. The control was then in fact in the hands of the princes, if of enlightened princes. But with the progress of enlightenment, the tutelage of the princes was no longer needed. Power could be entrusted to the people. It is true that the people did not always listen to the philosopher-scientists. But apart from the fact that the same was true of princes, society came to take on such a character that it was more and more compelled to listen to the philosopher-scientists if it desired to survive. Still there remained a lag between the enlightenment coming from above and the way in which the people exercised its freedom. One may even speak of a race: will the people come into full possession of its freedom before it has become enlightened, and if so, what will it do with its freedom and even with the imperfect enlightenment which it will already have received? An apparent solution was found through an apparent revolt against the enlightenment and through a genuine revolt against enlightened despotism. It was said that every man has the right to political freedom, to being a member of the sovereign, by virtue of the dignity which every man has as man—the dignity of a moral being. The only thing which can be held to be unqualifiedly good is not the contemplation of the eternal, not the cultivation of the mind, to say nothing of good breeding, but a good intention, and of good intentions everyone is as capable as everyone else, wholly independently of education. Accordingly, the uneducated could even appear to have an advantage over the educated: the voice of nature or of the moral law speaks in them perhaps more clearly and more decidedly than in the sophisticated who may have sophisticated away their conscience. This belief is not the only starting point and perhaps not the best starting point, but it is for us now the most convenient starting point for understanding the assertion which was made at that moment: the assertion that virtue is the principle of democracy and only of democracy. One conclusion from this assertion was Jacobin terror which punished not only actions and speeches but intentions as well. Another conclusion was that one must respect every man merely because he is a man, regardless of how he uses his will or his freedom, and this respect must be implemented by full political rights for everyone who is not technically criminal or insane, regardless of whether he is mature for the exercise of those rights or not. That reasoning reminds one of a reasoning which was immortalized by Locke's criticism and which led to the conclusion that one may indeed behead a tyrannical king, but only with reverence for that king. It remains then at the race between the political freedom below and the enlightenment coming from above.

Hitherto I have spoken of the philosopher-scientist. That is to say, I have pretended that the original conception, the seventeenth-century conception, has retained its force. But in the meantime philosophy and science have became divorced: a philosopher need not be a scientist, and a scientist need not be a philosopher. Only the title Ph.D. is left as a reminder of the past. Of the two henceforth divorced faculties of the mind, science has acquired supremacy; science is the only authority in our age of which one can say that it enjoys universal recognition. This science has no longer any essential connection with wisdom. It is a mere accident if a scientist, even a great scientist, happens to be a wise man politically or privately. Instead of the fruitful and ennobling tension between religious education and liberal education, we now see the tension between the ethos of democracy and the ethos of technocracy. During the last seventy years, it has become increasingly the accepted opinion that there is no possibility of scientific and hence rational knowledge of "values," that is, that science or reason is incompetent to distinguish between good and evil ends. It would be unfair to deny that, thanks to the survival of utilitarian habits, scientists in general and social scientists in particular still take it for granted in many cases that health, a reasonably long life, and prosperity are good things and that science must find means for securing or procuring them. But these ends can no longer claim the evidence which they once possessed; they appear now to be posited by certain desires which are not "objectively" superior to the opposite desires. Since science is then unable to justify the ends for which it seeks the means, it is in practice compelled to satisfy the ends which are sought by its customers, by the society to which the individual scientist happens to belong and hence in many cases by the mass. We must disregard here the older traditions which fortunately still retain some of their former power; we must disregard them because their power is more and more corroded as time goes on. If we look then only at what is peculiar to our age or characteristic of our age, we see hardly more than the interplay of mass taste with high-grade but strictly speaking unprincipled efficiency. The technicians are, if not responsible, at any rate responsive to the demands of the mass; but a mass as mass cannot be responsible to anyone or to anything for anything. It is in this situation that we here, and others in the country, raise the question concerning liberal education and responsibility.

In this situation the insufficiently educated are bound to have an unreasonably strong influence on education—on the determination of both the ends and the means of education. Furthermore, the very progress of science leads to an ever increasing specialization, with the result that a man's respectability becomes dependent on his being a specialist. Scientific education is in danger of losing its value for the broadening and the deepening of the human being. The only universal science which is possible on this basis—logic or methodology—becomes itself an affair of and for technicians. The remedy for specialization is therefore sought in a new kind of universalism—a universalism which has been rendered almost inevitable by the extension of our spatial and temporal horizons. We are trying to expel the narrowness of specialization by the superficiality of such things as general civilization courses or by what has aptly been compared to the unending cinema, as distinguished from a picture gallery, of the history of all nations in all respects: economic, scientific, artistic, religious, and political. The gigantic spectacle thus provided is in the best case exciting and entertaining; it is not instructive and educating. A hundred pages—no, ten pages—of Herodotus introduce us immeasurably better into the mysterious unity of oneness and variety in human things than many volumes written in the spirit predominant in our age. Besides, human excellence or virtue can no longer be regarded as the perfection of human nature toward which man is by nature inclined or which is the goal of his eros. Since "values" are regarded as in fact conventional, the place of moral education is taken by conditioning, or more precisely by conditioning through symbols verbal and other, or by adjustment to the society in question.

What then are the prospects for liberal education within mass democracy? What are the prospects for the liberally educated to become again a power in democracy? We are not permitted to be flatterers of democracy precisely because we are friends and allies of democracy. While we are not permitted to remain silent on the dangers to which democracy exposes itself as well as human excellence, we cannot forget the obvious fact that by giving freedom to all, democracy also gives freedom to those who care for human excellence. No one prevents us from cultivating our garden or from setting up outposts which may come to be regarded by many citizens as salutary to the republic and as deserving of giving to it its tone. Needless to say, the utmost exertion is the necessary, although by no means the sufficient, condition for success. For "men can always hope and never need to give up, in whatever fortune and in whatever travail they find themselves." We are indeed compelled to be specialists, but we can try to specialize in the most weighty matters or, to speak more simply and more nobly, in the one thing needful. As matters stand, we can expect more immediate help from the humanities rightly understood than from the sciences, from the spirit of perceptivity and delicacy than from the spirit of geometry. If I am not mistaken, this is the reason why liberal education is now becoming almost synonymous with the reading in common of the Great Books. No better beginning could have been made.

We must not expect that liberal education can ever become universal education. It will always remain the obligation and the privilege of a minority. Nor can we expect that the liberally educated will become a political power in their own right. For we cannot expect that liberal education will lead all who benefit from it to understand their civic responsibility in the same way or to agree politically. Karl Marx, the father of communism, and Friedrich Nietzsche, the stepgrandfather of fascism, were liberally educated on a level to which we cannot even hope to aspire. But perhaps one can say that their grandiose failures make it easier for us who have experienced those failures to understand again the old saying that wisdom cannot be separated from moderation and hence to understand that wisdom requires unhesitating loyalty to a decent constitution and even to the cause of constitutionalism. Moderation will protect us against the twin dangers of visionary expectations from politics and unmanly contempt for politics. Thus it may again become true that all liberally educated men will be politically moderate men. It is in this way that the liberally educated may again receive a hearing even in the market place.

No deliberation about remedies for our ills can be of any value if it is not preceded by an honest diagnosis—by a diagnosis falsified neither by unfounded hopes nor by fear of the powers that be. We must realize that we must hope almost against hope. I say this, abstracting entirely from the dangers threatening us at the hands of a barbaric and cruel, narrow-minded and cunning foreign enemy who is kept in check, if he is kept in check, only by the justified fear that whatever would bury us would bury him too. In thinking of remedies we may be compelled to rest satisfied with palliatives. But we must not mistake palliatives for cures. We must remember that liberal education for adults is not merely an act of justice to those who were in their youth deprived through their poverty of an education for which they are fitted by nature. Liberal education of adults must now also compensate for the defects of an education which is liberal only in name or by courtesy. Last but not least, liberal education is concerned with the souls of men and therefore has little or no use for machines. If it becomes a machine or an industry, it becomes undistinguishable from the entertainment industry unless in respect to income and publicity, to tinsel and glamour. But liberal education consists in learning to listen to still and small voices and therefore in becoming deaf to loud-speakers. Liberal education seeks light and therefore shuns the limelight.

NOTES

1. Cf. *Crito* 49d 2–5.
2. Ep. Ded., pp. 93–94, 164, 186.
3. Nos. 10, 35, 36, 55, 57, 62, 68.
4. *The Works of Edmund Burke* (Bohn Standard Library), I 407, II 7, 317–318, V 295.
5. James and John Stuart Mill, *On Education*, ed. by F. A. Cavenagh (Cambridge: University Press, 1931), pp. 151–157.
6. *Considerations on Representative Government* (London: Routledge, s.d.), pp. 93, 95, 101–102, 133–140, 155.

3 / The Liberalism of Classical Political Philosophy

Classical political philosophy—the political philosophy originated by Socrates and elaborated by Plato and by Aristotle—is today generally rejected as obsolete. The difference between, not to say the mutual incompatibility of, the two grounds on which it is rejected corresponds to the difference between the two schools of thought which predominate in our age, namely, positivism and existentialism. Positivism rejects classical political philosophy with a view to its mode as unscientific and with a view to its substance as undemocratic. There is a tension between these grounds, for, according to positivism, science is incapable of validating any value judgment, and therefore science can never reject a doctrine because it is undemocratic. But "the heart has its reasons which reason does not know," and not indeed positivism but many positivists possess a heart. Moreover there is an affinity between present-day positivism and sympathy for a certain kind of democracy; that affinity is due to the broad, not merely methodological, context out of which positivism emerged or to the hidden premises of positivism which positivism is unable to articulate because it is constitutionally unable to conceive of itself as a problem. Positivism may be said to be more dogmatic than any other position of which we have records. Positivism can achieve this triumph because it is able to present itself as very skeptical; it is that manifestation of dogmatism based on skepticism in which the skepticism completely conceals the dogmatism from its adherents. It is the latest form and it may very well be the last form in which modern rationalism appears; it is that form in which the crisis of modern rationalism becomes almost obvious to everyone. Once it becomes obvious to a man, he has already abandoned positivism, and if he adheres to the modern premises, he has no choice but to turn to existentialism.

Existentialism faces the situation with which positivism is confronted but does not grasp: the fact that reason has become radically problematic.

According to positivism, the first premises are not evident and necessary, but either purely factual or else conventional. According to existentialism, they are in a sense necessary, but they are certainly not evident: all thinking rests on unevident but nonarbitrary premises. Man is in the grip of powers which he cannot master or comprehend, and these powers reveal themselves differently in different historical epochs. Hence classical political philosophy is to be rejected as unhistorical or rationalistic. It was rationalistic because it denied the fundamental dependence of reason on language, which is always this or that language, the language of a historical community, of a community which has not been made, but has grown. Classical political philosophy could not give to itself an account of its own essential Greekness. Furthermore, by denying the dependence of man's thought on powers which he cannot comprehend, classical political philosophy was irreligious. It denied indeed the possibility of an areligious civil society, but it subordinated the religious to the political. For instance, in the *Republic*, Plato reduces the sacred to the useful; when Aristotle says that the city is natural, he implies that it is not sacred, like the sacred Troy in Homer; he reveals the precarious status of religion in his scheme by enumerating the concern with the divine in the "fifth and first" place: only the citizens who are too old for political activity ought to become priests.

Eric A. Havelock in his book *The Liberal Temper in Greek Politics* [1] approaches classical political philosophy from the positivistic point of view. The doctrine to which he adheres is, however, a somewhat obsolete version of positivism. Positivist study of society, as he understands it, is "descriptive" and opposed to "judgmental evaluation" (120, 368), but this does not prevent his siding with those who understand "History as Progress." The social scientist cannot speak of progress unless value judgments can be objective. The up-to-date or consistent positivist will therefore refrain from speaking of progress, and instead speak of change. Similarly Havelock appears to accept the distinction between primitive men or savages and civilized men (186–188), whereas the consistent positivist will speak not of savages, but of preliterate men and assert that preliterate men have "civilizations" or "cultures" neither superior nor inferior to those of literate men. It would be wrong to believe that the up-to-date positivist is entirely consistent or that his careful avoidance of "evaluative" terms is entirely due to his methodological puritanism; his heart tells him that once one admits the inequality of "cultures," one may not be able to condemn colonialism on moral grounds. Havelock is therefore perhaps only more intelligent or more frank than the consistent positivists when he describes his position as liberal, rather than as positivist. Yet this does not entirely dispose of the difficulty. "For the liberal man is to be taken as you find him and therefore his present political institutions are to be taken as given also." This means that here and now the liberals will take American democracy as given and will then "concentrate empirically and descriptively on this kind of political mechanism." This is a fair description of positivistic political science at its best. Yet Havelock praises the same liberals for writing "in defence of democracy" (cf. 123 and 155).

What then is a liberal? Was a German social scientist who in 1939 took "the present political institutions as given" and subjected them to "empirical analysis" for this reason by itself a liberal? If so, then a liberal is not a man of strong moral or political convictions, and this does not seem to agree with the common meaning of the word. Yet from Havelock's Preface it appears that the liberal regards all political and moral convictions as "negotiable" because he is extremely tolerant. Havelock applies the implicit maxim of conduct to the relations between the United States and Soviet Russia today. For all one can know from his book, he would have given the same advice during the conflict between the Western democracies and the fascist regimes at the time of the Munich conference. At any rate, he does not seem to have given thought to the question of whether Tolerance can remain tolerant when confronted with unqualified Intolerance or whether one must not fall back in the end on "moral convictions" which are not "negotiable." In almost all these points Havelock is liberal in the sense in which the word is commonly used here and now.

Originally, a liberal was a man who behaved in a manner becoming a free man as distinguished from a slave. According to the classic analysis, liberality is a virtue concerned with the use of wealth and therefore especially with giving: the liberal man gives gladly of his own in the right circumstances because it is noble to do so, and not from calculation; hence it is not easy for him to become or to remain rich; liberality is less opposed to prodigality than to meanness (greed as well as niggardliness). It is easy to see how this narrow meaning of liberality emerged out of the broad meaning. In everyday life, which is life in peace, the most common opportunities for showing whether one has the character of a free man or of a slave are afforded by one's dealings with one's possessions; most men honor wealth and show therewith that they are slaves of wealth; the man who behaves in a manner becoming a free man comes to sight primarily as a liberal man in the sense articulated by Aristotle. He knows that certain activities and hence in particular certain sciences and arts—the liberal sciences and arts—are choiceworthy for their own sake, regardless of their utility for the satisfaction of the lower kind of needs. He prefers the goods of the soul to the goods of the body. Liberality is then only one aspect of, not to say one name for, human excellence or being honorable or decent. The liberal man on the highest level esteems most highly the mind and its excellence and is aware of the fact that man at his best is autonomous or not subject to any authority, while in every other respect he is subject to authority which, in order to deserve respect, or to be truly authority, must be a reflection through a dimming medium of what is simply the highest. The liberal man cannot be a subject to a tyrant or to a master, and for almost all practical purposes he will be a republican. Classical political philosophy was liberal in the original sense.

It is not necessary for our present purpose to dwell on the successive changes which the word "liberal" has undergone since the early nineteenth century. Those changes follow the substitution of modern political philosophy—the ground as well as the consequence of modern natural science—for classical political philosophy. Before the substitution was completed, "liberality" sometimes meant lack of restraint, not to say profanity. By virtue of the more recent changes, "liberal" has come to mean almost the opposite of what it meant originally; the original meaning has almost vanished from "common sense." To quote Havelock, "It is of course assumed that by any common sense definition of the word liberal as it is applied in politics Plato is not a liberal thinker" (19). Havelock's understanding of liberalism hardly differs in either substance or mode from what is now the common-sense understanding. Liberalism, as he understands it, puts a greater stress on liberty than on authority; it regards authority as derivative solely from society, and society as spontaneous or automatic rather than as established by man; it denies the existence of any fixed norms: norms are responses to needs and change with the needs; the change of the needs and of the responses to them has a pattern: there is a historical process which is progressive without, however, tending toward an end or a peak, or which is "piece meal" (123); liberalism conceives of the historical process as a continuation of the evolutionary process; it is historical because it regards the human characteristics as acquired and not as given; it is optimistic and radical; it is "a genuine humanism which is not guilt-ridden"; it is democratic and egalitarian; accordingly it traces the historical changes and hence morality less to outstanding men than to groups and their pressures which "take concrete form in the educational activity of the members of the group"; it is in full sympathy with technological society and an international commercial system; it is empirical and pragmatic; last but not least it is naturalist or scientific, that is, nontheological and nonmetaphysical.

Havelock's understanding of liberalism differs from the vulgar understanding in two points. In the first place he regards it as necessary to look for the historical roots of liberalism in Greek antiquity. According to the common view, the sources of liberalism are found in writings like Locke's *Second Treatise of Government* and the Declaration of Independence. Havelock, however, feels that these writings convey a teaching which is not strictly speaking liberal since it is based on the assumption of natural right, that is, of an absolute; that teaching is therefore still too Platonic to be liberal (15–18). Pure liberalism exists either after the complete expulsion of Platonism or else before its emergence. As we would put it, there is a kinship between modern historicism and ancient conventionalism (the view that all right is conventional or no right is natural). Havelock contends that a pure liberalism existed in pre-Platonic or pre-Socratic thought; while implying "a brooding sense of natural justice among men" (377), it rejected natural justice. His historical opinion may be said to find its complete expression in the contention that whereas Plato and Aristotle as well as the Old Testament are responsible for the authoritarian strand in Western thought, the New Testament as well as certain Greek sophists, materialists, agnostics, or atheists are responsible for the liberal strand in it (259, 376). One might find it strange that a view according to which moral convictions are negotiable is suggested to be somehow in harmony with the New Testament. But perhaps Havelock thought chiefly of the New Testament prohibition or counsel against resisting evil and the failure of a pupil of Gorgias, as distinguished from a pupil of Socrates, to resort to the punishment of evildoers. Be this as it may, one is tempted to describe Havelock's liberalism as a classical scholar's Christian liberalism of a certain kind. But one must resist this temptation since Havelock deplores the "basic split between the moral or ideal and the expedient or selfish" which developed under "Christian other-worldly influences" (365, 14), unless one assumes that according to him "primitive Christianity" (18) was not otherworldly. The issue would seem to be settled by his remark that "religion, however humane, is always intolerant of purely secular thinking" (161).

There was a time when we were exposed to the opinion that Plato and Aristotle were related to the sophists as the German idealists were to the theorists of the French Revolution. This opinion could be shared by both friends and enemies of the principles of 1789. Havelock's contention is an up-to-date and therefore simplified version of that opinion. By speaking constantly of "the Greek liberals," he suggests that in Greek antiquity the battle lines were drawn in the same way as in modern times: liberals were up in arms against the orthodox and the authoritarians (18, 73). He explicitly contends that there existed in ancient Greece a "liberal-historical view"—a view which had become "a completed structure" by the time of Aristotle—and that the thinkers who set it forth combined in a nonaccidental manner a nontheological and nonmetaphysical anthropology or philosophy of history with faith in the common man or at any rate in democracy (11, 18, 32, 155). Everyone, we believe, grants or has granted that there were men prior to Plato who were "materialists" and at the same time asserted that the universe has come into being *opera sine divom* in any sense of the word "god." These men asserted therefore that man and all other living beings have come into being out of inanimate beings and through inanimate beings and that man's beginnings were poor and brutish; that, compared with its beginnings, human life as it is now presupposes a progress achieved through human exertions and human inventions; and that morality—the right and the noble—is of merely human origin. This doctrine or set of doctrines is, however, only the necessary but by no means the sufficient condition of liberalism. It is indeed common to present-day liberalism and its ancient equivalent. Yet once when speaking of a " 'Darwinian' and 'behaviorist' " ancient doctrine, Havelock says that in employing these adjectives he uses "a very loose analogy" (34). The mere mention of Darwinism might have sufficed to reveal the precarious character of the connection between evolutionism and liberalism. Above all, we are entitled to expect of a man who does not tire of speaking of science that he make abundantly clear the reason why the analogy is loose, or in other words that he make clear the fundamental difference between modern liberalism and its ancient equivalent. Havelock disappoints this expectation. He regards it as a thesis characteristic of liberals that "man is an animal" or "man is merely an animal" or "man is merely a special sort of an animal" (107–110), but, as Aristotle's definition of man sufficiently shows, this thesis cannot be characteristic of liberalism. Liberalism and nonliberalism begin to differ when the nonliberals raise the question regarding the significance of man's being "a special sort of animal." Let man be a mixture of the elements like any other animal, yet the elements are mixed in him from the beginning as they are in no other animal: man alone can acquire "the factors which distinguish him presently" from the other animals (cf. 75–76); he is the only animal which can look at the universe or look up to it; this necessary consequence of his "speciality" can easily lead to the nonliberal conclusion that the distinctly human life is the life devoted to contemplation as distinguished from the life of action or of production. Furthermore, if the universe has come into being, it will perish again, and this coming into being and perishing has taken place and will take place infinitely often; there were and will be infinitely many universes succeeding one another.

Here the question arises as to whether there can be a universe without man: is man's being accidental to the universe, to any universe? In other words, is the state of things prior to the emergence of man and the other animals one state of the universe equal in rank to the state after their emergence, or are the two states fundamentally different from each other as *chaos* and *kosmos?* The liberals assert that man's being is accidental to the universe and that *chaos* and *kosmos* are only two different states of *the* universe. But did their ancient predecessors—"the Greek anthropologists" —agree with them? Besides, just as the coming into being of the universe is succeeded by its perishing, the coming into being of civilization is succeeded by its decay: "the historical process" is not simply progressive but cyclical. As everyone knows, this does not affect the "flamboyant optimism" (69) of the liberals, but it may have affected their Greek predecessors; it may have led them to attach less importance to activity contributing to that progress of social institutions which is necessarily succeeded by their decay than to the understanding of the permanent grounds or character of the process or to the understanding of the whole within which the process takes place and which limits the progress (cf. 253); this limit is not set by man, and it surpasses everything man can bring about by his exertions and inventions; it is superhuman or divine. Moreover, one may grant that progress is due entirely to man's exertions and inventions and yet trace progress primarily to rare and discontinuous acts of a few outstanding men; "progressivism" is not necessarily identical with that "gradualism" which is apparently essential to liberalism. Finally, liberalism is empirical or pragmatic; it is therefore unable to assert that the principle of causality ("nothing can come into being out of nothing and through nothing") is evidently and necessarily true. On the other hand, it would seem that the Greek anthropologists or rather "physiologists" did regard that principle as evidently true because they understood the relation of sense perception and *logos* differently than do the liberals. It is no exaggeration to say that Havelock never meets the issue of the possible fundamental difference between the liberals and their Greek predecessors. For one cannot say that he meets that issue by asserting that the Greeks who believed in progress "may have retained this within the framework of a cosmic cycle" and that "the issue as it affects a basic philosophy of human history and morals is whether we *at present* are living in a regress or a progress" (405). It is obvious that this does not affect at all the considerations which have been indicated. Besides, in order to prove that a given Greek thinker was a liberal, Havelock is now compelled to prove that the thinker in question thought himself to live "in a progress." Contrary to his inclination, he cannot show this by showing that the thinker in question regarded his time as superior to the barbaric beginnings, for any time prior to the final devastation is superior to the first age. Nor can he show it by showing that the thinker in question believed himself to live at the peak of the process, for this belief implies that there will be no further progress to speak of. All this means that he cannot prove the existence of a single Greek liberal thinker.

Of one great obstacle to his undertaking Havelock is aware. To put it conservatively, very little is known of the Greek liberals; at most only fragments of their writings and reports about their teachings as well as about their deeds and sufferings survive. To overcome this difficulty, Havelock must devise an appropriate procedure. He divides the bulk of his argument into two parts, the first dealing with anthropology or philosophy of history and the second with political doctrine. He subdivides the first part completely and the second part to some extent in accordance with the requirements of the subject matter. Liberalism being preceded by orthodoxy (73), he presents first the orthodox or theological view, then the liberal or scientific view, and finally the compromise between the orthodox and the liberal views which is in fact the metaphysical view (of Plato and Aristotle). He thus tacitly replaces the Comtian scheme of the three stages by what would seem to be a dialectical scheme which bodes as ill for the future of liberalism as did Comte's. Given the great difficulty of interpreting fragments, especially when "the surviving scraps are . . . tenuous" (123), he wisely begins with complete books in which the liberal doctrine is believed to be embodied and only afterward turns to the fragments. But he does not take the complete works as wholes; he uses them as quarries from which he removes without any ado the liberal gems which, it seems, are immediately recognizable as such; if he is not confronted with fragments, he creates fragments. Furthermore, four of the ten complete books used in the first and basic part of his argument are poetic works, and poets are "not reporters"; one is a history which stems from the first pre-Christian century and which therefore is not obviously a good source of pre-Platonic thought (64, 73); the others are dialogues of Plato, who also is "not a reporter," and Aristotle's *Politics*. It would be petty to pay much attention to the fact that, on occasion, Havelock does not hesitate to assert without evidence that, in a given passage in which Plato does not claim to report, "Plato is reporting" (181). For on the whole, Havelock is very distrustful of Plato's and Aristotle's remarks about their predecessors. Hence it would seem that he cannot reasonably follow any other procedure in reconstructing pre-Platonic social science except to start from the complete prose works which are indubitably pre-Platonic, viz. from Herodotus and Thucydides. Havelock rejects this beginning apparently on the ground that Herodotus and Thucydides are historians and not scientists or that their works contain only "concrete observations" and not "generic schematizations" (405–406). But may "concrete observations" not be based on general premises? If a present-day historian of classical thought can know Bradley, Bentham, Bosanquet, Darwin, Dewey, Freud, Green, Grotius, Hegel, Hobbes, Hume, James, Kant, Leibniz, Locke, Machiavelli, Marx, Mill, Newton, Rousseau, Spencer (see the Index of Havelock's book), it is possible that Herodotus and Thucydides had heard of one or the other Greek anthropologist and that a careful reading of their histories will bring to light the "generic schematizations" which guided their "concrete observations." Havelock himself has occasional glimpses of this possibility (e.g. 414). What seems to protect him against the pitfalls of his procedure is his awareness that, at any rate as regards "the Elder Sophists," the sources are "imperfect and imprecise and the task of piecing them together to make a coherent picture requires philological discipline, a good deal of finesse, and also an exercise of over-all judgment which must be content to leave some things unsettled" (157, 230). We shall have to consider whether his deed corresponds to his speech, or whether he exhibits the virtues which he cannot help claiming to be indispensable to his enterprise.

Liberalism implies a philosophy of history. "History" does not mean in this context a kind of inquiry or the outcome of an inquiry, but rather the object of an inquiry or a "dimension of reality." Since the Greek word from which history is derived does not have the latter meaning, philological discipline would prevent one from ascribing to any Greek thinker a philosophy of history, at least before one has laid the proper foundation for such an ascription. Havelock thinks or acts differently. Since his authors do not speak of history in the derivative sense of the term, he makes them speak of it and thus transforms them into modern thinkers, if not directly into liberals. For instance, he translates "becoming" or "all human things" by "History" and he inserts "history," with brackets or without them, into the ancient sayings (62, 94, 108, 115).

The characteristic assertion of liberalism seems to be that man and hence also morality is not "a fixed quantity"; that man's nature and therewith morality are essentially changing; that this change constitutes History; and that through History man has developed from most imperfect beginnings into a civilized or humane being. The opponents of liberalism seem to assert that man's nature does not change, that morality is timeless or a priori, and that man's beginnings were perfect (27–29, 35, 40, 44–45). But it is not clear, and it has not been made clear by Havelock, that there is a necessary connection between the assertion that man's nature does not change and the assertion that man's beginnings were perfect, that is, superior to the present. The recollection, we do not say of Plato and Aristotle, but merely of eighteenth-century progressivism would have dispelled the confusion. Be this as it may, as is indicated by the titles of the pertinent chapters in Havelock's book, he is mainly concerned with the question regarding the status of man in the beginning.

The preliberal or orthodox position must be understood by Havelock as the belief that man's beginnings were simply perfect, that man's original state was the garden of Eden or the golden age, a state in which men were well provided for by God or gods and not in need of work and skills, and in which nothing was required of them except childlike obedience: imperfection or misery, and hence the need for work and the arts, arose through man's fault or guilt; but these merely human remedies are utterly insufficient. The orthodox regard History as Regress. "The classic Greek statement of the Eden dream" occurs in Hesiod's account of the golden age in the *Works and Days*. According to Havelock, the comparison of the golden age with the garden of Eden is not a loose analogy: "Hesiod's narrative conveys the inevitable suggestion that Eden was lost through eating of the fruit of the tree of knowledge" (36). Hesiod's "famous account of the five ages" contains "the story of three successive failures of three generations of men" (37), of failures which culminate in the present, the worst of all five ages. Havelock hears in Hesiod's account "the tone of genuine social and moral critique." Yet he cannot take him seriously: Hesiod's account of the fifth or present age "reads like the perennial and peevish complaint of an ageing conservative whose hardening habits and faculties cannot come to terms with youth or with changing conditions." Accordingly, he apologizes for having "lingered over Hesiod" after having devoted to him less than five pages, a considerable part of which is filled with a mere enumeration of items mentioned by Hesiod (40).

Havelock suggests then that according to Hesiod man lost Eden through his sin. Yet only three out of five successive races of men were "failures." The first and golden race was not a failure. There is no indication whatever that it came to an end through man's sin. The golden race lived under Kronos; the next race, the silver race, was hidden away by Zeus; and the three last races are explicitly said to have been "made" by Zeus. It would seem then, as Havelock notes in a different context, that when Zeus "succeeded to the throne of Kronos . . . human degeneration began" (53): the destruction of the golden race was due to Zeus's dethroning of Kronos. Zeus apparently did not wish or was not able to make a golden race of his own. It is, to say the least, not perfectly clear whether according to Hesiod the failure of the silver, bronze, and iron races was not due in the last analysis to Zeus's whim or his defective workmanship, rather than to man's fault. "Hebrew analogies . . . can often mislead" (137). However, one of the races made by Zeus, the fourth race, the race of the heroes or demigods, was by far superior to the three other races made or ruled by Zeus; some of the men of the fourth race are so excellent that they are again ruled by Kronos, if only after their death. Havelock does not explain why Hesiod assigned to the demigods the place between the inferior bronze race and the still more inferior iron race. When Plato adopted Hesiod's scheme in the *Republic*, he gave a reason why or intimated in what respect the fourth race, or rather the fourth regime, is almost equal to the first regime: the first regime is the rule of the philosophers, and the fourth regime is democracy, that is, the only regime apart from the first in which philosophers can live or live freely (546 e–547 al, 557d 4, 558a8). For reasons which need not be stated, one cannot use the Platonic variation for the understanding of the original. It is pertinent to say that according to Hesiod the fifth or iron race is not necessarily the last race: the age succeeding the iron age is likely to be superior to it or to the present age, which itself is not at all deprived of every goodness (*Works and Days* 174–175, 179). Could Hesiod have thought that a more or less better race is always succeeded by a more or less worse race which in its turn is always succeeded by a more or less better race and so on until the age of Zeus (or human life as we know it) comes to its end? On the basis of the evidence, this suggestion is more "inevitable" than the accepted interpretation. Under no circumstances is one entitled to say that Hesiod regarded "History as Regress."

How Hesiod's account of the five races must be understood depends on the context in which it occurs. As for its immediate context, it is the second of three stories; the first story is the account of Prometheus and Pandora, and the third story is the tale of the hawk and the nightingale.

Havelock refers in a few words to the first story, in which work may be said to be presented as a curse, but he does not say anything about the third story, although it is very pertinent to the history of Greek liberalism. The hawk said to the nightingale while he carried her high up in the clouds, having gripped her fast with his talons: "He is a fool who tries to withstand the stronger, for he will never vanquish him and he suffers pain besides the disgrace." The king believes that he disposes entirely of the fate of the singer, but the singer or the poet has a power of his own—a power surpassing that of the king (*Theogony* 94–103). As for the broad context of this story as well as of the story of the five races, it is the *Works and Days* as a whole. The poem as a whole tells when and how the various "works," especially of farming, must be done and which "days" are propitious and which not for various purposes; the account of the works and the days is preceded by exhortations to work as the only proper thing for just men and as a blessing, by answers to the question as to why the gods compel men to work, and by the praise of Zeus the king, the guardian of justice who blesses the just and crushes the proud if he wills (*W.D.* 267–273). There are, it seems, two ways of life: that of the unjust idlers and that of the just who work, especially as farmers. Closer inspection shows that there are at least three ways of life corresponding to the three kinds of men: those who understand by themselves, those who listen to the former and obey them, and those who understand neither by themselves nor by listening to others. The man who understands by himself and therefore can speak well and with understanding and is best of all is, in the highest case, the singer. The singer as singer neither works nor is idle. His deeds belong to the night, rather than to the "days." Song transcends the primary antithesis which must be transcended because of the ambiguity of work: work is both a curse and a blessing. Toil is the brother of Forgetting (*Theogony* 226–227), while the Muses are the daughters of Memory. Song transcends the primary antithesis because its highest theme—Zeus—transcends it.

Havelock is not concerned with the context of Hesiod's stories of the perfect beginning because he is too certain of his answers to all questions. "An early agricultural economy" combined with "disillusionment with sex" finds "wish fulfillment by projecting backwards"; and the "backward vision" combines "with an *a priori* epistemology" (36, 40). A psychology and a sociology derived from the observation of present-day Western man, or rather a certain type of present-day Western men, take the place of the authentic context and are used as the key to the character of men and societies of the past in such a way that phenomena, which are not allowed to exist by the "*a priori* epistemology" of these present-day pursuits, can never be noticed. The circle, being a circle, is necessarily closed. But the mind is closed too. The attempt is made to catch a profound and subtle thought in the meshes of a thought of unsurpassed shallowness and crudity.

As our quotations have abundantly proved, Havelock takes it for granted that the modern social scientist, but not Hesiod, understood what happened in Hesiod or to Hesiod. As for the assertion that Hesiod had an epistemology, it is not as preposterous as it sounds. Hesiod reflected on the sources of his knowledge. His *Works and Days* derives from three different sources: his experience, what people say, and what the Muses taught him. For instance, what he teaches regarding farming is derived from his experience, but since he had little experience of sailing, his teaching regarding sailing depends very much on instruction by the Muses (W.D. 646–662, 803). Instruction by the Muses seems to be indispensable for knowledge of the things that shall be and of the things that were in the olden times as well as of the gods who are always; that is, for knowledge hidden from man, who has experience only of what is now. The Muses, however, go abroad by night, veiled in thick mist. Or, as they said to Hesiod, they know how to say many lies which resemble the truth, but they also know, when they will, how to sing true things (*Theogony* 9–10, 27–28). As far as we can tell, the Muses did not always tell Hesiod which of their tales were true and which were not. Certainly Hesiod does not tell us which of his tales are true and which are not. The farmer, not the singer, must strip when doing his work (W.D. 391–392). Hesiod's teaching is ambiguous according to his knowledge, not to say according to his intention. One form in which the ambiguity appears is self-contradiction. Seeing that the Muses are the daughters of Zeus, we wonder whether they instructed the men of the age of Kronos as they instruct a few men of the iron age and whether the possible difference in this respect between the two ages did not affect Hesiod's private judgment about the golden age.

We conclude that it is not wise to open the discussion of the "regressivist" position with the interpretation of Hesiod. It is wiser to begin with the nonmusic and unambiguous discussion of the problem of progress which we find in the second book of Aristotle's *Politics*. Assuming as a fact that the change from the old manner in the arts and the sciences to the new manner has been beneficial, Aristotle wonders whether a corresponding change in the laws would be equally beneficial. He thus raises the question as to whether, as some people ("the Greek liberals") believe, there is a necessary harmony between intellectual progress and social progress. His answer is not unqualifiedly in the affirmative. By understanding his reasoning one will be enabled to begin to understand those Greek thinkers who both after and before the emergence of science were distrustful of social change and "looked backward."

Havelock tries to supplement Hesiod's "regressivist" statement by two Platonic statements of the same description. In the myth of the *Statesman*, Plato contrasts the present state of things, the state of things under Zeus, with the preceding state of things under Kronos. He modifies the old story by presenting the process as cyclical: the present age of Zeus will be succeeded by another age of Kronos, and so on. In spite of this, "the net effect upon the reader's imagination is less cyclical than regressive"; Plato "works on our values" in such a way that he "unmistakeably and ingeniously . . . denatures the activities of a technological culture and demotes it to the rank of a second-best" (42–43). While one must not neglect how Plato's "allegory" (47) affects the readers' imagination, one must also consider how it affects the reader's thought. Plato makes it clear that we have knowledge by perception only of the present age; of the age of Kronos we know only from hearsay (272b 1–3, 269a 7–8). Myths are told to children, and in the *Statesman*, a philosopher tells the myth of the ages of Kronos and of Zeus to a child or a youth who has barely outgrown childhood (268e 4–6; *Republic* 377a 1–6, 378d 1). As regards the only state of things of which we possess firsthand knowledge, the philosopher says that there is in it no divine providence, no care of God or gods for men (271d 3–6, 273a 1, 274d 3–6). The philosopher who indicates this thought, which is at variance with what other Platonic characters say elsewhere, is of course not Socrates, who merely listens in silence and refrains even at the end of the conversation from expressing his disagreement or agreement with what the strange philosopher had said. The stranger expresses a less disconcerting thought by saying that even if there were divine providence, human happiness would not be assured: the question of whether men led a blessed life under Kronos, when the gods took care of men, is left unanswered on the ground that we do not know whether men then used their freedom from care for philosophizing instead of telling one another myths; only a life dedicated to philosophy can be called happy (272b 3–d 4). Hesiod compelled us to raise a similar question regarding the golden age. Here we are compelled to raise the question as to whether philosophy would have been possible at all in the age of Kronos, in which there was no need for the arts, and hence the arts did not exist (272a); we recall that Socrates did not tire of talking, not indeed with shoemakers and physicians, but of shoemakers and physicians (*Gorgias* 491a 1–3) in order to make clear to himself and to others what philosophy is; he thus indeed "demoted [the arts] to the rank of a second-best," but this is a high rank. Above all, as Havelock recognizes, Plato admits in the myth of the *Statesman* the imperfect character of man's beginnings; that Plato has "borrowed" this view from "the scientific anthropologists" we shall believe as soon as we have been shown; we do not sufficiently know the limitations of Plato's mind to be able to say that he could not possibly have arrived at this view by his own efforts. Yet "then, illogically, but necessarily" he ascribes to fire, the arts, seeds, and plants divine origin (43). That the Eleatic Stranger thus contradicts himself is true, but we are not certain whether he does not contradict his contradiction in the same breath (274d 2–6), thus restoring the original position. And even while he speaks for a moment of divine gifts, Plato's Eleatic Stranger does not go so far as his

Protagoras who, on a similar occasion, speaks not only of the gifts of Prometheus but in addition of the political art as a gift from Zeus.

In the *Laws*, Plato's spokesman converses with old men who possess political experience. Again the story is told of how men lived under Kronos in abundance and were ruled by demons who cared for them. "This account which makes use of truth, tells even today" that not men, but a god or the immortal mind within us, must rule over men if the city is to be happy (713c 2–714a 2). Here men are indeed said to have led a blessed life under Kronos, but the conclusion from this is not that one must long for the lost age of Kronos, but that, in the decisive respect, the bliss of that age—rule of the divine—is equally possible now. When, in the *Laws*, Plato discusses man's first age thematically or, as Havelock says, "more ambitiously," he does not refer to the age of Kronos. Present-day life, including the great amounts of vice and of virtue which we find in it, has come into being out of the first men, the sparse survivors of a cataclysm (678a 7–9): the first men were not the golden race of Hesiod. Havelock contends that the paraphrased sentence "is really intended to suggest that the factor of novelty in human history does not exist" (45). He would be right if, in seeking the origin or the cause or the "out of which" of a thing, one implicitly asserts that the effect cannot differ from the cause.

Still, this time Havelock has some evidence for ascribing to Plato "a regressive concept of human history": "an Eden of innocence, not perfect in either virtue or vice, is later described as [possessing] three of the four cardinal virtues complete" (49). He would find us pedantic if we tried to stop him with the observation that Plato uses the comparative and not the positive (679e 2–3) and thus denies completeness to the cardinal virtues possessed by early men. Plato altogether denies to early man the first and highest of the cardinal virtues, wisdom or prudence. In some respects, he suggests, early men were superior to most present-day men, but in the decisive respect—as regards wisdom or the quest for wisdom—they were certainly inferior to the best of later men. To begin with, Plato praises early men highly: he praises them as highly as he praises the members of the city of pigs in the *Republic*. With some exaggeration one may therefore say that up to this point Havelock's interpretation would be tolerable if there were no philosophy. But Plato goes on to illustrate the political order of early man with that of Homer's Cyclopes. The interlocutor Megillus is intelligent enough to see that Plato's spokesman in fact describes early men as savages (680d 1–4) and even as cannibals (781e 5–782c 2). While, as we have seen, Havelock noticed that Plato's description of early men changes from a very qualified praise to a less qualified praise, he fails to see that it changes again and this time to the abandonment of all praise. Hence he judges that in Plato's account "the whole scientific perspective is . . . skillfully and totally corrupted by . . . wholly unscientific suggestion[s]" (48); given his prejudices, he cannot help reaching this result, except that he should not have spoken of Plato's "skill." From the fact that inventions have been made, Plato infers that men lacked the invented things at an earlier epoch; Havelock makes him "argue quite naively that though new invention has been achieved by man . . . it must come to a stop sometime": the notion of an "infinitely extended history" or of "human history as, so to speak, open at both ends is wholly alien to his imagination" (49). Whatever may be true of the liberal imagination, the liberal's science tells him that invention must come to a stop sometime, since the life of the human race will come to a stop sometime.

Following Havelock, we have completely disregarded the context of the "archeology" of the third book of Plato's *Laws* or the meaning of the work as a whole. As we can here only assert, consideration of the whole work would merely confirm what already appears from the passages used by Havelock, namely, that it is wholly unwarranted to say that according to Plato, man's early life is "a wholly admirable and happy thing" (58). Nevertheless Havelock is right in saying that "the net effect" of the passages in question "upon the reader's imagination" is the opposite. What "necessity" drove Plato, whose "systematic mind was, to say the least, not prone to contradiction" (100), to be "illogical"? Havelock suggests that Plato was compelled grudgingly to make concessions to the Greek anthropologists, but that his prejudice always reasserted itself and especially when he was old, that is, when he wrote the *Laws* in which "the Hesiodic nostalgia is in control" (44, 47). This explanation rests on the untenable assumption that Plato believed in the age of Kronos. Havelock also suggests, it seems, that Plato had to contradict himself because he could not contradict the Greek anthropologists "in open fight," for in doing so he would have been compelled to restate their doctrine and thus to contribute to the spreading of a dangerous doctrine (87–88). This explanation rests on the assumption, proved untenable by the tenth book of the *Laws*, for instance, that Plato was afraid openly to set forth dangerous or subversive doctrines to which he was opposed. Havelock might retort that the extreme view openly set forth and openly attacked by Plato was less dangerous in his eyes than the view of the Greek liberals; but until we know that there were Greek liberals we must regard it as possible that Plato failed to set forth the liberal view because the liberal view did not exist. We on our part suggest this explanation. Plato knew that most men read more with their "imagination" than with open-minded care and are therefore much more benefited by salutary myths than by the naked truth. Precisely the liberals who hold that morality is historical or of merely human origin must go on to say, with the sophist Protagoras as paraphrased by Havelock, that this invaluable acquisition which for later men is a heritage "must never be lost" or is "too precious to be gambled with" (187): the greatest enemies of civilization in civilized countries are those who squander the heritage because they look down on it or on the past; civilization is much less en-

dangered by narrow but loyal preservers than by the shallow and glib futur-
ists who, being themselves rootless, try to destroy all roots and thus do
everything in their power in order to bring back the initial chaos and pro-
miscuity. The first duty of civilized man is then to respect his past. This
respect finds its exaggerated but effective expression in the belief that the
ancestors—the Founding Fathers—were simply superior to the present
generation and especially to the present youth, and mere "logic" leads
from this to the belief in perfect beginnings or in the age of Kronos.

Havelock begins his attempt to disinter Greek liberalism by commenting
on three passages each of which is taken from a play of one of the three
tragedians. He contends that these passages present a progressivist view
of history and thus show the presence of "scientific anthropology"
(52). Aeschylus' *Prometheus* "offers a drastic correction of the Hesiodic
scheme." When Zeus dethroned Kronos, he desired to destroy the human
race and to plant a new one, but thanks to Prometheus' intervention,
which was inspired by love of man or by compassion for man, this plan was
frustrated. In Aeschylus' presentation Zeus's decision appears as "the whim
of a cruel and careless despot" (53). Aeschylus "underlines the philan-
thropy" of Prometheus because in his presentation man "is somehow gain-
ing in stature" (54). He says, as did Hesiod, that Prometheus' crime consisted in the theft of fire for the benefit of man, but he adds with emphasis
that the stolen fire, or the stolen source of fire, became man's teacher in
every art, that Prometheus has given man all arts, all of them great boons
to man, and, above all, that Prometheus gave man understanding. According to Havelock, then, Aeschylus makes two assertions. In the first place,
"so far from being created by the gods or descended from them [the
human species] emerged as we know it from a pre-human condition," and
it emerged from its prehuman condition through technology, that is,
through "human achievement" (57, 61). Second, "somehow, in the unfolding history of civilization, the cause of technology and the cause of
compassion are bound up together"; the threat of a "liquidation" of the
human race (by Zeus) was "a concomitant . . . of the total absence of
technology" (58). Aeschylus is, then, a believer in progressive evolution.
But did he believe only in progress achieved or did he have "the vistas of
infinite time," that is, of infinite future progress? Prometheus' condemnation and punishment by Zeus seem to show that Aeschylus "has retained
the Hesiodic pessimism"; but since in the end there will be a reconciliation
between Prometheus and Zeus, our faith in "the historical process" is restored (61). Havelock calls Prometheus' enumeration of the arts which he
gave to man "the catalogue of human achievement," just as he finds in the
play the view that man was not made by the gods. He does not even attempt to prove the second assertion (cf. *Prometheus* 235).

As for the first assertion, he admits that "on the surface of the drama"

Prometheus is a god, but he contends reasonably that if the fire which Prometheus stole is, as Prometheus himself says, the teacher of man in many or in all arts (*Prometheus* 109–110, 256), the arts are to some extent man's own achievement (63–65). What then is Prometheus' achievement? Who or what is Prometheus? "Prometheus is the embodiment of Intelligence" (64). Yet Prometheus says that he put blind hopes in men as a remedy for having made them stop to foresee their doom, their death (vv. 250–252). Similarly, he regards as his greatest invention the art of medicine by which men are enabled to ward off all diseases (vv. 478–483): does he claim that medicine can heal all mortal diseases or that he has abolished man's mortality? Is he a boaster? But he knows, or he has learned through his suffering, the limitation of all art: "Art is by far weaker than necessity" (vv. 514–518); Prometheus' love of man cannot overcome the power of necessity. There is then no "infinite progress." The well-meaning bringer of blind hopes is himself the victim of a blind hope: he did not foresee how harshly he would be punished by Zeus. The fore-thinker lacked forethought in his own case. In the struggle between Zeus and Kronos, between Guile and Strength, he sided with Zeus; he made a choice which seemed wise at the time, but which he now regrets (vv. 201–225, 268–271; cf. 1071–1079). He does not wish to tell Io her future fate because he knows that ignorance is sometimes better than knowledge or that man needs blind hopes, but he is easily persuaded to act against his better knowledge out of the kindness of his heart (vv. 624 ff.). Is Aeschylus' message so different from Hesiod's, who taught that Zeus is wilier than the wily Prometheus (vv. 61–62; *Theogony* 545–616)? Zeus, not Prometheus, teaches man to learn wisdom by suffering (vv. 585–586; *Agamemnon* 168–178) and not through the power of the arts. Is then the Zeus of the *Prometheus* a cruel tyrant?

The play is a part and certainly not the last part of a trilogy; Prometheus' antagonist does not appear in the play; Hermes states Zeus's case as well as he can; but we do not know how Zeus would have stated it. The very greatness of Prometheus, which is so powerfully exhibited in the play, may be meant to give us an inkling of the greatness of Zeus, of Zeus's wisdom. Zeus is so great that he cannot be understood, that he must appear as a cruel tyrant, before he has manifested himself. He found men—Kronos' men—as witless beings; the implication that Kronos' race of men was not golden, that the first men were witless, is part of the praise of Zeus. Zeus wished to destroy Kronos' men and to create new ones. Prometheus claims that he prevented the destruction of man by stealing fire for him. Did Zeus wish to create men worthy of him and free from blind hopes? Was it impossible for Zeus to undo the effect of Prometheus' deed, or did he decide to use Prometheus' kindhearted but not foreseeing deed in a foreseeing, in a royal manner? Did he decide, that is, to use Prometheus' increase of man's power as a means for teaching man true wisdom by the suffering coming from the very power of the arts? By dwelling on the "surface" of the play, one becomes aware of the contrast between the arts and true wisdom. Since the play presents the first men as most imperfect and since it seems to suggest that the arts are less divine gifts than human inventions, Havelock is certain that Aeschylus used a "scientific source" and as a consequence engages in speculations about the scientific anthropology which illumined the poet (61–64). With perhaps greater right could not one seek for the "scientific source" of the biblical account according to which the city and the arts were originated by Cain and his race? The Bible leaves much less doubt regarding the merely human origin of "civilization" than does Aeschylus. Havelock does not prove and cannot prove from Aeschylus the existence of "Greek liberalism." Aeschylus' changes of Hesiod's story are much more easily understood as the outcome of a somewhat different meditation on things divine-human than as due to the influence of science.

Havelock turns next to the choral song of the *Antigone* in which the chorus expresses its trembling admiration for man as the being which is supremely awful and supremely endangered: an awful crime against the law of the city has just been discovered. In describing man's awful or wondrous character, the chorus enumerates man's most outstanding inventions: "The figure of Prometheus has disappeared." This would prove the influence of science if it had been impossible for Greeks, or for men in general, who were not scientists or influenced by science to be somehow aware of the human origin of the human arts (cf. *Laws* 677d4). In two pages Havelock proves, in accordance with his standards of proof, three things. According to Havelock's Sophocles, man taught himself "consciousness"; hence Havelock forces the reader to wonder how an unconscious being can teach itself anything and in particular consciousness. The whole choral song in question expresses "flamboyant optimism." "The conclusion of the chorus carries us beyond the confines of anthropology to the borders of a liberal theory of morals and politics" (68–70). With equally "quick speech" he shows the influence of science as well as the "theistic" or "pietistic" perversion of science in a passage of Euripides' *Suppliants*. That passage is declared to be "a skillful rewrite" of a "scientific original" the existence of which we have by now learned to assume since we have so frequently been told to do so. The only remark which could possibly be stretched to be meant to be an attempt of a proof is the assertion that Euripides becomes involved "in unconscious paradox"—in a contradiction, since in theistically praising the kindness of heaven he speaks nontheistically of its harshness. In fact, Euripides makes his Theseus say that a god taught man to protect himself against a god, that is, another god. Havelock, however, knows that Euripides speaks "in the person of Theseus" (72).

For Havelock's purpose Diodorus Siculus is much more important than the three great tragedians. Diodorus—already an authority for Machiavelli and Hobbes—gives a coherent account of the origin of the universe and of man which is in fundamental agreement with "scientific naturalism," the inspiration of "the progressive . . . view of history" (75–76). In his sympathetic survey, Havelock mentions the fact that according to Diodorus the universe and man have come into being, whereas for Diodorus it is equally important that they will perish (I. 6. 3.): "progressivism" is not a precise description of his "view of history." Diodorus takes it for granted that man is by nature well endowed since he has as his helpers "hands and reason" (I. 8. 9); according to Havelock, he thus contradicts his "earlier naturalistic account of the origins of language" (78): as if reason, which is one and the same, and language, of which there are necessarily many, were the same thing; or, in other words, as if man's leading a brutish life at the beginning would prove that man was originally a brute. Hence Havelock is compelled to impute to Diodorus the desire to describe, not what man achieved by using his given hands and his given reason, but the genesis of the human hand and the genesis of the human reason (79). Since Diodorus speaks in his "prehistory" (75) only of nations or tribes, and not yet of the city, it follows that "the city-state could not have been for [the Greek anthropologists] the one essential form toward which all society tends" (80): what in fact follows is that the city is not "pre-historical." Diodorus repeatedly says that man progressed "little by little"; by this emphasis on "gradualism," Havelock contends, Diodorus opposes the myths according to which man's original condition was improved by gifts of the gods. Yet after having turned from a traditional speculation about man's origin, from "pre-history," to the description of actions which are remembered as having taken place in known localities of the inhabited earth (I. 8. 1 and 9. 1), Diodorus follows an Egyptian account according to which the arts are gifts of certain gods. Havelock is inclined to regard "this Egyptian fairy tale" as "a sort of parody," and he refers to "the whole question of why in antiquity it was so difficult for [the scientific] anthropologies to survive in their own stark scientific honesty" (84–85). We are not aware that he even tried to answer this question, although Diodorus is not silent about the usefulness of myths or untrue stories of a certain kind. If Havelock had not so airily dismissed Diodorus' "conflated and rather confused account of the mythical history of ancient Egypt" (83), he might have observed that Diodorus presents as part of the Egyptian lore the "Euhemeristic" explanation of the origin of the gods (cf. I. 13 with I. 17. 1–2 and I. 20. 5). He certainly does not avail himself of this opportunity for reflecting on a possible fundamental difference between ancient and modern "naturalism," between an approach or doctrine for which it was "difficult to survive in its own stark scientific honesty" and one for which it is extremely easy because it is allied with popular enlightenment. Such reflection might have led him to wonder whether the ancient predecessors did not conceive of the relation between science and society, and hence of the character of both science and society, in entirely different terms from those of the liberals. On the other hand it is gratifying to see that "gradualism" does not necessarily exclude the crucial importance of "gifted individuals" (93) and hence that "gradualism" may make allowance for sudden changes.

Having arrived at this point we are in a position to pass final judgment on Havelock's procedure. When speaking of Plato, he says: "we have spoken of his [scientific or naturalistic] source or sources. The case for their *existence* turns upon two factors: there is first the cross-comparison that can be made between the items of his historical analysis and those present in the reports of the dramatists and of Diodorus; second, there are the inner contradictions discoverable in [Plato's] pages" (100; the italics are not in the original). In recovering the teaching of the Greek anthropologists from Plato's writings, Havelock can already use the results of his analysis of the tragedies. But with what right did he assume the existence of "scientific" sources of the tragedians when he analyzed their plays? We assume that in his opinion some people have justified his assumption, but we cannot be certain that this is his opinion. We feel entitled to speak of an involuntary satire on scientific method and on scientific progress.

Since Havelock believes that Plato made greater concessions to the Greek anthropologists when he was not yet old than when he was old, he tries to reconstruct the teaching of these men from what seem to be the most promising sections of Plato's relatively early writings: the myth of the *Protagoras* and the second book of the *Republic*. The *Protagoras* is altogether the most important source for Havelock, as any degree of familiarity with the modern literature on the subject would have led one to expect. Read in his manner, the *Protagoras* supplies one with both the anthropology and the political theory of the Greek liberals. His whole thesis depends, as it depended in the writings of the scholars who maintained his thesis before him, on their interpretation of that dialogue. Havelock starts from the plausible assumption that Plato is not "a reporter" and therefore that the speech which Protagoras makes in the dialogue named after him is Plato's work. Yet if this speech is to supply us with information about the view of Protagoras himself, we must be in a position to distinguish its Protagorean elements from its Platonic elements. Since we know which teachings are peculiarly Platonic (or Socratic) and since the Platonic Protagoras makes use of peculiarly Platonic teachings, the only thing needed to discover Protagoras' teaching is a simple operation of subtraction. In his myth, the Platonic Protagoras asserts or suggests that there are essential or qualitative differences between various species of animals, and especially between man and the brutes, as well as within man between his intellectual power and his social or moral sense. According to Havelock, the emphasis on these differences is Platonic (or Socratic) and wholly incompatible with "previous Greek science," which asserted the primacy of "process" in general and of "the historical process" in particular as distinguished from the apparently essential distinctions between the products of the process (91). Yet we are dealing with a myth here, a popular statement, and Protagoras does not go beyond using the popular or common-sense distinctions of various kinds or races or tribes of living beings. If the incriminated remarks of the Platonic Protagoras prove Socratic influence, then the first chapter of Genesis was written under Socratic influence, to say nothing of Empedocles (B 71–76) and Democritus (B 164). When Havelock finds in the Platonic Protagoras' speech "the Platonic thesis . . . that men differ fundamentally from birth in mental capacity and aptitude," he himself admits that "this could be regarded as a truism of common sense" (97).

Furthermore, the Platonic Protagoras uses against Socrates what one may call the essential differences between the species and between the different parts of living beings in order to show the relativity or the "multi-colored" character of the good (333d 8–334c 6). In commenting upon this passage Havelock does not complain that Plato has adulterated the Protagorean teaching; he regards that passage as a reliable source, in fact as an "excerpt" from Protagoras, and draws infinite conclusions from it. He contends, however, that that passage contains, not "a classification of things in themselves in their genera and species," but a "classification . . . of acts and performances of things done by men in given situations" (205). We shall not quarrel with Havelock as to whether a classification does not presuppose the existence of classes. It suffices to say that the Platonic Protagoras classifies the useful things on the basis of a classification of the beings or parts of beings to which the useful things are useful. Moreover, Protagoras' most famous saying ("Man is the measure of all things") implies that not every being is the measure of all things and hence that there is a qualitative difference between man and the brutes. Above all, what is the status of the "species" and their "essential properties" according to the Platonic Protagoras? "The mortal races" are primarily mixtures of earth and fire and all that is mingled with fire and earth; as such they do not possess "natures," for the "natures" of the various races or kinds are the "powers" which they possess; primarily "the mortal races" are not even distinguished by size; the powers or natures or "essential properties" are secondary or derivative (*Protagoras* 320d 5, e 2–4, 321c 1). In this crucial point the teaching of the Platonic Protagoras is then not at all marred by "Socraticism," but is properly "naturalistic."

The second consideration by means of which Havelock tries to achieve the subtraction of the Platonic element from the Platonic Protagoras' speech starts from the fact that "in matters of religion [Protagoras] was a complete agnostic," and yet Plato's Protagoras ascribes to the gods the origin of all animals and especially of man and, above all, of the arts and of justice (92–94). Granted that Protagoras was "a complete agnostic," must he always have talked like a complete agnostic? Does he not sufficiently make clear where he stands by explicitly distinguishing his account of the origins as his myth from his *logos* (320c 6–7, 324d 6–7, 328c 3) and by treating the gods very differently in his myth on the one hand and in his *logos* on the other? It is in accordance with this, and it is not the consequence of Plato's defective "editorial skill" which does not succeed in reconciling a Platonic setting with a Protagorean content, that the Platonic Protagoras contradicts himself. He states to begin with that all animals, including man, were molded by the gods and later on that man in contradistinction to the brutes has "kinship with the gods" (92). He speaks of man's "kinship with the god" (not "with the gods") after he had shown how man had come to partake of a divine share or lot: man's kinship with the god is his participation in a divine lot. Man came to partake of a divine lot, not through Zeus's gift of right, but through Prometheus' theft of fire and technical wisdom from Hephaestus and Athena (321d 1–322a 4). Man owes his salvation or his being in the first place not to a gift of the gods but to a theft from the gods, to a kind of rebellion against the gods. This should be acceptable as a mythical expression of the "naturalistic" creed. But why does the Platonic Protagoras tell a myth at all?

In order to answer this question, one must consider the context. The city of Athens was rather liberal, but not so liberal as to tolerate every pursuit and every teaching. It seems that that city was so much opposed to Protagoras' activity that it had his writings burned and himself expelled. Plato's Protagoras was aware of the fact that he was in some danger in Athens since he was a stranger who engaged in an unpopular activity, in the activity of a "sophist." Havelock cannot consider this, although he cannot help noting the existence of a "prejudice" against the sophists (158) because he is compelled by his prejudice to imagine that the "model of Periclean Athens is there as the sophistic prototype of what a complete society really is" (187) or that there was perfect harmony between the sophists and the Athenian democracy. Granting for a moment that the sophists loved the Athenian democracy, it does not follow that the love was requited. The Platonic Protagoras at any rate had a strong sense of danger. In order to destroy the suspicion against the sophists, he decided to deviate from the practice of the earlier sophists who concealed their pursuit: he is the first man who professes to be a sophist, the first who speaks up, as his very name indicates. This does not mean that he says always and to everyone all that he thinks: apart from the precautionary measure of professing to be a sophist, he has provided himself with other precautionary measures. He does not tell what those other precautionary measures are. But the professed "agnostic" gives a sufficient indication of them by describing their intended result as follows: "under God, I shall not suffer anything terrible on account of my professing to be a sophist." The indication is indeed not sufficient for everyone, for, as he says, "the many do not, so to speak, notice anything" (316c 5–317c 1).

The third and final clue supplied by the speech of the Platonic Protagoras is his assertion that there is a fundamental difference between the arts and reverence or right: the latter are "universals," that is, all men must partake of them, while it is neither necessary nor desirable that everyone should be a physician, a shoemaker, and so on. Havelock finds this assertion incompatible with the assumed democratic creed of Protagoras (93). But does democracy, as distinguished from Marxism, require that every man be a jack of all trades? How does Havelock know that Protagoras' assumed theory of democracy demanded that everyone be a jack of all trades? The Platonic Protagoras' assertion that there is a fundamental difference between the arts and "man's moral sense" is meant to be the basis of democracy: all men are equal as regards that knowledge by which civil society as such stands or falls. Yet Plato's Protagoras describes reverence and right as gifts of Zeus, and how can "a complete agnostic" give a religious account of the origin and the validity of morality (93–94)? He explains his mythical account of the origin and validity of morality in what one may call the nonmythical part of his speech. The universal practice of mankind shows that everyone "in some way or another" partakes of justice, as distinguished from flute playing for instance; that is, that everyone must claim to be just, regardless of whether he is just or not (323a 5–c 2). Justice has in common with the arts that it is acquired by teaching and training; but the difference between the teaching and training by which the arts are acquired and the teaching and training by which justice is acquired appears from the fact that the latter consists chiefly in punishment: men become just "in some way or another" chiefly by punishment, or the threat of it, but also by praise, as distinguished from instruction proper (323d 6–324c 5, 324e 6–326a 4, 327d 1–2). What is mythically called a gift of Zeus is nonmythically described as "social compulsion," which as such cannot produce, at any rate in the case of thinking men, more than conformism or lip service. The assertion that morality rests on "social compulsion" or on "conditioning" (178) and not on natural inclination nor on calculation nor on intellectual perception should satisfy every behaviorist. It certainly satisfies Havelock after he has added a few touches of his own. When Plato's Protagoras says that the man who does not pretend to be just, whether he is just or not, is insane, Havelock adds "unless, *it is surely implied*, in temporary repentance" (171; the italics are not in the original). When the Platonic Protagoras is believed to have said that justice and virtue are useful, Havelock makes him say that morality is "pleasant" (185). Perhaps still more remarkable is his enthusiasm for what the Platonic Protagoras says regarding the purpose of punishment, namely, "that punishment only makes sense as a corrective or as a deterrent" (175). He takes it for granted that this teaching is genuinely Protagorean. But how does he know this? Because it is a liberal view? But the illiberal Plato held the same view. Besides, the same Platonic Protagoras teaches, just as Plato himself did, that there are incurable criminals who must be driven out of the city or be killed. Why did Plato entrust the rational teaching regarding punishment to Protagoras in particular? The context requires a praise of punishment, and the highest praise of punishment is its rational justification: the Platonic Protagoras presents his doctrine of punishment before he has formally concluded his myth (324d 6–7).

One cannot make a distinction between the Platonic and the Protagorean elements in the myth of the Platonic Protagoras because the contradictions occurring in that myth are perfectly intelligible as deliberate contradictions of the speaker. The same is true, *mutatis mutandis,* of the statement on the genesis of the city in the second book of the *Republic.* According to Havelock, Plato there uses the "naturalist-materialist principles" of the Greek anthropologists and finds therefore "the driving force behind the formation of society" and even of morality itself in "material and economic need." Yet Plato drops this approach "with some haste." Why then did he mention it "unless it occurred in his source and he has cited it almost by inadvertence?" (97.) This is obviously not a proof of the existence of a "naturalist" source. Understanding of the context would show that in a preliminary consideration one may limit oneself to the understanding of society and morality in terms of the bodily needs of man. After all, that section of the *Republic* which alone is discussed by Havelock deals with what is called there "a city of pigs." The city, as Aristotle says, "comes into being" for the sake of mere life but "is" for the sake of the good life. One may well begin the analysis of the city with its beginning, with its coming into being. Taking hypotheses for facts, Havelock has no difficulty whatever in accusing Plato of having "adulterated" his source (98–99). The only effort which he makes to prove his assertion starts from the "patent absurdity" which consists in Plato's attempt "to argue that a developed technical and commercial society is really a rustic Utopia committed to vegetarianism and the simple life": Plato follows the naturalists by tracing the development of society up to the development of technical and commercial society, but his obsession with primitive simplicity and innocence forces him to drop all luxuries in the same context. Similarly, Plato denies that in his original condition man waged war, "once more revealing his deeply regressive conception of history" (99–100). We disregard the fact that a society in which there is exchange of goods in the market place and which imports say salt and exports say timber is not by virtue of this a commercial society. While Havelock here goes so far as to impute to Plato's "city of pigs" the existence of "bankers," he says later on with equal disregard of the truth that "Plato omitted currency" (95, 97, 338). It is more important to understand the meaning of the whole discussion of the city of pigs as "the true city" or even as "the city" (372e 6–7,

433a). That city is not early society, but is the society according to nature which is sufficient for satisfying men's bodily needs without poverty, without compulsion (government), and without bloodshed of any kind; it is not a commercial society because it is not a competitive society, a competitive society presupposing the existence of government. Plato makes this experiment in order to show the essential limitations of society thus conceived. A society of this character may possess justice of some sort since its members exchange goods and services; it cannot possess human excellence: it is a city of pigs. Whereas its members sing hymns to the gods, they cannot sing the praises of excellent men because there cannot be excellent men in their midst (cf. 371e 9–372b 8 and 607a 3–4).

After he has completed his attempt to prove the existence of Greek progressivist philosophers from their alleged use or adulteration by the tragedians, Diodorus Siculus, and Plato, Havelock turns to the fragments of these alleged progressivists. Three very late reports on Anaximander and five fragments from Xenophanes are said to "hint at the presence in both [thinkers] of a scheme of cosmology which found perhaps its climax in the history of life and of man upon the earth. . . . The tentative conclusion can be drawn that . . . if the record of Anaximander guarantees the biological naturalism of Greek anthropology, that of Xenophanes does the same for its empirical pragmatic conception of the sources of human knowledge" (106–107). The unusual restraint of Havelock perhaps reflects the fact that according to a report to which he does not refer (21 A 49) Xenophanes regarded only reason itself, in contradistinction to sense perception, as trustworthy. He admits that "against these tentative conclusions should be set what we know of Xenophanes' 'theology.'" By this he does not mean Xenophanes' verses on the one god, the greatest among gods and men who does not resemble the mortals at all; he does not say a word about Xenophanes' Eleaticism or his denial of any coming into being; he merely means his "critical attack on Greek polytheism." To say nothing of the facts that according to a fragment and a report quoted by Havelock, Xenophanes did not limit his attack to the Greek popular notions of the gods and that he did not attack polytheism, Havelock wishes to believe that that "critical attack" "was a part of [Xenophanes'] reconstruction of the history of human institutions." Sympathizing with the spirit of present-day anthropology, Havelock "plays down" Xenophanes' concern with the question of the truth of what peoples believe.

As regards Anaxagoras, Havelock carefully avoids any reference to his doctrine regarding the ordering Intelligence which rules all things, knows all things, exists always and is unmixed, and is the cause of all things; he does not even take the trouble to deny the relevance of that doctrine for Anaxagoras' anthropology (107–112). To assimilate the Greek anthropologists to the liberals, Havelock must impute to Archelaus the view that "the historical process is . . . a natural growing process" and therefore dilute Archelaus' fundamental distinction between nature and convention ("the right and the base are not by nature but by convention" [112–114]). Similarly, when Democritus distinguishes between the "nature" of all animate beings, according to which they get themselves offspring "not for the sake of any utility" and endure hardship for it, and the assumption peculiar to men, according to which the parents derive benefit from their offspring (just as the offspring derives benefit from the parents), Havelock asserts that the peculiarly human "which is superimposed on *physis*, is not discontinuous with it" (115, 411); he is unconcerned with the difference with which Democritus is concerned: the difference between man and the brutes and the difference derived therefrom between nature and law or convention. When he is no longer under a compulsion to confront the reader with Democritean fragments, he takes courage to assert that for Democritus "nature and law did in fact coincide" (181). The fragment in question (B 278) appears to belong to the context, not of anthropological "description," but of "judgmental evaluation": Democritus questions the soundness of getting married and begetting children; the specifically human calculation which is meant to make the raising of children beneficial to the parents too, is not reliable (A 166, 169, 170; B 275–278). There is a close connection between this question and the question discussed in Aristophanes' *Birds* as to the inference to be drawn from the fact that the brutes do not respect their aged parents. Since Democritus notes that man has learned certain skills by imitating certain kinds of brutes, Havelock feels entitled to infer that according to Democritus "the possibility of any hero or master inventor . . . as having historical importance is decisively removed," although he makes Democritus speak of the "few with power of expression" who originated Greek "religious myth" (119–120; B 154 and 21). By translating "they proceeded" as "they took successive steps," he enables himself to ascribe to Democritus the "doctrine of historical gradualism" (116, 119).

So much about Havelock's account of the "philosophy of history" of the Greek anthropologists. We can be briefer in our examination of his account of the Greek liberals' political doctrine. He deals first with Democritus, then with those who are not "documented by their own utterances" (255), and finally with Antiphon. For the sake of convenience, we shall accept his assumption according to which the Democritean fragments embodied as authentic in Diels's edition are in fact authentic. The fragments which he uses to establish "the political doctrine of Democritus" are all or almost all rules of conduct which derive from common experience. While admitting that "Democritus makes a value judgment" here and there, he believes that he can discern in the fragments in question Democritus' "historical method": "the mind and method of Democritus [seek] to understand and to solve political problems simply by describing them" (131, 137, 138). He does not consider and does not even refer to Democritus' statement according to which "for all men good and true are the same, but pleasant differs from one man to another" (B 69; cf. A 166) "which no complete account of his philosophy can afford to ignore" (142); this statement would make clear that Democritus is not a historicist or a relativist, that for him the problem indicated by the distinction between factual and value judgments does not arise, and that one cannot intelligently solve a political problem by describing it if one does not know what is good for all men. As for Democritus' or Havelock's "historical method," we give two examples. Democritus' saying, "Faction within the tribe is bad for both sides," proves to Havelock that whereas Plato and Aristotle uncritically accepted "the virtual identification of nomos and polis," "Democritus true to his genetic method sees law generated as a solution to the problem which was already crystallizing . . . in the clan of blood kindred." Yet "depending on the context," "tribe" (*phyle*) "might refer [also] to all members of a polis" (135–136). Since we do not know the context in which the saying occurred, some modesty of assertion would be particularly proper, to say nothing of the fact that Plato and Aristotle only "virtually" "identified nomos and polis" (cf. *Laws* 681a–c and *Republic* 565e 4–7).

In another saying Democritus shows what good—compassion, fraternity, concord, and so on—follows or rather is already present when the powerful take heart to help the poor and to be kind to them. According to Havelock, this saying "constitutes the most remarkable single utterance of a political theorist of Hellas. Considering its epoch, it is as remarkable as anything in the history of political theory. Neither in content nor in temper has it a parallel in the better-known classical thinkers" (143). Apparently Havelock did not remember Plato's *Laws* 736d 4–e 2 and 936b 3–8 or Aristotle's *Politics* 1320a 35–b 11 (cf. *Rhetoric* II, 7–8). But forgetfulness does not explain the extraordinary assertion and the complete absence of a sense of proportion which it exhibits. He is driven to assertions of this kind by an inordinately strong prejudice and the ferocity which goes with such prejudices. When Democritus says that "poverty under democracy is as much to be preferred to the so-called prosperity which resides with lords or princes as freedom is to slavery," Havelock makes him say "poverty under democracy is better than any prosperity under oligarchy," takes him to prefer democracy to all other regimes, and finds it "hard to avoid the conclusion that when Thucydides penned the Funeral Speech of Pericles he was expressing an intellectual debt to Democritus" (146–147). He has strange notions of what is required for making a conclusion sound. Besides, the Funeral Speech does not strike one as a praise of "poverty under democracy." Havelock finds it unnecessary to comment on Democritus' relative praise of poverty, nor does he even allude to other fragments of Democritus which depreciate wealth (B 283–286). Those sayings would not confirm his contention that the position taken by the Greek liberals, among whom he counts Democritus,

is characterized by "a recurrent terminology of equality and good will
. . . of security, and leisure and wealth" (377). He does quote Democritus' statement according to which "ruling belongs by nature to the superior," and he rightly contends that Democritus understood by superiority
the superiority in understanding and in striving for the noble, although he
fails to refer to the Democritean sayings which confirm this contention (B
75, 56). He supplies from his own means without any effort a reconciliation of Democritus' recognition of "the aristocratic principle" with his presumed belief in democracy (148–149). He does not give any thought to
the possibility that the notion of natural rulers might have led Democritus,
as it led others, to the view according to which laws are "a bad after-
thought" and that "the wise man ought not to obey the laws as his rulers
but ought to live freely" (A 166)—to a view which is easily compatible
with the admission that law has "a virtue of its own" (B 248). Havelock's
horizon is blocked in every respect by his "a priori" certainty that Democritus was a liberal. As a matter of course he does not say a word about
Democritus' remarks asserting the inferiority of women (B 110–111,
273–274), for otherwise he could not so easily stigmatize the corresponding remarks of Aristotle as shockingly illiberal (326, 382).

In discussing the political theory of those Greek liberals of whom we
know chiefly if not exclusively through Plato, Havelock is confronted with
the fact that the thinkers in question are described by Plato as sophists. He
rightly states that the ambiguity of the word "sophist" has some analogy to
that of the present-day term "intellectuals," but since he has not reflected
on the problem of the intellectuals, he has no clue to what he calls Plato's
"denigration" of the sophists (157–158). He rightly suggests that for most
of their contemporaries Socrates was as much a sophist as Protagoras, but
he is too certain that those contemporaries were "the dispassionate"; it still
has to be proved that they were not the undiscerning (160). He rightly
wonders whether Plato was fair in censuring the sophists for taking pay for
their teaching. In this he can probably count on the applause of all professors since, as he hardheadedly notes, a professor "has got to live by his
trade like anybody else" (162) and would be in an awkward situation if
Plato's censure of the practice were sound. But the two cases are not altogether the same. If Havelock had not been so certain that there were
Greek liberals, or, in other words, if he had given some thought to the
peculiarities of the modern or liberal state, he would have become aware of
the significance of academic freedom which may be said to constitute the
specific difference between the sophist and the professor: the professor receives pay for teaching, not what his contemporaries wish to hear, but what
they ought to hear. To use the words of Havelock, it was Plato and Aristotle, and not the Greek liberals, who "had the compelling genius to in-
vent the idea of an institution of higher learning" (20). Havelock is right
in saying, and in fact agrees therein with Plato, that the theories of the

sophists had "their own specific integrity," but he does not seem to make much sense when he says that "the theories they taught and believed may or may not be possible of reconstruction, but they were at least serious theories, intellectually respectable" (160): how can one judge of the dignity of doctrines which become accessible only through reconstruction if their reconstruction is not possible? Given Plato's "fundamental hostility" (162) to the political theories of the liberals, Havelock would be unable to reconstruct them if he could not rely in his interpretation of the Platonic passages on that "portrait" of liberalism which he has painted with the assistance of a few fragments. But before connecting the Platonic evidence with the non-Platonic vision, true or feigned, of Greek liberalism, one must understand the Platonic evidence by itself. The *Protagoras* being the most important source for Havelock, he is under an obligation to interpret that dialogue. *Hic Rhodus hic salta.* Here is the occasion for displaying that "philological discipline," that "good deal of finesse," that "critical intuition," to say nothing of "the over-all judgment" to which he lays claim in this very context (157, 171).

Plato presents Protagoras as presenting his particular claim in a particular setting: in the house of a very wealthy Athenian, in the presence of his most formidable competitors, with a view to inducing a youth to become his pupil. A "pragmatist" (166) like Protagoras cannot but be influenced by this situation: we can only guess as to how he would have stated his claim if he had been closeted with Socrates or, for that matter, with the mathematician Theodorus. An author as much concerned with "logographic necessity" as Plato would not have prefaced the conversation between Socrates and Protagoras with the fairly extensive conversation between Socrates and young Hippocrates—to say nothing at all here of the conversation between Socrates and an anonymous "comrade" with which the dialogue opens—without a good reason. The conversation between Socrates and Hippocrates shows in the first place how much Protagoras appealed to a certain kind of young man and conversely how little Socrates appealed to those people or how little they appealed to Socrates; it permits us to size up Hippocrates. Protagoras is characterized by the fact that he is willing to accept as his pupil a youth of whom he knows nothing except what Socrates tells him in the youth's presence, namely, that he *comes* from a wealthy Athenian house, that as regards his nature he is *thought to be* a match for those of his age, that he *seems to Socrates* to desire to become famous in the city, and that he believes that he will most likely get what he wants if he joins Protagoras. "We know from Middle Comedy that Plato's Academy charged fees and high ones at that." Hence "by Platonic standards the sophists committed no offence" (162). The basis on which Havelock establishes the Platonic standard is somewhat narrow, and hence he misses the decisive point. For Protagoras it is sufficient to know that his potential customer can pay for his services; Socrates is concerned above everything else with whether his potential young friends have the right kind of "nature." In other words, Protagoras is at liberty to accept every wealthy young man as a pupil, whereas Socrates is not (cf. the *Theages* and *Memorabilia* I 6. 13). The place occupied in Socrates' thought by "nature" is taken in Protagoras' thought by "wealth." Havelock is unaware of this difference. According to Plato's presentation, Protagoras was insufficiently aware of it.

In his way Havelock admits then that Plato's presentation of Protagoras is fair. While he believes that Plato gives a reasonably fair account of Protagoras' claim, he contends that Plato "transfers [that claim] into a non-political context" (165, 168). Let us then consider the context. In his eagerness to acquire a new pupil of means, Protagoras was entirely unconcerned with inspecting the nature of Hippocrates; in spite of the caution of which he boasts, he did not stop to consider whether there was not a serpent lurking behind Hippocrates' alluring promise. Still less did he consider whether his claim did not bring him into conflict with the Athenian democracy. Socrates tactfully draws his attention to the fact that in Athens "rich and poor" are equally supposed to possess that political skill which Protagoras claims to teach (319c 8–e 1): Protagoras' claim is incompatible with democracy. Havelock sees here only "irony . . . at the expense of Athenian democratic practice" (168), although he observes when speaking of a term similar in meaning to "irony," namely, "playfulness," that it is "a term convenient to critics who have not understood Plato's mind" (100). It would be unbecoming to comment on his claim to have "understood Plato's mind." But we may say that strictly speaking every utterance of the Platonic Socrates is ironical since Socrates is always mindful of the qualities of his interlocutors and that for this reason Havelock is right when he intimates that one does not explain any particular utterance of the Platonic Socrates by describing it as ironical.

At any rate, Socrates forces Protagoras for the benefit of Protagoras (cf. 316c 5) to show that his claim is compatible with Athenian democracy. In the mythical part of his speech he defends or justifies democracy with that complete lack of qualification which is fitting in a mythical utterance; in the nonmythical part he defends or justifies democracy in a more qualified manner: he knows that some qualification of democracy is required if his claim is to be respectable or reasonable. If Protagoras had not given the unqualified justification of democracy, Socrates could not know, and the readers of the *Protagoras* could not know, whether Protagoras had understood the difficulty to which Socrates had alluded. According to Havelock, "the continuity [of the *logos*] with the myth is tenuous, simply because the myth is a myth" (168). He thus unwittingly suggests that Plato presented Protagoras as a very great blunderer; this suggestion is wrong. As for the qualification of democracy which is required for reconciling Protagoras' claim with democracy, Protagoras supplies it in a properly subdued manner by referring to the fact that in a democracy there are, after all, wealthy people who can afford to give their sons a rather expensive education and therefore, we must add, the education in that political art which he claims to supply. Havelock applauds the "pragmatic" wisdom "which any member of a liberal democracy is forced to accept: that educational opportunity tends to be available in proportion to family means" or that "leadership tends to fall into the hands of the privileged"; he applauds the sophists' "acceptance of a measure of plutocracy." But a democrat might well wonder whether Havelock is right in suggesting that a practice which is bound to increase the gulf between the rich and the poor "does not violate the ethos of democracy" (182–183, 248): "if there is inequality [of legal or social status], the function of amity is thereby inhibited" (397). All that one can say of Havelock's political theory is that if he is right, it is not for a liberal to be right in this point. As for his thesis that Protagoras was a defender of democracy, and even of "a craftsman democracy" (187), it must be restated so as to read that the Platonic Protagoras defended a mixture of democracy and oligarchy or that he deviated from democracy pure and simple in the direction of oligarchy. He might have defended oligarchy pure and simple if he had not been compelled to adapt his doubtlessly "negotiable" political convictions to a democracy. His criticism of democracy differs from Socrates' criticism because he takes the side of the wealthy, whereas Socrates takes the side of the gentlemen. We trust that Havelock is aware of this difference when he does not happen to write on "the Elder Sophists."

One would be unfair to the Platonic Protagoras if one did not stress more strongly than Havelock does that, according to him, the laws are, or should be, "the inventions of good and ancient lawgivers" (326d 5–6) as distinguished from the enactments of a chance multitude. However "radical" he may have been regarding the gods, he knew too well that reverence for antiquity and especially for the great "inventors" of antiquity is indispensable for society. But, as he says, "the many do not, so to speak, notice anything." It is due to the merit of those inventors that present-day man is separated by a gulf from the original savages. Protagoras must have noticed somehow that Socrates looked down on that political art which Protagoras claims to teach and of which he claims that every man possesses it. At any rate, he accuses Socrates of not properly appreciating that art or what one may call the progress of civilization: Socrates seems not to know that in the beginning human beings were worse than the worst criminals living in civilized society. "The reflection almost reads like a piece of Plato's own self-criticism; . . . here he lets the liberals have their say undiluted" (188). There is undoubtedly some kinship between the modern liberal and the ancient sophist. Both are unaware of the existence of a problem of civilization, although to different degrees. For Protagoras supplies his assertions with important qualifications which do not come out in Havelock's paraphrases. It would be painful and in no way helpful if we were to follow Havelock's analysis of the conversation between Socrates and Protagoras. As one would expect from his claim to have understood Plato's thought, he interprets Socrates' questions as dictated by Plato's "system" without listening patiently to what Socrates actually says in the context. Similarly, he interprets Protagoras' answers as dictated by a pragmatist or behaviorist epistemology or sociology. The utmost one can say about his whole discussion is that it may shed some light on present-day liberalism. Two examples must suffice.

The question discussed by Socrates and Protagoras is whether virtue is one or many. Common speech assumes that virtue is one: we speak of good men. At the same time common speech assumes that there are many virtues and that a man may possess one virtue while lacking all others. For instance, as Protagoras says, a man may be courageous and yet unjust or he may be just and not be wise. When Protagoras' attention is first drawn to the difficulty, he suggests immediately that the one virtue has many qualitatively different parts. Socrates seems to be surprised that Protagoras regards courage and wisdom too as parts of the one virtue. Protagoras replies emphatically in the affirmative and adds that wisdom is the greatest of all parts of virtue (329e 6–330a 2). Socrates' difficulty is not hard to understand: in his long speech Protagoras had been rather reticent regarding wisdom and especially reticent regarding courage; his emphasis had been on justice, moderation, and piety; for his chief subject had been "political virtue" (322e 2–323a 1, 323a 6–7), which is a special kind of virtue (323c 3–4). If one wishes to understand Protagoras, one must therefore make explicit what he implied by putting different emphases on justice, moderation, and piety on the one hand and wisdom and courage on the other. We suspect that one cannot achieve this if one does not reflect on the Platonic distinction between political virtue and genuine virtue. Who knows prior to investigation whether Protagoras did not admit the soundness of this distinction? Prior to further investigation it is clear that according to him only political virtue is a gift of Zeus, and yet there is also a virtue which is a gift of Prometheus (321d). Havelock carefully avoids this kind of reflection which would certainly complicate matters and might shake his confidence that Protagoras' thoughts about truth were thoughts about "the parliamentary process" or "the crystallization of public opinion."

At a certain point in the discussion Protagoras elaborates the obvious but not unimportant truth that different things are good for different beings or for different parts of those beings. Havelock finds therein a "pragmatic epistemology," a "pragmatic classification," a "sophistic economics," and a "pragmatic programme." He is therefore shocked by "the Socratic context." Socrates "virtually concludes 'Here is mere relativism . . .'" and "Plato next resorts to an artifice as unfair as anything anywhere in his dialogues. Socrates figuratively throws up his hands exclaiming: 'I cannot deal with long speeches.' . . . One would think that here, if anywhere, Plato's readers would get a little out of hand, and protest the propriety of his hero's attitude. But Plato is skillful—he must be, to judge by the procession of professors who have obediently followed the lead of this preposterous propaganda" (204–206). As Havelock virtually admits, the reason that Socrates almost breaks up the conversation is not that he is shocked by Protagoras' "relativism." Socrates and Protagoras had been discussing the admittedly delicate question of whether sobriety or prudence is compatible with acting unjustly. Protagoras did not like this discussion; he said that he would be ashamed to answer the question in the affirmative, and yet Socrates tries to compel him to defend the affirmative reply (333b 8–d 3). Was this wicked of Socrates? It would have been wicked if Protagoras had believed, as Havelock thinks he did, that justice and utility must coincide (203). But Protagoras had asserted that a man may have one virtue while lacking the others and that a man may be sober or sane without being just (323b). Not Protagoras simply, but an already somewhat chastened Protagoras, is ashamed to say in the present context that sobriety or prudence is compatible with acting unjustly. In his eagerness to defend Protagoras' pragmatic doctrine against Plato's static doctrine, Havelock overlooks the obvious fact that he is confronted with a Platonic dialogue and hence with a moving, not static, context. Socrates' apparently wicked action is in fact an act of reasonable punishment as Protagoras' liberal doctrine had defined it. For it is not sufficient that one is ashamed to pronounce a wicked proposition; one must learn to reject it in one's thought too; in order to learn this, one must make oneself, or one must be made by others, the defender of that proposition and take one's punishment for it. But Protagoras does not like to be punished: he mistakes punishment (improvement) for humiliation (defeat). Therefore he tries to evade the issue which is too hard for him to handle and to escape into an entirely different issue which is easy for him to handle. We do not deny that it might have helped both Havelock and simply inattentive readers if Socrates had protested, not against long speeches in general, but against long speeches which are irrelevant. But Plato had to think of all kinds of readers. Perhaps his Socrates felt that he should put a stop to a conversation which had already fulfilled its purpose, namely, to demonstrate to Hippocrates *ad oculos* that Protagoras was not such an excellent teacher of good counsel as he claimed to be and that a continuation which would stick to the issue so hard to handle would only embarrass Protagoras and needlessly mortify him. We cannot possibly do in a short review what Havelock has failed to do in a long book, namely, to give an interpretation of the *Protagoras* and, as a preparation for that, to explain what a Platonic dialogue is and how it is to be read. Havelock regards the Platonic dialogue as a vehicle for propaganda or even "preposterous propaganda." After all, his book is a liberal's book, not on Plato, but on liberalism.

After the conversation between Protagoras and Socrates had led to a conflict and to the threat of a breakup of the conversation and therewith of the society constituted by the conversation, the conflict becomes the concern of the whole society. Its outstanding members intervene either as partisans or as would-be arbiters. Immediately before the conflict Socrates and Protagoras had been speaking about justice. Now justice is presented in deed. In the words of Havelock, "the impasse which the dialogue has reached is treated as a parody of a situation in the *ecclesia*" (218). We pass over his vague speculations about the sophistic contribution to "parliamentary" techniques and the sophists' anticipation of "the necessity of the party system" (243). Instead we concentrate on his remarks about the speech of one of the would-be arbiters, Hippias. Hippias is frequently said to have stated in this context "the doctrine of man's common nature and brotherhood and world citizenship." Accepting this interpretation, Havelock finds that Plato's treatment of this doctrine "is not quite forgivable." If this interpretation were correct, Havelock would have presented to us the first example of a conflict between Plato and a Greek liberal. But alas, Havelock also says that Hippias teaches the common nature and brotherhood and common citizenship, not of all men, but of all Greeks. Yet can we be certain that Hippias taught even this much? He says that "all present" are "by nature, not by law" kindred and fellow citizens because like is by nature akin to like. "All present" are like to one another because they "know the nature of the things" or because they are exceptionally wise (337c 7–d 6; cf. 318e). Roughly speaking Hippias teaches then that by nature all wise men are kinsmen and fellow citizens, whereas all other kinship and fellow citizenship rests on law or convention. Plato ridiculed not this teaching but Hippias' childish belief that "all present know the nature of the things." Havelock, however, finds in Hippias' words the suggestion of an "epistemology of group communication" (225–229, 352).

Havelock's book culminates in, although it does not end with, his account of Antiphon. The account is based on "the mutilated record" supplied by two papyrus fragments which are now held to stem from the sophist Antiphon (256, 289, 416–418). Antiphon asserts that by nature all men, regardless of whether they are Greeks or barbarians, are alike in all respects and that the denial of this likeness is barbaric; he proves this likeness by the fact that as regards the things which are by nature necessary to all men, such as breathing through mouth and nose, there is no difference among men. Havelock admires Antiphon's "breathless logic" in which the distinction between "natural barbarians" and " 'the natural free man,' (that is, Greeks)" "dissolves like smoke" (257–258). He thus implies that Antiphon's liberal assertion is opposed to the view of the classics. His implicit criticism proceeds from a superficial understanding of certain passages in the first book of the *Politics* (351–352) and from a complete disregard, for instance, of the treatment of Carthage in the second book, to say nothing of Plato's description of the division of the human race into Greeks and barbarians as absurd, and of many other things. Antiphon's assertion, as distinguished from his proof, is not specifically liberal, but is implied in the understanding of philosophy as leaving the Cave. The difference between Antiphon and the classics appears from Havelock's overstatement: "In estimating man and his behaviour, you begin not with the mind but the lungs" (257). As for Antiphon, we have not given up hope that he did not stop at the lungs but proceeded to the mind. Those Greek thinkers who seemed to share the prejudice of their fellow Greeks against the barbarians meant by it that there were among the Greeks more men willing to learn from other nations and to understand the thought of other nations than there were among the other nations; barbarians are simply self-sufficient or self-contained in the decisive respect. Antiphon bears witness to this superiority of the Greeks: he calls it barbaric—un-Greek—to deny the fundamental unity of the human race.

Antiphon also questioned civil society itself. He seems to have argued as follows. Given that it is just not to wrong anyone if one has not been wronged by him first, it is unjust to bear witness against a criminal or to act as a judge in a law court against a criminal who has not wronged the potential witness or judge; besides, by testifying against a criminal or by condemning him, one makes him his lifelong enemy and thus does damage to oneself. The first argument would justify meeting hurt with hurt; the second argument seems to suggest that it is shrewd not to meet hurt with hurt. But the passage is so corrupt and Havelock's claim on behalf of his interpretation of it is so modest (262) that we may drop the matter with this observation: we fail to see that Antiphon is "tender-minded," a "utopist," and an anarchist (260, 263, 265, 290). Antiphon says that one should observe the laws of the city in the presence of witnesses and the laws of nature when one is alone. Havelock approaches this saying in the certainty, not supported by any evidence, that Antiphon is not "an immoralist." But he does not deny that in this saying Antiphon advocates "a flexible behaviour pattern which involves a double standard" or that "he has a large measure of sympathy [for] hypocrisy" or that according to him "one must give lip service" to the laws of the city or that those laws may be "flattered and evaded when they cannot be fought." As if Plato had never recommended "the noble lie," he proclaims that "idealists of all schools would violently object" to a "flexible behaviour pattern which involves a double standard." He then goes on to commit a *non sequitur* which in a sense does honor to him: "ripe civilizations . . . tend to nourish a split between private judgment and public observance. He is the first Greek candid enough to see this. In a sense, then, he is not a political theorist at all" (267–271; compare also this passage and the Preface with 376). The Antiphontic antithesis of law and nature gives him an occasion to express his dissatisfaction with Plato's suggestions regarding the use of that antithesis by certain individuals. He abstains from discussing the pertinent Platonic passages, and he does not even begin to consider whether Plato's own questioning of law—especially in the *Statesman*—as well as his simile of the Cave does not imply the same antithesis, although differently understood. He who had praised the sophists as "communication men" and blamed Plato for despising "discourse [as] a vehicle of group or collective opinion and decision" has the hardihood, and in a sense the consistency, to lump him together with the "group thinkers" for whom the polis is "the mistress adored" (194, 270). *Fiat liberalismus pereat Plato.*

All these lapses, however, fade into insignificance when compared with the great merit of an observation which, to the best of our knowledge, Havelock is the first classical scholar to make. "Any subject of a totalitarian state—and the city-state had its totalitarian aspects—and indeed the citizens of a democracy, in this present age of war and anxiety, know what Antiphon meant" (271). We dismiss the reference to "democracy in this age of war and anxiety" as out of place and even misleading. But in the main point Havelock is right. The polis, and even the celebrated Athens of Pericles, was not liberal or limited by a First Amendment, and Antiphon explicitly says that the law determines "for the eyes what they ought to see and what they may not see, and for the ears what they ought to hear and what they may not hear, and for the tongue what it ought to say and what it may not say." It is perhaps a pity that Havelock did not go on to wonder in the first place whether Antiphon's "candor," however praiseworthy on other grounds, does not have the disadvantage of being inconsistent with his insight because remarks like those quoted "fight" the law of the city in the presence of witnesses; and to wonder in the second place whether Antiphon's manner of writing was not perhaps affected by his insight or whether the obscurity of his style was not perhaps intentional—whether he appears to us as extraordinarily candid because a lucky or unlucky accident has saved for us a most shocking saying of his in isolation, while in the complete work it was perhaps hidden away in the middle of an innocent exposition or not presented by the author in his own name but entrusted to other people—whether therefore one should not read his fragments with a corresponding lack of innocence; and to wonder finally whether other Greek writers did not have the same insight (which after all is not of transcendent profundity) and hence composed their writings accordingly and hence must be read with much greater care and much less innocence than that with which they are usually read. A scholar who would have given these questions ever so little serious and unbiased consideration would have written an entirely different book—not a liberal book in the present-day sense, but a liberal book in the original sense.

To return to Havelock, he takes Antiphon's antithesis of law and nature to imply that law is not "framed by the virtue of inspired lawgivers," but "results from a social compact reached by society's members" (272). Antiphon says that the law or the usages of the city stem from agreement as distinguished from nature. This does not necessarily mean that the laws or usages are simply the product of "group opinion"; it does not exclude the possibility that the laws or usages are primarily the work of an outstanding man regarded as endowed with superhuman virtue whose proposals were accepted by human beings, and these human beings constituted themselves, by virtue of this acceptance, as members of one society. Havelock unintentionally reveals the fundamental difference between the modern liberal and the so-called Greek liberal by this question: "If law is a compact reached historically by human beings, why is it not natural and organic as are other items in man's progress?" (273.) For the liberal, "natural" is not a term of distinction: everything that is, is "natural"; for his Greek predecessors not everything that is, is "natural." Zeus "is," for otherwise one could not speak about him, distinguish him from Kronos, Hera, and so on; but in what sense "is" he? He is by virtue of opinion or establishment or agreement or law (cf. *Laws* 904a 9–b 1 with Antiphon B 44 A 2 line 27–28), whereas man, for instance, is not by virtue of law or opinion, but by nature or in truth. If the liberal rejoins, "But at any rate the law or opinion by virtue of which Zeus is, is not merely by law or opinion but is necessary for the people who adopted it or cling to it," his Greek predecessors would ask him how he knows this: is there no arbitrariness and hence in particular no arbitrary freezing, wise or unwise, of errors salutary or otherwise? While the ground of arbitrariness (the natural constitution of man as the rational animal) is natural, or, as was formerly said, while the conventional finds some place within the natural, certainly the product of the arbitrary act which establishes this or that convention is not natural. In other words, man fashions "a state within a state": the manmade "worlds" have a fundamentally different status from "the world" and its parts. The liberal view originally emerged through the combination of determinism with the assumption that the laws always correspond to genuine, not merely imagined, needs or that in principle all laws are sensible. The term "historical" as used by Havelock, which is almost the modern equivalent for "conventional," serves no other function than to obscure a very obscure event in the development of modern thought.

As for the specific meaning which Antiphon attaches to the antithesis of law and nature, Havelock is hampered in his understanding of it by his belief that Antiphon advocated justice in the sense of nonaggression or that he had "a deep feeling for the inviolability of the human organism." He infers the existence of this feeling from a saying of Antiphon which he renders, "To be alive is a natural condition," while Antiphon says, "To live and to die is from nature" (275): "the human organism" is by nature most violable. Similarly, Antiphon's saying that life comes from the useful or suitable, and dying from the damaging or unsuitable, is taken by Havelock to bespeak "reverence for life" (280). In fact Antiphon explains what the good by nature is as distinguished from the good by convention: the good by nature is that which is conducive to life, and therefore the good by nature is ultimately the pleasant. "The human organism" is violable in particular by other "human organisms"; the laws claim to protect the innocent; Antiphon questions the truth of this claim. Havelock admits that Antiphon's statement on this subject could "easily" be understood to mean that it is according to nature "to adopt the initiative in aggression" in order not to become the helpless victim of aggression. He rejects this possibility on the ground that according to Antiphon "nature does not seek to create enemies" (284), although he also says that Antiphon questioned the benign character of "nature's rule" (294). Antiphon merely says that what is just must be universally beneficent; he does not say that justice thus understood is possible, and he certainly does not say that justice thus understood is implied in "the laws of nature." He also appears to have pointed out the essential inconveniences of marriage, and he may very well have questioned the natural character of marriage. Havelock interprets the passage in question, after having excised portions of it "which better reflect the tradition" than they reflect Antiphon (293), in the same spirit in which he interprets his questioning the laws of the city. "The twentieth-century note in his teaching is there. It sounds almost uncanny. Was he an apostle of the new education? Would he have approved a progressive school? Is it possible that in his Greek we catch, across the centuries, the accents of Sigmund Freud?" (294.) The "almost" is inspired not by reasonable restraint, but by the liberal temper: Sigmund Freud can be relied upon a priori to show in each case that what appears to be uncanny is not truly uncanny.

Some readers may blame us for having devoted so much time and space to the examination of an unusually poor book. We do not believe that their judgment of the book is fair. Books like Havelock's are becoming ever more typical. Scholarship, which is meant to be a bulwark of civilization against barbarism, is ever more frequently turned into an instrument of rebarbarization. As history suggests, scholarship is, as such, exposed to that degradation. But this time the danger is greater than ever before. For this time the danger stems from the inspiration of scholarship by what is called a philosophy. Through that philosophy the humane desire for tolerance is pushed to the extreme where tolerance becomes perverted into the abandonment of all standards and hence of all discipline, including philological discipline. But absolute tolerance is altogether impossible; the allegedly absolute tolerance turns into ferocious hatred of those who have stated most clearly and most forcefully that there are unchangeable standards founded in the nature of man and the nature of things. In other words, the humane desire for making education accessible to everyone leads to an ever increasing neglect of the quality of education. No great harm is done, or at least there is no new reason for alarm, if this happens in disciplines of recent origin; but the situation is altogether different if the very discipline which is responsible for the transmission of the classical heritage is affected. True liberals today have no more pressing duty than to counteract the perverted liberalism which contends "that just to live, securely and happily, and protected but otherwise unregulated, is man's simple but supreme goal" (374) and which forgets quality, excellence, or virtue.

NOTE

1. New Haven: Yale University Press, 1957.

4 / On the *Minos*

The *Minos* has come down to us as a Platonic work immediately preceding the *Laws*. The *Laws* begins where the *Minos* ends: the *Minos* ends with a praise of the laws of the Cretan king Minos, the son and pupil of Zeus, and the *Laws* begins with an examination of those laws. The *Minos* thus appears to be the introduction to the *Laws*. The *Laws* more than any other Platonic dialogue needs an introduction, for it is the only Platonic dialogue in which Socrates is not mentioned or which is set far away from Athens, in Crete. The *Minos* thus also appears to be entirely preliminary. Yet it is the only work included in the body of Platonic writings which has no other theme than the question "What is law?" and the answer to it. It could appear strange, and it ought to appear strange, that this grave question which is perhaps the gravest of all questions is, within the body of the Platonic writings, the sole theme only of a preliminary work. But we must remember that in Xenophon's Socratic writings Socrates never raises the question "What is law?"; according to Xenophon, it was Socrates' ambiguous companion Alcibiades who raised that Socratic question in a conversation with Pericles while Socrates was absent. The strangeness is enhanced by the fact that Plato's Socrates raises his question concerning law, not as is his wont, after proper preparation, but abruptly; he seems to jump at an unsuspecting companion with his bald question. He thus brings it about that nothing accidental or particular—like the question of Socrates' own law-abidingness in the *Crito*—distracts our attention from the universal question in all its gravity. We are not even distracted by the name of the companion; that companion remains nameless and faceless; we perceive only what he says. Since no one else appears to be present at the conversation, the work could not carry as its title, as most Platonic dialogues do, the name of a participant in a Socratic conversation or of a listener to it:

65

the name which is mentioned in the title is the name of a man of the remote past who is only spoken about in the conversation.

While the question with which Socrates opens the conversation is abrupt, it cannot be said to be unambiguous. It is not clear whether he asks the companion, "What in our opinion is law?" or "What is the law to which we [we Athenians (?)] are subject?" The first question might be called universal or theoretical, and the second question might be called practical or particular. The practical question is again ambiguous; it may refer to a whole legal order or to any particular law. While being distinct, the theoretical and the practical questions are inseparable from each other. One cannot know to which law one is subject without having some knowledge, however vague and dim, of law as such; one cannot know what law as such is without possessing at least a directive toward the law to which one is subject. For the time being Socrates makes his initial question unambiguous by limiting the conversation to the theoretical question. But the practical question is only driven underground: the dialogue ends with the suggestion that the law deserving the highest respect is the law, not of Athens, but of Crete.

Socrates illustrates the question "What is law?" first by the question "What is gold?" and then by the question "What is stone?" Gold is most valuable, and a stone may be entirely worthless. "Gold" is never used in the plural, whereas "stone" is; one cannot say "a gold" as one can say "a stone": there are wholes each part of which is a whole or complete, and there are wholes no part of which is complete. We are thus induced to wonder whether law, properly understood, is more like gold or more like stone. But regardless of whether any particular law or even any particular code can be said to be a whole, Socrates' question is concerned with a whole—the whole comprising all laws. Just as gold does not differ from gold in respect of being gold and stone does not differ from stone in respect of being stone, law does not differ from law in respect of being law. Does this mean that a bad law is as much law as a good law?

The companion's first answer to Socrates' comprehensive question is to the effect that the law is the whole consisting of whatever is "held" or whatever is established by law. Socrates convinces him by suitable parallels that just as in other cases what we may call the acts of the human soul are not the same as the things in which these acts issue, law as an act of the soul is not the same as that in which that act issues. Law is then so far from being something inanimate (like gold or stone) that it is an act of the soul: is it manifestation or science or is it finding (invention) or art? In his answer (the second and central answer to Socrates' comprehensive question) the companion does not meet the issue. He says that law is the decision of the city. He means by this that the law is not an act of the soul, but something in which certain acts of the soul issue. Yet it is now clear to him that law is the outcome of some act of the soul, whereas his first answer would have been compatible with the view that law is custom of which no one knows whence it came or, as one might say, which is not "made" but has "grown." Socrates rephrases the second answer in such a way as to make it an answer to the particular question which he had addressed to the companion: the act of the soul which is law has the character, neither of science nor of art, but of opinion; it is the city's opining about the affairs of the city.

A simple consideration suffices to show that this answer is insufficient. We assume that there is a connection between law and justice. Perhaps a man may be law-abiding without being just, but surely a lawless man is unjust. In a way law and justice seem to be interchangeable; hence law will be something high. But a city's opinions may be low. We are then confronted with a contradiction between two most audible opinions which are so audible because they are opinions of the city: the opinion that the law is the opinion of the city and the opinion that the law is something high. Socrates, without any hesitation and without giving any reason, chooses the second opinion and therewith tacitly rejects the opinion that the law is the opinion of the city. Since the opinions of the city are self-contradicting, even the best of citizens cannot simply bow to them. Law is indeed an opinion, according to Socrates; but he does not yet say whose opinion it is; for the time being he only says that it is a high opinion, hence a true opinion, and hence the finding out of what is. "Finding out," and hence law, appears to be between "finding" or art on the one hand and "manifestation" or science on the other.

Only one more step is needed in order to bring us to the third and final definition of law, the only definition proposed by Socrates: the law wishes to be the finding out of what is. The last step is a step back. Socrates qualifies the apparent result according to which the law is the finding out of what is. He does not give a reason for his qualification, but the compelling reason comes to sight immediately afterward: if the law were the finding out (the having found out) of what is, and what is (what is without any admixture of nonbeing) is always the same, law would be simply unchangeable, and hence all or most of the things which we call laws and which differ from time to time and from place to place would not be laws at all. But if law only wishes, or tends, to be the finding out of what is, if no law is necessarily the finding out of what is, there can be an infinite variety of laws which all receive their legitimation from their end: The Truth. The companion fails to grasp the qualification; he believes that Socrates has left it at suggesting that law is the finding out of what is. Given the fact, he argues, that we constantly find out the same things as things which are (sun, moon, stars, men, dogs, and so on), all men should always use the same laws, and they manifestly do not. Socrates replies to the effect that the variety in question is due to the defects of human beings and does not affect the law itself. The implied distinction between the infallible law

and the fallible human beings suggests to us that law is indeed an act of
the soul, but perhaps not necessarily of the human soul. Besides, Socrates
regards it as an open question whether human beings do use different laws
at different places and in different times. He thus compels the companion
to prove the fact that laws vary. But when he has completed that proof,
Socrates seems to reject it as an irrelevant "long speech." In brief, Socrates
tries to be silent about the variety of laws—about a fact which had induced
him to say that the law wishes to be—that is, is not necessarily—the finding out of what is.

The companion proves the variety of laws by the examples of laws concerning sacrifices and burials; the examples concern sacred things. They
confirm to some extent Socrates' definition of law; they show that at any
rate the most awe-inspiring laws are based on more or less successful attempts to find out what is in the highest sense, namely, the gods and the
soul and hence what the gods demand from men and what death means.
The examples show the great difference between present Athenian practice
and the practice of the earliest past, of the age of Kronos, as it were. They
seem to show that in the beginning men were savage, whereas in present-
day Athens they are gentle; hence present-day Athenian laws will be superior to the oldest laws, Greek or barbarian. This finding obviously presupposes that laws differ temporally and locally. Perhaps Socrates treats the
changeability of law in so gingerly a manner because it is the premise of
the finding mentioned—of a finding with which he is not satisfied.

Socrates attempts now to bring about a meeting of minds with the companion by means of short speeches, or short questions and answers. The
companion prefers to answer Socrates' questions rather than to question
Socrates. He grants to Socrates that people everywhere and always hold
that the just things are just, the noble things are noble, the unjust things
are unjust, and the base things are base—just as all people, regardless of
whether they hold it lawful or impious to bring human sacrifices, hold that
the things that weigh more are heavier and the things that weigh less are
lighter. The final result of this reasoning confirms the unqualified definition of law according to which law does not merely wish but is the finding
out of what is. The companion, who through his own fault is compelled to
give short and rather quick answers and cannot, as we can, read and reread
Socrates' questions, is unable to lay bare the sophism to which Socrates
draws our attention while committing it: the universal agreement regarding the opposition of the just or noble things to the unjust or base things
does not establish universal agreement as to the content of "the just and
the noble." Nevertheless, the companion remains entirely unconvinced, for
Socrates' result manifestly contradicts what the companion himself observes with his own eyes in Athens every day, namely, that "we" (that is,
we Athenians) unceasingly change the laws.

What one may call Socrates' second proof of his definition of law is not a mere repetition of the first. In the second proof Socrates tactily contrasts "the just things" and "the heavier things"; he thus draws our attention to two questions: (1) Can justice be a matter of degree as is weight? (2) Is disagreement regarding weight as widespread and as profound as disagreement regarding justice? Besides, the first proof was still related to the opinion that law is the opinion of the city; that opinion plays no role in the second proof. We are thus being prepared for the suggestion that law is the mental act, not of the city (that is, of the assembly of the citizens) or of the citizen, but of men of a different description.

Reading on, we observe that what we have called Socrates' second proof of his definition of law is in fact the first section of his tripartite defense of his definition of law; that tripartite defense forms the second or central part of the dialogue. At the beginning of the central section of the central part, Socrates abruptly turns to the writings of men who possess an art. We can discern the reason for the apparent change of the subject. Socrates had raised the question whether law is a science or an art. He assumes now that law is an art. He seems to justify this assumption as follows. Laws are prescriptive writings; but the arts, being a kind of perfect, final, fixed knowledge which is the same for all, necessarily find their appropriate expression in prescriptive writings; hence laws belong to the same genus as the arts. This reasoning suffers from an obvious flaw: it is not necessary for either arts or laws to present themselves in writings. For instance, the farmers, that is, the experts in farming, do not necessarily compile or even read writings on farming.

If laws belong to the same genus as the arts and are therefore prescriptive writings composed by experts of a certain kind, namely, the kings (or statesmen), there is no reason why laws should be the work of the city or of Greeks: neither citizens nor Greeks are, as such, experts in the kingly art. The prescriptions ordinarily called "laws" may differ from place to place; but regarding things of which men possess knowledge, all knowers agree, as Socrates asserts, regardless of where they live or whether they are Greeks or barbarians. When the companion emphatically assents to this assertion, Socrates praises him for the first time. Furthermore, the prescriptions ordinarily called "laws" may differ from time to time; but where there is knowledge, there is no change of thought; or vice versa, where there is change of thought, there is no knowledge; the frequent change of "laws" for which Athens was so notorious is then a clear proof that the Athenian legislature is ignorant, and hence its findings or decisions do not deserve to be called laws or to be respected as laws; in fact those "laws" must be particularly bad. The companion does not object to this tacit result; in other words, he has now become convinced of the truth of Socrates' definition of law or, more precisely, of the fact that law is an art. It looks as if Socrates has succeeded in appealing from his pro-Athenian prejudice to his antidemocratic prejudice. We on our part realize that the answer to the theoretical question "What is law?" has supplied at least a negative answer to the practical question "What is the law to which we are subject?" In spite of the agreement reached, there remains at least one difference between Socrates and the companion—a difference which comes to light in the very center of the dialogue: the companion is more certain than Socrates that cookery is an art; Socrates' uncertainty regarding the status of cookery is matched in the *Minos* only by his uncertainty regarding the status of soothsaying, that is, of the art by which men claim to know what goes on in the minds of the gods. The companion is also more certain, at least to begin with, that knowers agree always and everywhere than that experts agree always and everywhere; perhaps he knew in advance that good legislation requires knowledge of the subject matter to be regulated by law, but was doubtful that that knowledge must be expert knowledge: knowledge of the pertinent facts as distinguished from their causes may be sufficient for good legislation.

In the last section of the central part Socrates proves that law is an art by assuming that art consists in distributing properly the parts of some whole to the parts of another whole—of a herd, as it were. In some cases the distributor assigns to each member of the herd the same quantity of the whole to be distributed as to every other member. In other arts, however, the distributor must consider the fact that the "herd" consists of qualitatively different parts or that different things are good for different parts or different individuals. What human beings call laws would then be the distributing, say, of punishments and rewards to the members of the city or in the best case the distributing of the proper food and toil to the souls of human beings by the king. The king assigns to each the work best for him, that is, most conducive to his becoming a good man: he does not treat the human beings whom he rules as parts of a herd. But if to be a good man is the same as to be a good citizen, a good member of the city, one can also say that the king assigns each man to the place or the work for which he is best fitted. In this section writings are no longer mentioned: assigning to each soul what is good for it cannot be done well except orally, by the king on the spot. It would be more simple to say that such assigning cannot be done well by any law. Socrates prefers to say that it is best done by the best laws, the laws of the king. He thus implies that laws ought to be infinitely variable. Whereas according to the preceding argument, law as art entails that law must be always and everywhere the same and hence that at least almost all so-called laws do not deserve to be called laws, according to the present argument, law as art entails that law must be as variable as the individuals and their individual situations and hence that no so-called law deserves to be called law. On the other hand, by now speaking of the best laws Socrates restores the common view according to which certain decisions of ignoramuses or of assemblies of ignoramuses may also be regarded and respected as law. Yet the best laws prove to be unwritten laws of a certain kind—not indeed the unwritten laws of unknown origin which say the same things always and everywhere, but certain acts of a wise soul.

Socrates had opened the central part of the dialogue with the suggestion that there is universal agreement regarding the just and the noble things. This suggestion taken by itself could be thought to refer to the unwritten laws which are always and everywhere acknowledged to be laws and which for this reason cannot be the work of human legislators (Xenophon, *Memorabilia* IV. 4. 19). But the *Minos* is silent about the unwritten laws thus understood. One may say that in this dialogue Socrates turns from unwritten laws of unknown origin first to written laws and then to unwritten laws of known origin, viz. the distributing by the king of the proper food and toil to each man's soul.

The third and last part of the *Minos* deals with the laws of Minos. The transition is not explained and is therefore abrupt. We are supposed to have learned what law is and what makes a law good; we must then seek the best laws. What we have learned may have made us doubtful whether the best laws can be of human origin. The lesson conveyed through the last part of the dialogue may provisionally be said to be that the best laws are the laws of Minos because Minos received them from the highest god, his father Zeus. What must surprise us is that the laws of Zeus do not consist in assigning to each man's soul the food and toil best fitted for him, and besides that Zeus did not communicate his laws to all men: he communicated them only to a single privileged man, to Minos, whom he appointed also as the highest judge of the dead (*Gorgias* 523e–524a). Perhaps Zeus did not wish to rule directly so that man, within certain limits left to himself, would be compelled or enabled to choose as long as he lives. Furthermore, if Zeus had communicated his law to men directly, men would necessarily be able to know the thoughts of Zeus, that is, soothsaying would necessarily be a genuine art; but there is no need for soothsaying if there is an intermediary between Zeus and men, an intermediary like Minos who, as participating in divinity, does not need a human art to be aware of the thoughts of his father and as participating in humanity can communicate his father's thoughts to men just as human legislators communicate their laws to men.

Socrates leads up to the laws of Zeus by speaking first not simply of the best laws but of laws (prescriptive and distributive acts) both good and ancient regarding flute playing. As we could have learned from the companion's long speech, the good is in no wise the same as the ancient: certain ancient laws commanded human sacrifices to the then highest god. But an ancient law which is now still in force approximates the unchangeability which appeared to be a mark of goodness. Law must be not only good or wise but also stable: could the best laws be laws which are both wise and stable? The example of flute playing—of an art which reminds most forcibly of speech and yet which cannot be practiced while one speaks—draws our attention to the quality of the divine as distinguished from the ancient and the good. The flute songs invented by certain ancient barbarians are most divine because they alone move and bring to light those who are in need of the gods; yet the divine character of those flute songs explains why they still retain their force. Not everything ancient is divine, but perhaps everything divine necessarily lasts for a very long time. Could the stability of the best laws be due to the unspeakable or mysterious power of the divine which rules chance and may rule it in favor of the good? We are thus prepared for Socrates' suggestion that the oldest Greek laws—the laws which Minos gave to his fellow Cretans, rather than, for instance, the Egyptian laws or the Lacedaemonian laws which were popularly traced to Apollo, the victor over Marsyas and his art of flute playing—combine the qualities of oldness, goodness, and divinity.

The companion, who has been brought to admit that law is an art and hence that the Athenian laws are either not laws at all or in the best case only bad laws, refuses to bow to the Cretan laws. He does not deny that Minos was an ancient king of divine origin, but he denies that he was a good king. Socrates tells him that he is under the spell of an Athenian myth; he sets out to liberate him from the spell of the Athenian myth as he has liberated him from the spell of the Athenian laws. In a speech whose length surpasses by far the length of the companion's long speech, Socrates appeals from the Athenian tragic poets who had originated the myth, according to which Minos was bad, to Homer and Hesiod, the most ancient poets, and thus proves that Minos and hence his laws are good. From Homer, Socrates has learned that Minos was the only one of the children of Zeus educated by Zeus in his art, the noble art of sophistry, which may be identical with the legislative art and certainly is identical with the kingly art; the education took place in a cave, if in the cave of Zeus. Law is so far from being the opinion of the city that it is, or is based upon, an art, the highest art, the art of the highest god. In order to judge of Socrates' contention, one would have to consider in their contexts the few Homeric verses to which he appeals; one would have to see whether they express the view of Homer or of a Homeric character; in the latter case one would have to consider whether that character can be presumed to possess both the knowledge and the truthfulness required in a matter of such importance. As Socrates indicates, the decisive Homeric passage could be thought to mean that Minos associated with his father Zeus, not in speeches devoted to education in virtue, but in drinking and playing. He disposes of the suggestion that Minos associated with Zeus in drinking to the point of drunkenness by a consideration which, it must be admitted, is not free from begging the question. He does not dispose of the suggestion that Zeus and Minos associated for other purposes which have nothing in common with education to virtue. It is not advisable to speculate on the alternatives which are not mentioned. It suffices to say that, as Socrates makes clear at the very end, the whole conversation is based on ignorance of the function of the good legislator: the whole praise of Minos' laws must be reconsidered, as it is in the *Laws*.

The audible proof of Minos' goodness is balanced by an inaudible doubt of that goodness. The difference between proof and doubt corresponds to the difference between two Socratic exhortations. The proof is preceded by an exhortation to piety, for Socrates challenges the Athenian myth regarding Minos in the name of piety: it is impious for a human being to speak ill of Minos, that is, a hero who was the son of Zeus; the god may resent this more than if one speaks ill of him. The proof is followed by an account of how the myth of Minos' badness arose: Minos waged a just war against Athens, defeated Athens, and compelled the Athenians to pay "that famous ransom": to send fourteen young Athenians at regular intervals to Crete as a kind of human sacrifice; hence Minos became hateful to "us," the Athenians, and we take our revenge on him through the tragic poets who present him as bad; this revenge is effective because tragedy is in its way as pleasing to the people and as apt to lead the soul as flute playing itself. While stating these things, Socrates addresses his second exhortation to the companion—the exhortation to be on his guard, not against acts of impiety, but against incurring the hatred of any patriotic poet. As is shown by the example of Minos, one cannot comply in all cases with both exhortations, although each exhortation demands compliance in all cases. While complying with his first exhortation Socrates was compelled to praise most highly the most ancient enemy of Athens to whom he will owe, if indirectly, the postponement of his execution decreed by the city of Athens (cf. *Phaedo* 58a–c).

The end of the dialogue renders doubtful its chief result. This ending is not entirely unexpected, for the suggestion that Minos' laws are the best laws implies the view that law can be the finding out of what is and hence can be unchangeable, whereas Socrates' definition of law implies the view that law can never be more than the attempt to find out what is and hence is necessarily changeable. According to the first view, men can be experts —can possess full knowledge—regarding the matter with which law is concerned; according to the second view, men are ignorant regarding that matter. One can resolve this difficulty by suggesting that while men cannot be experts regarding that matter, they necessarily are knowers of it. The fundamental difficulty can also be stated as follows: law is always and everywhere the same and therefore one; law must be as variable as the needs of individuals and therefore infinitely many. If one accepts the second view, one reaches this conclusion: whereas in the case of man, justice, dog, the one (man as such, justice as such, dog as such) is of higher dignity than the many (the individual men, just things, dogs); in the case of law the one (the universal rule) is of lower dignity than the many (the assignment of the proper food and toil to each man's soul) and in fact spurious.

We could touch only on some of the things which the reader of the *Minos* must consider much more carefully than we have been able to do here. For instance, we did not speak of the circumstances in which Socrates and the companion address each other by name or in other ways. The companion addresses Socrates eight times by name and never in any other way. Socrates never addresses the companion by name (which does not necessarily mean that he does not know his name), but addresses him three times by an expression which we may render "you excellent one." In conversations between two men one uses the name of the other especially in two cases: when the other says something apparently absurd and one tries to call him back to his senses, and when one is pushed to the wall by the other and begs for mercy. Socrates addresses the companion twice as "you excellent one" immediately after the companion has addressed him as "O Socrates"; the first time the companion was dissatisfied with Socrates' praise of Minos, and the second time the companion failed to understand how the good Minos could have acquired the reputation of being bad. As for the character of the companion, we suspect that he was no longer quite young, that he was concerned with civic fame, that he was what one might call free from prejudices, and that he believed that one can be just while being savage and unaccommodating.

The *Minos* raises more questions than it answers. In order to see how the thoughts suggested by the *Minos* are best continued, one must turn to the other dialogues. It is of little use to look up parallels in the other dialogues to this or that passage of the *Minos*, for the meaning of the parallels depends on their contexts, that is, on the whole dialogues within which they occur. One must then study the other dialogues. With every other dialogue a new land comes to sight; the experience resembles that of one's becoming aware of an unexpected turn of the road at what seemed to be the end of the road. The dialogue most akin to the *Minos* is the *Hipparchus*. The *Minos* and the *Hipparchus* are the only dialogues between Socrates and a single nameless companion. They are the only dialogues whose titles consist of the name of someone who is not present at the conversation but was dead a long time before the conversation; their titles resemble the titles of tragedies. They are the only dialogues which open with Socrates' raising a "what is" question. While the *Minos* begins with the question "What is law?", the *Hipparchus* begins with the question "What is the quality of gain-loving? Who are the gain-loving ones?" If the beginning of the *Minos* corresponded strictly to the beginning of the *Hipparchus*, it would read: "What is the quality of lawful? Who are the law-abiding ones?" If not law itself, surely law-abidingness is generally praised, while love of gain is generally blamed: the *Minos* need not vindicate law-abidingness and law, while the *Hipparchus* is devoted to vindicating love of gain. While the *Minos* may be said to end in the praise of the Cretan legislator Minos, the *Hipparchus* may be said to culminate in the praise of the Athenian tyrant Hipparchus. The vindication of the love of gain is the vindication of tyranny, if the tyrant is the most outstanding lover of gain (cf. Aristotle, *Politics* 1311a 4–11). Tyranny is the opposite of law or rule of law; the *Minos* and the *Hipparchus* together deal with the two fundamental alternatives. The connection which we indicated between "love of gain" and "Hipparchus" is not made explicit in the *Hipparchus*. Hipparchus is mentioned there because a saying of Hipparchus throws light on the conversational situation. Socrates charges the companion with trying to deceive him, and the companion charges Socrates with in fact deceiving him. (No such charge is made in the *Minos*.) Thereupon Socrates quotes, after proper preparation, the saying of Hipparchus "Do not deceive a friend." The saying does not disapprove of deceiving people who are not friends. From the context it would appear that not deceiving friends is a part of justice or, in other words, that justice consists in helping one's friends and hurting one's enemies. Love of gain is generally despised because it seems inseparable from deception. However this may be, Socrates praises the Athenian tyrant Hipparchus as a good and wise man, the great educator of the Athenians in wisdom, whose reign resembled the age of Zeus's father Kronos. If we put the *Minos* and the *Hipparchus* together, we become haunted by the suggestion that an Athenian tyrant rather than the Athenian law (and even than the Cretan law) was good and wise. Accordingly, just as in the *Minos* Socrates explicitly rejects the Athenian myth regarding Minos, in the *Hipparchus* he takes issue with what "the many" in Athens say about Hipparchus: Harmodios and Aristogeiton, who were magnified as liberators by the people of Athens, murdered Hipparchus for no other reason than because they were envious of his wisdom and his effect on the young; the nonlegal murder of Hipparchus foreshadows the legal murder of Socrates.

The *Hipparchus* questions the view that love of gain is simply bad, just as the *Minos* may be said to question the view that law is simply good: a law may be bad just as gain may be good. These facts recommend the view that both law and gain by themselves are neutral just as man may be said to be neutral: a high-class man is not more nor less a man than a low-class man (*Hipparchus* 230c). But just as the *Minos* leads up to the view that a bad law is not a law, the *Hipparchus* leads up to the view that a bad gain is not a gain. With what right do we then say of a low-class human being that he is nevertheless a human being?

5 / Notes on Lucretius

I. Ascent

1. The Opening (I 1–148)

Lucretius' work is a poetic exposition of Epicurean philosophy. The reader who opens the book for the first time and peruses its opening does not know through firsthand knowledge that it is devoted to the exposition of Epicureanism. The poet leads his reader toward Epicureanism; he makes him ascend to Epicureanism. Accordingly he begins his work by appealing to sentiments which are not peculiar to Epicureans or by making statements which are not peculiarly Epicurean. The reader of the poem is in the first place its addressee, Memmius, a Roman of noble descent. The importance of his being a Roman is shown by the word which opens the poem: *Aeneadum*. He is to ascend from being a Roman to being an Epicurean.

The ascent from being a Roman to being an Epicurean requires that there be a link between Romanism and Epicureanism. Being a Roman must be more than being a member of one city among many or of any city other than Rome. The Romans, the Aeneads, are the descendants of the goddess Venus who alone guides the nature of things (21). Being a Roman means to have a kinship, denied to other men, with the guide or ruler of the whole. The goddess Venus is the joy not only of the Romans but of gods and men simply; she is the only being that guides the birth or growth not only of Romans and beings subject to Roman rule but of all living beings simply; she brings life, calm, lucidity, beauty, smiling, and light everywhere, although not at all times; she arouses fond sexual love everywhere on earth; nothing glad and lovely emerges without her anywhere (1–23). Lucretius opens his poem with a praise of Venus because that goddess—and not, for instance, Jupiter Capitolinus—is the link between Rome and all living beings; through Venus, and only through Venus, does one ascend from Romanism to Epicureanism.

Lucretius' praise of Venus also serves the more obvious purpose of making her willing to grant him two favors. Since nothing glad and lovely emerges without her, the poet asks her to help him in writing his poem by granting abiding charm to what he will say. He tries to induce her to grant him this favor by telling her that his poem will deal with the nature of things, that is, her mighty empire, and that it is to benefit Memmius, who has always been her favorite (21–28). He further asks Venus to grant peace everywhere, to all mortals; she alone can restore peace since Mars, the god of war, can be subdued only by his desire for Venus; when his desire will have been fully aroused, he will not be able to refuse her request to grant peace to the Romans; for as long as the fatherland is in the grip of war, Lucretius will lack the equanimity needed for writing his poem as perfectly as he wishes and Memmius, compelled to come to the assistance of the common weal, will lack the leisure needed for listening to the poet's verses (29–43). Only Venus can give charm to Lucretius' poem, and only Venus can restore the peace which is required for writing and enjoying that poem. This is the reason that Lucretius, although he speaks of Mars, is silent about the fact that the Romans are descendants not only of Venus but of Mars as well: Venus, not Mars, is the link between Romanism and Epicureanism.

Lucretius concludes his invocation of Venus by supporting his prayer for peace with a reminder of what she owes to herself not because she is Venus but because she is a divine being: all gods enjoy deathless life in perfect peace. By this he means in the first place that since all gods enjoy perfect peace, they all are able and willing to grant peace to men. But he also means something else: the gods enjoy perfect peace because they are self-sufficient, free from all pain and all danger, in no wise in need of men and therefore not to be swayed by men's good or bad deeds; they are altogether remote from the affairs of men (44–49). The six verses which conclude the invocation of Venus must be understood as part of their pre-Epicurean context. The poet will repeat them literally in an Epicurean context; there he introduces them by stating explicitly that the view of the gods which they convey contradicts the popular view (II 644–645). No such statement accompanies the verses when they occur first. In their pre-Epicurean context they do not exclude the possibility that the gods, who do not need men in any way and cannot be swayed by any human merits and demerits, bestow blessings on some men from sheer kindness whenever it pleases them, just as Venus has always willed to bestow the greatest blessings on Memmius (26–27) and has succeeded in doing so. In asking Venus to grant abiding charm to his verses and peace to the Romans, the poet is not necessarily trying to arouse the goddess to action; he may merely wish to guide her in the action which she herself spontaneously started, the action of benefiting Memmius; he merely shows her how her entirely unsolicited wish to benefit Memmius can be fulfilled most perfectly. After all, he never suggested that Venus is omniscient; he never asked her to be his Muse or to inspire him with knowledge of the Epicurean doctrine. The six verses do cast doubt on the divinity of Mars, who does not always enjoy peace and who cannot be free from all pain since he suffers from the everlasting wound of sexual desire.[1] Be this as it may, we remain closer to the accepted view if we assert that the verses in question render doubtful the immediately preceding prayer to a divine being and the poet's singling out of Venus as worthy of higher praise than any other deity; nay, that they render doubtful the very being of all gods as worshiped by the Romans and men in general. The verses thus understood would indicate that the invocation of Venus and especially the praise of Venus is a falsehood, if a beautiful falsehood (cf. II 644–645). They would point toward the end of a movement which begins with the turning to Venus and to Venus alone: not all gods as worshiped by the Romans are equally remote from the true gods; Venus, the joy of the gods as worshiped by the Romans, comes closer to the true gods than any other gods worshiped by the Romans. Since Venus owes her predominance in the opening of Lucretius' poem primarily to her being the ancestress of the Romans, the movement from Venus to the true gods cannot but affect profoundly the status of Rome.

After the poet has addressed Venus in forty-nine verses, there remains one more thing for him to do before he can begin to expound the Epicurean doctrine: he must address Memmius. He must make it as certain as he can that Memmius will listen to the true account with a mind free from all cares and not reject it with contempt before he has grasped it. He tries to arouse Memmius' attention by indicating to him the grandeur of the poem's theme. That theme will indeed not be Venus. The poet will "begin" to speak to Memmius about "the highest ground of heaven and the gods," and he will reveal the origins from which nature creates the things and makes them grow and into which she dissolves them again— those origins which "we" call *materies*, *genitalia corpora*, and *semina rerum*, but also, without any reference to life or sex, the first bodies, since everything else that is comes from them (50–61). The nature which creates the things out of the first bodies and dissolves the things into the first bodies cannot be herself a first body; one must pause for a moment to wonder whether the creative-destructive nature is not a god dwelling in heaven; being destructive as well as creative, he could not be Venus as celebrated in the very beginning; but the end of the passage seems to make it certain that the gods too stem from the first bodies. The first bodies cannot be expected to possess the splendor and the charm of the gods; they cannot be expected to be attractive. Why then should Memmius become concerned with those bodies? Why indeed should he not turn his back on Lucretius' poem with contempt?

In order to see why knowledge of the unattractive origins of everything including heaven and gods is most attractive, one must consider how men lived before the quest for these origins started. Before that event human life was abject, crushed as it was by dreadful religion. It was a Greek who first dared to face the terror of religion and to take a stand against it. He was not deterred by the dreadful tales about the gods nor by dreadful sights or sounds from on high. He was encouraged to his daring deed not only by his loathing of religion or suffering from it but also by his desire for honor, for being the first: he wished to be the first to free himself from the common bondage or imprisonment. Thanks to the power of his mind he succeeded in breaking through the walls of the world and traversing in mind the boundless whole and in bringing back to "us" knowledge of what is possible and impossible: the gods as experienced in religion are impossible. Hence "we" no longer grovel upon the earth, but equal the highest (62–79).

Lucretius fears that Memmius might fear that, by acquiring the knowledge which is gained through rising against religion and which justifies that rising, he would commit a crime. His reply is simple: religion has caused crimes more frequently than irreligion. He gives a single example: Agamemnon sadly but pitilessly sacrificed his utterly terrified virgin daughter Iphigenia, his first-born child, in order to appease the virgin goddess Diana who would not otherwise permit the sailing of the Greek fleet against Troy (80–101). By reminding us of Diana's savage demand the poet justifies once more his turning toward Venus. Apart from this, his single example would appear to be neither sufficient nor the most appropriate, for the event with which he deals occurred in the remote past; it did not occur in Rome; and there is no reason to believe that the abolition of human sacrifice was due to philosophy. Provisionally one may reply that Lucretius chooses the Greek example since it was a Greek who liberated man from religion. He thus underlines the fact that Greekness is the link between Romanism and Epicureanism, or that after having turned to Venus, the ancestress of the Romans, the Roman must turn to Greeks, to men belonging to a foreign people now enslaved by Rome, in order to become free: it was a Greek who won the greatest of all victories, a victory surpassing all Roman victories.

Whatever may be true of the crimes caused by religion, its terrors seriously endanger Memmius' happiness. Lucretius is certain that religious fear will induce Memmius to try to turn his back on the truth even after he has listened to it, for he will be exposed to the fear-inspiring inventions of seers regarding everlasting punishments after death. Even "our" Ennius, the first Roman poet who won immortal fame, speaks—not without contradicting himself—of the pale and miserable shades in Acheron and says that the shade of Homer rose to him and "began" to shed bitter tears and to reveal to him the nature of things. The only way to liberate oneself from such saddening and terrifying dreams is knowledge of the nature of the soul, of its mortality, and of how it comes that "we" seem to see and hear the dead as if they were still alive; therefore man also needs knowledge of all things above and below (102–135). It would seem that Memmius is threatened less by fear of the gods than by fear of what might happen to him after death; one is led to wonder whether the fear of what might happen to men after death may not be independent of the fear of gods or even precede it. By referring to Ennius, Lucretius does not supply an example of Roman crimes caused by religion, unless one were to say that spreading terrifying tales is a crime. Besides, however much Lucretius disapproves of the dangerous falsehoods propagated by Ennius, he admires that poet: well-executed fables as such, even if they serve the untruth, are praiseworthy (cf. II 644). It is more immediately important to note that the first great Roman poet traced his knowledge of the nature of things to the first of the Greek poets: in turning to Greek wisdom Lucretius follows a most respectable Roman precedent. The opening of the poem is not the place to speak proudly, not to say to boast, of the poet's innovation or originality (cf. I 922–934, V 335–337).

Lucretius is to some extent an imitator of Ennius: he will transmit the obscure findings of the Greeks to the Romans in a poem. He is aware of the difficulty of his task—a difficulty due to the poverty of his native tongue and the novelty of the matter. He is induced to undergo the labor by the worth of Memmius and the prospect of friendship with him: friendship in the true sense requires that the friends think alike about the weightiest things. The poetic presentation serves the purpose of enlightening Memmius so that he can grasp thoroughly what otherwise would remain deeply hidden (136–145).

The findings of the Greeks are obscure only for those who have not grasped them, who therefore live in darkness and are gripped by fear of what might happen to them after death. That darkness and terror cannot be dispelled by Venus or anything else resembling her or akin to her and in particular not by poetry as such, but only by nature coming to sight and being penetrated (146–148).

Lucretius leads Memmius from Rome via Venus to the victorious Greek. In the remote past the Greeks defeated and destroyed Troy, protected by Venus, through religion, that is, the sacrifice of Iphigenia; this victory led to the founding of Rome, which defeated Greece, but did not altogether destroy it. At their peak some Greeks won through philosophy the most glorious victory possible.

The opening of the poem leads from Venus, the joy of gods and men, to the promise of the true joy which comes from the understanding of nature. The poem itself is meant to fulfill that promise. Let us turn at once to its ending in order to see how the promise has been fulfilled.

2. *The Ending* (VI 1138–1286)

The last Book of the poem is the only one that begins and ends with
"Athens." It almost goes without saying that no Book begins and ends
with "Rome." The beginning of the last Book shows Athens' greatness,
and the end shows Athens' misery. Athens of outstanding fame first gave
men corn, an elevated kind of life, and laws; she first gave men sweet solace
of life when she brought forth the highly gifted man who by teaching wisdom and thus liberating men from anguish showed them the way to happiness. This praise of Athens must be read in the light of the beginning of
the preceding Book. There Lucretius has spoken of the story that Ceres has
taught men how to grow corn and of the fact that the god Epicurus has
taught men how to become wise. By correcting himself in the parallel passage the poet shows that he can, if with some difficulty, resist the temptation to deify the greatest benefactor of the human race, the most venerable
among the departed.[2] He is grateful, not to any god, but in the first place
to Athens and to no other city.

The last Book ends with a description of the plague which had struck
Athens and which had been rendered immortal by Thucydides. This is not
the ending which one would have expected, the happy ending. The poet
had promised a copious speech on the gods (V 155), a speech which would
have made a happy ending. For some reason he replaced the speech on the
gods, the only beings that are perfectly happy, by the description of extreme misery.

Lucretius' description of the plague differs most strikingly from its
Thucydidean model in being completely silent about the fact that the
plague occurred during a war and even owed its extremely destructive character to that war:[3] the plague was altogether a natural phenomenon, the
work of nature. As a consequence the plague as presented by Lucretius is
not less but more terrible than it is according to Thucydides. Since Lucretius does not present the plague in its context—in what we would call its
"historical" context—since he does not present the events preceding it and
following it, but describes it in isolation at the end of his poem, he presents it as if it were the end of the world; he is silent on the cessation of
the plague. He presents to his readers in fact a recorded experience which
could give them a notion of the unrecordable end of the world. He is less
explicit than Thucydides about the fact that there were many who survived
the plague.[4] He dwells more than Thucydides does on the fear of death
which gripped those exposed to the plague—their fear of death, not of
what might happen to them after death—and he is silent about their (not
necessarily unsuccessful) attempts, emphasized by Thucydides, to snatch
some pleasures without any regard to law before it was too late.[5] He does
follow Thucydides' description of the breakdown of fear of the gods and of

respect for the sacred laws regarding burial. Yet this description takes on a somewhat different meaning in the Lucretian context; one cannot say of Thucydides' work what one can say of Lucretius' work: that its most important purpose is to liberate men from religion.

In order to reveal the magnitude of his enterprise, the poet returns at the end of his poem for a moment to a still more pre-Epicurean view than the one from which he started. He says that those who, from too great a desire for life and fear of death, failed to take care of their sick were punished afterward with a shameful death since they themselves were neglected and left without help when they fell sick; although he does not speak of divine punishment, he suggests it. Yet he corrects himself immediately thereafter: those who from a sense of shame did take care of their sick died no less miserably than the shameless.[6] As a consequence of the misery everywhere, neither the rites thought to be of divine origin nor the gods themselves counted for much: they did not count for nothing. For while the Athenians disregarded the customs of burial which they had always observed, they did not desert the bodies of their dead kinsmen.[7] At any rate, the breakdown of religion is presented by Lucretius, as it is by Thucydides, as a sign of extreme misery: there is something worse, much worse, than religion.[8] In the Lucretian context this means that the plague which occurred in the heyday of Athenian civilization was more terrible than the sacrifice of Iphigenia which occurred far from Athens in the obscure past: the witnesses of Iphigenia's slaughter were sad and terrified; they were not in a state of utter despondency; they could hope that Diana would be appeased, and to the best of their knowledge this hope was fulfilled. And while the story of Iphigenia's sacrifice may or may not be true, the truth of the account of the plague in Athens is vouched for by one of the most sober observers that ever was—by a man who was singularly free from religious fear. The fact that Thucydides observed and described the plague which struck him down could seem to show that philosophy, the study of nature, is possible under the most unfavorable circumstances. Lucretius' description of the plague, however, taken by itself, is far from suggesting this. It rather suggests that the mind of the philosopher stricken by the plague would lose all its powers, become filled with anguish, pain, and fear, and disintegrate before he died.[9] The plague occurred prior to Epicurus' birth, but Lucretius does not in the slightest degree suggest that Epicurus or an Epicurean would have withstood it better than anybody else.

By contrasting directly the opening of the poem with its ending we gain the impression that the poem moves from the sweetest natural phenomenon to the saddest and ugliest or that at the beginning the poet abstracts entirely from the evils in order to accumulate them at the end. At the beginning he praises Venus, the giver of joy, charm, and peace, as the ruler of nature; at the end he speaks, not even of Mars, but of the plague. Near the beginning he speaks of the sacrifice of Iphigenia which was demanded by Diana and appeared to appease that goddess. At the end he speaks of the plague which could be thought to have been sent by Apollo, but the stark terror of which is not relieved by any hope that one could appease the god who might have sent it. The poem appears to move from beautiful or comforting falsehoods to the repulsive truth. There is undoubtedly a certain falsehood implied in the isolation of the plague: the plague is as much a work of nature as procreation, but not more than the latter. The plague is as much the work of nature as the golden deeds of Venus, nay, as the understanding of nature. It is doubtful whether philosophy has any remedy against the helplessness and the debasement which afflicts anyone struck by such events as the plague. By revealing fully the nature of things, philosophy proves to be not simply a "sweet solace" (V 21). Nevertheless, the movement from Venus to nature, which is destructive as it is creative, is an ascent.

3. *The Function of Lucretius' Poetry (I 926–950 and IV 1–25)*

The movement from the untruth to the truth is not simply a movement from unrelieved darkness and terror to pure light and joy. On the contrary, the truth appears at first to be repulsive and depressing. A special effort is needed to counteract the first appearance of the truth. This special effort is beyond the power of philosophy; it is the proper work of poetry. The poet Lucretius follows the philosopher Epicurus; he imitates him; he belongs as it were to a weaker and lower species than the teacher of the naked truth.[10] Yet precisely for this reason the poet can do something which the philosopher cannot do.

Lucretius' poetry makes bright and sweet the obscure and sad findings of the Greeks, that is, of the philosophers.[11] The contrast between the sweetest and most exhilarating celebrated at the beginning of his poem and the saddest and most depressing described at its end—a contrast which we understand as indicative of the movement the reader must undergo—is the most striking example of the character of Lucretius' poetry.

Lucretius speaks of the character of his poetry most clearly in twenty-five verses which occur first immediately before his exposition of infinity and which are repeated with very minor changes at the beginning of Book IV, the Book devoted to what we may call the acts of the soul or the mind. His subject, we learn, is dark, but his poem is bright. The doctrine which he sets forth seems often to be rather sad to those not initiated into it, and the multitude shrinks from it with horror. Therefore he sets it forth in a sweet poem, giving the doctrine as it were a touch of the sweet honey of the Muses. In so doing he acts like a physician who attempts to give children repulsive wormwood to drink and first touches the rim of the cup with sweet honey; thus the unsuspecting children are deceived for their benefit and do not sense the bitterness of the drink which heals them.

The potential Epicurean whom Lucretius addresses may be a man of rare worth according to ordinary standards, and he may have an excellent mind; in the most important respect he is, to begin with, quite immature. Therefore the poet must deceive him by adding something to the doctrine which he expounds, something which is alien to the doctrine and which is meant to conceal the sad, repulsive, and horrible character of the doctrine. The comparison of honey and wormwood on the one hand with the poetry and the doctrine on the other does not hold in every respect: children do not necessarily learn that it was the bitter medicine which cured them, whereas those readers of Lucretius' work who grasp its meaning necessarily learn that it is the doctrine which makes them sound and happy. The comparison surely holds in that in both cases the patient tastes the sweet first: thanks to the poetry, what the reader tastes first is sweet. But does the reader ever taste the repulsive? Is what is primarily repulsive, if tasted by itself, noticed only after it is no longer repulsive? Will its taste eventually even be sweet? The example of Venus at the beginning and of the plague at the end would seem to show that whereas the sweet is sensed first, the repulsive or sad is sensed even at the end, but in such a way that it is more bearable for the sensitive reader after he has digested the doctrine than before. Furthermore, the child may take the honeyed wormwood merely for the sake of the honey, or he may take it because he is uncomfortable; he surely is not so uncomfortable as to be willing to take the bitter potion by itself. Similarly, the potential Epicurean may be attracted to the Epicurean doctrine only because of the sweetness of Lucretius' poetry, or he may be attracted by it because he suffers from the terrors of religion; surely those terrors are not so great as to make him willing to swallow the naked truth. After all, he does not live in the age in which Agamemnon sacrificed his beloved daughter. We conclude that poetry is the link or the mediation between religion and philosophy.

How can religion be more attractive than philosophy if religion is nothing but terrifying? To answer this question, one must reconsider what the poet says at the beginning in the light of what he says later on how men lived before the emergence of philosophy; one must consider the function of religion. Originally men lived like wild beasts, depending entirely on the spontaneous gifts of the earth, without fire and the arts as well as without laws and language, unable to conceive of a common good. They feared death because they clung to the sweet light of life, but apparently not because they feared what might happen to them after death. Nor did they fear that the sun might not rise again after it had set; the thought that sun and earth might be destructible had not occurred to them.[12] That thought occurred to them only after they had acquired language and the arts and established society and laws; then they began to doubt whether the sun would always rise and set and whether the earth would last forever:

whether the world would come to an end and hence whether it did not have a beginning. There is only one protection against the fear that the walls of the world will someday crumble: the will of gods. Religion thus serves as a refuge from the fear of the end or the death of the world; it has its root in man's attachment to the world. Lucretius himself wishes, not to say prays, that the day on which the huge machine of the world will fall down with a dreadful sound will not come soon. The world to which man is attached is not the boundless whole but the visible whole—heaven and earth and what belongs to them—which is only an infinitesimal part of the boundless whole: there are infinitely many worlds both simultaneously and successively; everything to which a man can be attached—his life, his friends, his fatherland, his fame, his work—implies attachment to the world to which he belongs and which makes possible the primary objects of his attachment.[13] The recourse to the gods of religion and the fear of them is already a remedy for a more fundamental pain: the pain stemming from the divination that the lovable is not sempiternal or that the sempiternal is not lovable. Philosophy transforms the divination into a certainty. One may therefore say that philosophy is productive of the deepest pain. Man has to choose between peace of mind deriving from a pleasing delusion and peace of mind deriving from the unpleasing truth. Philosophy which, anticipating the collapse of the walls of the world, breaks through the walls of the world, abandons the attachment to the world; this abandonment is most painful. Poetry on the other hand is, like religion, rooted in that attachment, but unlike religion, it can be put into the service of detachment. Because poetry is rooted in the prephilosophic attachment, because it enhances and deepens that attachment, the philosophic poet is the perfect mediator between the attachment to the world and the attachment to detachment from the world. The joy or pleasure which Lucretius' poem arouses is therefore austere, reminding of the pleasure aroused by the work of Thucydides.[14]

II. ON THE FIRST BOOK

In giving an account of things "we" refer them to the first bodies (I 59). The first bodies are not immediately known; they become known only through an ascent (or descent). Prior to the ascent people render an account of things, or at least of many things, by tracing them to gods. What we have indicated regarding the first stage of the ascent can be stated in general terms as follows. Primarily men are under the spell of ancestral opinion; they act on the assumption that the true and the good is the ancestral. A flexible man who by traveling has become aware of the thought of many peoples will have become doubtful of the equation of the true and good with the ancestral. Yet since all peoples trace at least some things to gods, he will still believe in active gods. The second stage of the ascent consists then in an insight which cannot be acquired by traveling, but only while sitting or standing still; it is the realization that activity is incompatible with the bliss of gods. For some reason Lucretius does not use this theological insight at the beginning of his exposition of the truth.

Lucretius opens his account of nature with the assertion that nothing ever comes into being out of nothing through gods. He thus opposes the opinion of "all mortals" who trace to gods the numerous happenings of which they cannot see the causes. He does not establish the principle that nothing happens without a cause; all men take that principle for granted as they take it for granted that there are things. The question concerns exclusively the causality of gods, or, more precisely, the question is exclusively whether one is entitled to identify the invisible causes with the gods. To refute the opinion primarily held by all mortals, he will show that nothing ever comes into being out of nothing; by showing this he shows that nothing ever comes into being out of nothing through gods. He seems to dismiss without argument the possibility that the gods create things from something: is coming into being through gods the same as coming into being through nothing? He cannot be said to presuppose the true view of the gods according to which activity is incompatible with their bliss, for, as we have seen, the verses in the proem (44–49) which intimate this view do not in their context exclude the possibility that the self-sufficient gods bestow their favors from kindness or whim, without any effort, as it were playfully, on beings which are not self-sufficient. Lucretius says that when we have seen that nothing can be created out of nothing, we shall understand whence each thing can be created and how all things come to be without the labor of gods: he will prove that all things come into being from something in such a way that there is no room for any divine activity or interference (149–158); this proof makes unnecessary the inference from the gods' bliss; it makes unnecessary the assertion of the gods' bliss.

Lucretius establishes the view that nothing can come into being out of nothing as follows. If things could come into being out of nothing, they could *a fortiori* come into being out of anything: things of every kind could come into being out of things of every other kind; at any season, suddenly, they could be born full-grown; their coming into being would not require the fulfillment of any specific conditions; the various kinds of things would not have peculiar sizes and powers; human art would not have any rhyme or reason. As it is, however, it is manifest that things come into being from fixed seeds and the like; hence, they cannot come into being out of nothing (159–214). Lucretius achieves the transition from "they do not" to "they cannot" by starting from this disjunction: things come into being either from nothing (or anything) or else from fixed seeds; but they come into being only from fixed seeds; hence they cannot come into being from nothing. One could say that his argument is defective because he gives only a few examples; he would probably ask the objector to produce a single example of coming into being out of nothing or even of metamorphoses which are not natural processes, for such metamorphoses would be in the decisive respect emergences out of nothing. Still, his selection of examples is in need of an explanation.

All examples adduced by him in support of the six arguments which are meant to prove that nothing comes into being out of nothing are taken from animals and plants. In the fifth argument he uses as sole example the size and power of men; he could as well have chosen the size and power of lions, cows, or mice; he chooses man in order to prepare the transition from natural beings [15] to art. But why does he limit his choice in the whole passage to living beings (animals and plants)? [16] Let us consider the context or rather the immediate sequel. After having proved that nothing comes into being out of nothing, he proves in four arguments that nothing perishes into nothing (215–264); the examples by which he supports these arguments are taken from animate and inanimate things (such as earth and sea) alike. Furthermore, he now speaks of Venus as well as of Father Ether and Mother Earth; no reference of this kind had occurred in his speech about coming into being. Finally, the second half of the fundamental reasoning is adorned by the sketch of a pleasing rural spectacle, a sketch which fills one-third of the fourth argument; there is no parallel to this in the first half. We suggest this explanation. In the first half Lucretius deals with birth, and in the second he deals with death. Birth is more pleasing, more beautiful, than death. One way of mitigating or concealing the repulsive is by generalization: inanimate things perish, but do not die. The poet speaks of Venus in that argument in which he speaks of what time removes through old age and what is brought back in a manner by Venus: Venus compensates and comforts for death; it is indeed no longer possible to speak of Venus as the sole ruler of the nature of things (21). The poet speaks of Father Ether and Mother Earth, and he draws a pleasing picture in the argument in which he speaks of the consequences of a certain "passing away," namely, the passing away of rain; these consequences are altogether exhilarating: a rich vegetation which nourishes the animals and which renders possible the generation of offspring and the healthy growth of the young animals. Death—be it only the death of rain—loses its sting if it is seen to lead to life or to the only possible eternity. We have not yet learned that there will be an end of the cycle of births and deaths on our earth. At any rate, in presenting his fundamental reasoning Lucretius follows the rule that the sweet must precede the sad and that the sad must be sweetened.

Lucretius fears that his addressee or reader might "begin" to distrust what he is told since the causes to which he is led (the eternal and indestructible first bodies) are invisible; his teacher reminds him therefore of invisible bodies of which he cannot help admitting that they are. His first example is the unseen bodies of wind; he describes their devastating power and compares it to the devastating power that the soft nature of water acquires through abundance of rain (265–297); he speaks of the devastating effect of rain only after having spoken of its exhilarating effect; and when speaking of the devastating effect of storms or floods he does not mention explicitly their destroying animals in general and men in particular. Only one argument in this section deals exclusively and explicitly with the disappearance of invisible bodies, that is, with destruction; this argument is supported only by examples taken from inanimate things and chiefly from artifacts (305–321). The last argument in this section deals with both growth and decay; the only example mentioned here is the decay of rocks (322–328).

Lucretius next turns to proving the being of the void, that is, of the only kind of nothing that is. The speech about the void does not seem to require any sweetening, although, as we learn later, the void belongs to the "steep" things (658–659). If one compares the central argument establishing the being of the void with its repetition in the last Book (I 348–355, VI 942–955), one sees that in the first statement there is no explicit mention of the void in man, whereas in the second statement the void in man is emphasized; the second statement is directly linked to the description of the plague. Although the doctrine of the void does not need sweetening, it will not be accepted by Memmius without a special effort on the part of both the pupil and the master. The section on the void is the first in which the poet engages in explicit polemics against "some" (371; cf. 391), and it is the first in which he addresses Memmius by name; he also uses there the second person singular with greater frequency than at any time since he began to address him. In concluding his reasoning regarding the being of the void, Lucretius indicates that he is not sure that he has convinced Memmius. He urges him to discover additional arguments on the basis of the poet's slight suggestions. Yet Memmius may be ever so little slack. In that case will he remain exposed to the terrors of religion? This is not what the poet says: one can overcome the terrors of religion without asserting the void. Considering the fact that the fundamental reasoning which, without being theological, leaves no room for divine action is not specifically Epicurean, we may say that according to Lucretius one can overcome the terrors of religion without being an Epicurean; it is sufficient for this purpose to become a *physiologos* in general. Lucretius does not threaten Memmius with anything should he be slack; if he is, Lucretius promises that he will hear further arguments from the poet till the end of their lives. Or could one call this promise a threat? It is hard to know which alternative Memmius is likely to choose. When encouraging him to discover additional arguments, Lucretius compares Memmius' ability to draw the truth from its hiding places to the ability of dogs to find the lair of a wild beast that ranges the mountains (402–411); this comparison is the second occurring in the poem, the first being the comparison of devastating storms to devastating floods (280–290).

There is no nature, nothing self-subsisting, apart from bodies and the void; for whatever is by itself must either be susceptible of being sensed by "the common sense" (or, perhaps more precisely, it must touch and be touched), and then it is body, or it cannot be touched, and then it is the void; or, whatever is by itself is either able to act and to be acted upon, and then it is body, or it is that within which or through which acting and being acted upon take place, and then it is the void (418–448). What is, but is not by itself, is either the property of a body or the void, that is, cannot be separated from the body in question or the void without the body in question or the void being destroyed, or it is an accident of body or of the void. Among the examples of properties which Lucretius gives there is none that is peculiar to man and even to living beings; but the examples which he gives of accidents are all peculiar to men: "the human things" are all accidents. He mentions slavery and freedom, poverty and wealth, war and peace. He does not mention life, for it is a property of living beings. He throws no light on the status of death. Regarding time, he makes clear that it is not self-subsisting. Past events—his examples are Paris' desire for Helen, the rape of Helen, the Greeks' nocturnal conquest of Troy with the help of the wooden horse, and their destruction of Troy—were accidents of the human beings in question; they are now as little as those human beings themselves are (449–482). The poem opens with a presentation of Venus as the life-giving goddess who bends Mars to her will. The present examples correct that presentation. Paris was the favorite of Venus then, just as Memmius is her favorite now. Paris brought about the ruin of his city or the victory of the Greeks; Memmius is to contribute to the victory of Greek wisdom in Rome. Could Lucretius' poem be comparable to the Trojan horse? This much is certain: the whole dimension of things Greek and Roman qua Greek and Roman is a small part of the sphere of accidents. We are at the opposite pole of the thought, stated in the proem, that the Romans and only the Romans are akin to that deity who is the only guide of the nature of things.

Lucretius proceeds to show that the first bodies whose character he has left hitherto undetermined are atoms. They are absolutely solid, that is, they do not include any void, and hence are eternal and indestructible, whereas all other bodies are perishable: everything we see is more quickly destroyed than built up, as the poet here observes in passing (556–557). The atoms are indivisible; the fact that there is a limit to the division of bodies is at the bottom of every finiteness and fixedness such as the specific limitations of the growth and the life span of the various kinds of living beings and of what each kind can and cannot do by virtue of the "covenants" or "laws" of nature (551–598). Finiteness is meant to be a source of comfort.[17] In accordance with this Lucretius does not yet make clear that the visible world as a whole is perishable; he only alludes to it (502); he rather seems to suggest the eternity of the species (584–598) and hence of the visible world. No atoms, no species. The poet speaks therefore in this section of "nature creating things" or of "matter which generates" (629, 632–633) as distinguished not only from Venus (277–278) but also from nature as both creative and destructive (56–57). While the atoms are indivisible, they consist of parts, but these parts cannot be separated from one another (599–634).

The teachings regarding the void and the atoms are the first teachings presented by Lucretius which are not accepted by all students of nature. When speaking of the void he indicates that Memmius might be impressed by the fictions of those who deny the void (370–376, 391, 398–399). Such indications are almost completely avoided in the verses dealing with the atoms (624). Lucretius does not speak explicitly of possible objections of the addressee to the doctrine of atoms because he turns to alternatives to atomism after having stated the atomistic doctrine; in the latter context he voices the objections of the addressee in a more emphatic form than he has voiced his previous objections, hesitations, or misgivings: he makes Memmius voice them.[18]

The alternatives to atomism which Lucretius regards as worthy of consideration are these: the first bodies are (1) one or two of the four elements, (2) the four elements (Empedocles), and (3) the homoeomeria of Anaxagoras. The most famous upholder of the first alternative is Heraclitus, who taught that fire is the matter of things. His fame is bright among the empty or lightheaded of the Greeks—*inanes a negando inane* (658)— as distinguished from the weighty or ponderous ones who seek the truth. The reason is not that fire tends upward,[19] but that Heraclitus' language is dark; fools admire and love particularly those things which they can see hidden beneath words turned upside down, and they set up for true what can prettily tickle the ears and is adorned with the help of make-up supplied by charming sounds (635–644). Lucretius does not say that Heraclitus spoke obscurely in order to be admired and loved by fools; nor does he deny that Heraclitus' words sound well; Lucretius himself is eager to charm the reader with his language so as to enable him to understand an obscure teaching.[20] Did then Heraclitus employ the charm of his language in order to prevent the understanding of an obscure teaching? The Epicureans surely were proud of their outspokenness.[21] At any rate, Lucretius' bark is somewhat worse than his bite; he must counteract Heraclitus' renown.

After he has concluded his attack on Heraclitus, he chants the praise of Empedocles, whom he regards as superior to all other deniers of the atoms and the void; Empedocles' teaching is indeed not according to nature, but it surely is in accordance with the nature of his native Sicily.[22] Thereafter Lucretius makes it clear that those to whom he has referred before mentioning Empedocles—among them Heraclitus is the only one whom he has

mentioned by name—were great men since they found many things divinely, in a more holy manner, and by a much more certain reasoning than
Apollo's Pythia ever does (734–739). In accordance with this he does not
criticize Heraclitus, Empedocles, and Anaxagoras on the ground that their
doctrines support or do not destroy the terrors of religion. To wonder how
this can be reconciled with what we know through the fragments especially
of Empedocles means to wonder how Lucretius read Empedocles, but one
cannot begin to study how Lucretius read Empedocles before one knows
how Lucretius wrote. We have seen earlier that according to Lucretius one
can overcome the terrors of religion without becoming an Epicurean. Perhaps his amazing silence about Plato and Aristotle (as distinguished from
Heraclitus, Empedocles, and Anaxagoras) signifies that they are not helpful in the fight against religion.

The central argument of Lucretius against all nonatomists is this: all
things which we perceive are changeable and hence perishable bodies;
hence the indestructible first bodies cannot be perceptible; but the four
elements (fire, earth, water, air) and the characteristics of the homoeomeria (bones, flesh, blood, gold, earth, fire, water, and so on) are perceptible. In other words, the first bodies must have a different nature from
that of "the things"; they must have a secret and unseen nature; only if the
nature of the first things differs from that of "the things" can the character
of "the things" as changeable and perishable be preserved.[23] There remains the difficulty not discussed by Lucretius that size and shape—
characters of both the atoms and the things—are as such sensible and
hence destructible. Be this as it may, Lucretius does not say that the alternatives to atomism must be rejected because they favor religion and its
terrors; his objection to them is purely theoretical; but by making
Memmius defend them in direct speech,[24] the poet presents him as making a last-ditch stand in defense of the ultimate dignity of "the things,"
"the world," "the walls of the world," after he has failed to rise in defense
of Romanism. But Memmius succumbs to Lucretius' powerful assault.

This is the situation in which the poet, taking breath, speaks about his
art and its function by comparing himself to a physician who has to give a
bitter potion to children and deceives them for their benefit by sweetening
the repulsive drink. He speaks about what he is doing after he has been
doing it, and after the reader has been exposed to it, for a considerable
time. The critique of the nonatomistic doctrines has in fact shown that
atomism is the most bitter or sad of all doctrines; the completion of that
critique is therefore a kind of climax, surely a place for rest and reflection.
The poet introduces the verses which deal with his art and its function by
proudly proclaiming the novelty of his undertaking: he is the first to write
a poem openly devoted to the liberation of the mind from the bonds of
religion, and he wishes to be the first; he is spurred by a great hope of
praise; he goes so far as to say that that great hope has made him love the

Muses (922–925). Originally (140–141) he has said that he is spurred by his hope for Memmius' friendship. But originally he has spoken only of the exhilarating character of his undertaking and has been silent about its saddening character. As he discloses the true character of the true doctrine, he discloses his true motive: if the true doctrine were simply gratifying, his love of Memmius would be a sufficient motive for writing the poem; but since it is not simply gratifying, it is not certain that Memmius or any other man known to the poet will be gratified by it; he can reasonably hope only for praise, that is, for praise by indeterminate readers.

In other words, however sad the truth may be, to be the first discoverer of the sad truth is not sad, for to be the first to achieve a great victory, a victory of a new kind, is worthy of praise, and praise is gratifying. The Greek who was the first to vanquish religion also wished to be the first to win that victory (71 ff.). However sad the truth may be, to be the first who speaks about the sad truth in charming verses is not sad. Since the poet makes bright the dark discoveries of the Greeks (136–145), the fame for which he longs may even be brighter than the fame of that Greek. He surely possesses an art which his master lacked. This art presupposes a deep understanding of the feelings which obstruct the acceptance of the true doctrine by most men—an understanding which the master did not necessarily possess. Hence in a respect which is not unimportant, the pupil may be wiser than the master; he may not be the master's pupil in every respect. Therefore we should not expect Lucretius to follow his master or his school in every point. Was there ever a pupil, wise or foolish, who in fact agreed with his master in every point?

The passage under discussion is less a conclusion to what precedes it than an introduction to what follows it (921). What follows requires a keener listening, a higher degree of understanding, of ability to overcome one's attachments, of the addressee's co-operation with the poet,[25] than what precedes. What follows is the proof that the whole is infinite; it is infinite in extent, and there are infinitely many atoms. Finiteness is comforting; infinity is terrifying. Yet without infinity there cannot be "things," that is, finiteness. There cannot be a world without limits, without walls; yet the walls owe their stability which is precarious to the infinity beyond them; in the last resort we live in "an unwalled city." The comparison of the true doctrine to wormwood is a fit introduction to the section on infinity. After having shown that space is infinite, Lucretius argues as follows. In infinite space there must be infinitely many atoms or else there will be no compulsion for the atoms to come together for the formation of finite things, for the atoms, being mindless or blind, cannot intend to come together;[26] nor are the atoms attracted by one another; they are brought together and kept together only by colliding with one another, by buffeting one another; since by themselves they are in constant motion, only a limitless supply of atoms can keep the world, or the worlds, in being, partly by inflicting blows on the worlds from outside. The examples which Lucretius gives of the things that are created by the mindless meeting of the mindless atoms and that could not last for ever so short a time if the atoms were not replaced constantly from without are the sea, the earth, the sky, the race of mortals, and the sacred bodies of the gods (1014–1016). The gods are then not strictly speaking self-sufficient. The context (1019–1020, 1027–1031) suggests that the gods have come into being like all things other than the atoms and the void. The gods being created by the atoms in the same manner as the world (heaven and earth and what belongs to them) or the worlds, one cannot resort to the gods for assurance that the world is everlasting. It is perhaps more important to note that Lucretius still fails to make clear that the human race or the world will not last forever; since he mentions the human race together not only with heaven and earth but with the gods as well, he would have seemed to deny the imperishability of the gods by asserting the perishability of the world. This is to say nothing of the fact that if the worlds are perishable, it is hard to see how the *intermundia*—the places where the gods are asserted to live in eternal security—can be imperishable.

Lucretius does not fear that these or similar implications might induce Memmius to rebel against the doctrine of infinity. He fears that Memmius, whom he now addresses by name for the second time,[27] might be attracted by the view of "some" according to which the stability of the world is brought about, not by any blows by atoms from the outside, but by the desire of everything for the center of the world. There cannot be a center of the world, that is, of the universe, if the universe is infinite (1052–1082). What makes this view attractive would seem to be the *horror infiniti* or, perhaps more precisely, man's need for regarding himself and his world as the center of the universe. In trying to reduce that view *ad absurdum,* Lucretius points out that, as a consequence of its implications, the whole world would perish, that is, nothing would remain but space and the atoms (1083–1113): he does not say here that this is the inevitable fate of the world precisely on the basis of Epicureanism; he does not say here that the gate of death is not shut on the world.[28]

III. On Book II

The First Book opens with the praise of Venus as both the ancestress of the Romans and the sole guide of the nature of things; the Second Book opens with a praise of that life of man as man which is in accordance with nature. Nature calls for nothing but that the body be free from pain and that the mind, freed from care and fear, enjoy pleasure. Bodily nature can be gratified at little cost; it does not require luxury, wealth, noble birth, or regal power. Nor are things of this kind needed or useful for the well-being of the mind. What the mind needs is freedom from the terrors of religion and from fear of death—evils which are removed, not by political and military power,[29] but only by reason; reason alone, the study of nature, can give man tranquillity of mind (14–61). Nature and the study of nature are the sole sources of happiness.

In the first thirteen verses Lucretius speaks of a great boon about which he is silent in the rest of the proem; we must not forget that gratification while listening to his description of human happiness. It is sweet or gratifying, he says, to behold others in the grip of evils from which oneself is free. He gives three examples: the man on land who sees another struggling in the wind-tossed sea, the man in safety who watches armies in battle, and the pupil of wise men who from his heights looks down on the unwise struggling for superiority with one another. Of these spectacles the last is the most gratifying; in fact it is second to nothing else in sweetness. Lucretius does not speak of a man in bodily health who sees others suffering from disease. He says that it is not the distress of others which is pleasant, but only the beholding of evils from which one is free. Yet he does not speak of evils from which oneself has suffered before, for one cannot strictly speaking behold those evils; hence one must admit that our pleasure or happiness is enhanced by our seeing the pains and dangers of others. The sad is necessary as a foil for the sweet, for sensing the sweet. Does the gods' supreme happiness—their complete freedom from pain and danger (I 47)—require that they behold the misery of men? Is it desirable or even possible that all men should be happy, that is, philosophers? We have seen how much Lucretius is concerned with receiving praise for being the first, with superiority: his happiness requires the inferiority of others. We cannot say whether he regards this kind of pleasure as natural, for he speaks of nature only afterward (II 17, 20, 23). Certainly nature will not be the source of happiness if it is not also the source of unhappiness. Man's happiness requires that he be free from "the blind night" in which he finds himself prior to philosophy; yet philosophy discovers the roots of all things in empty space and the "blind" atoms (I 1110, 1115–1116).[30] Nothing is more alien to wisdom than that with which wisdom is above everything else concerned: the atoms and the void. The first things are in no way a model for man.

Lucretius turns at once to the questions concerning the movement by which the atoms generate the various things and dissolve them again, concerning the force which compels them to do this, and concerning the speed with which they move in the void. He asks for the reader's attention in a commanding tone. That the atoms are in motion is shown by the fact that "we" see that "all" things decay and disappear and other things of the same kind take their place (II 62–79). Lucretius obviously thinks, not of the sun and the species of animals, but of individual animals and nations. While he now mentions destruction first, he sees it only as a stage in the cycle through which "the sum of things [the present world] always renews itself." [31] Nor does he mention death. He goes on to show how the atoms, moving in the boundless void, never come to rest, how some of them colliding with one another either bounce back or unite with one another, how by uniting in different ways they produce different kinds of things. He illustrates the process by an explicit likeness and image: the movement of minute bodies in the sun's rays when those rays enter a dark room; those bodies mingle in many ways and, as it were having formed troops, engage in everlasting battle. It goes without saying that the atoms' clashes do not take place in the light of the sun; the likeness sweetens the likened. The clashes of the atoms are fights in the dark, blind fights of blind atoms, blind blows which the blind atoms inflict on one another (80–141). The fundamental movements resemble less the deeds of Venus than those of Mars.[32] We see once more how one-sided, how misleading is the invocation of Venus at the beginning of the work despite or because of its necessity. We also see how appropriate it is that the central example at the beginning of Book II is a man not engaged in fighting who watches fighting.

Lucretius underlines the importance of his general characterization of the atomic movements by what he does immediately afterward. Both near the beginning of the next section (142–183) and near its end he addresses Memmius by name. He has addressed him by name twice in Book I (411, 1052). The section thus distinguished consists of two parts. The first part is devoted to the speed with which the atoms move in the void. How great that speed is one can gather by considering the speed with which the light of the sun travels; since it does not travel in the void, the speed of the atomic motions must be much, much greater than the speed of the light of the sun. The poet stresses the contrast between the movement of the sun's light and that of the atoms by alluding to the birds' celebration of sunrise. It is reasonable to think that it is the enormous speed with which the atoms travel that accounts for the full fury and violence of their clashes; it is then that fury and violence which contributes to, or rather accounts for, the emergence of the "things." According to the diametrically opposite view the world is the work of the greatest awakeness, circumspection, and care. It is this view against which Lucretius turns in the second part of the section. According to "some," [33] we are told, only beings of superhuman wisdom and power, only gods, can have formed the world out of matter, atomic or nonatomic: only through the activity of gods can the world possess that perfect harmony with the needs of man which it is seen to possess; only in this way can it be understood that nature prevents the death of the human race by inducing men through divine pleasure, through the deeds of Venus, to generate offspring—this wonderful harmony between the individual's sweetest pleasure and the most common good. Lucretius rejects this view as utterly false. The reason is not that he is an Epicurean: even if he did not know what the origins of the things are, that is, if he did not know that they are the atoms and the void, he would dare to assert from the very manner of working of heaven as well as from many other things that the nature of the world is not created for our bene- fit by divine power; by nature the world abounds in defects (167–182). Not wise gods or gods of wisdom, not even Venus, are at the helm or are the originators; at the origin there is the fury and violence of the blind atoms' blind fights. There is a radical disharmony between the atomic movements and even the *rationes caeli* on the one hand and the *rationes humanae* or the *rationes vitae* on the other.[34] The theological view tries to establish a harmony between the *rationes caeli* and the *rationes humanae*; it wishes to be comforting. Lucretius fights religion less on account of its terrors and crimes than of the defective character of the world; he does not fight religion primarily because he holds Epicureanism and in particular Epicurean theology to be true. What the poet tacitly suggested at the be- ginning of his argument (see pages 85–86 above) he now says almost ex- plicitly: there is no need for recourse to the fundamental theologoumenon in order to refute the theological account. It goes without saying that the realization of the badness of the world does not induce Lucretius for a moment to think of rebellion or conquest: misery is as necessary to human life as happiness.

Lucretius continues his account of the atomic movements by showing first that the atoms move downward and then that they swerve. The atoms are of different weight, but in the void they all fall with equal speed; they would never clash and thus bring about the emergence of compounds but for the fact that they spontaneously swerve a little at times and in places which are in no way fixed: the movement after the swerve does not in a fixed manner arise from the movement before it. Atoms are so little attrac- tive that they do not even attract one another. The alternative to the swerve would be that everything is determined by fate, and this is incom- patible with the freedom with which every living being on earth follows "the will of [its] mind," that is, where pleasure leads it, or originates motion (216–293). When Epicurus takes issue with the physicists who assert that everything is determined by fate or necessity, he says that the belief in fate is worse than the belief in the tale of the gods since fate is inexorable, whereas the gods of the tale are not.[35] Lucretius does not fol- low his master in this point. His statement on the swerve of the atoms does not read as if it were directed against any school of thought (cf. 225). He does not wish to present the Epicurean teaching as pleasing or comforting, as more pleasing and comforting than other teachings set forth by students of nature. The doctrine of the swerve as Lucretius presents it is not meant to bring the *rationes* of the atoms into harmony with the *rationes humanae*. A sign of this is that the "freedom" which he tries to vindicate by that doctrine is not peculiar to man, but is common to all animals.

The swerve of the atoms might cast doubt on the fixedness of the natural order. To dispel that doubt Lucretius asserts that while the atoms are always in motion, the universe is in a sense at rest. No atom comes into being or perishes, nor do the kinds of their movements change, hence also not the outcome of those movements, that is, the production of the things of various kinds. Lucretius is again silent about the destruction of the kinds of things or of the world. The fact that the whole is seen to be at rest while all its parts are in motion is strange. To remove that strangeness, Lucretius adduces two gratifying ("white" or "glimmering") examples: a herd of grazing sheep and their lambs running around on a faraway hill, and military units engaged in a war game—not in war proper—on a plain as seen from high mountains (299–332).

There are infinitely many things and infinitely many atoms. Yet the things are related to the atoms as the infinitely many words or combinations of words are to the small numbers of letters (cf. I 823–829): the infinitely many atoms fall into classes of which there are not infinitely many. Lucretius starts from the infinitely many natural things, both animate and inanimate, each of which differs in shape from the others of its kind. He speaks at the greatest length of animals, especially of the fact that a mother can tell its offspring from any other young animal of its kind and the offspring its mother, and still more especially of the sad spectacle of a cow vainly seeking its calf which has been slaughtered before the altars of the gods. He thus prepares the reader for the detailed discussion (in II 398 ff.) of the atomic causes of the painful things on the one hand and of the pleasant on the other. He infers from the infinite variety of shapes of things that there must be a great variety of shapes of atoms: uniformity is the outcome of purposeful action, of human production that is guided by a single model (because it is guided by a single end), rather than of nature (333–380). The variety of atomic shapes is shown in a more precise manner especially by the different ways in which different things affect us with pleasure or pain; pleasure and pain are due to the different shapes of atoms. Lucretius is thus led to exclaim that "touch, yea touch, o holy majesties of the gods, is the sense of body" (434–435). The reference here to the gods needs an explanation. The poet had spoken earlier (I 1015) of "the holy bodies of the gods" (cf. I 38). In the present context he mentions a deity by name. He speaks of the pleasant feelings which go with the discharge of the semen "born in the body" "through the generative acts of Venus"; he does not yet refer to a deity when speaking in the same context of feelings of pain (II 435–439). The reference to Venus barely reminds us of the praise of Venus as "the joy of men and gods" at the beginning of the poem; we are more than sufficiently prepared for any weakening of that praise (cf. 172–173). Can we still believe that the gods enjoy the deeds of Venus? Above all, only twenty-five verses later Lucretius speaks of the bitter or nauseous body of Neptune, that is, of sea water—of the body of a god which can be dissolved into its ingredients even by human means (471–477). Certain it is that our awareness of the gods must be understood in the last analysis in terms of our sense of touch.

One cannot help wondering regarding the size and shape especially of those atoms which compose the bodies of the gods. We learn from Lucretius that the number of atomic shapes or forms is limited, that the sizes of the atoms keep within unchangeable and rather narrow bounds, and that therefore there cannot be atoms of gigantic, not to say boundless, size. Similarly, none of the things created by the clash of atoms can surpass others of those things infinitely in beauty and splendor.[36] What this means regarding the gods is obvious. On the other hand, as we hear again, there are infinitely many atoms of each form. This is compatible with the fact that there are many fewer individuals of some kinds of things than of others. Even if there were a terrestrial species of which there is only one individual, infinitely many atoms of the appropriate shapes would be needed so that that individual could be formed and preserved, given the fact that the atoms move in what the poet now calls that vast and faithless sea. In fact, the movement of the atoms in the infinite void is comparable to that of the parts of a wrecked ship in the sea: as little as those parts, which are small in number, could ever be put together again through being tossed hither and thither by the waves, so little could atoms of a finite number ever be brought together and kept together to form a thing (522–568). All the terrors of the ocean, which after all has limits, are as nothing compared with the terrors of the void. Infinity achieves what wise gods could not have achieved: the production of a world of very deficient goodness. In particular, the balance between birth and death is due to the war which the atoms carry on with one another from infinite time. This balance is least perfect in the case of man with whom wise gods would be especially concerned: man begins his life crying, and laments accompany him to his grave.[37]

Lucretius is still silent about the death of the world—about the death of the species as distinguished from the death of individuals. He goes on to speak about the atomic composition of the earth without drawing the obvious conclusion that, being a compound, the earth is bound to perish sooner or later. He starts from the facts that nothing whose nature is manifestly seen consists only of one kind of atom and that the larger the number of powers a thing possesses within itself, the larger the number of kinds of atoms of which it will consist. The earth possesses within itself the greatest variety of powers; it gives rise to water, fire, and vegetation and it sustains man as well as wild beasts. Hence the earth alone has been called the Great Mother of the gods, of the wild beasts, and of our body (581–599).[38] Lucretius draws our attention to beings whose nature is not manifestly seen and which may consist of one kind of atoms only; one wonders whether the gods are beings of that kind, although (or because) this would imply that the gods are the least powerful beings in the universe. The sequel surely suggests that the earth has much greater powers, or at least a much larger number of powers, than the gods and that the gods are terrestrial beings. At any rate, the earth understood as a goddess seems to be the clearest case of a terrestrial animal species of which there is only one member (cf. 541–543).

Of all these questions Lucretius answers immediately and explicitly only one; he denies the divinity of the earth. He prefaces this denial with a rather detailed description of the terror-inspiring, savage, and exotic procession of the Great Mother. That procession had been described by the ancient and learned poets of the Greeks who explained the meaning of its various features. Lucretius mentions seven items. The central one is the fact that the Great Mother is called the Mother of Mount Ida and that she is given as companions Phrygian bands, because, "as they say," corn was first produced in that part of the earth. The Trojans, from whom the Romans are derived, were Phrygians (I 474), but the Romans owe their knowledge of the remarkable Phrygian cult in question to the Greeks. It is in accordance with this that Lucretius traces the growing of corn to Athens (VI 1–2). The second item conveys encouragement to parents regarding the education of their children; the fifth conveys a condemnation of, and severe threat to, people who have violated the majesty of the mother and have been found ungrateful to their parents.[39] The sixth item serves the purpose of filling with fear the ungrateful minds and the impious hearts of the multitude through the divine majesty of the goddess; the context leaves it in doubt whether this goal is achieved. Lucretius himself is doubtful regarding the last feature of the procession which he mentions; it may refer to the tale told of the salvation of the infant Jupiter from the danger that his father Saturnus might devour him, to the everlasting grief [40] of the Great Mother, or it may intimate the goddess' proclaiming that men should defend their fatherland (their paternal earth) and protect and adorn their parents (600–643). Lucretius bestows high praise, if not on the procession itself, at least on the thoughts which the Greek poets found in some of its features. Yet he rejects those thoughts as quite wrong. His reason is that the gods are free from all pain and danger and that they are wholly unconcerned with men, with their merits or crimes (644–651). We may add that if the gods are born, they also will die.

The reason stated by Lucretius had been stated by him in the same words near the beginning of the poem (I 44–49), but the second statement, despite its being literally identical with the first, has a different meaning from that of the first. In the first place, the second statement is much richer in meaning than the first by virtue of what we have learned from Lucretius in the meantime; above all, the first statement concludes the invocation of Venus and does not call into question the divinity of Venus, whereas the second statement concludes the speech on the Great

Mother and is meant to justify the denial of her divinity. Yet the fundamental theologoumenon is not the sole reason why Lucretius denies the divinity of the Great Mother, or, if you wish, that theologoumenon implies a verity which the poet has not yet made explicit. The fundamental theologoumenon articulates the perfection, the happiness of the gods without making explicit that perfect happiness is not possible without perception or feeling. Lucretius denies the divinity of the earth on the ground that the earth lacks perception or feeling at all times (II 652). He thus makes us wonder whether a being ceases to be a god if it lacks perception or feeling from time to time as in sleep. Be this as it may, Lucretius rejects the deification of the earth (or of the sea, of corn, and of wine) with much less asperity than he rejects religion in general (655–660). To understand this, one must compare the present section with its parallels.

The statement on the Great Mother is closely connected with the attack on the theologico-teleological account of nature in II 165–182. The connection is indicated by the fact that no explicit polemic occurs between these two polemical passages. As we have observed, the problem of the gods is present in the whole discussion between the two passages, that is, in the discussion of the atomic composition of all things and hence also of the gods. Lucretius rejects the theologico-teleological account of nature as wrong, as a theoretical error, without saying anything about its roots in human life and its effect on it. When he speaks of the deification of the earth, however, he indicates clearly the function of that error; he thus throws new light on religion. The terror which the cult of the Great Mother causes is meant to be salutary. Lucretius does not say that it is not salutary. Religion thus appears to be a human invention which serves the purpose of counteracting the indifference of the whole to man's moral and political needs, for not all men are or can be philosophers; this is to say nothing of the question as to whether philosophy, that is, Epicurean philosophy as Lucretius understood it, enjoins patriotism and gratitude to parents. The section on the Great Mother also reminds one of the section on Venus at the beginning of the poem; to say the least, Venus, who is not mentioned in the section on the Great Mother, is not as obviously a goddess concerned with political morality as is the Great Mother; the unqualified rejection of religion which follows the invocation of Venus (I 62 ff.) is therefore less surprising than an unqualified rejection of religion following the speech on the Great Mother would be. The section on the Great Mother surely leaves us with the sting of the question as to how the unphilosophic multitude will conduct itself if it ceases to believe in gods who punish lack of patriotism and of filial piety. One wonders in particular what will happen to Memmius' patriotism or concern with the common weal (I 41–43) if Lucretius should succeed in converting him to Epicureanism.

Despite the fact that there is only a limited, if large, number of shapes of atoms, their number (and especially the still larger number of combinations of atoms of various shapes) is sufficient to account for the enormous variety of the things which are produced by the atoms. Yet not every combination which one might imagine is possible; there are no monsters like Chimaeras, for instance. Lucretius does not speak in this section (II 661–729) of the gods, but the question of the atomic composition of the gods is present in it since he speaks here of the composition of all species of living beings: the variety of shapes of atoms must be such as to account for the fact that "all things" are born of fixed seeds, preserve their kinds, and are in need of specific food. The application to the conceit of children stemming from the intercourse of gods and men like Aeneas is obvious. One might think that the gods are not living beings. The force of this objection is destroyed by Lucretius' declaring that "these laws," which obtain regarding the coming into being and the preservation of living beings, obtain *mutatis mutandis* regarding inanimate things as well.

Lucretius turns next to the qualities which the atoms lack. They lack colors, sounds, tastes, smells, as well as hot and cold. All these qualities are changeable and perishable and cannot therefore belong to the unchangeable and imperishable atoms (749–756, 862–864). The exposition of this doctrine continues and deepens the critique of the nonatomistic doctrines which was presented in Book I, but the poet no longer engages in explicit polemics against actual or potential opponents: there is no longer any sign of resistance on the part of Memmius. The discussion of colors is far more extensive than that of all the other qualities in question taken together; in the case of colors the contrast between the things and the atoms is particularly striking: no colors without light, and the atoms exist in blind darkness (795–798).

The next step requires a somewhat greater effort.[41] The reader must now be brought to admit that the atoms, which are the origins of all living beings, lack sense or feeling—are lifeless. That animate beings emerge under certain conditions out of inanimate ones is shown by experience: worms emerge from stinking dung. In this context the poet remarks that just as inanimate things (of a not noisome character) serve as food for cattle and thus change into cattle, and the cattle into human bodies, our bodies frequently serve as food for wild beasts and birds (871–878). It is not clear whether he refers here to wild beasts and birds killing men or merely, as is more likely, to their feeding on human corpses.[42] The atoms must be lifeless in order to be deathless: to be a living being and to be mortal is the same (919). The teaching according to which the causes of all things are lifeless is sweetened to some extent in the verses with which the poet ends his speech about the qualities which the atoms lack. He draws the somewhat unexpected conclusion that we all are of heavenly origin: we all—plants, men, and wild beasts—owe our being to the rain which is sent down from the regions of the ether and which fertilizes the earth. Ether is our common father, and Earth is our common mother. Lucretius shows that the earth is deservedly called mother: thanks to the earth, the wild beasts, to say nothing of human beings, feed their bodies, pass a sweet life, and propagate their kinds; he does not show that heaven is deservedly called father (991–1001). When we compare these verses with the Euripidean verses of which they remind us,[43] we see that Lucretius does not, as Euripides does, call Ether the progenitor of men and gods in contradistinction to the Earth who gives birth to the mortals: throughout his poem Lucretius puts a stronger emphasis on Earth than on Ether because he does not wish to speak explicitly of the origin of the gods. As father and mother, Ether and Earth would be living beings, hence mortal; hence they could not be the ultimate origins of "us all": the ultimate origin is matter, that is, the atoms; not Ether and Earth, but the atoms are the origins of everything, as Lucretius states again in the immediate sequel in which he ascribes to heaven and earth no higher status than to the sea, the rivers, the sun, the crops, the trees, and living beings (1002–1022). In his earlier speech on Mother Earth he had made clear that the earth, which lacks sense or feeling, is not a divine being (641–652). But the same is true of the ether.[44] If heaven and earth were gods, the things brought forth by them would not be as defective as they are (180–181). In other words, the world, nay, the boundless whole, grounded in nothing but the atoms and the void, is not divine. Only some parts of the whole can possibly be divine: the gods. Whatever Lucretius' doctrine of the gods may mean, it surely means that the whole or the world is not divine.[45]

The last section of Book II deals, like the last section of Book I, with the infinity of the whole. Accordingly, it is introduced by a statement (1023–1047) which is comparable to the "wormwood and honey" passage in Book I (921–950). In both introductions the poet speaks of a special effort which the reader must make in order to understand the immediate sequel. In all other respects the two introductions differ profoundly. In the second introduction the poet mentions the subject which he is about to discuss, whereas he had failed to do this in the first one. In the first introduction he had spoken of his innovation through which the harsh doctrine will be sweetened; he had spoken of a gratifying novelty without speaking of the novelty of the doctrine. Now he speaks of the novelty of the doctrine to be set forth, a repulsive novelty. Novelty as such, we are told, is disconcerting; a doctrine may even be frightening merely because it is new and as long as it is new. Lucretius urges the addressee not to reject the doctrine to be expounded merely because he is frightened by its novelty; he ought to examine it and accept it if it appears to him to be true or reject it if it is false. He seems to be less concerned with making him an Epicurean than with liberating him from fear of the new as new.[46] He creates the impression that the doctrine to be expounded can be repulsive only because it is new or as long as it is new, or that it is not in itself repulsive. On the other hand he surely does not say that it is, or will become, exhilarating.

The new doctrine follows from the doctrine of infinity as set forth in Book I. Given the infinity of the void and of matter on the one hand and the finiteness of our world on the other, given also that our world is the work of nature or chance, there must be many worlds, nay, infinitely many worlds. There are many heavens, earths, and humankinds, just as there are within each world many individuals of the same animal species: every heaven, every earth, every animal species, has a fixed life span just as do the individuals of the species (1048–1089). The introductory verses made us expect some resistance to this doctrine on the part of the addressee or some polemics against the believers in a single world on the part of the author.[47] This expectation is disappointed. The new doctrine, which was announced so emphatically, is presented in not more than forty-two verses. One must admit that the new doctrine is upsetting: more than anything that went before, it "destroys our importance," the importance of "our" human race—and therewith of "History"—by presenting our human race as one individual among infinitely many of the same kind. The poet has his remedy ready and does not hesitate for a moment to use it: surely a whole consisting of innumerably many worlds cannot be ruled by the gods, those proud tyrants, that is, the gods of the vulgar. The infinity of the world, however unattractive in another respect, is a small price to pay for the liberation from religion. Invoking the true gods—"the holy hearts of the gods" [48]—who live in perfect tranquillity and therefore do not rule anything, he asserts that no being could possibly rule the boundless whole, take care of the innumerable heavens and earths, to say nothing of governing with justice the innumerable humankinds: not even our humankind is justly governed by gods (1090–1104). To say nothing of other defects of this reasoning, why could there not be infinitely many groups of gods, each group ruling some part of the boundless whole? Must there not be many groups of gods located in different parts of the universe if gods are to be sensed by all humankinds in the infinitely many and infinitely distant worlds?

Lucretius has not yet completed the exposition of the new teaching which he has announced. In the rest of the section he no longer speaks of the infinity of the worlds, but of an implication of this subject. He speaks of the growth of "the great world"—our world—and of its decay. By limiting himself to our world, he brings his lesson home to us. He shows that the growth and decay of the world parallels that of individual living beings. The world has already reached its old age, as is shown by the aging of the earth. The earth no longer brings forth, as it did in its youth, the huge bodies of wild beasts, but barely tiny worms; it no longer produces spontaneously rich harvests, but barely, despite men's toil, poor ones. No one knows this better than the aged plowman who can compare the present with the past and who sees the decay of the soil going hand in hand with the decay of piety: the latifundia have ruined Italy; everything passes to the grave (1105–1174). What every old peasant knows to some extent cannot be frightening because of its novelty. By generalizing the observations of old peasants about the decay of agriculture and piety into the doctrine of the decay of the world, Lucretius may even be said to sweeten the sad doctrine in accordance with the feelings of the true Roman: the decay or end of Rome is the decay or end of the world. When he repeats the doctrine of the future destruction of the world at much greater length later on, in a more advanced stage of Memmius' education, Lucretius takes away this scaffolding: in his opinion our world is still in its youth (V 330–337). The decay of Italian agriculture and piety does not announce the speedy end of the world. Lucretius does not deny that piety and Italian agriculture are no longer what they were; but surely some of the arts are still progressing; philosophy is of recent origin, and it enters Rome only now, through Lucretius' poem.

IV. On Book III

This Book is the only one in which the poet addresses Epicurus. He does this in the proem (1–30) and nowhere else. It is also the only Book in which he mentions the name of Epicurus (1042): he never addresses Epicurus by name. One may say that throughout the work Epicurus remains the nameless *Graius homo* (I 66), or rather the nameless "glory of the Greek race" (III 3), if not a nameless god (V 8). In the present proem Lucretius apostrophizes Epicurus with the vocative *inclute* (I 10); in the proem to Book I he has apostrophized Venus in the same way (40), and in the proem to Book V he will do the same to Memmius (8); the movement from Venus to Epicurus is an ascent, and the movement from Epicurus to Memmius is a descent; the whole movement is an ascent followed by a descent. If one counts I 925–950 as the second proem,[49] the proem to Book III will be the central proem. The peak is in the center.

The praise of Epicurus at the beginning of Book III serves in the first place the purpose of bringing out the difference of rank between Epicurus and Lucretius. Lucretius is a follower, an imitator of Epicurus; he could as little rival Epicurus as a swallow could rival swans or kids a horse; as regards both beauty and force Lucretius' work belongs to a different species, to a lower species than Epicurus' work. Yet "thou art the father, the discoverer of the things." Lucretius merely profits from the discovery; Epicurus' mind is divine, whereas Lucretius receives through the master's teaching "some divine pleasure and a dread or horror."[50] Thanks to Epicurus' complete discovery of the nature of things, the terrors of the mind are dispelled and the walls of the world part asunder. Thus the majesty of the gods comes to sight; they are seen to dwell in tranquil and beautiful abodes, of which those of the Homeric gods on Olympus give an inkling, beyond the walls of the worlds; nature is seen to supply the gods with everything. Whereas Epicurus' discovery reveals the perfect bliss of the gods, it reveals the nonexistence of Hades. As for the nonexistence of Hades, of a miserable life after death, Lucretius is going to prove it in Book III. He does not say that, and where, he will prove the existence of the gods. He surely has not proved it before; he merely has proved, or attempted to prove, that the nature of things does not leave room for divine action on the world and its ingredients. We observe that nature is said to supply the gods with everything: nature does not supply men with everything.

In order to drive out the fear of Hades which utterly confounds human life and spoils all pleasures, Lucretius will lay bare the nature of the soul on the basis of the principles set forth in the first two Books. Men frequently say that there are things worse than hell and that they know the nature of the soul without having engaged in studies, so that they do not need Epicurean philosophy. But this is an idle boast. As soon as they have committed a crime and as a consequence suffered the disgrace of which they formerly said that it is worse than death, they cling to life and sacrifice to the dead and the gods of the dead, that is, turn to religion (31–58). Lucretius did not take issue with people who deny that they need Epicurean philosophy in order to get rid of fear of the gods: common experience seems to show that one fate befalls the just and the unjust, or that the gods do not rule the human race; but this does not exclude the possibility that the fates of the just and the unjust will be greatly different after death or that only through fear of punishment after death does the fear of the gods reach its full power. Memmius at any rate seems to be more threatened by fear of hell than by fear of the gods as such (page 80 above).

Lucretius speaks with special emphasis of the criminals' religious fear. He thus makes us wonder again whether by attempting to take away that fear he does not weaken a salutary restraint. He answers this objection as well as he can in the immediate sequel. He comes close to suggesting that the primary phenomenon is not the fear of hell, but the fear of death, and that crimes which seem to be a cause of the fear of hell are in fact a consequence of the fear of death (59–86).[51] That is to say, by freeing men from the fear of death, one does not emancipate crime from a powerful restraint; one rather contributes to the abolition of crime. We are left with the suspicion that prior to Epicurus, and in Rome even prior to Lucretius, religion served a good purpose. Given the fact that many men, nay, almost all men, will always refuse to listen to the Epicurean teaching, religion will always serve a good purpose. Lucretius concludes his statement of the subject of Book III with the same seven verses with which in Books II and VI he concludes the proems as distinguished from the statements of the subjects of those Books: just as children fear everything in the dark, "we" sometimes fear in the light things which are no whit more dreadful than what children tremble at in the dark and imagine that it will happen; this terror must be dispelled, not by the rays of the sun, but by nature coming to sight and being penetrated. Book III is *the* Book devoted to the overcoming of "our" childish fear.

Lucretius tells his reader that the soul is a part of man like the hand and therefore located in a determinate part of the body. It is not, as some Greeks have asserted, a harmony of the whole body (94–135). It is not Lucretius' manner as we have hitherto had occasion to observe it to begin his presentation of a teaching with polemics against philosophic doctrines. The polemic against "harmonism" is firm, but free from harshness or sarcasm: harmonism is as good for establishing the mortality of the soul as Epicureanism; [52] it is the first doctrine explicitly discussed which is rejected merely because it is wrong and not at the same time with a view to its effect on man's feelings. If any doubt were left, the discussion of harmonism would show that Epicureanism is not needed for liberating the mind from the terrors of religion.

The soul is a single nature consisting of the *animus* and the *anima*. The *animus*, or the mind, is located in the breast, is the ruler of the whole body, and is at the same time that through which we suffer fear, joy, and the like; the understanding and the passions belong together. The *anima* is spread through the whole body and obeys the *animus*. The distinction is meant to explain that there is what one may call a particular freedom of man. The *animus* alone and by itself can understand and can feel pleasures and pains which are not pleasures and pains of the body (136–160). Both parts of the soul must be bodily, as is shown by the fact that they affect our body and are affected by it, for nothing can affect a body and be affected by it without touch, and nothing can touch or be touched except body (161–176). Since the acts of the *animus* are capable of unrivaled swiftness and nimbleness, it must consist of very round, very smooth, and very tiny parts. This insight into the nature of the *animus* is of very great importance, as the poet indicates both explicitly and by addressing the reader in a unique way (*o bone*). Things which consist of such parts are more easily dissolved than things consisting of parts of the opposite description. The fact that the *animus* through which we can sense or feel is of such a fine texture and can be contained in a very small place explains why the contours and the weight of a man immediately after his death do not differ from his contours and weight immediately before it. The same fact proves that the *anima* too consists of very tiny particles. The poet compares the soul in this respect to the flavor of wine, or as he puts it here, of Bacchus; this is the first time that he mentions a god or a pseudo god by name in the

Book (177–230). In no other Book are gods as rarely mentioned with or without name as in Book III.

The soul consists of heat, air, and wind and of a fourth nature which is nameless and which accounts for sensing and thinking (231–257). Lucretius opens his explanation of how those ingredients are mingled with one another by apologizing again for the defects of his exposition, which are due to the poverty of his "paternal speech." The second reference to "the paternal speech" (260) differs from the first (I 832) since it follows the sole reference to "the paternal precepts" (III 9–10), namely, the precepts given by Epicurus; Lucretius has two fathers or fatherlands, one by virtue of language (or blood) and another by virtue of the mind; the precepts which bind or guide him stem exclusively from the latter. Of the four ingredients of the soul the nameless one is the soul of the soul and rules the whole body. As for the three other ingredients, each of them predominates in different species of animals. Here Lucretius tacitly makes clear for the first time that his doctrine of the soul is not merely a doctrine of the human soul;[53] he is, however, silent on the specific difference of the human soul.[54] Men, like oxen, stand in the middle between the hot-hearted and angry lions and the coldhearted and fearful deer. There are natural differences in this respect also between the individuals of the same species, at least of the human species. Training or education can make some men equally refined; it cannot eradicate the fundamental, natural diversity or inequality. But reason is strong enough to expel the traces of those natural defects so that nothing stands in the way of a life worthy of gods (262–322). Does Lucretius mean that every man, however dull-witted he may be, can grasp the Epicurean doctrine and thus be enabled to lead a life worthy of the gods? Would this throw any light on the intelligence of the gods? Does he mean that, as a matter of principle, every human being can live in freedom from religion? Is this true even of children who tremble at everything and fear it when it is dark (87–88)? As a matter of fact, all men were under the spell of the terrors of religion prior to the daring act of a Greek who had a divine mind, and presumably all Romans are still in that condition before they have read Lucretius' poem. The primary addressee of the poem is Memmius, who is supposed to possess a keen mind (I 50, IV 912). Now it seems that Memmius would not have to possess a keen mind in order to derive the greatest benefit from Lucretius' poem. Are we entitled to doubt Memmius' native excellence? Such a doubt would be compatible with the fact that Lucretius wishes his potential friend to share in his most cherished possession. Yet he addresses, of course, indefinitely many Romans, most of whom will be men of mean capacities: he attempts to propagate Epicurean philosophy in Rome. The motive of this attempt, we submit, is not merely love of praise (cf. pages 91–92 above); even a philosopher who does not care for the city is in need of support or protection by politically active and powerful men.

The section with which Lucretius concludes his exposition of the nature of the soul consists of three parts. He shows first that the soul cannot be without the body and vice versa. Body and soul come into being together and perish together. No sensation or feeling is possible without the co-operation of body and soul. It is true that the soul is the immediate cause of sensing, but it is an error to hold that only the soul senses while using the body merely as an instrument (323–369). In the central part Lucretius takes issue with the view of Democritus regarding the local order of the body atoms and the soul atoms. The treatment of the Democritean doctrine near the end of the discussion of the nature of the soul reminds of the treatment of harmonism at its beginning: the Democritean doctrine would not render questionable the mortality of the soul. Lucretius indeed treats Democritus or his doctrine with much greater respect than harmonism; he applies to him or to his doctrine the epithet "sacred"; Democritus is the only human being to whom or to whose doctrine he ever applies that epithet unqualifiedly; [55] he never applies it to Epicurus. He fails to apply it to Democritus in the central reference to him (III 1037) where Democritus' inferiority to Epicurus is clearly brought out. This throws light on his calling "sacred" the gods' bodies, their *numina*, and so on. Finally, the poet restates the supremacy of the *animus* over the *anima* and the body (396–416). While he is primarily concerned with the mortality of the soul, he is very much concerned with its being the ruling part in man, nay, in all living beings. Since he holds the soul to be as corporeal as the body, he is not compelled to regard the acts of the soul as mere epiphenomena of the body; he can leave intact the "common-sensical" distinction between soul and body.

The center of Book III (417–829) is devoted to the proof that the souls are born and die. That proof consists of a large number of arguments which are more or less independent of one another. In no other case does Lucretius devote so many verses and so many arguments to the proof of a single proposition. One could think that the coming into being and perishing of the souls is sufficiently established by the fact that they are compounds of atoms. Yet the gods are also compounds of atoms and nevertheless supposed to be immortal. It is true that the Epicurean gods do not live within the world or worlds, while the souls do. But could the souls not live within the world and then, if they have lived piously here, withdraw to the *intermundia* in which the gods dwell, to Islands of the Blessed, as it were? Lucretius turns therefore to reasonings based on the specific characters of the soul which, after all, are better known to him than those of the gods. In introducing these reasonings he reminds us that his verses are to be worthy of Memmius' "life" (420) without, however, mentioning Memmius' name; he reminds us of his esteem for Memmius. The first argument makes clear that the soul is mortal because it is a compound of particularly small and mobile atoms which are kept together by the body;

but the body is manifestly mortal. In what looks at first glance like an excursus, Lucretius illustrates the mobility of the soul by the ease with which it is moved through slender causes; it is moved not only by smoke and clouds but even by images of smoke and clouds; for instance, when asleep we see high altars breathing steam and sending up their smoke (425–444).

When attempting to prove the mortality of the soul, Lucretius cannot help presenting to us vividly the sad spectacles of men's sudden or slow deaths, of their diseases and decay, although he never comes near to that accumulation of horrors which he has reserved for the end of his work. He makes no attempt to sweeten the sad; the sweetening thought is the consideration, which now indeed remains unexpressed, that death, however slow and painful, is preferable to the terrors of Hades. This thought remains so little expressed that Lucretius now uses men's great unwillingness to die, their eagerness to clutch at the last tie of life, as a proof of the mortality of the soul: if our souls were immortal, we would not mind dying (597–614). However unreasonable the fear of death may be, it seems to be quite natural.[56] We may note some slight signs of resistance on the part of the addressee,[57] but the poet does not engage in explicit polemics against other schools of thought while proving the mortality of the soul (425–669); he engages in such polemics while attempting to refute the belief in the pre-existence of the soul (670 ff.).[58] The reason is that he does not take seriously the belief in the immortality of the soul if it is not accompanied by the belief in its pre-existence: only an eternal soul can be immortal (cf. 670–673).

The reference to men's revulsion from death as a proof or sign of the mortality of the soul occurs shortly before the end of the section that deals with the soul's immortality as distinguished from its pre-existence. It is followed by three more arguments in support of mortality. The two last of these arguments refer in very different ways to hearsay. According to Lucretius, one cannot assert the immortality of the soul without asserting the immortality of the five senses and hence of their organs; the painters and writers of old presented the souls in Acheron as endowed with the senses; but the senses cannot exist without the whole body (624–633). The implication is that the painters and writers of old acted more reasonably than the more recent philosophers who assert the immortality of the soul bereft of the senses. Lucretius is silent here about the ancient writers' presenting the souls as undergoing eternal punishment in Hades (I 111). In the last argument (634–669) he uses his knowledge through hearsay of the maiming and killing caused by scythe-bearing chariots. We do not know whether Memmius had firsthand knowledge of battles in which such chariots were used; Lucretius surely had not. This is not to deny that the poet may have observed other kinds of battles from afar (II 5–6).

The antepenultimate argument in support of mortality (615–623) is repeated and enlarged in the argument that concludes the central part of

Book III (784–829). The thought which Lucretius repeats is that everything has its place outside of which it cannot be; the mind cannot be in the shoulders or in the heels, for instance; still less can it be outside the whole body. He enlarges this thought by the consideration that the eternal or immortal cannot be linked with the mortal. He then raises the question as to what kinds of things are immortal and finds that the soul does not belong to them. He identifies three kinds of immortal things: the atoms, the void, and the universe. He does not mention the gods. But he compels us to think of the gods by raising the question as to what kinds of things are, or can be, immortal. He may allude to the gods by saying that things may be eternal if there is no place without into which their parts may scatter or if there are no bodies which could assault them; for this condition could be thought to be fulfilled in the *intermundia* in which the gods are said to dwell. At any rate, the central part of Book III begins and ends with allusions not so much to the gods as to the problem of the gods.

In the last part of Book III Lucretius draws the practical conclusion from his proof of the soul's mortality: death is nothing to us. The conclusion does not follow from the proof since we naturally recoil from death as from a very great evil. Lucretius must therefore show in addition that our revulsion from death is due to a delusion. It could be thought that by liberating us from this delusion he weakens our concern with preserving our lives. Besides, the brutes too recoil from death; are they too under the spell of a delusion? Yet Lucretius both as an atomist and as a human being knows the power of death or the eagerness with which men cling to "the sweet light of life" (V 989). He shows that he has considered the objections to his thesis by the way in which he concludes the passage under discussion; he concludes it by opposing "immortal death" to "mortal life." The delusion is said to consist in our believing that we are still alive and feeling while we no longer are. We can be as little affected by what happens after our death as we were affected by what happened before we were born: we were not affected by the Punic Wars when the rule over all men was at stake between the Carthaginians and the other side (830–869). Lucretius opens the last part of Book III with a somewhat subdued reassertion of Romanism.[59] In the same context he touches briefly on the possibility that the same atomic compound which is a given man was frequently produced long before his time. He disposes of it by the consideration that the same atomic compound was not the same man since no memory links the earlier and the later. He does not speak of the possibility of a return of the same compound.

Lucretius next shows us a man who pities himself by imagining the terrible or disgraceful things which will happen to him, that is, to his body, after his death; that man imagines that he himself can stand by his corpse and look at it; he imputes to his corpse the feelings which he, a living man, has (870–893). Lucretius next presents to us living men addressing a man who just died, pitying him for what he has lost. They do not add, Lucretius observes, that the dead man no longer yearns for what he has lost; Lucretius states in their direct speech what they ought to say to the dead man, just as he has stated in their direct speech what they do say to him. He then makes them say to the dead man what they would say if they were to consider that he is not aware of anything: thou hast no reason to grieve, but we have reason for everlasting grief. He finds fault with what he makes them, or rather one of them, say—no one has reason for everlasting grief —but he does not address this reproach to them; he never speaks to them. Instead he makes them state another of their untutored speeches, and he again refutes it without addressing them. At the end of this refutation he calls death "the chill stopping of life" (894–930). His next action is still more extraordinary than the one which we just described: he makes the nature of things speak to any one of us, to whom she applies the vocatives "thou mortal" and "thou fool" (933, 939). Nature herself is made to proclaim how unreasonable it is to regard death as a great evil, regardless of whether one has lived hitherto happily or miserably. Lucretius, having listened together with his reader to Nature's speech, finds that the only answer which "we" can give to Nature is that she is right. He then makes Nature address an oldish man who fears death more than it is just to do; she naturally deals more harshly with him than with the younger men; she applies to him the vocative "thou criminal" (955). Having listened to Nature's second and last speech, Lucretius finds again that Nature would be right in making her reproaches. He then gives the reader or addressee additional reasons why Nature's verdict and action are sound: the old must give way to the new; if we look at death in the light of Nature, death ceases to be terrible. Neither Lucretius nor the addressee or reader speaks to Nature—which does not mean that Nature does not speak to the addressee.

There is a noteworthy contrast between the central section of the last part of Book III—the section in which Nature is made to speak and Lucretius comments on her speeches (931–977)—and the next section, which is altogether undramatic, that is, in which not even the second person is ever used (978–1023). The poet speaks now of the terrors of hell, the denial of which seemed to be the primary reason for denying the possibility of a life after death; these terrors have proved to be of secondary importance. While it is true that only through the fear of hell does the fear of the gods acquire its full power, and hence Memmius is threatened by the fear of hell rather than by the fear of the gods as such (see page 105 above), it appears that not the fear of hell, but the fear of death, is the enemy of our happiness; the fear of hell threatens, not man as man, but the unjust. This means that Lucretius ascribes some importance to the terrors of hell: he does not even take the trouble to deny in so many words that a blessed life after death is reserved for the just; he wishes to remain silent about religion as a possibly pleasant and salutary delusion. He need not give a special proof in order to deny that there is a hell after he has proved the mortality of the souls. He limits himself therefore to explaining the stories of hell in terms of the evils of human life. To cite only the central example, the true Sisyphus is the man who runs for public office, for he wishes to lay hold on a power which always eludes him, that is, which always remains precarious.

After the interlude on the terrors of hell, which was necessary in order to bring out the peculiarity regarding both subject matter and manner of treatment of the surrounding sections, Lucretius turns to telling the reader something which he should tell himself from time to time: the reader is to play the role previously played by men in general and, above all, by Nature. Yet what he is to tell himself reads as if Lucretius were telling it to him, as if Lucretius were addressing him. It is then Lucretius who tells his address-ee, whom he apostrophizes now as "thou knave," that much better men than he have died and that therefore he should not make any fuss about his dying. The language which he uses is stronger than the language previously used by Nature. He reminds the reader of six men who have died. The first three are political men: the Roman king Ancus, the Persian king Xerxes, whose name and country are not mentioned, and Scipio, the terror of Carthage. The last three men are philosophers and poets: Homer, Democritus, and Epicurus; Epicurus' genius surpassed that of all other men. The men of outstanding minds are all Greeks (1024–1052). The political men are all non-Greeks: they are all barbarians. Romanism is a kind of barbarism. It is proper that Lucretius should make some effort to entrust this speech to somebody else.

The sequel—the end of Book III—is as undramatic or nearly so as the interlude that deals with the terrors of hell; it tacitly takes up the theme that hell is the life of the fools here. Men live in the way they do because they suffer from a burden the causes of which they do not know; hence no one knows what he wants and changes from one thing or place to another; everyone runs away from himself, but he cannot escape from himself; he is sick without knowing the cause of his sickness; if he knew that cause, he would leave everything else and first attempt to know the nature of things, for what is at stake is his condition in eternity—the "eternal death" from which he cannot escape and from which he foolishly attempts to escape. The flight from oneself is the flight from one's death (1053–1094). To study nature means to learn to accept one's death without delusion or rebellion and hence to live well.

The last part of Book III tells us what the right posture toward death is. In this context Lucretius presents seven utterances of beings other than the poet in direct speech. Direct speech of beings other than Lucretius occurs only here and twice in Book I (803–808, 897–900), but in Book I the speaker in question is the addressee, and he speaks in defense of philosophic doctrines, that is, within the context of Lucretius' polemics against philosophic doctrines; whereas in Book III the polemic is directed against common, nay universal, opinion, and the speakers are men in general, Nature, and the addressee as a mask for Lucretius. In the speeches of Nature and of the addressee as a mask for Lucretius there occurs an unusually large number of vocatives; those speakers apostrophize their addressee as "thou mortal," "thou fool," "thou criminal," and "thou knave." Lucretius himself has apostrophized his addressee earlier in Book III (206) as "thou good one." It so happens that Lucretius apostrophizes the addressee after Book III only in Book V, where he apostrophizes him five times "o Memmius." (He apostrophizes him "o Memmius" altogether nine times in the poem.) The difference between the manner in which Lucretius, speaking in his own name on the one hand and speaking through a mask on the other, apostrophizes his addressee deserves notice, although it is not surprising.[60]

V. On Book IV

The proem almost literally repeats the wormwood-honey passage in Book I. The most obvious change consists in the omission of the remark on the poet's desire for praise (I 922–923). The most important change is the change of the context, for, as we have observed more than once, the context, the place where a statement occurs, may be crucial for its meaning; identically the same statement may have a different meaning in a different context. The same verses which were first used for introducing the discussion of infinity now open a whole Book. While their meaning at their first occurrence must be understood also in the light of their immediate sequel, their meaning at their second and last occurrence cannot be so understood. The proem to Book IV deals with the relation of Lucretius' poetry to Epicurean philosophy. So does the proem to Book III. The proem to Book IV supplements, and therewith corrects, the proem to Book III, just as the proem to Book II may be said to correct the proem to Book I (cf. note 29). Lucretius or his work does not, as we were told in the proem to Book III, unqualifiedly belong to a lower species than Epicurus or his work. In the proem to Book III, Lucretius had compared himself to a swallow and Epicurus to a swan. From now on he compares himself to a swan (IV 181, 910). The proem to Book IV does not contain a praise of Epicurus.

The subject of Book IV or of its first part, as stated by the poet, is the proper sequel to the discussion of the soul in the preceding Book: [61] the likenesses of things; for those likenesses which fly through the air frighten us when we are awake and also in sleep, when we behold wondrous shapes and the likenesses of the departed. One must explain the likenesses of things lest "we" believe that something of us remains after death in Hades or elsewhere (26–44). This seems to mean that the many proofs given in Book III are not quite sufficient to establish the mortality of the souls. But how could this be? The belief in punishment after death presupposes not only the immortality of the souls but the existence of punishing gods as well. Perhaps the explanation of the likenesses throws light on the belief in such gods or in gods in general. In the proem (6–7) Lucretius has reminded us of his purpose to liberate the mind from the bondage of religion. The only way in which we can know, according to the Epicurean doctrine, of the gods' being and their nature is through their likenesses or images which reach us after they have passed through the flaming walls of the world. Someone might say that Lucretius' discussion of the likenesses or images in Book IV has no relation whatever to his teaching regarding the gods since the very terms "likenesses" (*simulacra*) and "images" (*imagines*) do not occur in his statement about how men have come to know of the gods.[62] This objection could at least as well be used in support of the opposite assertion. Paintings and statues of the gods are also called "likenesses" and "images." [63] The difficulty which we have indicated may explain why Lucretius gives a second justification of his present theme by linking the subject "the likenesses of things," not to the doctrine of the soul, but to the atomistic doctrine in general (45–53).

The likenesses or images are minute bodies on the surface of the things; they are hurled forward by pressure from within the things; each likeness is propelled immediately by the succeeding one; the succession never ceases; the likenesses are carried away with incredible speed in all directions; they are so tiny that they cannot be seen. Streaming from the surfaces of the things, they preserve the things' shapes and colors without alteration. If certain conditions are fulfilled, they literally transmit to us faithful images or copies of the shape and color of the thing in question. Yet not all likenesses stream directly from things. Some likenesses are formed in the air; they can be compared to the shapes which clouds sometimes take on like those of giants and other fear-inspiring things. Besides, genuine likenesses are deformed by the air on their way from the things to our eyes. Our shadows seem to walk and to gesticulate, whereas, being lifeless, they are incapable of walking and gesticulating (129–142, 168–175, 352–378).

A square tower seen from afar looks round; this means that the likeness of the tower has become round on its way from the tower to our eyes; it is as genuine as the square likeness which hits us when we are near the tower. This is to say that not the eyes are deceived, but the mind, for it is the reasoning of the mind, not the eyes, through which we can know the nature of the things. In a sense we see everything (462) which appears to us as visible, regardless of whether we are awake or asleep at the time, and this fact can easily shake our trust in the senses. Yet it is not the fault of the senses if we do not distinguish between the things manifest—the likenesses as such—and the things dubious—what the mind adds of its own. This fault is indeed hard to avoid since nothing is harder than to make that distinction intelligently, especially, we may add, when the appearances are wondrous (33–36). Lucretius indicates or imitates the difficulty by his use of the passive forms of *videre* which mean here (379–468) in all cases but one (428) "to seem" or, as the poet makes clear, "to be believed" (387– 388, 401–402), or "merely to seem" (433–434), or "to be contrary to the truth" (444–446). The section under discussion contains the greatest density of *videri* that occurs in the whole work [64] while it does not contain a single mention of *simulacra* or *imagines*. Lucretius concludes his discussion of the likenesses by restating the case for the trustworthiness of the senses against two views; his polemic does not claim, however, to be directed against philosophic schools. If one does not trust the senses, one is led to deny the possibility of knowledge altogether; but apart from the fact that by denying the possibility of knowledge one asserts that one possesses knowledge, one cannot deny the possibility of knowledge without knowing what knowledge is, without having experienced knowing. The other alternative to trust in the senses is trust in reason, but reason is wholly founded on the senses; hence if the senses cannot be trusted, reason cannot be trusted; without trust in the senses, reason, nay, life itself, collapses. Trust in the senses is the first of all trusts (469–521).

Lucretius turns next to the question as to how each of the other senses perceives what belongs to it. He speaks first of hearing. The principle of explanation is the same as in the case of sight, which does not mean that Lucretius does not pay some attention to the peculiarities of hearing (cf. 595–614). He is more concerned with voices than with sounds in general. He is very much concerned with proving the corporeal character of voices. Within the central part of the section on hearing he explains the echo. In giving this explanation he addresses the reader in an unusual manner; he says to him that if he understands the explanation well, he can give an account of the phenomena in question to himself and to others (572–573); he reckons with the possibility that at least a part of his teaching will be transmitted by his reader or readers to men who are not his readers. The explanation of the echo permits Lucretius to explain the sounds traced especially by rustics living in lonely places to satyrs, nymphs, fauns, and in particular to Pan; beings of this kind exist only in speech or are known only through hearsay (580–594). It seems that people may believe in gods without having been moved to do so by any images, however deformed. Differently stated, no sound ever heard by us stems from gods. This does not contradict the fact that we are supposed to know that the Epicurean gods utter "haughty sounds" (V 1173–1174). However haughty their sounds may be, the gods cannot be our "haughty lords" (II 1091)—if for no other reason, then at least because their sounds cannot reach us since they would have to travel through the flaming walls of the world.

Lucretius turns next, not, as one would expect, to smell, but to taste; he does not discuss touch at all. As a consequence, the discussion of taste occupies the center of the section devoted to the senses other than sight. Lucretius is particularly concerned with the fact that the same food tastes sweet or bitter to different kinds of beings, that is, to different kinds of atomic compounds. He opens his discussion of this subject by another unusual expression; his discussion serves the purpose, he says, "that we may see how and why for different beings there is different food" (633–634); [65] it looks as if the poet himself were listening to his own instruction or as if he were still learning while teaching.[66] Things taste differently to different kinds of beings, that is, the tastes are not copies of the qualities of the things; when one sees the things, their shapes and colors are preserved; but one destroys the things when tasting them. As for smells, they come from the interior of the things smelled and not, as the likenesses, from their surface; the same kinds of smells attract or repel different species of living beings. In addition, the species differ in regard to the keenness of their power of smelling. Men are less apt to discern wholesome food by their sense of smell than are wild beasts, while in other respects men's senses are superior to those of other animals.

Lucretius turns next to the question as to by what and whence the mind (*mens*) is moved. This section too is opened by an unusual expression.[67] We understand this section better if we look forward to the fact that "the nature of the gods is subtle and far removed from our senses" (V 148–149). "The subtle nature of the mind" is moved to the perception peculiar to it by "subtle" likenesses of things which wander in the air and become linked with one another; those combined likenesses are more subtle than the likenesses which cause the vision of the eyes. In this way we "see" Centaurs, Scyllas, Cerberus, and the likenesses of the dead. We recall that the explanation of such sights is the guiding purpose of the discussion of likenesses in general (IV 29 ff.). The expression "we see" is justified to the extent that the awareness of beings like the Centaurs is caused by likenesses just as the awareness of ordinary things is. Needless to say, there are no Centaurs and the like; the likenesses of Centaurs are produced by chance meetings of the likenesses of horses with those of men. A single image of this kind is sufficient to stir our mind, which is exceedingly subtle and mobile. The mind's "seeing" is more powerful when we are asleep than when we are awake: it is in our dreams that "we seem to behold," or that "our mind believes it sees," the dead (722–776). All this does not mean that there are no likenesses affecting the mind which copy things that are as they are; without such likenesses true thinking would be impossible.

Up to this point the chief subject of Book IV is the likenesses or images. What the chief subject of the second half of the Book is, is not easy to say. The first half may be said to consist of three parts: (1) the likenesses and vision, (2) the three other senses discussed, (3) thought. The second half also consists of three parts: (1) critique of the teleological view (823–857); (2) explanation (*a*) of the need for food, (*b*) of how we are able to move our limbs in various ways, (c) of sleep and dreams (858–1036); and (3) explanation and critique of love (1037–1287). Lucretius first attacks the view that the parts of the body were brought into being for their use (the eyes for the sake of seeing, for instance); according to him their usefulness and the awareness of it are consequent upon their having come into being; only in the case of artifacts does awareness of usefulness precede the coming into being. This criticism does not present itself as directed against a philosophic school. More important, it is the only criticism of teleology occurring in the work which contains no reference whatever to the gods. The poet desires to remain silent on the gods in the present context. But not to mention the gods is not the same as not to think of them. We have stated earlier that in no other Book are gods as rarely mentioned with or without name as in Book III. We must now correct this statement with a view to the fact that the poet speaks very frequently in the last section of Book IV of Venus, meaning by this word not the goddess, but simply sexual love.

Let us now consider the central part of the last half of Book IV. "Food" had already been discussed from a different point of view in the central part of the first half of Book IV, namely, when the sense of taste was being considered. But then "food" occupied the central place, a place taken in the second half by "movement of the limbs." Movement of the limbs is the action most emphatically ascribed to the gods in the section par excellence devoted to the gods: "men ascribed sense to the gods because the gods were seen to move their limbs" (V 1172–1173); the gods' moving their limbs is the *ratio cognoscendi* of the gods' sensing (and perhaps thinking), or of the gods' being living beings. There is no difficulty in reconciling this with the facts that the likenesses of the dead seem to move their limbs when they appear to us in our dreams and that our shadows seem to walk (IV 364–369, 756–770). The difficulty is this. Our voluntary movements are preceded by images or likenesses of those movements; these images are very small bodies, and yet they set in motion the whole large bulk of our bodies. Lucretius disposes of this difficulty with ease. For all we know, he explained the gods' moving their bodies, which are of wondrous bulk (V 1171), in the same manner, but he is silent as to how the gods can move their limbs. As for food, all living beings need food in order to repair the losses which they incur especially through their exertions. The gods are seen in our dreams to accomplish many wondrous things without undergoing any toil (V 1181–1182); hence they would not seem to be in need of food; Lucretius is silent on this subject.

Dreams were first discussed in connection with thinking; in the repetition they are discussed in connection with sleep. The discussion of sleep is introduced with nine verses in which Lucretius speaks of how he will treat that subject—he will treat it in sweet verses rather than in many—and urges his reader, who is again assumed to possess a keen mind, to listen carefully and thus to accept the true teaching. Sleep, we are told, liberates the mind from its cares. Thus one might think that it is a most desirable state. Lucretius does not draw this conclusion. Sleep is due to a disordering of the positions of the body atoms and the mind atoms (IV 943–944). This disordering brings about a disturbance of the soul and hence in particular the suspension of sensing. Lucretius speaks here in all cases but one (944) of the *anima,* and not of the *animus,* thus permitting us to imagine that the *animus* can perceive the gods (V 1170–1171) while the *anima* is dormant. Surely in his first discussion of dreams (IV 722–822), in which he has spoken of our seeing Centaurs and the like, he has spoken only of *animus* and *mens.* In the second discussion he gives seventeen examples of dreams or kinds of dreams; in the ninth example (1008) there occurs the only mention of "gods" or of "divine" that occurs between verses 591 and 1233. He now states that we mostly dream of the thing with which we were preoccupied while we were awake or that the likenesses which enter the mind when we are asleep are the same as those which we previously apprehended with the senses. What we dream depends on "interest and will." The same is true of the beasts. Dogs, for instance, dream of hunting wild beasts, and after they have been awakened by such dreams they still pursue "the empty likenesses of stags"; puppies behave in their dreams "as if they beheld unknown forms and faces." Other examples show that what living beings dream of depends on their fears. Sometimes the likenesses believed to be seen do not precede the emotions or the movements of the limbs, but are called forth by them. The likenesses of every body which appear to males ripe for the discharge of the semen seem to announce "a glorious face and a beautiful color" and thus to facilitate that discharge (962–1036). One is tempted to say that it is not only fear but love too which gives rise to visions of superhuman beings, of beings of superhuman beauty and splendor; but it is wise to resist such temptations. Certain it is that both Lucretian discussions of dreams do not in any way suggest that through dreams we have an access (or a superior access) to beings that are and to which we have no access (or only an inferior access) while we are awake.

The last part of Book IV is devoted to Venus, who, according to the beginning of the poem, is the deity par excellence. We have learned in the meantime that Venus, so far from being a deity, is nothing but a personification of sexual love (cf. II 655–657 and 437). We also have learned what to think of favorites of Venus like Paris. We learn now that sexual love, so far from being divine, is a great threat to our happiness, although perhaps not as great a threat as fear of death. The attack on love in the last section of Book IV corresponds to the attack on the fear of death in the last section of Book III, and the deepest reason for this correspondence might well be the fact that both fear and love are roots of the belief in gods. The fate of Venus in the poem indicates the fate of all gods in it; Venus is related to the true gods as the true gods are to the truth about the true gods. Love is a wound of the mind, the beloved like a mortal enemy. Love promises pleasure, but the pleasure which it gives is followed by chilly care. From this we draw the conclusion that the gods cannot feel love, just as they do not need food or sleep; Lucretius does not draw this conclusion. Love is love of one, boy or woman; in order to enjoy the fruit of Venus without suffering from the cares which she brings with her, one must separate sexual pleasure from love. The ingredient of enmity in love reveals itself in the very act of embrace. The lovers hope that by their embrace their desire will be stilled, but this hope cannot be fulfilled, for the beauty which arouses the love is only a delicate likeness which cannot enter the body like food or drink; the lovers are mocked by images just as the thirsty man who dreams of drinking (1048–1120). The sufferings of lovers are aggravated by their self-deception; the lover ascribes to his beloved more than it is right to ascribe to any mortal; he regards her as Venus herself or as some other entirely flawless being which has nothing whatever to conceal. Hence one frees oneself from the fetters of love best by thinking of the defects of mind and body which the beloved is bound to have (1153–1191). All this does not mean that venereal desire and pleasure is not natural; brutes have no less a share in it than men (1192–1208). We may say that it is as natural as the fear of death. Sterility is not due to divine action and therefore cannot be counteracted by sacrifices to the gods (1233–1247). Nor is it due to divine action that sometimes a woman of indifferent attractiveness comes to be loved (1278–1287). Philosophy counteracts love as it counteracts fear. There is no link between philosophy and *eros*.

VI. On Book V

The proem to Book V is devoted, as is the proem to Book III, to the praise of Epicurus. But in the proem to Book V Lucretius does not address Epicurus; he praises Epicurus while addressing Memmius by name. He indicates again that his work is inferior to that of Epicurus: no poem can match "the grandeur of the things and the discoveries" of Epicurus; surely no one formed of a mortal body can produce a poem which fits Epicurus' deserts. It would seem that only a god could chant Epicurus' praises adequately, for is not Epicurus himself a god? If one must speak in accordance with what the known grandeur of the things itself demands, one must say that Epicurus was a god, for he was the greatest benefactor of men that ever was. In order to see that Epicurus was a god, it suffices that one compare his discoveries with the divine discoveries of others which were made in antiquity, with the discoveries said to have been made by Ceres and Liber. Those discoveries are not necessary for life; there are said to be peoples which live without bread and wine. Epicurus' discovery, however, is necessary for living well; it makes possible happiness amidst great peoples. It is safe to assume that those great peoples include not only the Greeks but the Romans as well. In accordance with this Lucretius indicates here that the Romans are not barbarians and in Book V, as distinguished from the two preceding Books, addresses Memmius by name. Lucretius then compares Epicurus' benefactions with the famous deeds of Heracles. By killing the famous monsters Heracles and others have not disposed of the wild beasts and other terrors with which the earth still abounds. Epicurus, however, has taught men how to cleanse their hearts from desires and fears, from the vices of all kinds. Therefore he deserves to be ranked among the gods. He deserves this rank above all since he was wont to utter well and divinely many sayings about the immortal gods themselves and to reveal in his sayings the whole nature of things (1–54). Epicurus was then a god, if we understand by a god not a being which is deathless, but a supreme benefactor of men. He is, or was, not the only god: he deserves to be ranked among the gods. But are those gods, the immortal gods, also benefactors of the human race? Does the notion underlying the praise of Epicurus as a god not render doubtful the notion underlying the Epicurean conception of the gods? Is the praise of Epicurus as a god not tantamount to saying that Epicurus was a god because he denied the godness of the gods? Why does Lucretius praise here most highly, not Epicurus' revealing the whole nature of things, but his speeches about the immortal gods? [68]

Lucretius follows Epicurus to the extent that he teaches by what law "everything" has been created; he does not say here that he will reproduce his master's well and divinely framed sayings about the immortal gods. He has shown before that the mind is mortal because it is inseparable from a body which has come into being. He must show now that the world is mortal because it has come into being; he must show how all its parts have come into being. The human things belong to those parts; of the human things Lucretius mentions here only speech and religion; the genesis, the atomic composition, of reason has been not indeed discussed but intimated before, in Book III; reason and religion are the most important human phenomena. He will also explain how nature steers the courses of sun and moon lest "we" think that those bodies move of their own will in order to favor the crops and the living beings or that those bodies are moved by gods. That the heavenly bodies cannnot be moved by gods follows indeed from the fundamental theologoumenon, but if one does not know precisely how they are moved, one is tempted time and again to relapse into the ancient fears of harsh, omnipotent lords (55–90). Epicurus' divine sayings about the immortal gods are less useful for the liberation from religion than his astronomy.

Lucretius begins to fulfill his promise that he will prove the mortality of the world by telling Memmius, whom he again addresses by name, that sea, earth, and heaven, those three bodies so different from each other, will perish on a single day. That heaven and earth will perish is a novel and hence incredible assertion; it is not supported by Memmius' experience. Yet perhaps he will soon be a witness of an earthquake which will shake his confidence in the stability of the world. The doctrine of the mortality of the world is frightening not only because it is novel but because the destruction of the world is terrible in itself (91–109).[69] The teaching that the soul is mortal is gratifying because it relieves us from the fear of hell. The teaching that the world is mortal is not gratifying because, so far from relieving us from any fear, it adds to our fears. Yet can the world be immortal if it is not the work of gods, and will these gods not be harsh lords? Yet as preservers of the world will they not also be beneficent?

Before taking on this difficulty Lucretius makes two more promises. He promises to prove the mortality of the world, or rather to reveal the future destiny of mankind in a more sacred and in a much more certain manner than the Pythia. But before he will proclaim this superior revelation, he will supply the reader with many solaces (110–114). That is to say, he promises to show that the mortality of the world is preferable to its immortality, just as the mortality of the soul is more desirable than its immortality. Yet the reader needs first some comfort against his fear that by denying the immortality and hence the divinity of the world or of its most conspicuous parts he will commit a monstrous crime and be punished like the giants of old. Lucretius, who is not averse to repeating himself, no longer retorts that religion rather than its rejection is a crime or responsible for crimes.[70] He limits himself to proving that religion is based on untruth. Heaven, sea, and earth, sun, moon, and stars are not divine because they lack vital motion and sense or mind. By gods we understand beings which possess vital motion and sense or mind, and such beings must possess appropriate bodies such as none of those parts of the world possess (114–145). This argument would prove that the gods must have bodies resembling human bodies, if Lucretius did not ascribe mind (*mens*) also to brutes.[71] He goes on to assert that no part of the world can be an abode of the gods; the world is in no sense divine. The abodes of the gods must fit the gods' subtle nature, which is not accessible to our senses, but is barely seen by the mind. Lucretius promises the reader to prove in a copious speech what he has said about the nature and the abodes of the gods (146–155); he does not promise that he will prove the existence of the gods. Nor does he keep his promise, although he had said that the speeches about the immortal gods are his master's greatest achievement (52–54).

Not only is the world not divine; it is not even the work of gods. People say that the gods have willed to fashion the glorious nature of the world for the sake of man and hence that the world is immortal. Lucretius again takes issue with the view that it is sinful to deny the immortality of the world, and he again fails to counter it by referring to the crimes caused by religion. But in discussing the divine origin of the world as distinguished from its divinity he again addresses Memmius by name. He argues as follows. The gods, as perfectly self-sufficient beings—as *entia perfectissima* —have no reason whatever to create the world, to do anything for our sake. Blessed beings have no reason for being kind. Nor would it have been unkind of the gods not to create us, for beings which are not do not suffer from not being. Besides, it is hard to see how the gods could have had a pattern of things to be created, and in particular of man, or how they could have known how to produce the world out of the atoms, if nature itself had not supplied them with such a pattern (156–194). This argument leads one to wonder whether the self-sufficient gods can have any knowledge of the world and in particular of man.[72]

The reasoning just summarized is based to some extent on Epicurean premises and therefore not evident to all readers. Lucretius repeats therefore while enlarging it an argument which is not dependent on Epicurus' teaching: the nature of things has not been made by divine power for our benefit, for that nature abounds in defects (195–199).[73] The largest part of the world is unfit for human life or habitation. That part which is useful for man would be covered by nature with thorns if man did not resist nature with his sweat and toil, and all his toil is frequently frustrated by exorbitant heat, inundations, and hurricanes. Why does nature give food and increase to the frightful race of wild beasts, the enemies of man? Why does she make men die before their time? Why is it that man alone of all animals is born completely helpless, like a sailor cast away by the cruel waves (200–234)? Man alone is nature's stepchild. This thought, which was at most intimated in Book II, is stated without any concealment or sweetening in Book V. This progress in explicitness and emphasis agrees with the corresponding progress in regard to the teaching as to the end of the world. It is a progress from the sweet or less sad to the sad. Lucretius may have succeeded in showing that the view according to which the gods have produced the world and preserve it forever for the sake of man is not true; he did not show, and he did not mean to show, that that view is frightening. On the contrary, he has tacitly shown that religion is comforting, for on his own showing religion asserts that man is the end or purpose of creation or that man alone, at least among the earthly beings, is akin to the highest beings. The truth which he teaches is much harsher than the teaching of religion.

Lucretius proves the mortality of the world in four arguments. The first and the last arguments make use of the doctrine of the four elements. This causes no difficulty since the elements can be understood as atomic compounds, but it is not necessary that they be so understood. It seems that Lucretius attempts to prove the mortality of the world on the broadest possible ground. In the last argument (380–415) he conceives of the world as constituted by the continuous unholy war among the elements; their contest will be ended by the complete victory of one or another element, that is, by the destruction of the world. According to the stories, there was once a time when fire won out and another when water won out (the deluge). The ancient Greek poets presented the temporary victory of fire in the story of Phaëthon, according to which the omnipotent father (Jupiter) prevented the destruction of the world by his timely intervention. Lucretius rejects as untrue this story and its implication that the death of the world can or will be prevented by the gods. The omnipotent father himself would be mortal (cf. 318–323 and 258–260).

The second argument in support of the mortality of the world (324–350) is likewise not based on specifically Epicurean premises. The world and hence also the human race are mortal because each had a beginning, and that the world had a beginning is shown by the fact that the past which men remember does not go beyond the Theban and Trojan wars. In fact, the world is young as is shown by the recent origin of some of the arts and especially of philosophy. One cannot explain these facts by cataclysms which left the world itself (heaven, earth, and the species of animals) intact, for if all the works of men and almost all men could be destroyed by a weaker cause, a more grievous cause can destroy all men and the world itself. The third argument (351–379) proves the mortality of the world by showing that the world does not belong to the beings which are necessarily immortal. Lucretius' enumeration of the immortal beings agrees almost literally with the one which he had given when proving the mortality of the soul (III 806–818). The immortal beings are the atoms, the void, and the infinite universe (as distinguished from the world or worlds). But the world does not possess the perfect solidity of the atoms, nor is it void, nor is it the universe; hence the gate of death is not shut on the world, but stands open and looks toward the world with huge wide-gaping maw. This argument would imply that the mortality of the world can be established only on the basis of atomism and therefore that atomism, or rather Epicureanism, is the indispensable basis for denying the divine origin of the world or divine intervention in the world, that is, for liberating the mind from the terrors of religion.

Since the world is mortal, it must have come into being (V 373–376). The proof of the mortality is followed by an exposition of how the world came into being. This exposition seems to complete the proof of the Epicurean doctrine; the infinitely many atoms moving in infinite time through the infinite void explain the world as we know it, since they explain how it came into being: the world is one of the many arrangements of atoms which in a very long time came about through the furious clashes of the blind atoms without the intervention of an ordering mind or a peaceful agreement between the atoms; and once it has come about, it preserves itself for a long time. Order comes out of disorder, discord, war—a war due to the dissimilarity of the atoms and their mutual repulsion (416–448). Owing to its specific atomic composition the earth emerged first and came to occupy the lowest place in the center of the visible world. As a consequence of its emergence those atoms or atomic compounds which were to form the stars and the ether were driven from the earth and began to form those upper bodies; this change in its turn led to the emergence of the sea and thus to the earth's taking on its final shape. Lucretius speaks in this context of the living bodies of sun and moon, but he means by this no more than that they are not stationary in contrast to the earth which is stationary (449–494; cf. 125). The temporary quasi divinization of sun and moon serves the purpose of bringing out the low estate of the earth, allegedly the Great Mother, the place of man who is allegedly the favorite of the creating gods: the defects of nature, which prove that it is not the work of gods, are above all the defects of the earth.[74]

After having sketched the coming into being of the main parts of the world, Lucretius turns to the heavenly bodies. He begins his discussion of them with the words, "Now let us sing what is the cause of the motions of the stars." The expression "let us sing" occurs nowhere else in the poem. On the only other occasion on which Lucretius speaks of his "singing" (VI 84), he means his exposition of other phenomena aloft.[75] Since he "sings" of the motions of the stars, he is entitled to speak of "the stars of the eternal world" and shortly thereafter even of the earth as "living" (V 509, 514, 538; cf. 476). Singing means magnifying and embellishing. Yet beyond the two examples mentioned Lucretius cannot be said to magnify or embellish the heavenly bodies or their motions. He does not hesitate to speak of Matuta's spreading rosy dawn (656–657), of the moon's beholding the sun setting (709), of Venus or Cupid (737), of Mother Flora (739), and of Ceres and Bacchus (741–742), but the exercise of this poetic license is in no way peculiar to the astronomic part of the poem. One might say that Lucretius exclaims, "Let us sing," when he "sings" least and therefore can indicate in an inconspicuous manner what "singing" means.

What then is peculiar to the astronomic part? Lucretius does not give "the cause" of the motions of the stars, but a variety of incompatible causes; he gives a variety of possible causes since it is impossible to know which is truly the cause (526–533). Strictly speaking, he does not know "the cause of the motions of the stars." Yet ignorance of that cause gives rise to religion (1185–1186) or is the chief justification of religion. Hence it would seem that the human mind is insufficient in the decisive respect. One is therefore tempted to say that one "sings" when one does not know. But the insufficiency mentioned is not peculiar to our knowledge of things aloft (VI 703–711). It would be better to say that Lucretius does not discuss in detail the genesis of the heavenly bodies and their motions, but speaks of them as they are after their genesis has been completed, whereas, as regards the terrestrial beings, he presents their genesis in detail. But why does he proceed so differently in the two cases? The heavenly bodies and their motions are one of the chief reasons, nay, the chief reason, why men believe that there are gods acting on the world or in the world, and to destroy that belief is one of the two primary purposes of the whole poem.[76] It is therefore all the more remarkable that the astronomic part of the poem is completely free from the attacks on religion in which the poet engages so often. Or, to speak more generally, in the astronomic part Lucretius is completely silent about the nonexistence of the vulgar gods or the existence of the true gods. Lucretius' "singing" means here his complete silence about the problem of the gods. This leaves us with the question with what right singing thus understood can still be described as magnification or embellishment.

After the completion of the astronomic part Lucretius "returns to the youth of the world" (780) in order to give an account of how the terrestrial things came into being. This is the only occasion on which the poet speaks of his "returning" to something; the uniqueness of "I return" corresponds to the uniqueness of "let us sing"; he returns now to nonsinging. The astronomic part is a digression within the context of a Book devoted to the coming into being of the world and its parts. The coming into being of the world and its parts, we recall, is the reverse side of the mortality of the world. The mortality of the world seemed to be incredible because of the belief in gods who created the world. This belief is refuted long before the beginning of the astronomic part and independently of any peculiarly Epicurean assumptions (195–234). The "digression" has the subordinate function of counteracting the impression made by the visible (and completed) heavenly bodies and their motions—an impression which leads to the belief in the gods of religion. Precisely because the "digression" has this subordinate function, it is all the more remarkable that it is more emphatically a "song" than any other part of the first five Books.

The earth brought forth first the plants and then the animals. Even now the earth brings forth some small animals; it is therefore not surprising that in the spring of the world, when the earth was of youthful fertility, that is, when heat and moisture abounded everywhere and yet a mild climate prevailed everywhere, the earth should have brought forth all kinds of animals (783–820). The earth is therefore deservedly called the mother of all living beings; in her youth she was almost literally their mother; through aging she lost her primeval power. In her youth she gave birth to many kinds of monsters or freaks which proved to be unable to procreate and even to live for any length of time; those kinds perished. Only those kinds survived which from the beginning were able to live and to propagate. Some of those kinds survived through their own powers, others because they were entrusted to the protection of man, who preserves them since they are useful to him. When speaking of the species which are entrusted to man's tutelage, Lucretius addresses Memmius for the fourth time in this Book by name (821–877). In the three preceding cases, as well as in the two cases occurring in Book II, he had addressed Memmius by name in antitheological contexts.[77] We assume therefore that the present context is likewise antitheological. The poet uses here the language of teleology in order to deny teleology: the domestic animals are entrusted to man, not by nature or gods, but by man himself; man has made it his business to protect them because they are useful to him; nothing is useful to the gods (166); [78] nature produces the most absurd monsters in the same way in which she produces man, whom one might call the whole source of purposefulness in the universe. We must add at once that the critique of theology or rather of teleology [79] is here almost completely concealed. We also note that Lucretius is silent here on the peculiarity of man or on the peculiar "gift" of nature which enabled the human race to survive (cf. 857–863 with III 294–306).

As we have observed, it was necessary for Lucretius to assert that in the beginning the earth had produced various kinds of monsters. It is equally necessary for him to deny that there ever were beings like the Centaurs, the Scylla, or the Chimaera: even in her youth the earth could never have brought forth beasts of different kinds mingled together. The species emerged at the beginning with their distinctive, incommunicable, and unchangeable characters (878–924). This applies, of course, to man as well as to the other animals. The earthborn men and even their progeny partook of the hardness of the earth more than the later generations; they were stronger, healthier, and of greater power of resistance than latter-day men. They lived miserably from what the earth spontaneously offered. They did not know the use of fire or any arts; they had no notion of a common good or of customs and laws; everyone lived by himself for himself alone. They did not know of lasting unions of men and women. They did not fear gods (for they took for granted the necessity of the sun's setting and rising), but they feared wild beasts. The only deity that acted on them was Venus.[80] They did not fear what might happen to them after death, but they feared death unless unbearable pain made them long for death. Yet as they lacked the advantages of life in common and of the arts, they did not suffer from the evils which these cause (925–1010).

Five things brought it about that the human race first began to soften: huts, skins, fire, the living together of men and women, and (the consequence of that living together) the fact that both parents knew their offspring and paid attention to it. On this basis neighboring families began to form friendship with one another by making wordless contracts to the effect that they would not hurt one another, and men began to approve of pity with the weak, that is, with their women and children. Thus men came to live rather peacefully together in small societies (1011–1027). They would have been unable to live together if they had not been able to indicate to one another their various feelings by various sounds. This use of the tongue was not the invention of some individual—man or god—but is as natural in the case of men as in that of the beasts which likewise utter different sounds when impelled by different feelings (1028–1090). Lucretius is almost completely silent on the conventional ingredient of language which was admitted by Epicurus; [81] he does not deny it, of course.

Lucretius next discusses one of the changes which led to the softening of the human race or to prepolitical society, namely, the invention of fire. He takes up this subject explicitly with regard to a possible silent question of the addressee. This is the only place in which he explicitly refers to a silent question of the addressee. It was lightning, the poet says, that first of all brought fire to the earth for men: lightning, this fear-inspiring happening (1125, 1127, 1219–1221), originally brought men the gift of heat; man's acquaintance with fire is as much the work of nature as his uttering of sounds. Man was taught by the sun to cook food (1091–1104).

After the digressions on language and fire Lucretius returns to his account of human life or living together. The transition from prepolitical society to political society was effected by men of superior minds. Kings founded cities and assigned property to each man; they did not give equal shares to all, but considered in their distribution above all beauty and strength and to a lesser degree intelligence. With the invention of hereditary property and of the use of gold the rich took the place of the beautiful and strong. One might say that the qualities by nature good were replaced by the qualities good only by convention. This change eventually led to the destruction of kingship and to a condition in which everyone sought for himself governmental power. The ensuing violence and discord were ended when men listened to some who taught them to establish magistracies and laws. This, however, was not simply a blessing. Laws entail punishments for transgressions of the laws. Henceforth the fear of punishment mars the prizes of life. To understand this apparently strange statement of the poet, it is sufficient to think of the Epicurean withdrawal from political life of which the law in principle disapproves. It is not easy for the lawbreakers to lead a quiet life. Their crimes may not be noticed by gods or men, but the criminals can never be certain of that; at least people say that many criminals have betrayed themselves in their sleep or when raving in disease (1105–1160). Lucretius does not say that it is impossible for the lawbreaker to lead a quiet life; [82] the view that it is impossible is a salutary convention. He does not contradict himself by referring to the possibility that crimes might be observed and punished by the gods, [83] for that possibility is believed in by many criminals (cf. III 48–54) and that belief can therefore sometimes act as a restraint. This means, however, that according to Lucretius religion is of a utility which is not altogether negligible.

Just as the passage dealing with prepolitical society was followed by a discussion of the origin of language and of the use of fire, the passage dealing with political society is followed by a discussion of the origins of religion and the arts. Fire and the arts belong together. It is reasonable to expect that language and religion belong together. Language as discussed by

Lucretius is, so to speak, entirely by nature; calculation, consideration of utility, or convention is barely mentioned (1028–1029). Religion as discussed by Lucretius is entirely by nature; he is altogether silent on its utility, although he has drawn our attention to it immediately before beginning his discussion of religion; he is altogether silent on a possible conventional ingredient of religion.

The discussion of religion (1161–1240) is, according to Bailey,[84] "the longest and fullest treatment of the nature of the gods and the causes and function of religion in the poem." It comes closer than any other section to being the copious speech proving "the tenuous nature" of the gods and of their abodes which the poet had promised in V 148–155. It is prepared by the remarkable silence on the problem of the gods which he had observed since V 110–234, that is, since the passage which contains the most elaborate critique occurring in the poem of the divinity or the divine origin of the world. The discussion of religion is the only passage in which Lucretius tells the reader precisely what we know experientially, or more specifically by sight, of the gods' being and nature. In an earlier remark (III 16–18) he had made one expect that we have direct knowledge not only of the gods' being but even of their abodes. Strictly speaking, however, the present passage gives an account, not of the gods' being and nature, but of the cause which has spread among great nations the powers of the gods and filled the cities with divine worship proceeding from shuddering awe. The account of what precisely we know of the gods' being or nature is a subordinate part of the account of how that knowledge came into being in the past: the whole account is framed in the imperfect tense. The discussion of religion, in contradistinction to the astronomic part, is devoted to coming into being.

Lucretius is prepared to state "the cause" of men's awareness of the gods and of their worshiping the gods. But he states two causes. We recall that at the beginning of the astronomic part he promised to expound "the cause" of the motions of the stars and then stated more than one cause (508–533). The present case is different. According to Bailey,[85] Lucretius "assigns two reasons for [the universal belief in gods], though he does not, as he should have done, explain that one of these reasons is true and the other false." As a rule it is wise to abstain from telling a superior man what he should have done. Transgressions of this rule cannot be traced to democracy, but stem from a frailty which is effective in all regimes. The two reasons given by Lucretius are to explain not only "the universal belief in gods" but divine worship as commonly practised in the cities as well; perhaps "the true reason" is not sufficient for explaining that divine worship. Besides, "the true reason" explains how men came to believe in beautiful gods, but men do not universally believe in beautiful gods.[86]

Even then, Lucretius tells us, the races of mortals saw with their mind while being awake and still more in sleep the glorious forms or faces of the gods and the marvelous sizes of their bodies. This much and not more is unambiguously said to have been "seen" and still to be "seen" of the gods by men awake. The beautiful forms and the great bulk do not by themselves prove that their owners are living beings; gods must be capable of feeling or sensing. Men did not "see" that the gods sense, but they "attributed" sense to the gods because they "saw" the gods moving their limbs. Yet this inference is of questionable validity. Men see the gods chiefly in sleep; in sleep they also "see" dead men moving their limbs, that is, they seem to see this or they believe they see it (IV 757–772). Accordingly Lucretius does not unambiguously say that the gods were seen to move their limbs; the expression which he uses (*videbantur*) can as well mean that the gods seemed to move their limbs. The whole sentence reads as follows: "They attributed sense to the gods because they seemed to move their limbs and to utter haughty sounds befitting their resplendent form and their ample strength." The gods' sensing, that is, living, is not experienced, but a human "addition" to the experienced (cf. V 1195 and IV 462–468); the experience in itself is in fact not more than a seeming.

What is true of the gods' sensing is also true of their eternal life: men "gave" them eternal life, and "they believed" that gods possessing such great strength could "not easily" be overcome by any force; beings which are not easily overcome by any force are not necessarily eternal. "They believed" the gods to be outstanding in good fortune because none of the gods was ever troubled by fear of death, and "in sleep they saw them achieve many wondrous things without undergoing any toil" (V 1169–1182). One is curious to know whether men saw while awake that the gods were never troubled by fear of death, and which wondrous things the gods were seen to do; there is no suggestion that they were seen to think or to understand or in any other way to know the truth. There is also no suggestion that they were seen to be simply self-sufficient and hence unable to act on the world and within it and in particular to act on men. On the contrary, since the first cause of religion as presented by Lucretius consists to a considerable extent of human additions to what was genuinely seen or experienced, there is no reason why men should not have imagined also that the beings possessing beautiful faces and enormous sizes, which appeared to them in their dreams and seemed to utter haughty sounds, were not also their haughty lords threatening them with terrible punishments. This may be the reason why Lucretius declares that he will set forth "the cause," that is, a single cause, of religion. However this may be, he is concerned with pointing to a cause which has nothing whatever to do with men's dreams; therefore he adduces the following cause: men were induced by their beholding the celestial phenomena, of which they do not know the causes, to trace those phenomena to the gods. In particular, frightening and nocturnal phenomena of this kind were held to be threats on the part of the gods or proofs of their anger. In the light of "the longest and fullest treatment of the nature of the gods and the causes and function of religion in the poem" as well as of our previous observations,[87] we shall say that the fundamental theologoumenon is meant to articulate in the most adequate manner our notion of the gods as *entia perfectissima:* the most perfect beings cannot possibly act on the world or in the world; the fundamental theologoumenon, in contradistinction to the ontological proof, is not meant to prove the existence of gods; their existence is not known.

This result is not contradicted by those writings of Epicurus that have come down to us in nonfragmentary form. In the case of fragments we cannot know how the thoughts expressed in them would appear in the light of the whole to which they belonged. The *Principal Opinions* never speaks of gods or of the divine.[88] According to the first of those *Opinions,* "that which is blessed and indestructible suffers no trouble nor does it cause trouble to any other; hence it is not affected by fear or favor; for everything of this kind occurs only in what is weak." This statement is ordinarily taken as an assertion of the fundamental theologoumenon; but there are "immortal goods" which wise men can enjoy.[89] The *Letter to Herodotus,* which is an epitome of Epicurus' teaching on nature, never speaks of gods or of the divine; it does say that "in the indestructible and blessed nature there can in no way be anything which can bring about dissolution or confusion" (78); this statement could be made by a monotheist as well as by an atheist. The *Letter to Herodotus* also teaches that one must not believe that the same things are blessed and indestructible and at the same time will or do or cause things that are incompatible with bliss and indestructibility (81). The *Letter to Pythocles,* which is a summary of Epicurus' teaching about the things aloft, warns its reader against having recourse to "the divine nature" in order to explain celestial phenomena: one must leave the divine nature unmolested in its complete bliss (97; cf. 113 and 115–116). The utmost one can say is that the *Letter to Pythocles* uses the fundamental theologoumenon as a bulwark against mythical explanations, but those explanations are known to be impossible independently of the fundamental theologoumenon (cf. 104). The *Letter to Pythocles* refers once to the *intermundia* (89) without even alluding to their being the abodes of the gods. Epicurus sets forth his teaching regarding the gods and especially their existence in his *Letter to Menoeceus* (123–124), which is in fact devoted to ethics; he has found no place for it in his physics, that is, his teaching regarding the whole. No one in his right mind will say that the Epicurean gods are postulated by practical reason: Epicurus did not "find it necessary to deny knowledge in order to make room for faith."

To return to Lucretius, according to what one may call his official teaching the truth is sad because the world is not divine nor of divine origin, but the truth is attractive or comforting above all because the most lovable is sempiternal since there are gods, blessed and immortal beings that are akin to man rather than to any other beings. Yet if the gods are not, the most divine being, the being most resplendent, most beneficent, and most high in rank is the wise man with his frail happiness. The frailty of human happiness cannot be overcome by any conquest of nature, by the subjection of the whole to human use, for this would require among other things the emancipation of the desires for unnecessary things and therefore the certainty of human misery, of the fate of Sisyphus. Besides, the Epicurean sage has as little incentive to charity—to feeding the hungry and clothing the naked—as the Epicurean gods; like the Epicurean gods he is beneficent by being what he is rather than by doing anything. It is in agreement with this that Lucretius' "political philosophy" is only an account of the coming into being of political society; it does not deal with the question of the best regime: no regime deserves to be called good; philosophy cannot transform, or contribute toward transforming, political society.

Religion is presented by Lucretius as belonging to political society (V 1161–1162, 1222; cf. 1174 and 1111), which does not mean that it does not have ingredients antedating political society. It belongs to political society because laws, punishment, and fear of punishment belong to political society (1136–1151). Fear of punishment and fear of the gods belong together; fear of the gods is fear of divine punishment. Fear of the gods leads to men's despising themselves; Lucretius no longer says that it leads to crimes; [90] he says now that it leads to the sacrifice of beasts; he no longer speaks, as he did at the beginning, of human sacrifices. Ignorance of the causes of the motions of the heavenly bodies is not the sole or sufficient cause of men's believing in angry gods. (Hence astronomy is not sufficient for liberating men from the fear of the gods.) At least as important in this respect is men's bad conscience; for instance, the awareness of haughty kings that they have done or said haughty things which deserve punishment (1194–1240). We see again that religion may exert a salutary restraint. It is surely greatly preferable that the restraint be exerted by philosophy, which restrains the desires while it takes away the fear of the gods. This implies, however, that philosophy belongs to political society no less than religion does or that philosophy is impossible in prepolitical society: philosophy presupposes a high development of the arts. In prepolitical society Venus alone held sway. In political society, just as in nature, Mars rather than Venus holds sway.[91] Prepolitical society is in one sense more natural than political society; but it cannot be "the state of nature" since man lives according to nature only by virtue of philosophizing. The same man who in prepolitical society would have been a member of his tribe, like everybody else, may in political society lead the strictly private life of the philosopher.

At the beginning of his account of the genesis of the arts Lucretius speaks of the discovery of copper, gold, and iron as well as of silver and lead. The discovery of gold was an important step in the transition from the rule of those by nature superior to the rule of the rich (1113–1114). Through trial and error men learned to prefer copper to gold and silver because of its greater usefulness; the now prevailing preference for gold emerged at a later date (1241–1280). The use of iron was discovered last. When speaking of the discovery of the nature of iron Lucretius apostrophizes Memmius by name for the last time in the poem. He says: "It is easy for you to know by yourself, Memmius, how the nature of iron was discovered" (1281–1282). The poet had not used the second person since verse 1091. No such rarity of the use of the second person occurs anywhere else in the poem.[92] The present use of the second person is emphasized by the simultaneous use of the vocative of Memmius. The poet had apostrophized Memmius by name after Book I only in antitheological contexts; the present context is even less visibly antitheological than the preceding one (cf. pages 125–126 above). But between the present use of the vocative of Memmius and of the second person and the preceding use of the vocative of Memmius or of the second person there occurred the statement par excellence on the gods: Lucretius saw no need for emphasizing the importance of that statement. Lucretius mentions Memmius for the last time when speaking of the discovery of iron; iron is particularly useful in war; the connection between Memmius and war was indicated near the beginning of the poem (I 40–43). How much Lucretius is concerned with opening his account of the genesis of the arts with the theme "war" is shown by the fact that the sequel to what he says on the discovery of the metals deals with the various stages in which beasts were employed in war. Lucretius uses this occasion to indicate how much the progress of the arts takes place through error and trial; he makes us imagine for a moment that men foolishly tried to use bulls, boars, and even lions against their enemies, perhaps because, despairing of victory, they wished to harm their enemies while committing suicide (1281–1349).

Lucretius turns from the progress of the art or arts of war to weaving. By this he does not mean to turn from a man's art to a woman's art—the superior sex invented even the art of weaving, which is thought to be a preserve of the inferior sex—but from the arts of war to the arts of peace. Still, the peaceful art exercised commonly by men and hence higher in rank than weaving is agriculture, which is the next subject of the poet. The first teacher of agriculture and arboriculture was indeed nature herself, but men improved on the first lessons. Nature also taught men the rudiments of music, and reason raised the rustic Muse to its height. Lucretius presents the emergence of the various arts in accordance with the order of their rank. He therefore turns from music to knowledge of the seasons, that is, of one of the most visible signs of the sure order of nature; this knowledge is the last discovery discussed by him in any detail. In discussing music (as distinguished from knowledge of the seasons) he alludes to the fact that the enjoyments of the rustic Muse, despite their rudeness, embody some of the purest subphilosophic enjoyments of present-day men.[93] While this kind of music survives into the present in an improved form, present-day men are not happier than the earthborn men at the beginning who could not suffer from the lack of pleasures which they did not know. Progress within many arts is due to the desire for novel or even greater pleasures, that is, by the ignorance of the term of true pleasure. Hence this kind of progress goes hand in hand with the progress of war. This is not to deny that the progress of the arts is on the whole a progress of knowledge, a progress which culminates in Epicurus' work. The order of the arts as presented at the end of Book V follows the same principle as the order of outstanding men which occurred near the end of Book III (1024–1044).[94]

VII. On Book VI

The proem to this Book [95] is a corrective of the proem to Book V, just as the proem to Book IV is a corrective of the proem to Book III, and the proem to Book II is a corrective of the proem to Book I. Lucretius now praises Epicurus again as a man, as a mortal (cf. I 66–67); he no longer praises him as a god. He had praised him as a god with a view to the fact that he was the greatest benefactor of men; but one cannot be a god while being a benefactor of men. What survives Epicurus is his "divine discoveries" and his glory. Lucretius is silent about himself and his poetry. He praises Epicurus as a guide toward the highest good, as men's liberator from care or fear; he does not speak here in so many words of Epicurus' having liberated men from fear of gods or of hell. He alludes to those fears by saying that the race of men for the most part suffers from unfounded cares: a human life simply without care is impossible. In accordance with this Lucretius makes it clear that Epicurus' discoveries came at the end or near the end of that progress of the arts which is necessary to supply men with what they need and for making human life as safe as possible (1–42).

Lucretius next reminds us of what he has done in the preceding Book: he has shown that the world is mortal or has come into being, and he has expounded most of what necessarily happens in heaven. He is silent about the second half of Book V in which he has set forth the coming into being of the world or its parts. He promises to discuss in Book VI a certain kind of terrestrial and celestial things (43–50). This means that he will no longer deal with the coming into being of the world or its parts; the expositions given in Book VI are therefore akin to those given in the astronomic part of Book V, as distinguished from those given in the second half of Book V; they are cosmologic, rather than cosmogonic. The cosmogonic second half of Book V which contains the theological statement par excellence is thus surrounded by cosmologic portions. To the extent to which this is true, Book VI makes us forget the coming into being, and therewith the death, of the world. Lucretius has reminded us of that sad truth even in the latter part of Book V, which is so single-mindedly devoted to coming into being as distinguished from perishing, by speaking of the ambiguity of the progress of the arts. Yet at the very end of Book V (1440–1457) he has become silent about that ambiguity. But it suffices to compare the last verses of Book V with the last verses of Book VI in order to see that the poet's use of honey is judicious; he does not permit the honey to make us insensitive to the wormwood.

The phenomena to be dealt with in Book VI are traced by men to the gods whom they believe to be their dreadful masters. It is undoubtedly true that the gods lead a life free from all care and that fear of the gods is incompatible with pure worship or perception of the gods. Yet it is also true that the error which leads to fear of the gods is uprooted only by the *verissima ratio*, that is, by the natural explanation of the phenomena which induce ignorant men to believe in divine wrath. The expression *verissima ratio* occurs nowhere else in the poem. One of the things which Lucretius must therefore do is to "sing" of the true causes and effects of storms and lightnings. He invokes the Muse Calliope, who is "rest to men and joy to gods," to be his leader (51–95). Calliope now takes the place of Venus; Venus is not even mentioned any more in Book VI. Calliope had been the Muse invoked by Empedocles. Empedocles was both a philosopher and a poet. He was surpassed by Democritus and above all by Epicurus. Yet in surpassing Empedocles, Democritus and Epicurus had separated philosophy entirely from poetry. Poetry became at best the handmaid of philosophy. Yet the poet possesses insights which Epicurus may have lacked, above all the understanding of men's attachment to the world and what this implies. By restoring the union of philosophy and poetry, by presenting the true and final philosophic teaching poetically, Lucretius may be said to surpass Epicurus; the Lucretian presentation of the truth is superior to the Epicurean presentation. Yet if we consider the crucial importance of the Epicurean gods in the Epicurean presentation of the truth, are we not driven to say that in the decisive respect Epicurus too is a poet? Do the Epicurean gods not magnify or embellish the whole?

Lucretius explains thunder (96–159) and lightning (160–218) in order to explain the thunderbolt (219–378), for the thunderbolt, being the strongest of all fires, is together with its concomitants the most frightening thing coming from heaven. The explanation of the thunderbolt naturally leads up to an attack on the Tyrrhenian kind of divination (which had been taken over by the Romans) and, more generally, on the theological view: thunderbolts strike the innocent as well as the guilty; nay, they strike the likenesses and images of the gods (379–422). One need not be an atomist in order to be impressed by arguments of this kind. Lucretius explains thereafter at some length three phenomena akin to thunderstorms: the waterspouts, which are a kind of abortive thunderstorm, as well as clouds and rain which go together with thunderstorms (423–534). In explaining these phenomena Lucretius does not emphasize that they are frightening (430). The case of earthquakes, to which he turns next (535–607), is different; earthquakes are directly linked with the poet's primary and fundamental concern; they offer the most massive proof of the possibility of the death of the world; they give as it were a foretaste of that death.[96] Lucretius does not speak here, as he did in the section on the thunderbolt, of men's tracing the terrifying phenomenon to the wrath of the gods; he only alludes to men's believing that the gods in their kindness vouch for the sempiternity of the world (601–602); on the other hand, he says explicitly that men "fear to believe" that the world will die a natural death (565–567).[97] It is this fear for the world, that is, for this world, for everything that is a man's own or his nation's own, which gives rise to the belief in gods and therewith also to the fear of the gods; the fear of gods is not the fundamental fear. The fundamental fear gives rise in the first place to fear of that very fear, to fear of the most terrible truth. The poet, having exposed himself to the fear of the terrible truth, can calmly face that truth. His courage is not in need of support by belief in social progress between now and the death of the world or by other beliefs. The verses under discussion are the central digression occurring in the body of Book VI; they prepare the end of the poem, the description of the plague.[98]

Men wonder, Lucretius continues, that nature does not make the sea bigger since all rivers from every quarter fall into the sea. There is only one step from this wondering to fear of a deluge that destroys all life on land. Lucretius disregards this apparent possibility (608–638). The eruptions of Mount Etna are frightening to the tribes living nearby. Those eruptions as well as earthquakes and similar phenomena are frightening because of their gigantic size; but they are of very small size compared with the infinite whole of which a whole world is an infinitesimal part. The discussion of the eruptions of Mount Etna opens the discussion of other local phenomena or of other phenomena indicated by place names: the flood of the Nile, the Avernian Lake, the spring near the shrine of Ammon and the one within the sea at Aradus, and finally the magnet (cf. 906–909). Lucretius thus prepares the description of the plague in Athens—a description reasonably preceded by an explanation of pestilences in general. The only subject treated in the second half of Book VI which he explicitly connects with his primary concern is the Avernian places; these places must not be thought to be places from which the gods of the dead lead the souls to the shores of Acheron (749–768). In giving the true reason for this phenomenon (769–780), Lucretius makes it clearer than ever before that the earth is as much the destroyer as the mother of all living beings. The last Book is, less than any other Book, concerned with embellishment.

NOTES

1. Cf. Hesiod, *Theogony* 11–21: Ares is not explicitly mentioned among the gods praised by the Muses. Cf. *Works and Days* 145–146.
2. Cf. the *virum* in VI 5 with the *deus ille fuit, deus* in V 8.
3. Cf. especially 1259–1263.
4. Cf. 1197–1204, 1210–1211, 1226–1229 with Thucydides II 49.8 and 51.6.
5. 1183, 1212; cf. 1208–1212 with Thucydides II 49.8; consider the fact that there is no passage in Lucretius which corresponds to II 53.
6. Cf. 1239–1246 with Thucydides II 51.5.
7. Cf. 1278–1286 (consider especially the last words of the poem) with Thucydides II 53.4, beginning and 52.4. Cf. Epicurus' unconcern with his burial: Diogenes Laertius X 118.
8. In his letter to Menoeceus (134) Epicurus says that there is something worse than the tale of the gods: the fate or necessity of which the *physikoi* speak.
9. Cf. 1156–1162, 1182–1185, 1212.
10. III 1–30.
11. Cf. I 117–119, 121, 124, 136–137, 143–145.
12. V 925–1010, 1087–1090; cf. VI 601–602.
13. V 1211–1217, 1236–1240, 91–109, 114–121, 373–375, 1186–1187; VI 565–567, 597–607, 650–652, 677–679.
14. Cf. Thucydides I 22.4.
15. Hence the conclusion of the whole reasoning in 205–207. The fourth argument is the only one which shows that many first bodies are common to many things as letters ("elements") are common to words, that is, that there is something more common than the heterogeneous seeds of the various kinds of animals and plants.
16. Lucretius does not regard plants as living beings: I 774 (cf. 821 and II 702–703).
17. Cf. I 107–108. Cf. the emphasis on numbers, that is, on small numbers, in 419–420, 432, 445–446, 449–450, 503.
18. I 803–808, 897–900. Cf. 770.
19. Cf. II 185–190.
20. I 28, 136–145, 933–934.
21. Cicero, *De republica* III 26; *De finibus* II 15.
22. I 716–725; cf. VI 680 ff.
23. I 675–678, 684–689, 778–781, 848–856, 915–920.
24. I 803–808 and 897–900. In I 803–808 the addressee tries to prove that without the four elements there could not be growth of plants and animals; Lucretius strengthens this argument by stating that without the four elements there could not be human life. In the parallels in IV 633–672 and VI 769–780 he also speaks of diseases and death.
25. Cf. the *evolvamus* and *pervideamus* in I 954 and 956.
26. I 1021–1022; cf. 328 and 1110.
27. I 1052.
28. Cf. I 1112 with V 373–375.
29. Only in this context does Lucretius refer to things Roman in the proem to Book II. He no longer refers to things Roman in the proems to the following Books.
30. Cf. also the implicit contrast between the wandering or restless atoms and the wandering mind in II 82–83. Cf. also the contrast between the fall of the atoms

and the fall of certain philosophers (I 741). The void is motionless or quiet (II 238); yet this quietness has no kinship with the quietness which the mind needs (cf. I 639).

31. Cf. also the emphasis on generating in II 62–64. Cf. the *semper* in II 76 with the *nunc* in V 194.
32. Cf. I 1025; II 573–576, V 380–381, 391–392.
33. In the two cases in which the poet addressed Memmius by name in Book I he also did this while polemicizing against "some," that is, while indicating Memmius' likely resistance to Epicureanism. The same is true of the two cases in Book I (803–808, 897–900) in which he presents Memmius as opposing Epicureanism in direct speech.
34. II 169, 178, I 105. Consider again the initial statement about the theme of the whole poem in I 54–55. Cf. Spinoza, *Tr. theol.-pol.* XVI 10–11 (Bruder).
35. Letter to Menoeceus 134.
36. II 481–482, 496–507; cf. V 1171, and 1177 (*auctos.*). Consider the unusual section-beginnings in II 478–479 and 522–523.
37. II 569–580; cf. 174–181 and V 220–234.
38. Cf. IV 761: the dead are held by "death and earth."
39. As for the difference between the second and the fifth items, cf. Democritus (Diels) B 278.
40. Literally, "the everlasting wound"; cf. "the everlasting wound" of Mars in I 34, that is, shortly before the first statement of the fundamental theologoumenon.
41. Cf. II 886–888, 902–903, 931, 983.
42. Cf. III 879–889.
43. Cf. Bailey's edition and commentary (Oxford: 1947), p. 956.
44. Cf. V 115–125, 144–145.
45. Cf. Cicero, *De natura deorum* I 52.
46. Note the contrast with I 398–417, the conclusion of the section dealing with the void.
47. Cf. I 1052–1053 in the parallel.
48. He does not invoke the gods in order to confirm a theologoumenon; cf. the parallel case in II 434 (*pro divom numina sancta*). No other reference to the hearts of the gods occurs in the poem.
49. Cf. Bailey, *op. cit.*, p. 761.
50. "Lucretius is a poet not to be suspected of giving way to superstitious terrors; yet when he supposes the whole mechanism of nature laid open by the master of his philosophy, his transport on this magnificent view, which he has represented in the colours of such bold and lively poetry, is overcast with a shade of secret dread and horror." Burke, *The Sublime and Beautiful*, II sect. 5.
51. Reconsider from this point of view I 80–83.
52. Cf. Plato, *Phaedo* 86c2–d4 (Simmias). Cf. the sarcasm in Lucretius' critique of pre-existence (the premise of Cebes' argument) in III 776–783.
53. Just as "we all" who "stem from heavenly seed" (II 991) are not merely "all we human beings." Cf. also page 96 above.
54. Cf. III 753.
55. III 371, V 622. Of Empedocles he says that Sicily does not seem to have possessed something more sacred than him (I 729–730).
56. Cf. V 177–178.
57. Expressions like *fateare necessest, cur credis, quod si forte putas, quid dubitas, quod si forte credis* do not occur in the first part of Book III (31–424), but occur in the second part.
58. Cf. 754, 760, 765–766.
59. Note the contrast between the avoidance of the first person plural in the verses

dealing with the Punic Wars (833–837) and the frequency of the first person plural ("we," that is, we human beings, not we Romans) in the rest of the passage.

60. Compare the procedure of the Xenophontic Socrates who apostrophizes Xenophon and no one else as "you wretch" and "you fool" (*Memorabilia* I 3.11,13). Cf. Plato, *Republic* 595c10–596al.

61. Cf. also I 130–135.

62. V 1161–1193. Cf. VI 76–77.

63. II 609; VI 419–420.

64. Passive forms of *videre* occur here seventeen times with the unambiguous meaning of "to seem." Cf. I 726 (*videtur*) and 727 (*fertur*).

65. Cf. the "we" in 37. Cf. VI 970–972.

66. Cf. IV 969–970.

67. *Nunc age . . . accipe . . . percipe* (722–723).

68. Cf. III 12–27.

69. Cf. II 1023–1047.

70. Cf. I 80 ff.

71. III 294–301. Cf. II 265–268 and V 1325.

72. Cf. II, 478–484.

73. Cf. II, 175–182. The promise there made to Memmius is fulfilled in the present context.

74. Cf. especially 233–234 with 198. Cf. 495–505. This step is prepared by the transition from 258–260 (the earth is the parent of all) to 318–323 (the sky is the parent of all). Cf. II 598–599 with 991–998.

75. VI 84; cf. 255, 259, 376. Verbal forms of *canere* occur ten times; in nine cases the word is applied to human singing or music. *Cantus* occurs four times and *canor* twice.

76. V 1183–1193, 1205–1221, 83–87; cf. I 62–69.

77. Cf. pages 95–96, 119–120, 121–123 above.

78. This is so despite the fact that nature supplies everything to the gods (III 23).

79. Cf. pages 116–117 above.

80. Bailey, *op. cit.*, p. 1474 note, refers to Empedocles (B 128, lines 1–3): "for those men Ares was not god nor Kydoimos nor Zeus the king nor Kronos nor Poseidon but only Kypris the queen." Lucretius indicates the absence of Zeus, Ares, and Poseidon in V 958–959 and 999–1006.

81. *Letter to Herodotus* 75–76.

82. Cf. Plato, *Republic* 365c6–dl. Cf. the *plerumque* in V 1153 and the *ferantur* in 1159.

83. Cf. Cicero, *De finibus* I 51.

84. *Op cit.*, p. 1507.

85. *Ibid.*, p. 67.

86. Cf. Xenophanes B 16.

87. See pages 99–100, 114–115, 117–118, 121–122 above. Cf. I 132–135.

88. The *Gnomologium Vaticanum* differs in this respect from the *Principal Opinions*; cf. Nos. 24, 33, and 65.

89. *Letter to Menoeceus*, end; *Gnomologium Vaticanum* No. 78.

90. Cf. pages 121–122 above.

91. Cf. page 95 above.

92. If I am not mistaken, the second person is used in Book I (consisting of 1117 verses) 91 times; in Book II (1174), 122 times; in Book III (1094), 112 times; in Book IV (1287), 89 times; in Book V (1457), 49 times; and in Book VI (1286), 62 times. I disregarded the cases in which the second person is used of Venus, Epicurus, or Calliope.

93. Cf. 1392–1411 with II 29–33.
94. Cf. also the ascent from political life to poetry in 1440–1445; cf. also 1448–1451 and 332–337.
95. Cf. page 81 above.
96. Cf. V 95–109 and 1236–1240.
97. Cf. Aristotle, *Metaphysics* 1050b22–24; cf. *On the Heaven* 270b1–16.
98. Cf. page 81 above.

6/ How To Begin To Study
The Guide of the Perplexed

I believe that it will not be amiss if I simply present the plan of the *Guide* as it has become clear to me in the course of about twenty-five years of frequently interrupted but never abandoned study. In the following scheme Roman (and Arabic) numerals at the beginning of a line indicate the sections (and subsections) of the *Guide*, while the numbers given in parentheses indicate the Parts and the chapters of the book.

A. VIEWS (I 1–III 24)
A′. VIEWS REGARDING GOD AND THE ANGELS (I 1–III 7)
    I. Biblical terms applied to God (I 1–70)
    Terms suggesting the corporeality of God (and the angels) (I 1–49)
        1. The two most important passages of the Torah that seem to suggest that God is corporeal (I 1–7)
        2. Terms designating place, change of place, the organs of human locomotion, etc. (I 8–28)
        3. Terms designating wrath and consuming (or taking food) that if applied to divine things refer to idolatry on the one hand and to human knowledge on the other (I 29–36)
        4. Terms designating parts and actions of animals (I 37–49)
    Terms suggesting multiplicity in God (I 50–70)
        5. Given that God is absolutely one and incomparable, what is the meaning of the terms applied to God in nonfigurative speech? (I 50–60)
        6. The names of God and the utterances of God (I 61–67)
        7. The apparent multiplicity in God consequent upon His knowledge, His causality, and His governance (I 67–70)
    II. Demonstrations of the existence, unity, and incorporeality of God (I 71–II 31)

1. Introductory (I 71–73)
2. Refutation of the Kalām demonstrations (I 74–76)
3. The philosophic demonstrations (II 1)
4. Maimonides' demonstration (II 2)
5. The angels (II 3–12)
6. Creation of the world, i.e., defense of the belief in creation out of nothing against the philosophers (II 13–24)
7. Creation and the Law (II 25–31)

III. Prophecy (II 32–48)
1. Natural endowment and training the prerequisites of prophecy (II 32–34)
2. The difference between the prophecy of Moses and that of the other prophets (II 35)
3. The essence of prophecy (II 36–38)
4. The legislative prophecy (of Moses) and the Law (II 39–40)
5. Legal study of the prophecy of the prophets other than Moses (II 41–44)
6. The degrees of prophecy (II 45)
7. How to understand the divine actions and works and the divinely commanded actions and works as presented by the prophets (II 46–48)

IV. The account of the Chariot (III 1–7)

A″. VIEWS REGARDING BODILY BEINGS THAT COME INTO BEING AND PERISH, AND IN PARTICULAR REGARDING MAN (III 8–54)

V. Providence (III 8–24)
1. Statement of the problem: matter is the ground of all evils and yet matter is created by the absolutely good God (III 8–14)
2. The nature of the impossible or the meaning of omnipotence (III 15)
3. The philosophic arguments against omniscience (III 16)
4. The views regarding providence (III 17–18)
5. Jewish views on omniscience and Maimonides' discourse on this subject (III 19–21)
6. The book of Job as the authoritative treatment of providence (III 22–23)
7. The teaching of the Torah on omniscience (III 24)

B. ACTIONS (III 25–54)
VI. The actions commanded by God and done by God (III 25–50)
1. The rationality of God's actions in general and of His legislation in particular (III 25–26)
2. The manifestly rational part of the commandments of the Torah (III 27–28)

      3. The rationale of the apparently irrational part of the com-
         mandments of the Torah (III 29–33)
      4. The inevitable limit to the rationality of the commandments
         of the Torah (III 34)
      5. Division of the commandments into classes and explanation
         of the usefulness of each class (III 35)
      6. Explanation of all or almost all commandments (III 36–49)
      7. The narratives in the Torah (III 50)
  vii. Man's perfection and God's providence (III 51–54)
      1. True knowledge of God Himself is the prerequisite of provi-
         dence (III 51–52)
      2. True knowledge of what constitutes the human individual
         himself is the prerequisite of knowledge of the workings of
         providence (III 53–54)

The *Guide* consists then of seven sections or of thirty-eight subsections.
Wherever feasible, each section is divided into seven subsections; the only
section that does not permit of being divided into subsections is divided
into seven chapters.

The simple statement of the plan of the *Guide* suffices to show that the
book is sealed with many seals. At the end of its Introduction, Maimonides
describes the preceding passage as follows: "It is a key permitting one to
enter places the gates to which were locked. When those gates are opened
and those places are entered, the souls will find rest therein, the eyes will
be delighted, and the bodies will be eased of their toil and of their labor."
The *Guide* as a whole is not merely a key to a forest but is itself a forest, an
enchanted forest, and hence also an enchanting forest: it is a delight to the
eyes. For the tree of life is a delight to the eyes.

The enchanting character of the *Guide* does not appear immediately. At
first glance the book appears merely to be strange and in particular to lack
order and consistency. But progress in understanding it is a progress in
becoming enchanted by it. Enchanting understanding is perhaps the highest form of edification. One begins to understand the *Guide* once one sees
that it is not a philosophic book—a book written by a philosopher for
philosophers—but a Jewish book: a book written by a Jew for Jews. Its first
premise is the old Jewish premise that being a Jew and being a philosopher
are two incompatible things. Philosophers are men who try to give an
account of the whole by starting from what is always accessible to man as
man; Maimonides starts from the acceptance of the Torah. A Jew may
make use of philosophy, and Maimonides makes the most ample use of it;
but as a Jew he gives his assent, where as a philosopher he would suspend
his assent (cf. II 16).

Accordingly, the *Guide* is devoted to the Torah or more precisely to the
true science of the Torah, of the Law. Its first purpose is to explain biblical

terms, and its second purpose is to explain biblical similes. The *Guide* is then devoted above all to biblical exegesis, although to biblical exegesis of a particular kind. That kind of exegesis is required because many biblical terms and all biblical similes have an apparent or outer and a hidden or inner meaning; the gravest errors as well as the most tormenting perplexities arise from men's understanding the Bible always according to its apparent or literal meaning. The *Guide* is then devoted to "the difficulties of the Law" or to "the secrets of the Law." The most important of those secrets are the Account of the Beginning (the beginning of the Bible) and the Account of the Chariot (Ezek. 1 and 10). The *Guide* is then devoted primarily and chiefly to the explanation of the Account of the Beginning and the Account of the Chariot.

Yet the Law whose secrets Maimonides intends to explain forbids that they be explained in public, or to the public; they may only be explained in private and only to such individuals as possess both theoretical and political wisdom as well as the capacity of both understanding and using allusive speech; for only "the chapter headings" of the secret teaching may be transmitted even to those who belong to the natural elite. Since every explanation given in writing, at any rate in a book, is a public explanation, Maimonides seems to be compelled by his intention to transgress the Law. There were other cases in which he was under such a compulsion. The Law also forbids one to study the books of idolaters on idolatry, for the first intention of the Law as a whole is to destroy every vestige of idolatry; and yet Maimonides, as he openly admits and even emphasizes, has studied all the available idolatrous books of this kind with the utmost thoroughness. Nor is this all. He goes so far as to encourage the reader of the *Guide* to study those books by himself (III 29–30, 32, 37; *Mishneh Torah*, H. 'Abodah Zarah II 2 and III 2). The Law also forbids one to speculate about the date of the coming of the Messiah; yet Maimonides presents such a speculation or at least its equivalent in order to comfort his contemporaries (*Epistle to Yemen*, 62, 16 ff., and 80, 17 ff. Halkin; cf. Halkin's Introduction, pp. xii–xiii; *M.T.*, H. Melakhim XII 2). Above all, the Law forbids one to seek for the reasons of the commandments; yet Maimonides devotes almost twenty-six chapters of the *Guide* to such seeking (III 26; cf. II 25). All these irregularities have one and the same justification. Maimonides transgresses the Law "for the sake of heaven," that is, in order to uphold or to fulfill the Law (I Introd. and III Introd.). Still, in the most important case he does not, strictly speaking, transgress the Law, for his written explanation of the secrets of the Law is not a public but a secret explanation. The secrecy is achieved in three ways. First, every word of the *Guide* is chosen with exceeding care; since very few men are able or willing to read with exceeding care, most men will fail to perceive the secret teaching. Second, Maimonides deliberately contradicts himself, and if a man declares both that *a* is *b* and that *a* is not *b,* he cannot be said to declare anything.

Lastly, the "chapter headings" of the secret teaching are not presented in an orderly fashion, but are scattered throughout the book. This permits us to understand why the plan of the *Guide* is so obscure. Maimonides succeeds immediately in obscuring the plan by failing to divide the book explicitly into sections and subsections or by dividing it explicitly only into three Parts and each Part into chapters without supplying the Parts and the chapters with headings indicating the subject matter of the Parts or of the chapters.

The plan of the *Guide* is not entirely obscure. No one can reasonably doubt, for instance, that II 32–48, III 1–7, and III 25–50 form sections. The plan is most obscure at the beginning, and it becomes clearer as one proceeds; generally speaking, it is clearer in the second half (II 13–end) than in the first half. The *Guide* is then not entirely devoted to secretly transmitting chapter headings of the secret teaching. This does not mean that the book is not in its entirety devoted to the true science of the Law. It means that the true science of the Law is partly public. This is not surprising, for the teaching of the Law itself is of necessity partly public. According to one statement, the core of the public teaching consists of the assertions that God is one, that He alone is to be worshiped, that He is incorporeal, that He is incomparable to any of His creatures, and that He suffers from no defect and no passion (I 35). From other statements it would appear that the acceptance of the Law on every level of comprehension presupposes belief in God, in angels, and in prophecy (III 45) or that the basic beliefs are those in God's unity and in creation (II 13). In brief one may say that the public teaching of the Law, insofar as it refers to beliefs or to "views," can be reduced to the thirteen "roots" (or dogmas) which Maimonides had put together in his Commentary on the Mishnah. That part of the true science of the Law which is devoted to the public teaching of the Law or which is itself public has the task of demonstrating the roots to the extent to which this is possible or of establishing the roots by means of speculation (III 51 and 54). Being speculative, that part of the true science of the Law is not exegetic; it is not necessarily in need of support by biblical or talmudic texts (cf. II 45 beginning). Accordingly, about 20 per cent of the chapters of the *Guide* contain no biblical quotations, and about 9 per cent of them contain no Hebrew or Aramaic expressions whatever. It is not very difficult to see (especially on the basis of III 7 end, 23, and 28) that the *Guide* as devoted to speculation on the roots of the Law or to the public teaching consists of sections II–III and V–VI as indicated in our scheme and that the sequence of these sections is rational; but one cannot understand in this manner why the book is divided into three Parts, or what sections I, IV, and VII and most, not to say all, subsections mean. The teaching of the *Guide* is then neither entirely public or speculative nor entirely secret or exegetic. For this reason the plan of the *Guide* is neither entirely obscure nor entirely clear.

Yet the *Guide* is a single whole. What then is the bond uniting its exegetic and its speculative ingredients? One might imagine that while speculation demonstrates the roots of the Law, exegesis proves that those roots as demonstrated by speculation are in fact taught by the Law. But in that case the *Guide* would open with chapters devoted to speculation; yet the opposite is manifestly true. In addition, if the exegesis dealt with the same subject matter as that speculation which demonstrates the public teaching par excellence, namely, the roots of the Law, there would be no reason why the exegesis should be secret. Maimonides does say that the Account of the Beginning is the same as natural science and the Account of the Chariot is the same as divine science (that is, the science of the incorporeal beings or of God and the angels). This might lead one to think that the public teaching is identical with what the philosophers teach, while the secret teaching makes one understand the identity of the teaching of the philosophers with the secret teaching of the Law. One can safely say that this thought proves to be untenable on almost every level of one's comprehending the *Guide:* the nonidentity of the teaching of the philosophers as a whole and the thirteen roots of the Law as a whole are the first word and the last word of Maimonides. What he means by identifying the core of philosophy (natural science and divine science) with the highest secrets of the Law (the Account of the Beginning and the Account of the Chariot) and therewith by somehow identifying the subject matter of speculation with the subject matter of exegesis may be said to be the secret par excellence of the *Guide.*

Let us then retrace our steps. The *Guide* contains a public teaching and a secret teaching. The public teaching is addressed to every Jew, including the vulgar; the secret teaching is addressed to the elite. The secret teaching is of no use to the vulgar, and the elite does not need the *Guide* for being apprised of the public teaching. To the extent to which the *Guide* is a whole, or one work, it is addressed neither to the vulgar nor to the elite. To whom then is it addressed? How legitimate and important this question is appears from Maimonides' remark that the chief purpose of the *Guide* is to explain as far as possible the Account of the Beginning and the Account of the Chariot "with a view to him for whom (the book) has been composed" (III beginning). Maimonides answers our question both explicitly and implicitly. He answers it explicitly in two ways; he says on the one hand that the *Guide* is addressed to believing Jews who are perfect in their religion and in their character, have studied the sciences of the philosophers, and are perplexed by the literal meaning of the Law; he says on the other hand that the book is addressed to such perfect human beings as are Law students and perplexed. He answers our question more simply by dedicating the book to his disciple Joseph and by stating that it has been composed for Joseph and his like. Joseph had come to him "from the ends of the earth" and had studied under him for a while; the interruption of the oral instruction through Joseph's departure, which "God had decreed," induced Maimonides to write the *Guide* for Joseph and his like. In the Epistle Dedicatory addressed to Joseph, Maimonides extols Joseph's virtues and indicates his limitation. Joseph had a passionate desire for things speculative and especially for mathematics. When he studied astronomy, mathematics, and logic under Maimonides, the teacher saw that Joseph had an excellent mind and a quick grasp; he thought him therefore fit to have revealed to him allusively the secrets of the books of the prophets, and he began to make such revelations. This stimulated Joseph's interest in things divine as well as in an appraisal of the Kalām; his desire for knowledge about these subjects became so great that Maimonides was compelled to warn him unceasingly to proceed in an orderly manner. It appears that Joseph was inclined to proceed impatiently or unmethodically in his study and that this defect had not been cured when he left Maimonides. The most important consequence of Joseph's defect is the fact, brought out by Maimonides' silence, that Joseph turned to divine science without having studied natural science under Maimonides or before, although natural science necessarily precedes divine science in the order of study.

The impression derived from the Epistle Dedicatory is confirmed by the book itself. Maimonides frequently addresses the reader by using expressions like "know" or "you know already." Expressions of the latter kind indicate what the typical addressee knows, and expressions of the former kind indicate what he does not know. One thus learns that Joseph has some knowledge of both the content and the character of divine science. He knows, for example, that divine science in contradistinction to mathematics and medicine requires an extreme of rectitude and moral perfection, and in particular of humility, but he apparently does not yet know how ascetic Judaism is in matters of sex (I 34, III 52). He had learned from Maimonides' "speech" that the orthodox "views" do not last in a man if he does not confirm them by the corresponding "actions" (II 31). It goes without saying that while his knowledge of the Jewish sources is extensive, it is not comparable in extent and thoroughness to Maimonides' (II 26, 33). At the beginning of the book he does not know that both according to the Jewish view and according to demonstration, angels have no bodies (I 43, 49), and he certainly does not know, strictly speaking, that God has no body (I 9). In this respect as well as in other respects his understanding necessarily progresses while he advances in his study of the *Guide* (cf. I 65 beginning). As for natural science, he has studied astronomy, but is not aware of the conflict between the astronomical principles and the principles of natural science (II 24), because he has not studied natural science. He knows a number of things that are made clear in natural science, but this does not mean that he knows them through having studied natural science (cf. I 17, 28; III 10). From the ninety-first chapter (II 15) it appears that while he knows Aristotle's *Topics* and Fārābī's commentary on that work, he does not know the *Physics* and *On the Heaven* (cf. II 8). Nor will he acquire the science of nature as he acquires the science of God and the angels while he advances in the study of the *Guide*. For the *Guide*, which is addressed to a reader not conversant with natural science, does not itself transmit natural science (II 2). The following remark occurring in the twenty-sixth chapter is particularly revealing: "It has been demonstrated that everything moved undoubtedly possesses a magnitude and is divisible; and it will be demonstrated that God possesses no magnitude and hence possesses no motion." What "has been demonstrated" has been demonstrated in the *Physics* and is simply presupposed in the *Guide*; what "will be demonstrated" belongs to divine science and not to natural science; but that which "will be demonstrated" is built on what "has been demonstrated." The student of the *Guide* acquires knowledge of divine science, but not of natural science. The author of the *Guide* in contradistinction to its addressee is thoroughly versed in natural science. Still, the addressee needs some awareness of the whole in order to be able to ascend from the whole to God, for there is no way to knowledge of God except through such ascent (I 71 toward the end); he acquires that awareness through a report of some kind (I 70) that Maimonides has inserted into the *Guide*. It is characteristic of that report that it does not contain a single mention of philosophy in general and of natural science in particular. The serious student cannot rest satisfied with that report; he must turn from it to natural science itself, which demonstrates what the report merely asserts. Maimonides cannot but leave it to his reader whether he will turn to genuine speculation or whether he will be satisfied with accepting the report on the authority of Maimonides and with building on that report theological conclusions. The addressee of the *Guide* is a man regarding whom it is still undecided whether he will become a genuine man of speculation or whether he will remain a follower of authority, if of Maimonides' authority (cf. I 72 end). He stands at the point of the road where speculation branches off from acceptance of authority.

Why did Maimonides choose an addressee of this description? What is the virtue of not being trained in natural science? We learn from the seventeenth chapter that natural science had already been treated as a secret doctrine by the pagan philosophers "upon whom the charge of corruption would not be laid if they exposed natural science clearly": all the more is the community of the Law-adherents obliged to treat natural science as a secret science. The reason why natural science is dangerous and is kept secret "with all kinds of artifices" is not that it undermines the Law—only the ignorant believe that (I 33), and Maimonides' whole life as well as the life of his successors refutes this suspicion. Yet it is also true that natural science has this corrupting effect on all men who are not perfect (cf. I 62). For natural science surely affects the understanding of the meaning of the Law, of the grounds on which it is to be obeyed, and of the weight that is to be attached to its different parts. In a word, natural science upsets habits. By addressing a reader who is not conversant with natural science, Maimonides is compelled to proceed in a manner that does not upset habits or does so to the smallest possible degree. He acts as a moderate or conservative man.

But we must not forget that the *Guide* is written also for atypical addressees. In the first place, certain chapters of the *Guide* are explicitly said to be useful also for those who are simply beginners. Since the whole book is somehow accessible to the vulgar, it must have been written in such a way as not to be harmful to the vulgar (I Introd.; III 29). Besides, the book is also meant to be useful to such men of great intelligence as have been trained fully in all philosophic sciences and as are not in the habit of bowing to any authority—in other words, to men not inferior to Maimonides in their critical faculty. Readers of this kind will be unable to bow to Maimonides' authority; they will examine all his assertions, speculative or exegetic, with all reasonable severity; and they will derive great pleasure from all chapters of the *Guide* (I Introd.; I 55, 68 end, 73, tenth premise).

How much Maimonides' choice of his typical addressee affects the plan of his book will be seen by the judicious reader glancing at our scheme. It suffices to mention that no section or subsection of the *Guide* is devoted to the bodies that do not come into being and perish (cf. III 8 beginning, and I 11), that is, to the heavenly bodies, which according to Maimonides possess life and knowledge, or to "the holy bodies," to use the bold expression used by him in his Code (*M.T.*, H. Yesodei ha-Torah IV 12). In other words, no section or subsection of the *Guide* is devoted to the Account of the Beginning in the manner in which a section is devoted to the Account of the Chariot. More important, Maimonides' choice of his typical addressee is the key to the whole plan of the *Guide*, to the apparent lack of order or to the obscurity of the plan. The plan of the *Guide* appears to be obscure only so long as one does not consider the kind of reader for which the book is written or so long as one seeks for an order agreeing with the essential order of subject matter. We recall the order of the sciences: logic precedes mathematics, mathematics precedes natural science, and natural science precedes divine science; and we recall that while Joseph was sufficiently trained in logic and mathematics, he is supposed to be introduced into divine science without having been trained properly in natural science. Maimonides must therefore seek for a substitute for natural science. He finds that substitute in the traditional Jewish beliefs and ultimately in the biblical texts correctly interpreted: the immediate preparation for divine science in the *Guide* is exegetic rather than speculative. Furthermore, Maimonides wishes to proceed in a manner that changes habits to the smallest possible degree. He himself tells us which habit is in particular need of being changed. After having reported the opinion of a pagan philosopher on the obstacles to speculation, he adds the remark that there exists now an obstacle that the ancient philosopher had not mentioned because it did not exist in his society: the habit of relying on revered "texts," that is, on their literal meaning (I 31). It is for this reason that he opens his book with the explanation of biblical terms, that is, with showing that their true meaning is not always their literal meaning. He cures the vicious habit in question by having recourse to another habit of his addressee. The addressee was accustomed not only to accept the literally understood biblical texts as true but also in many cases to understand biblical texts according to traditional interpretations that differed considerably from the literal meaning. Being accustomed to listen to authoritative interpretations of biblical texts, he is prepared to listen to Maimonides' interpretations as authoritative interpretations. The explanation of biblical terms that is given by Maimonides authoritatively is in the circumstances the natural substitute for natural science.

But which biblical terms deserve primary consideration? In other words, what is the initial theme of the *Guide?* The choice of the initial theme is dictated by the right answer to the question of which theme is the most urgent for the typical addressee and at the same time the least upsetting to him. The first theme of the *Guide* is God's incorporeality. God's incorporeality is the third of the three most fundamental truths, the preceding ones being the existence of God and His unity. The existence of God and His unity were admitted as unquestionable by all Jews; all Jews as Jews know that God exists and that He is one, and they know this through the biblical revelation or the biblical miracles. One can say that because belief in the biblical revelation precedes speculation, and the discovery of the true meaning of revelation is the task of exegesis, exegesis precedes speculation. But regarding God's incorporeality there existed a certain confusion. The biblical texts suggest that God is corporeal, and the interpretation of these texts is not a very easy task (II 25, 31, III 28). God's incorporeality is indeed a demonstrable truth, but, to say nothing of others, the addressee of the *Guide* does not come into the possession of the demonstration until he has advanced into the Second Part (cf. I 1, 9, 18). The necessity to refute "corporealism" (the belief that God is corporeal) does not merely arise from the fact that corporealism is demonstrably untrue: corporealism is dangerous because it endangers the belief shared by all Jews in God's unity (I 35). On the other hand, by teaching that God is incorporeal, one does not do more than to give expression to what the talmudic Sages believed (I 46). However, the Jewish authority who had given the most consistent and the most popularly effective expression to the belief in God's incorporeality was Onqelos the Stranger, for the primary preoccupation of his translation of the Torah into Aramaic, which Joseph knew as a matter of course, was precisely to dispose of the corporealistic suggestions of the original (I 21, 27, 28, 36 end). Maimonides' innovation is then limited to his deviation from Onqelos' procedure: he does explicitly what Onqelos did implicitly; whereas Onqelos tacitly substituted noncorporealistic terms for the corporealistic terms occurring in the original, Maimonides explicitly discusses each of the terms in question by itself in an order that has no correspondence to the accidental sequence of their occurrence in the Bible. As a consequence, the discussion of corporealism in the *Guide* consists chiefly of a discussion of the various biblical terms suggesting corporealism, and, vice versa, the chief subject of what Maimonides declares to be the primary purpose of the *Guide*, namely, the explanation of biblical terms, is the explanation of biblical terms suggesting corporealism. This is not surprising. There are no biblical terms that suggest that God is not one, whereas there are many biblical terms that suggest that God is corporeal: the apparent difficulty created by the plural *Elohim* can be disposed of by a single sentence or by a single reference to Onqelos (I 2).

The chief reason why it is so urgent to establish the belief in God's incorporeality, however, is supplied by the fact that that belief is destructive of idolatry. It was, of course, universally known that idolatry is a very grave sin, nay, that the Law has, so to speak, no other purpose than to destroy idolatry (I 35, III 29 end). But this evil can be completely eradicated only if everyone is brought to know that God has no visible shape whatever or that He is incorporeal. Only if God is incorporeal is it absurd to make images of God and to worship such images. Only under this condition can it become manifest to everyone that the only image of God is man, living and thinking man, and that man acts as the image of God only through worshiping the invisible or hidden God alone. Not idolatry, but the belief in God's corporeality, is a fundamental sin. Hence the sin of idolatry is less grave than the sin of believing that God is corporeal (I 36). This being the case, it becomes indispensable that God's incorporeality be believed in by everyone, whether or not he knows by demonstration that God is incorporeal. With regard to the majority of men it is sufficient and necessary that they believe in this truth on the basis of authority or tradition, that is, on a basis that the first subsections of the *Guide* are meant to supply. The teaching of God's incorporeality by means of authoritative exegesis, that is, the most public teaching of God's incorporeality, is indispensable for destroying the last relics of paganism: the immediate source of paganism is less the ignorance of God's unity than the ignorance of His radical incorporeality (cf. I 36 with M.T., H. 'Abodah Zarah I 1).

It is necessary that we understand the character of the reasoning that Maimonides uses when he determines the initial theme of the *Guide*. We limit ourselves to a consideration of the second reason demanding the teaching of incorporeality. While the belief in unity leads immediately to the rejection of the worship of "other gods," but not to the rejection of the worship of images of the one God, the belief in incorporeality leads immediately only to the rejection of the worship of images or of other bodies, but not to the rejection of the worship of other gods: all gods may be incorporeal. Only if the belief in God's incorporeality is based on the belief in His unity, as Maimonides' argument indeed assumes, does the belief in God's incorporeality appear to be the necessary and sufficient ground for rejecting "forbidden worship" in every form, that is, the worship of other gods as well as the worship of both natural things and artificial things. This would mean that the prohibition against idolatry in the widest sense is as much a dictate of reason as the belief in God's unity and incorporeality. Yet Maimonides indicates that only the theoretical truths pronounced in the Decalogue (God's existence and His unity), in contradistinction to the rest of the Decalogue, are rational. This is in agreement with his denying the existence of rational commandments or prohibitions as such (II 33; cf. I 54, II 31 beginning, III 28; *Eight Chapters* VI). Given the fact that Aristotle believed in God's unity and incorporeality and yet was an idolater (I 71, III 29), Maimonides' admiration for him would be incomprehensible if the rejection of idolatry were the simple consequence of that belief. According to Maimonides, the Law agrees with Aristotle in holding that the heavenly bodies are endowed with life and intelligence and that they are superior to man in dignity; one could say that he agrees with Aristotle in implying that those holy bodies deserve more than man to be called images of God. But unlike the philosophers he does not go so far as to call those bodies "divine bodies" (II 4–6; cf. Letter to Ibn Tibbon). The true ground of the rejection of "forbidden worship" is the belief in creation out of nothing, which implies that creation is an absolutely free act of God or that God alone is the complete good that is in no way increased by creation. But creation is according to Maimonides not demonstrable, whereas God's unity and incorporeality are demonstrable. The reasoning underlying the determination of the initial theme of the *Guide* can then be described as follows: it conceals the difference of cognitive status between the belief in God's unity and incorporeality on the one hand and the belief in creation on the other; it is in accordance with the opinion of the Kalām. In accordance with this, Maimonides brings his disagreement with Kalām into the open only after he has concluded his thematic discussion of God's incorporeality; in that discussion he does not even mention the Kalām.

It is necessary that we understand as clearly as possible the situation in which Maimonides and his addressee find themselves at the beginning of the book, if not throughout the book. Maimonides knows that God is incorporeal; he knows this by a demonstration that is at least partly based on natural science. The addressee does not know that God is incorporeal; nor does he learn it yet from Maimonides: he accepts the fact that God's incorporeality is demonstrated, on Maimonides' authority. Both Maimonides and the addressee know that the Law is a source of knowledge of God; only the Law can establish God's incorporeality for the addressee in a manner that does not depend on Maimonides' authority. But both know that the literal meaning of the Law is not always its true meaning and that the literal meaning is certainly not the true meaning when it contradicts reason, for otherwise the Law could not be "your wisdom and your understanding in the sight of the nations" (Deut. 4:6). Both know, in other words, that exegesis does not simply precede speculation. Yet only Maimonides knows that the corporealistic expressions of the Law are against reason and must therefore be taken as figurative. The addressee does not know and cannot know that Maimonides' figurative interpretations of those expressions are true: Maimonides does not adduce arguments based on grammar. The addressee accepts Maimonides' interpretations just as he is in the habit of accepting the Aramaic translations as correct translations or interpretations. Maimonides enters the ranks of the traditional Jewish authorities: he simply tells the addressee what to believe regarding the meaning of the biblical terms. Maimonides introduces reason in the guise of authority. He takes on the garb of authority. He tells the addressee to believe in God's incorporeality because, as he tells him, contrary to appearance, the Law does not teach corporeality, because, as he tells him, corporeality is a demonstrably wrong belief.

But we must not forget the most important atypical addressee, the reader who is critical and competent. He knows the demonstration of God's incorporeality and the problems connected with it as well as Maimonides does. Therefore the exegetic discussion of God's incorporeality which is presented in the first forty-nine chapters of the *Guide*, and which is prespeculative and hence simply public as far as the typical addressee is concerned, is postspeculative and hence secret from the point of view of the critical and competent reader. The latter will examine Maimonides' explanations of biblical terms in the light of the principle that one cannot establish the meanings of a term if one does not consider the contexts in which they occur (II 29; cf. *Epistle to Yemen* 46, 7 ff.) or that while grammar is not a sufficient condition, it is surely the necessary condition of interpretation. For while the competent reader will appreciate the advantages attendant upon a coherent discussion of the biblical terms in question as distinguished from a translation of the Bible, he will realize that such a discussion may make one oblivious of the contexts in which the terms occur. He will also notice contradictions occurring in the *Guide*, remember always that they are intentional, and ponder over them.

The readers of the *Guide* were told at the beginning that the first purpose of the book is the explanation of biblical terms. They will then in no way be surprised to find that the book opens with the explanation of biblical terms in such a way that, roughly speaking, each chapter is devoted to the explanation of one or several biblical terms. They will soon become habituated to this procedure: they become engrossed by the subject matter, the What, and will not observe the How. The critical reader, however, will find many reasons for becoming amazed. To say nothing of other considerations, he will wonder why almost the only terms explained are those suggesting corporeality. It is perhaps not a matter of surprise that one chapter is devoted to the explanation of "place" and another to the explanation of "to dwell." But why is there no chapter devoted to "one," none to "merciful," none to "good," none to "intelligence," none to "eternity"? Why is there a chapter devoted to "grief" and none to "laughter"? Why is there a chapter devoted to "foot" and another to "wing," but none to "hand" nor to "arm"? Assuming that one has understood Maimonides' selection of terms, one still has to understand the order in which he discusses them. To what extent the explanation of terms is limited to terms suggesting corporeality appears with particular clarity when one considers especially those chapters that are most visibly devoted to the explanation of terms, the lexicographic chapters. By a lexicographic chapter I understand a chapter that opens with the Hebrew term or terms to be explained in the chapter regardless of whether these terms precede the first sentence or form the beginning of the first sentence and regardless of whether these terms are supplied with the Arabic article *al-* or not. The lexicographic chapter may be said to be the normal or typical chapter in the discussion of God's incorporeality (I 1–49); thirty out of the forty-nine chapters in question are lexicographic, whereas in the whole rest of the book there occur at most two such chapters (I 66 and 70). All these thirty chapters occur in I 1–45: two-thirds of the chapters in I 1–45 are lexicographic. Thus the question arises why nineteen chapters of the discussion of God's incorporeality—and just the nineteen chapters having both the subject matters and the places that they do—are not lexicographic. Why do ten of these thirty lexicographic chapters begin with Hebrew terms preceding the first sentence and twenty of them begin with Hebrew terms forming part of the first sentence? Thirteen of the terms in question are nouns, twelve are verbs, and five are verbal nouns: why does Maimonides in some cases use the verbs and in other cases the verbal nouns? Within the chapters, generally speaking, he discusses the term that is the subject of the chapter in question, first in regard to the various meanings it has when it is not applied to God and then in regard to the various meanings it has when applied to God; he proves the existence of each of these meanings in most cases by quoting one or more biblical passages; those quotations are sometimes explicitly incomplete (ending in "and so on") and more frequently not; the quotations used to illustrate a particular meaning of a particular term do not always follow the biblical order; they are frequently introduced by "he said," but sometimes they are ascribed to individual biblical authors or speakers; in most cases he does not add to the name of the biblical author or speaker the formula "may he rest in peace," but in some cases he does; sometimes "the Hebrew language" or "the language" is referred to. In a book as carefully worded as is the *Guide* according to Maimonides'

emphatic declaration, all these varieties, and others that we forgo mentioning, deserve careful consideration. It goes without saying that there is
not necessarily only one answer to each of the questions implied in each of
these varieties; the same device—for example, the distinction between lexicographic and nonlexicographic chapters or the tracing of a biblical quotation to an individual biblical author—may fulfill different functions in
different contexts. In order to understand the *Guide*, one must be fully
awake and as it were take nothing for granted. In order to become enabled
to raise the proper questions, one does well to consider the possibility that
there exists the typical chapter or else to construct the typical chapter, that
is, to find out which of the varieties indicated are most in accordance with
the primary function of the chapters devoted to the explanation of biblical
terms: only the other varieties are in need of a special reason.

The first chapter of the *Guide* is devoted to "image and likeness." The
selection of these terms was necessitated by a single biblical passage: "And
God said, Let us make man in our image, after our likeness. . . . So God
created man in his image, in the image of God created he him, male and
female created he them" (Gen. 1:26–27). The selection of these terms for
explanation in the first chapter is due to the unique significance of the passage quoted. That passage suggests to the vulgar mind more strongly than
any other biblical passage that God is corporeal in the crudest sense: God
has the shape of a human being, has a face, lips, and hands, but is bigger
and more resplendent than man since He does not consist of flesh and
blood, and is therefore in need, not of food and drink, but of odors; His
place is in Heaven from which He descends to the earth, especially to high
mountains, in order to guide men and to find out what they do, and to
which He ascends again with incredible swiftness; He is moved, as men
are, by passions, especially by anger, jealousy, and hate, and thus makes
men frightened and sad; His essence is Will rather than Intellect. (Cf. I
10, 20, 36–37, 39, 43, 46, 47, 68.) Maimonides tells his addressee that
ṣelem (the Hebrew term which is rendered by "image") does not mean, if
not exactly in any case, but certainly in the present case, a visible shape; it
means the natural form, the specific form, the essence of a being: "God
created man in his image" means that God created man as a being endowed with intellect or that the divine intellect links itself with man.

Similar considerations apply to the Hebrew term rendered by "likeness."
The Hebrew term designating form in the sense of visible shape is *to'ar*,
which is never applied to God. After having dispelled the confusion regarding "image" Maimonides says: "We have explained to thee the difference
between *ṣelem* and *to'ar* and we have explained the meaning of *ṣelem*."
He thus alludes to the twofold character of his explanation here as well as
elsewhere: one explanation is given to "thee," that is, to the typical
addressee, and another is given to indeterminate readers; the latter explanation comes to sight only when one considers, among other things, the

context of all biblical passages quoted. To mention only one example, the second of the three quotations illustrating the meaning of *to'ar* is "What form is he of?" (I Sam. 28:14). The quotation is taken from the account of King Saul's conversation with the witch of Endor, whom the king had asked to bring up to him the dead prophet Samuel; when the woman saw Samuel and became frightened and the king asked her what she saw, she said: "I saw gods (*elohim*) ascending out of the earth." The account continues as follows: "And he said unto her, What form is he of? And she said: an old man cometh up; and he is covered with a mantle." Maimonides himself tells us in the next chapter that *elohim* is an equivocal term that may mean angels and rulers of cities as well as God; but this does not explain why that term is also applied to the shades of the venerable departed—beings without flesh and blood—which frighten men either because those shades do not wish to be "disquieted," that is, they wish to rest in peace, or for other reasons. To say nothing of other reasons, the rational beings inhabiting the lowest depth are in truth not men who have died, but all living men, the Adamites, that is, the descendants of Adam, who lack Adam's pristine intellectuality (cf. I 2 with I 10). It looks as if Maimonides wished to draw our attention to the fact that the Bible contains idolatrous, pagan, or "Sabian" relics. If this suspicion should prove to be justified, we would have to assume that his fight against "forbidden worship" and hence against corporealism is more radical than one would be inclined to believe or that the recovery of Sabian relics in the Bible with the help of Sabian literature is one of the tasks of his secret teaching.

However this may be, his interpretation of Genesis 1:26 seems to be contradicted by the fact that the Torah speaks shortly afterward of the divine prohibition addressed to man against eating of the fruit of the tree of knowledge: if man was created as an intellectual being and hence destined for the life of the intellect, his Creator could not well have forbidden him to strive for knowledge. In other words, the biblical account implies that man's intellectuality is not identical with man's being created in the image of God, but is a consequence of his disobedience to God or of God's punishing him for that sin. As we are told in the second chapter, this objection was raised, not by the addressee of the *Guide*, but by another acquaintance of Maimonides, a nameless scientist of whom we do not even know whether he was of Jewish extraction and who was apparently not very temperate in regard to drink and to sex. (Compare the parallel in III 19.) Maimonides tells his addressee that he replied to his objector as follows: the knowledge that was forbidden to man was the knowledge of "good and evil," that is, of the noble and base, and the noble and base are objects not of the intellect, but of opinion; strictly speaking they are not objects of knowledge at all. To mention only the most important example, in man's perfect state, in which he was unaware of the noble and base, although he was aware of the naturally good and bad, that is, of the pleasant and painful, he did not regard the uncovering of one's nakedness as disgraceful.

After having thus disposed of the most powerful objection to his interpretation of Genesis 1:26, or after having thus taught that the intellectual life is beyond the noble and base, Maimonides turns to the second most important passage of the Torah that seems to suggest that God is corporeal. More precisely, he turns both to the terms applied in that passage to God and to kindred terms. The passage, which occurs in Numbers 12:8, reads as follows: "he (Moses) beholds the figure of the Lord." He devotes to this subject three chapters (I 3–5); in I 3 he discusses explicitly the three meanings of "figure," and in I 4 he discusses explicitly the three meanings of the three terms designating "beholding" or "seeing"; in one of the biblical passages partly quoted, the Lord is presented as having appeared to Abraham in the guise of three men who yet were one. Maimonides tells the addressee that the Hebrew terms designating "figure" and "beholding" (or their equivalents) mean, when they are applied to God, intellectual truth and intellectual grasp. The relation of I 5 to I 3–4 resembles the relation of I 2 and I 1. The view that man was created for the life of the intellect was contradicted by the apparent prohibition against acquiring knowledge. Similarly, "the prince of the philosophers" (Aristotle) apparently contradicts his view that man exists for the life of the intellect by apologizing for his engaging in the investigation of very obscure matters: Aristotle apologizes to his readers for his apparent temerity; in fact, he is prompted only by his desire to know the truth. This restatement of an Aristotelian utterance affords an easy transition to the Jewish view according to which Moses was rewarded with beholding the figure of the Lord because he had previously "hid his face; for he was afraid to look upon God" (Exod. 3:6). The pursuit of knowledge of God must be preceded by fear of looking upon God or, to use the expression that Aristotle had used in the passage in question (*On the Heaven* 291b 21 ff.) and that does not occur in Maimonides' summary, by sense of shame: the intellectual perfection is necessarily preceded by moral perfection—by one's having acquired the habit of doing the noble and avoiding the base—as well as by other preparations. Maimonides' emphasis here on moral perfection, especially on temperance, as a prerequisite of intellectual perfection is matched by his silence here on natural science as such a prerequisite. The weeding out of corporealism proceeds *pari passu* with the watering of asceticism.

Having arrived at this point, Maimonides does something strange: he abruptly turns to the explanation of the terms "man and woman" (I 6) and "to generate" (I 7). The strangeness, however, immediately disappears once one observes that I 6–7 are the first lexicographic chapters after I 1 and one remembers that I 2 is merely a corollary of I 1: the explanation of "man and woman" and of "to generate" forms part of the explanation of Genesis 1:26–27. There it is said that "in the image of God created (God man); male and female created he them." Literally understood, that saying might be thought to mean that man is the image of God because he is bisexual or that the Godhead contains a male and a female element that generate "children of God" and the like. Accordingly, the last word of I 7 is the same as the first word of I 1: "image." Maimonides does not discuss the implication which was stated, for it is one of the secrets of the Torah, and we are only at the beginning of our training. The explanation of the key terms (or their equivalents) occurring in Genesis 1:26–27 surrounds then the explanation of the key terms (or their equivalents) occurring in Numbers 12:8. The discussion of the most important passages of the Torah regarding incorporeality forms the fitting subject of the first subsection of the *Guide*. That subsection seems to be devoted to five unconnected groups of terms; closer inspection shows that it is devoted to two biblical passages: Maimonides seems to hesitate to sever the umbilical cord connecting his exegesis with Onqelos'.

At first glance the theme of the second subsection is much easier to recognize than that of the first. This seems to be due to the fact that that theme is not two or more biblical passages, but biblical terms designating phenomena all of which belong essentially together: place as well as certain outstanding places, occupying place, changing place, and the organs for changing place. Nineteen of the twenty-one chapters of the second subsection are manifestly devoted to this theme. The discussion begins with "place" (I 8), turns to "throne" (I 9), a most exalted place that if ascribed to God designates not only the temple but also and above all the heaven, and then turns to "descending and ascending" (I 10). While this sequence is perfectly lucid, we are amazed to find that, whereas I 8 and 9 are lexicographic chapters, I 10 is not a lexicographic chapter. This irregularity can be provisionally explained as follows: when Maimonides treats thematically several verbs in one lexicographic chapter, those verbs are explicitly said to have the same or nearly the same meaning (I 16, 18); when he treats thematically verbs that primarily designate opposites, but do not designate opposites if applied to God, he treats them in separate chapters (I 11, 12, 22, 23); but "descending" and "ascending" designate opposites both in their primary meaning and if applied to God: God's descending means both His revealing Himself and His punitive action, and His ascending means the cessation of His revelation or punitive action (cf. the silence on "returning" at the beginning of I 23). Maimonides indicates the unique character of the subject "descent and ascent" by treating it in a nonlexicographic chapter surrounded on the one side by four and on the other side by three lexicographic chapters. On the basis of "the vulgar imagination" God's natural state would be sitting on His throne, and sitting is the opposite of rising. "Sitting" and "rising" (I 11 and 12) designate opposites, but do not designate opposites if applied to God: although God's "sitting" refers to His unchangeability, His "rising" refers to His keeping His promises or threats, it being understood that His promises to Israel may very well be threats to Israel's enemies. A talmudic passage that confirms Maimonides' public explanation and in which "sitting" is mentioned together, not with "rising," but with "standing up" naturally leads to the discussion of "standing up" (I 13), which term, according to Maimonides, means, if applied to God, His unchangeability—an unchangeability not contradicted, as he indicates, by God's threats to destroy Israel.

Having arrived at this point, Maimonides interrupts his discussion of verbs or of other terms that refer to place and turns to the explanation of "man" (I 14). A similar interruption occurs shortly afterward when he turns from "standing" and "rock" (I 15 and 16) to an explanation of the prohibition against the public teaching of natural science (I 17). Although these chapters are subtly interwoven with the chapters preceding and following them, at first glance they strikingly interrupt the continuity of the argument. By this irregularity our attention is drawn to a certain numerical symbolism that is of assistance to the serious reader of the *Guide*: 14 stands for man or the human things and 17 stands for nature. The connection between "nature" and "change of place" (or, more generally, motion), and therewith the connection between the theme of I 17 and the subsection to which that chapter belongs, has been indicated before. The connection between "14" and the context cannot become clear before we have reached a better understanding of the relation between nature and convention; at present it must suffice to say that I 7 deals with "to generate." Although I 26 obviously deals with terms referring to place, it also fulfills a numerological function: the immediate theme of that chapter is the universal principle governing the interpretation of the Torah ("the Torah speaks according to the language of human beings"); 26 is the numerical equivalent of the secret name of the Lord, the God of Israel; 26 may therefore also stand for His Torah. Incidentally, it may be remarked that 14 is the numerical equivalent of the Hebrew for "hand"; I 28 is devoted to "foot": no chapter of the *Guide* is devoted to "hand," the characteristically human organ, whereas Maimonides devotes a chapter, the central chapter of the fourth subsection, to "wing," the organ used for swift descent and ascent. In all these matters one can derive great help from studying Joseph Albo's *Roots*. Albo was a favorite companion living at the court of a great king.

Of the twenty-one chapters of the second subsection sixteen are lexicographic and five (I 10, 14, 17, 26, 27) are not. Of these sixteen chapters two begin with Hebrew terms supplied with the Arabic article (I 23 and 24). Thus only seven of the twenty-one chapters may be said to vary from the norm. In seven of the fourteen chapters beginning with a pure Hebrew term, that term precedes the first sentence, and in the seven others the Hebrew term forms part of the first sentence. Seven of these chapters begin with a verb and seven with a noun or a verbal noun. It is one thing to observe these regularities and another thing to understand them. The distinction between the verbs and the verbal nouns is particularly striking, since lexicographic chapters beginning with verbal nouns occur only in one subsection. Furthermore, of the three lexicographic chapters of the first subsection, one opens with nouns preceding the first sentence, one with nouns forming part of the first sentence, and one with a verb preceding the first sentence; orderliness would seem to require that there be a chapter opening with a verb that forms part of the first sentence. One of the chapters of the second subsection (I 22) begins with a verb preceding the first sentence, but the first sentence opens with the verbal noun (supplied with the Arabic article) of the same verb; there occurs no other case of this kind in the whole book. If we count this ambiguous chapter among the chapters beginning with a verbal noun forming part of the first sentence, we reach this conclusion: the second subsection contains four chapters beginning with verbs or verbal nouns preceding the first sentence and eight chapters beginning with verbs or verbal nouns forming part of the first sentence. Furthermore, the second subsection contains six chapters beginning with verbs and six chapters beginning with verbal nouns; of the latter six chapters three begin with pure verbal nouns and three begin with verbal nouns supplied with the Arabic article. The second subsection surpasses the first subsection in regularity especially if I 22 is properly subsumed. From all this we are led to regard it as possible that I 22 somehow holds the key to the mystery of the second subsection.

The first chapter of the second subsection (I 8) is devoted to "place," a term that in postbiblical Hebrew is used for designating God Himself. To our great amazement Maimonides is completely silent about this meaning of "place." His silence is all the more eloquent since he quotes in this very chapter postbiblical Hebrew expressions containing "place," since he admonishes the readers in this very chapter to consult regarding his explanation of any term not only "the books of prophecy" but also other "compilations of men of science"—Talmud and Midrash are such compilations—and since he has concluded the preceding chapter with a quotation from the Midrash. In the only other lexicographic chapter devoted to a term used for designating God Himself—in I 16, which is devoted to "rock"—he does not hesitate to say that that term is also used for designating God, for that meaning of "rock" is biblical. We see then how literally he meant his declaration that the first intention of the *Guide* is to explain terms occurring in "the books of prophecy," that is, primarily in the Bible: he is primarily concerned with the theology of the Bible in contradistinction to postbiblical Jewish theology. He is alive to the question raised by the Karaites. As he puts it, not only does criticism of the talmudic Sages do no harm to them—it does not even do any harm to the critic or rather to the foundations of belief (I Introd., 5 end, 19 end, 46 end; cf. *Resurrection* 29, 10–30, 15 Finkel). This observation enables us to solve the difficulty presented by I 22.

I 18–21 opened with verbs; I 22 marks the transition from chapters opening with verbs to chapters opening with verbal nouns supplied with the Arabic article; I 23–24 open with verbal nouns supplied with the Arabic article. I 25 opens again with a verb. That verb is "to dwell." The transition made in I 22 and the procedure in I 23–24 make us expect that I 25 should open with the verbal noun "the dwelling," the *Shekhinah*, the postbiblical term particularly used for God's indwelling on earth, but this expectation is disappointed. Maimonides makes all these preparations in order to let us see that he is anxious to avoid as a chapter heading the term *Shekhinah*, which does not occur in the Bible in any sense, and to avoid the Hebrew term *Shekhinah* in its theological sense within the most appropriate chapter itself: when speaking there of the *Shekhinah* theologically, he uses the Arabic translation of *Shekhinah*, but never that Hebrew term itself. He does use the Hebrew term *Shekhinah* in a theological meaning in a number of other chapters, but *Shekhinah* never becomes a theme of the *Guide*: there are no "chapters on the *Shekhinah*" as there are "chapters on providence" or "chapters on governance" (I 40 and 44). It should also be noted that the chapter devoted to "wing" does not contain a single reference to the *Shekhinah* (cf. particularly Maimonides' and Ibn Janāḥ's explanation of Isaiah 30:20 with the Targum *ad loc.*). In the chapter implicitly devoted to the *Shekhinah*, which is the central chapter of the part devoted to incorporeality (I 1–49), Maimonides had mentioned the *Shekhinah* together with providence, but *Shekhinah* and providence are certainly not identical (cf. I 10 and 23). One should pay particular attention to the treatment of the *Shekhinah* in the chapters obviously devoted to providence strictly understood (III 17–18 and 22–23). With some exaggeration one may say that whereas the *Shekhinah* follows Israel, providence follows the intellect. In other words, it is characteristic of the *Guide* that in it *Shekhinah* as a theological theme is replaced by "providence," and "providence" in its turn to some extent by "governance," "governance" being as it were the translation of *Merkabah* ("Chariot"), as appears from I 70. Needless to say, it is not in vain that Maimonides uses the Arabic article at the beginning of I 23 and 24. He thus connects I 23 and 24 and the context of these chapters with the only other group of chapters all of which begin with a Hebrew term supplied with the Arabic article: III 36–49. That group of chapters deals with the individual biblical commandments, that is, with their literal meaning, rather than their extrabiblical interpretation, as is indicated in the chapter (III 41) that stands out from the rest of the group for more than one reason and that is devoted to the penal law. One reason why that chapter stands out is that it is the only chapter whose summary, in III 35, is adorned with a biblical quotation, III 35 being the chapter that serves as the immediate introduction to III 36–49. To repeat, the second subsection of the *Guide* draws our attention to the difference between the biblical and the postbiblical

Jewish teaching or to the question raised by the Karaites. Maimonides, it need hardly be said, answered that question in favor of the Rabbanites, although not necessarily in their spirit. It suffices to remember that not only *Shekhinah* but also "providence" and "governance" are not biblical terms.

Like the first subsection, the second subsection is based on two biblical passages, although not as visibly and as clearly as the first. The passages are Exodus 33:20–23 and Isaiah 6. In the former passage the Lord says to Moses: "Thou canst not see my face; for there shall no man see me, and live: . . . thou shalt see my back parts: but my face shall not be seen." Accordingly, Moses sees only the Lord's "glory pass by." In the latter passage Isaiah says: "I saw the Lord sitting upon a throne, high and lifted up. . . . Mine eyes have seen the king, the Lord of hosts." Isaiah does not speak, as Moses did, of "the figure of the Lord" or of "the image of God." Nor is it said of Isaiah, as it is said of Moses, Aaron, Nadab, Abihu, and seventy of the elders of Israel: "they saw the God of Israel: *and there was under his feet etc.* . . . And the nobles of the children of Israel . . . saw God, *and did eat and drink*" and thus suggested that the vision was imperfect (cf. I 5 with Albo's *Roots* III 17). We are thus induced to believe that Isaiah reached a higher stage in the knowledge of God than Moses or that Isaiah's vision marks a progress beyond Moses'. At first hearing, this belief is justly rejected as preposterous, not to say blasphemous: the denial of the supremacy of Moses' prophecy seems to lead to the denial of the ultimacy of Moses' Law, and therefore Maimonides does not tire of asserting the supremacy of Moses' prophecy. But the belief in the ultimacy of Moses' Law and even in the supremacy of Moses' prophecy in no way contradicts the belief in a certain superiority of Isaiah's speeches to Moses' speeches—to say nothing of the fact that Maimonides never denied that he deliberately contradicts himself. The following example may prove to be helpful. In his *Treatise on Resurrection*, Maimonides teaches that resurrection, one of the thirteen roots of the Law, is clearly taught within the Bible only in the book of Daniel, but certainly not in the Torah. He explains this apparently strange fact as follows: at the time when the Torah was given, all men, and hence also our ancestors, were Sabians, believing in the eternity of the world, for they believed that God is the spirit of the sphere, and denying the possibility of revelation and of miracles; hence a very long period of education and habituation was needed until our ancestors could be brought even to consider believing in that greatest of all miracles, the resurrection of the dead (26, 18–27, 15 and 31, 1–33, 14 Finkel). This does not necessarily mean that Moses himself did not know this root of the Law, but he certainly did not teach it. At least in this respect the book of Daniel, of a late prophet of very low rank (II 45), marks a great progress beyond the Torah of Moses. All the easier is it to understand that Isaiah should have made some progress beyond Moses.

The reason why progress beyond the teaching of the Torah is possible or even necessary is twofold. In the first place, the Torah is the law par excellence. The supremacy of Moses' prophecy—the superiority of Moses' knowledge even to that of the Patriarchs—is connected with its being the only legislative prophecy (I 63, II 13, 39). But precisely because his prophecy culminates in the Law, it reflects the limitations of law. Law is more concerned with actions than with thoughts (III 27–28; I Introd.). Mosaic theology reflects this orientation. According to the opinion of many of our contemporaries, Maimonides' theological doctrine proper is his doctrine of the divine attributes (I 50–60). In that subsection he quotes passages from the Torah only in that single chapter (I 54) in which he discusses the thirteen divine attributes revealed to Moses (Exod. 34:5–7); those attributes—all of them moral qualities—constitute the Mosaic theology; they express positively what in negative expression is called in the same context "God's back parts." Although God's goodness had been revealed to Moses in its entirety, the thirteen attributes articulate only that part of God's goodness which is relevant for the ruler of a city who is a prophet. Such a ruler must imitate the divine attributes of wrath and mercy, not as passions—for the incorporeal God is above all passion—but because actions of mercy or wrath are appropriate in the circumstances, and he must imitate God's mercy and wrath in due proportion. The ruler of a city, on the other hand, must be more merciful than full of anger, for extreme punitiveness is required only because of the necessity, based on "human opinion," to exterminate the idolaters by fire and sword (I 54). Following another suggestion of Maimonides (I 61–63) one could say that the adequate statement of Mosaic theology is contained in the divine name YHVH—a name by which God revealed Himself for the first time to Moses as distinguished from the Patriarchs: "I appeared unto Abraham, unto Isaac, and unto Jacob, by the name of God Almighty, but by my name YHVH was I not known to them" (Exod. 6:3). Maimonides recognizes that this verse asserts or establishes the superiority of Moses' prophecy to that of the Patriarchs (II 35), but he does not explain that verse: he does not explain, at least not clearly, which theological verities other than the thirteen attributes were revealed to Moses, but were unknown to the Patriarchs. Only this much may be said to emerge: Abraham was a man of speculation who instructed his subjects or followers, rather than a prophet who convinced by miracles and ruled by means of promises and threats, and this is somehow connected with the fact that he called "on the name of YHVH, the God of the world" (Gen. 21:33) (I 63, II 13), that is, the God of the transmoral whole rather than the law-giving God. It is this Abrahamitic expression that opens each Part of the *Guide* as well as other writings of Maimonides. Considering all these things, one will find it wise to limit oneself to saying that the Mosaic theology par excellence is the doctrine of the thirteen moral attributes.

Second, the Mosaic legislation was contemporary with the yet unbroken and universal rule of Sabianism. Therefore the situation in the time of Moses was not different from the situation in the time of Abraham, who disagreed with all men, all men having the same Sabian religion or belonging to the same religious community. The innovation was naturally resisted, even with violence, although it was not a principle of Sabianism to exterminate unbelievers. Yet the Torah has only one purpose: to destroy Sabianism or idolatry. But the resistance by the Sabians proper was less important than the inner Sabianism of the early adherents of the Torah. It was primarily for this reason that Sabianism could be overcome only gradually: human nature does not permit the direct transition from one opposite to the other. To mention only the most obvious example, our ancestors had been habituated to sacrifice to natural or artificial creatures. The sacrificial laws of the Torah are a concession to that habit. Since the simple prohibition or cessation of sacrifices would have been as unintelligible or distasteful to our ancestors as the prohibition or cessation of prayer would be now, God provided that henceforth all sacrifices be transferred to Him and no longer be brought to any false gods or idols. The sacrificial laws constitute a step in the gradual transition, in the progress from Sabianism to pure worship, that is, pure knowledge, of God (cf. I 54, 64); the sacrificial laws were necessary only "at that time." The Sabians believed that success in agriculture depends on worship of the heavenly bodies. In order to eradicate that belief, God teaches in the Torah that worship of the heavenly bodies leads to disaster in agriculture, whereas worship of God leads to prosperity. For the reason given, the open deprecation of sacrifices as such occurs not yet in the Torah, but in the prophets and in the Psalms. Conversely, the Torah is less explicit than the later documents regarding the duty of prayer (III 29, 30, 32, 35–37).

No less important an adaptation to Sabian habits is the corporealism of the Bible. For Sabianism is a form of corporealism; according to the Sabians, the gods are the heavenly bodies or the heavenly bodies are the body of which God is the spirit (III 29). As for the Bible, Maimonides' teaching on this subject is not free from ambiguity. The first impression we receive from his teaching is that according to it the corporealistic understanding of the Bible is a mere misunderstanding. For instance, *ṣelem* simply does not mean visible shape, but only natural form, and even if it should sometimes mean visible shape, the term must be considered to be homonymous, and it certainly does not mean visible shape, but natural form, in Genesis 1:26–27 (I 1; cf. I 49). In other cases, perhaps in most cases, the primary meaning of the term—say, "sitting"—is corporealistic, but when it is applied to God, it is used in a derivative or metaphoric sense; in those cases the meaning of the text, the literal meaning, is metaphoric. Generally stated, the literal meaning of the Bible is not corporealistic. But there are also cases in which the literal meaning is corporealistic, for instance, in the many cases in which the Bible speaks of God's anger (cf. I 29). One must go beyond this and say that generally speaking the literal meaning of the Bible is corporealistic because "the Torah speaks in accordance with the language of the children of Man," that is, in accordance with "the imagination of the vulgar," and the vulgar mind does not admit, at least to being with, the existence of any being that is not bodily; the Torah therefore describes God in corporealistic terms in order to indicate that He is (I 26, 47, 51 end). The Bible contains indeed innumerable passages directed against idolatry (I 36), but, as we have seen, idolatry is one thing and corporealism is another. The corporealistic meaning is not the only meaning, it is not the deepest meaning, it is not the true meaning, but it is as much intended as the true meaning; it is intended because of the need to educate and to guide the vulgar and, we may add, a vulgar that originally was altogether under the spell of Sabianism. What is true of the biblical similes is true also of the metaphoric biblical terms. According to the talmudic Sages, the outer of the similes is nothing, while the inner is a pearl; according to King Solomon, who was "wiser than all men" (I Kings 5:11), the outer is like silver, that is, it is useful for the ordering of human society, and the inner is like gold: it conveys true beliefs (I Introd.). Hence it is not without danger to the vulgar that one explains the similes or indicates the metaphoric character of expressions (I 33). For such biblical teachings as the assertions that God is angry, compassionate, or in other ways changeable, while not true, yet serve a political purpose or are necessary beliefs (III 28).

A third possibility emerges through Maimonides' thematic discussion of providence. There he makes a distinction between the view of the Law regarding providence and the true view (III 17, 23). He could well have said that the true view is the secret teaching of the Law. Instead he says that the true view is conveyed through the book of Job, thus implying that the book of Job, a nonprophetic book whose characters are not Jews and that is composed by an unknown author (II 45; *Epistle to Yemen* 50, 19–52, 1 Halkin), marks a progress beyond the Torah and even beyond the prophets (cf. III 19). We recall that the simple co-ordination, taught by the Torah, of the worship of the Lord with agricultural and other prosperity was merely a restatement of the corresponding Sabian doctrine. As Maimonides indicates when explaining the account of the revelation on Mount Sinai, the beautiful consideration of the texts is the consideration of their outer meaning (II 36 end, 37). This remark occurs within the section on prophecy in which he makes for the first time an explicit distinction between the legal (or exegetic) and the speculative discussion of the same subject (cf. II 45 beginning). Accordingly, he speaks in his explanation of the Account of the Chariot, at any rate apparently, only of the literal meaning of this most secret text (III Introd.). Or to state the matter as succinctly as Maimonides does in the last chapter, the science of the

Law is something essentially different, not only from the postbiblical or at any rate extrabiblical legal interpretation of the Law, but from wisdom, that is, the demonstration of the views transmitted by the Law, as well.

Undoubtedly Maimonides contradicts himself regarding Moses' prophecy. He declares that he will not speak in the *Guide* explicitly or allusively about the characteristics of Moses' prophecy because or although he has spoken most explicitly about the differences between the prophecy of Moses and that of the other prophets in his more popular writings. And yet he teaches explicitly in the *Guide* that Moses' prophecy, in contradistinction to that of the other prophets, was entirely independent of the imagination or was purely intellectual (II 35, 36, 45 end). His refusal to speak of Moses' prophecy has indeed a partial justification. At least one whole subsection of the section on prophecy (II 41–44) is devoted to the prophecy of the prophets other than Moses, as is indicated by the frequent quotation in that subsection of this passage: "If there be a prophet among you, I the Lord will make myself known unto him in a vision, and will speak unto him in a dream"; for the Bible continues as follows: "My servant Moses is not so, who is faithful in all my house" (Num. 12:6–7). Still the assertion that Moses' prophecy was entirely independent of the imagination leads to a great difficulty if one considers the fact, pointed out by Maimonides in the same context (II 36; cf. II 47 beginning), that it is the imagination that brings forth similes and, we may add, metaphors, as well as the fact that the Torah abounds, if not with similes, at any rate with metaphors. To mention only one example, Moses' saying that Eve was taken from one of Adam's ribs or that woman was taken out of man (Gen. 2:21–23) or derived from man reflects the fact that the word *ishah* (woman) is derived from the word *ish* (man), and such substitutions of the relation of words for the relation of things are the work of the imagination (cf. II 30 and 43; I 28; and *M.T.*, H. Yesodei ha-torah I).

In order to understand the contradiction regarding Moses' prophecy, we must return once more to the beginning. Maimonides starts from accepting the Law as seen through the traditional Jewish interpretation. The Law thus understood is essentially different from "demonstration" (II 3), that is, the views of the Law are not as such based on demonstration. Nor do they become evident through "religious experience" or through faith. For, according to Maimonides, there is no religious experience, that is, specifically religious cognition; all cognition or true belief stems from the human intellect, sense perception, opinion, or tradition; the cognitive status even of the Ten Commandments was not affected by or during the revelation on Mount Sinai: some of these utterances are and always remained matters of "human speculation," while the others are and always remained matters of opinion or matters of tradition (I 51 beginning and II 33; *Letter on Astrology* §§ 4–5 Marx; and *Logic* chap. 8). As for faith, it is, according to Maimonides, only one of the moral virtues, which as such do not belong to man's ultimate perfection, the perfection of his intellect (III 53–54). The views of the Law are based on a kind of "speculative perception" that human speculation is unable to understand and that grasps the truth without the use of speculative premises or without reasoning; through this kind of perception, peculiar to prophets, the prophet sees and hears nothing except God and angels (II 38, 36, 34). Some of the things perceived by prophets can be known with certainty also through demonstration. While for instruction in these things nonprophetic men are not absolutely in need of prophets, they depend entirely on prophets regarding those divine things that are not accessible to human speculation or demonstration. Yet the nonrational element in the prophetic speeches is to some extent imaginary, that is, infrarational. It is therefore a question how nonprophetic men can be certain of the suprarational teaching of the prophets, that is, of its truth. The general answer is that the suprarational character of the prophetic speeches is confirmed by the supranatural testimony of the miracles (II 25, III 29). In this way the authority of the Law as wholly independent of speculation is established wholly independently of speculation. Accordingly the understanding or exegesis of the Law can be wholly independent of speculation and in particular of natural science; and considering the higher dignity of revelation, exegesis will be of higher rank than natural science in particular; the explanations given by God Himself are infinitely superior to merely human explanations or traditions. This view easily leads to the strictest biblicism. "The difficulty of the Law" may be said to arise from the fact that the miracles do not merely confirm the truth of the belief in revelation but also presuppose the truth of that belief; only if one holds in advance the indemonstrable belief that the visible universe is not eternal can one believe that a given extraordinary event is a miracle (II 25). It is this difficulty that Maimonides provisionally solves by suggesting that Moses' prophecy is unique because it is wholly independent of the imagination, for if this suggestion is accepted, the difficulty caused by the presence of an infrarational element in prophetic speeches does not arise. Yet if Moses' prophecy alone is wholly independent of the imagination, the Torah alone will be simply true, that is, literally true, and this necessarily leads to extreme corporealism. Since corporealism is demonstrably wrong, we are compelled to admit that the Torah is not always literally true and hence, as matters stand, that the teaching of the other prophets may be superior in some points to that of Moses.

The fundamental difficulty of how one can distinguish the suprarational, which must be believed, from the infrarational, which ought not to be believed, cannot be solved by recourse to the fact that we hear through the Bible, and in particular through the Torah, "God's book" par excellence (III 12), not human beings but God Himself. It is indeed true in a sense that God's speech gives the greatest certainty of His existence, and His declaring His attributes sets these attributes beyond doubt (cf. I 9 and 11, II

11); but God Himself cannot explain clearly the deepest secrets of the Torah to flesh and blood (I Introd., 31 beginning); He "speaks in accordance with the language of the children of man" (I 26); things that might have been made clear in the Torah are not made clear in it (I 29); God makes use of ruses and of silence, for only "a fool will reveal all his purpose and his will" (I 40; cf. III 32, 45 and 54); and, last but not least, as Maimonides explains in the *Guide,* God does not use speech in any sense (I 23), and this fact entails infinite consequences. One is therefore tempted to say that the infrarational in the Bible is distinguished from the suprarational by the fact that the former is impossible, whereas the latter is possible: biblical utterances that contradict what has been demonstrated by natural science or by reason in any other form cannot be literally true, but must have an inner meaning; on the other hand, one must not reject views the contrary of which has not been demonstrated, that is, which are possible—for instance, creation out of nothing—lest one become thoroughly indecent (I 32, II 25).

Yet this solution does not satisfy Maimonides. Whereas he had originally declared that the human faculty that distinguishes between the possible and the impossible is the intellect, and not the imagination, he is compelled, especially in his chapters on providence, to question this verdict and to leave it open whether it is not rather the imagination that ought to have the last word (I 49, 73, III 15). He is therefore induced to say that the certainty of belief is one's awareness of the impossibility of the alternative or that the very existence of God is doubtful if it is not demonstrated or that man's intellect can understand what any intelligent being understands (I 50 and 51 beginning, 71, III 17). This is acceptable if the Account of the Beginning and the Account of the Chariot are indeed identical with natural science and divine science and if these sciences are demonstrative. But this enigmatic equation leaves obscure the place or the status of the fact of God's free creation of the world out of nothing: does this fact belong to the Account of the Beginning or to the Account of the Chariot or to both or to neither? (Cf. *Commentary on the Mishnah,* Ḥagigah II 1.) According to the *Guide,* the Account of the Chariot deals with God's governance of the world, in contradistinction not only to His providence (cf. I 44 on the one hand, and on the other I 40, where Maimonides refers to III 2 and not, as most commentators believe, to the chapters on providence, just as in III 2 he refers to I 40) but also to His creation. By considering the relation of the Account of the Beginning and the Account of the Chariot, one is enabled also to answer completely the question that has led us to the present difficulty: the question concerning the order of rank between the Mosaic theophany and the Isaian theophany. The Account of the Beginning occurs in the Torah of Moses, but the Account of the Chariot, which is identical with the divine science or the apprehension of God (I 34), occurs in the book of Ezekiel and in its highest form precisely in the sixth chapter of Isaiah (III 6; cf. also the quotations from the Torah on the one hand and from other biblical books on the other in III 54).

Once one has granted that there is an intrabiblical process beyond the teaching of Moses, one will not be compelled to deny the possibility of a postbiblical progress of this description. The fact of such a progress can be proved only if there are characteristic differences between the Bible and the postbiblical authoritative books. We could not help referring, for instance, to Maimonides' tacit confrontation of the talmudic view according to which the outer of the similes is "nothing" and of Solomon's view according to which it is "silver," that is, politically useful; taken by itself this confrontation suggests that Solomon appreciated the political to a higher degree than did the talmudic Sages. The differences in question are to some extent concealed, since the postbiblical view ordinarily appears in the guise of an explanation of a biblical text. Maimonides discusses this difficulty in regard to homiletic, rather than legal, explanations; he rejects both the opinion that these explanations are genuine explanations of biblical texts and the opinion that since they are not genuine explanations, they ought not to be taken seriously; in fact the talmudic Sages used a poetic or a charming device, playing as it were with the text of the Bible, in order to introduce moral lessons not found in the Bible (III 43). He indicates that he will not stress his critique of the talmudic Sages (III 14 end). Since the emphasis on serious differences between the Bible and the Talmud could appear in the eyes of the vulgar as a criticism of the talmudic Sages, he has spoken on this subject with considerable, although not extraordinary, restraint. Whenever he presents a view as a view of the Law, one must consider whether he supports his thesis at all by biblical passages and, if he does so, whether the support is sufficient according to his standards as distinguished from traditional Jewish standards. In other words, in studying a given chapter or group of chapters one must observe whether he uses therein any postbiblical Jewish quotations at all and what is the proportion in both number and weight of postbiblical to biblical quotations.

In the first chapter explicitly dealing with providence (III 17), he speaks of an "addition" to the text of the Torah that occurs "in the discourse of the Sages"; as one would expect, he disapproves of this particular "addition." This statement is prepared by an immediately preceding cluster of talmudic quotations that are in manifest agreement with the teaching of the Torah and that strike us with particular force because of the almost complete absence of talmudic quotations after the end of III 10. In this twofold way he prepares his silence on the future life in his presentation of the Torah view on providence: the solution of the problem of providence by recourse to the future life is more characteristic of the postbiblical teaching than of the Bible. According to the talmudic Sages, "in the future life there is no eating, nor drinking" and this means that the future life is incorporeal (*M.T.*, H. Teshubah VII 3). It follows that the Talmud is freer from corporealism than the Bible (I 46, 47, 49, 70, II 3). Accordingly certain talmudic thoughts resemble Platonic thoughts and are expressed with the help of terms of Greek origin (II 6). Similarly it was Onqelos the Stranger who more than anyone else made corporealism inexcusable within Judaism and may well have thought that it would be improper to speak in Syriac (that is, Aramaic), as distinguished from Hebrew, of God's perceiving an irrational animal (I 21, 27, 28, 36, 48; cf. II 33). The progress of incorporealism is accompanied by a progress of asceticism. To mention only one example, the Talmud is, to say the least, much clearer than the Bible about the fact that Abraham had never looked at his beautiful wife until sheer self-preservation compelled him to do so (III 8, 47, 49). There is a corresponding progress in gentleness (I 30 and 54). Finally, the Talmud is more explicit than the Bible regarding the value of the intellectual life and of learning for men in general and for prophets in particular (II 32, 33, 41, III 14, 25, 37, 54).

But even the Talmud and Onqelos do not contain the last word regarding the fundamentals, as Maimonides indicates by a number of remarks (I 21, 41, II 8–9, 26, 47, III 4–5, 14, 23). One example for each case must suffice. The talmudic Sages follow at least partly the opinion according to which the Law has no other ground than mere Will, whereas "we," says Maimonides, follow the opposite opinion (III 48). "We" is an ambiguous term. As Maimonides has indicated by as it were opening only two chapters (I 62 and 63) with "we," the most important meanings are "we Jews" and "Maimonides." As for Onqelos, he removes through his translation the corporealistic suggestions of the original, but he does not make clear what incorporeal things the prophets perceived or what the meaning of a given simile is; this is in accordance with the fact that he translated for the vulgar; but Maimonides explains the similes, and he is enabled to do so because of his knowledge of natural science (I 28). Progress beyond Onqelos and the Talmud became possible chiefly for two reasons. In the first place, the ever more deepened effect of the Torah on the Jewish people as well as the rise and political victory of Christianity and Islam have brought it about that the Sabian disease has completely disappeared (III 49, 29). Second, the fundamental verities regarding God are genuinely believed in by nonprophetic men only when they are believed in on the basis of demonstration, but this requires for its perfection that one possess the art of demonstration, and the art of demonstration was discovered by the wise men of Greece or the philosophers, or more precisely by Aristotle (II 15). Even Kalām, that is, what one may call theology or more precisely the science of demonstrating or defending the roots of the Law, which is directly of Christian origin, owes its origin indirectly to the effect of philosophy on the Law. In spite of its defects, the Kalām is very far from being entirely worthless; and properly understood, as prior to Maimonides it was not, it is even indispensable for the defense of the Law. Kalām entered Judaism long after the talmudic period, in the Gaonic period (I 71, 73). All the more must the introduction of philosophy into Judaism be regarded as a great progress, if it is introduced in due subordination to the Law or in the proper manner (that is, as Maimonides introduced it to begin with in his legal works). One must also consider the considerable scientific progress that was made by both Greeks and Muslims after Aristotle's time (II 4, 19). All this does not mean, however, that Maimonides regarded his age as the peak of wisdom. He never forgot the power of what one may call the inverted Sabianism that perpetuates corporealism through unqualified submission to the literal meaning of the Bible and thus even outdoes Sabianism proper (I 31); nor did he forget the disastrous effect of the exile (I 71, II 11): "If the belief in the existence of God were not as generally accepted as it is now in the religions [that is, Judaism, Christianity, and Islam], the darkness of our times would even be greater than the darkness of the times of the sages of Babylon" (III 29). This is to say nothing of the fact that Sabianism proper was not completely eradicated and could be expected to have a future (cf. I 36). It goes without saying that Maimonides also never forgot the Messianic future, a future that may or may not be followed by the end of the world (cf. I 61 with II 27). In spite of this, one is entitled to say that Maimonides regarded the step that he took in the *Guide* as the ultimate step in the decisive respect, namely, in the overcoming of Sabianism. As he modestly put it, no Jew had written an extant book on the secrets of the Law "in these times of the exile" (I Introd.). At the beginning, the power of Sabianism was broken only in a limited part of the world through bloody wars and through concessions to Sabian habits; those concessions were retracted almost completely by the post-Mosaic prophets, by the Aramaic translators, and by the Talmud, to say nothing of the cessation through violence of the sacrificial service and the conversion of many pagans, which was assisted by military victories, to Christianity or Islam. Now the time has come when even the vulgar must be taught most explicitly that God is incorporeal. Since the Bible suggests corporealism, the vulgar will thus become perplexed. The remedy for this perplexity is the allegoric explanation of the corporealistic utterances or terms that restores the faith in the truth of the Bible (I 35), that is, precisely what Maimonides is doing in the *Guide*. But the progress in overcoming Sabianism was accompanied by an ever increasing oblivion of Sabianism and thus by an ever increasing inability to remove the last, as it were, fossilized concessions to Sabianism or relics of Sabianism. Maimonides marks a progress even beyond the post-Mosaic prophets insofar as he combines the open depreciation of the sacrifices with a justification of the sacrificial laws of the Torah, for his depreciation of the sacrifices does not as such mean a denial of the obligatory character of the sacrificial laws. He is the man who finally eradicates Sabianism, that is, corporealism as the hidden premise of idolatry, through the knowledge of Sabianism recovered by him. He recovered that knowledge also through his study of Aristotle, who after all belonged to a Sabian society (II 23).

If the *Torah for the Perplexed* thus marks a progress beyond the Torah for the Unperplexed, Maimonides was compelled to draw the reader's attention at an early stage to the difference between the biblical and the postbiblical teaching. In that stage that difference alone was important. Hence to begin with he treats the Bible on the one hand and the postbiblical writings on the other as unities. Generally speaking, he introduces biblical passages by "he says" (or "his saying is") and talmudic passages by "they say" (or "their saying is"). He thus suggests that in the Bible we hear only a single speaker, while in the Talmud we hear indeed many speakers who, however, all agree, at least in the important respects. Yet in the first chapter of the *Guide* "he" who speaks is in fact first God, then the narrator, then God, and then "the poor one"; in the second chapter "he" who speaks is the narrator, the serpent, God, and so on; God "says" something, and the narrator "makes clear and says." But the *Guide* as a whole constitutes an ascent from the common view, or an imitation of the common view, to a discerning view. Accordingly, Maimonides gradually brings out the differences concealed by the stereotyped, not to say ritual, expressions. For instance, in I 32 he introduces each of four biblical quotations by the expression "he indicated by his speech"; only in the last case does he give the name of the speaker, namely, David; the saying of David is somewhat more akin in spirit than the preceding three sayings (of Solomon) to a saying of the talmudic Sages quoted immediately afterward; the talmudic Sages had noted that Solomon contradicted his father David (I Introd. toward the end). In I 34 he introduces by the expression "they say" the saying of a talmudic Sage who tells what "I have seen." The unnamed "he" who, according to I 44, spoke as Jeremiah's providence was Nebuchadnezzar. In I 49 he quotes five biblical passages; in two cases he gives the names of the biblical authors, in one of the two cases adding "may he rest in peace" to the name. In I 70 he introduces a talmudic passage with the expression "They said," while he says at the end of the quotation, "This is literally what he said." Names of biblical teachers occur with unusual frequency in some chapters, the first of which is II 19 and the last of which is III 32. Near the beginning of II 29 Maimonides notes that every prophet had a diction peculiar to him and that this peculiarity was preserved in what God said to the individual prophet or through him. The prophet singled out for extensive discussion from this point of view is Isaiah; thereafter six of the other prophets are briefly discussed in a sequence that agrees with the sequence of their writings in the canon; only in the case of the prophet who occupies the central place (Joel) is the name of the prophet's father added to the name of the prophet. One must also not neglect the references to the difference between the Torah proper and the Mishneh Torah, that is, Deuteronomy (cf. II 34–35 and III 24). Maimonides' link with the Torah is, to begin with, an iron bond; it gradually becomes a fine thread. But however far what one may call his intellectualization may go, it always remains the intellectualization of the Torah.

Our desire to give the readers some hints for the better understanding of the second subsection compelled us to look beyond the immediate context. Returning to that context, we observe that after Maimonides has concluded the second subsection, he again does something perplexing. The last chapter of the second subsection dealt with "foot"; that passage of the Torah on which the second subsection is based speaks emphatically of God's "face" and His "back"; nothing would have been simpler for Maimonides than to devote the third subsection to terms designating parts of the animate body or of the animal. Instead he devotes the fourth subsection to this subject; the first two chapters of the fourth subsection are devoted precisely to "face" and to "back" (I 37 and 38). The third subsection, which deals with an altogether different subject, thus seems to be out of place or to be a disconcerting insertion. Furthermore, the third subsection is the least exegetic or the most speculative among the subsections devoted to incorporeality; six of its eight chapters are not lexicographic; five of them are in no obvious sense devoted to the explanation of biblical terms and do not contain a single quotation from the Torah; one of these chapters (I 31) is the first chapter of the *Guide* that does not contain a single Jewish (Hebrew or Aramaic) expression, and another (I 35) does not contain a single quotation of Jewish (biblical or talmudic) passages. One is tempted to believe that it would have been more in accordance with the spirit of the book if the most speculative among the subsections devoted to incorporeality had formed the end of the part devoted to that subject.

In order to understand these apparent irregularities, it is best to start from the consideration that, for the general reason indicated, Maimonides desired to divide each of the seven sections of the *Guide* into seven subsections and that for a more particular reason he decided to treat unity in three subsections; hence incorporeality had to be treated in four subsections. Furthermore, it was necessary to place almost all lexicographic chapters within the part treating incorporeality, or conversely it was necessary that the majority of chapters dealing with incorporeality should be lexicographic. For the reasons given where they had to be given, it proved convenient that the majority of chapters of the first subsection should be nonlexicographic and the majority of chapters of the second subsection should be lexicographic. It is this proportion of the first two subsections that Maimonides decided to imitate in the last two subsections devoted to incorporeality: the majority of chapters of the third subsection became nonlexicographic, and the majority of chapters of the fourth subsection became lexicographic, but—for a reason to be indicated presently—in such a way that the third subsection is more predominantly nonlexicographic than the first, and the fourth subsection is more predominantly lexicographic than the second. It is reasonable to expect that the distribution of lexicographic and nonlexicographic chapters among the four subsections has some correspondence to the subject matter of those subsections. If one defines their subject matter by reference to the subject matter of their lexicographic chapters, one arrives at this result: the first subsection deals with the specific form, the sexual difference, and generating, while the third subsection deals with sorrow and eating; the second subsection deals chiefly with acts of local motion or rest, while the fourth subsection deals chiefly with the parts of the animate body and sense perception. To understand this arrangement it suffices both to observe that the first quotation regarding sorrow is "in sorrow thou shalt bring forth children" (Gen. 3:16) and to read Maimonides' explanation (in I 46) of the relation that links the parts of the animal and its acts to the ends of preservation. Furthermore, it would be a great mistake to believe that the emphasis on sorrow and eating is weakened because these two themes are the only lexicographic themes of the subsection in which they are discussed. Finally, Maimonides used in the most appropriate manner the lexicographic chapters devoted to sorrow and to eating as an introduction to the first series of speculative chapters occurring in the *Guide* and thus brought it about that the third subsection (in contradistinction to the first and the second) ends with nonlexicographic chapters (I 31–36); he thus prepared a similar ending of the fourth subsection (I 46–49); this enabled him to indicate by the position of the next lexicographic chapter (I 70), which is the last lexicographic chapter, as clearly as possible the end of the first section or the fact that I 1–70 form the first section.

The term '*aṣab*, which we thought convenient in our context to render by "sorrow," as well as the term "eating," may refer to God's wrath with those who rebel against Him or to His enmity to them. Since His wrath is directed exclusively against idolatry and since His enemies are exclusively the idolaters (I 36), the two terms refer indirectly to idolatry. But "eating" is used also for the acquisition of knowledge. With a view to this second metaphoric meaning of "eating," Maimonides devotes to the subject of human knowledge the five speculative chapters immediately following the explanation of "eating" (I 30). In the last chapter of the subsection (I 36) he reconsiders the prohibition against idolatry on the basis of what has emerged in the five speculative chapters. The third subsection deals then with both idolatry and knowledge in such a way that the discussion of idolatry surrounds the discussion of knowledge. This arrangement affects the discussion of knowledge: Maimonides discusses knowledge with a view to its limitations, to the harm that may come from it, and to the dangers attending it. One can say that the first series of speculative chapters occurring in the *Guide* deals with forbidden knowledge (cf. particularly I

32)—forbidden to all or to most men—within the context of forbidden worship.

The third subsection throws light on the relation between the Bible and the Talmud. Since we have treated this subject before, we limit ourselves to the following remark. In the chapter dealing with "eating," Maimonides explicitly refuses to give an example of the use of the word in its primary meaning: the derivative meaning according to which the word designates the taking of noncorporeal food has become so widespread as to become as it were the primary meaning (cf. the quotation from Isa. 1:20 with Isa. 1:19). Regarding the meaning of "eating" as consuming or destroying, which he illustrates by four quotations from the Torah and two quotations from the prophets, he says that it occurs frequently, namely, in the Bible; regarding the meaning of "eating" as acquiring knowledge, which he illustrated by two quotations from Isaiah and two from the Proverbs, he says that it occurs frequently also in the discourse of the talmudic Sages, and he proves this by two quotations. No talmudic quotation has illustrated the meanings of 'aṣab. The talmudic Sages compared the acquisition of knowledge of the divine things to the eating of honey and applied to that knowledge the saying of Solomon: "Hast thou found honey? Eat so much as is sufficient for thee, lest thou be filled therewith, and vomit it." They thus taught that in seeking knowledge one must not go beyond certain limits: one must not reflect on what is above, what is below, what was before, and what will be hereafter—which Maimonides takes to refer to "vain imaginings" (I 32): Maimonides, who explains what is meant by the fact that man has a natural desire for knowledge (I 34), warns, not against the desire for comprehensive knowledge, but against seeming knowledge.

With regard to the fourth subsection, we must limit ourselves to the observation that it is the first subsection that lacks any reference to philosophy or philosophers. On the other hand the expression "in my opinion" ('indī), which indicates the difference between Maimonides' opinion and traditional opinions, occurs about twice as frequently in the fourth subsection as in the first three subsections taken together. Another substitute is the references to grammarians in I 41 and 43—references that ought to be contrasted with the parallels in I 8 and 10—as well as the rather frequent references to the Arabic language. One grammarian is mentioned by name: Ibn Janāḥ, that is, the Son of Wing who with the help of Arabic correctly interpreted the Hebrew term for "wing" as sometimes meaning "veil" and who may therefore be said to have uncovered "Wing." Another substitute is the reference (in I 42) to an Andalusian interpreter who, in agreement with Greek medicine, had explained as a natural event the apparent resurrection of the son of a widow by the prophet Elijah. Through his quotations from the Bible in the same chapter Maimonides refers among other things to a severe illness caused by the circumcision of adults as well as to the biblical treatment of leprosy. The chapter in question deals with the Hebrew term for "living"; that term is the only one occurring in the lexicographic chapters of this subsection that is not said to be homonymous; this silence is pregnant with grave implications regarding "the living God" (cf. I 30 and 41).

The last chapter of the fourth subsection is the only chapter of the *Guide* that opens with the expression "The angels." This chapter sets forth the assertion that the angels are incorporeal, that is, it deals with the incorporeality of something of which there is a plurality. Maimonides thus makes clear that incorporeality, and not unity, is still the theme as it had been from the beginning. The next chapter opens the discussion of unity. Incorporeality has presented itself as a consequence of unity; unity has been the presupposition, an unquestioned presupposition. Unity now becomes the theme. We are told at the beginning that Unity must be understood clearly, not, as it is understood by the Christians, to be compatible with God's trinity, or, more generally stated, with a multiplicity in God (I 50). In the fifth subsection Maimonides effects the transformation of the common, not to say traditional, understanding of unity, which allowed a multiplicity of positive attributes describing God Himself, into such an understanding as is in accordance with the requirements of speculation. The fifth subsection is the first subsection of the *Guide* that may be said to be entirely speculative. Hence the discussion of unity, in contradistinction to the discussion of incorporeality, is characterized by a clear, if implicit, distinction between the speculative and the exegetic discussion of the subject. In the first four subsections there occurred only one chapter without any Jewish expression; in the fifth subsection five such chapters occur. In the first forty-nine chapters there occurred only nine chapters without any quotation from the Torah; in the eleven chapters of the fifth subsection ten such chapters occur. In spite of its speculative character the fifth subsection does not demonstrate that God is one; it continues the practice of the preceding subsections by presupposing that God is one (I 53, 58, 68). Yet from this presupposition it draws all conclusions and not merely the conclusion that God is incorporeal: if God is one, one in every possible respect, absolutely simple, there cannot be any positive attribute of God except attributes describing His actions.

Maimonides knows by demonstration that God is one. The addressee, being insufficiently trained in natural science (cf. I 55 with I 52), does not know unity by demonstration, but through the Jewish tradition and ultimately through the Bible. The most important biblical text is "Hear, O Israel, the Lord is our God, the Lord is one" (Deut. 6:4; cf. *M. T.*, H. Yesodei ha-Torah I 7). To our very great amazement, Maimonides does not quote this verse a single time in any of the chapters devoted to unity. He quotes it a single time in the *Guide*, imitating the Torah, which, as he says, mentions the principle of unity, namely, this verse, only once (*Resurrection* 20, 1–2). He quotes the verse in III 45, that is, the 169th chapter, thus perhaps alluding to the thirteen divine attributes ("merciful, gracious . . .") proclaimed by God to Moses. Whatever else that silence may mean, it certainly indicates the gravity of the change effected by Maimonides in the understanding of unity. The demonstrated teaching that positive attributes of God are impossible stems from the philosophers (I 59, III 20); it clearly contradicts the teaching of the Law insofar as the Law does not limit itself to teaching that the only true praise of God is silence, but it also prescribes that we call God "great, mighty, and terrible" in our prayers. Hence the full doctrine of attributes may not be revealed to the vulgar (I 59) or is a secret teaching. But since that doctrine (which includes the provision that certain points that are made fully clear in the *Guide* are not to be divulged) is set forth with utmost explicitness and orderliness in that book, it is also an exoteric teaching (I 35), if a philosophic exoteric teaching.

As Maimonides indicates, the meaning of "the Lord is one" is primarily that there is no one or nothing similar or equal to Him and only derivatively that He is absolutely simple (cf. I 57 end with I 58). He develops the notion of God's incomparability, of there being no likeness whatsoever between Him and any other being, on the basis of quotations from Isaiah and Jeremiah as distinguished from the Torah (cf. I 55 with I 54). He is silent here on Deuteronomy 4:35 ("the Lord he is God; there is none else beside him"), on a verse that he quotes in a kindred context in his Code (H. Yesodei ha-Torah I 4) and in different contexts in the *Guide* (II 33, III 32 and 51). Yet absolute dissimilarity or incomparability to everything else is characteristic of nothing as well as of God. What is meant by God's absolute dissimilarity or incomparability is His perfection; it is because He is of incomparable perfection that He is incomparable; it is because He is of unspeakable perfection that nothing positive can be said of Him in strict speech and that everything positive said of Him is in fact (if it does not indicate His actions rather than Himself) only the denial of some imperfection. The meaning of the doctrine of attributes is that God is the absolute perfect being, the complete and perfectly self-sufficient good, the being of absolute beauty or nobility (I 35, 53, 58, 59, 60 end, II 22). If this were not so, Maimonides' doctrine of attributes would be entirely negative and even subversive. For that doctrine culminates in the assertion that we grasp of God only that He is and not what He is in such a manner that every positive predication made of Him, including that He "is," has only the name in common with what we mean when we apply such predications to any being (I 56, 58, 59, 60). If we did not know that God is absolutely perfect, we would ascribe we know not what to what we do not know, in ascribing to Him "being," or we would ascribe nothing to nothing; we certainly would not know what we were talking about. What is true of "being" is true of "one," that is, of the immediate presupposition of the whole argument of the first section of the *Guide*. Let no one say that Maimonides admits attributes of action as distinguished from the negative attributes; for, not to enter into the question whether this distinction is ultimately tenable (cf. I 59), through the attributes of action God is understood as the cause of certain effects, and it is difficult to see how "cause," if applied to God, can have more than the name in common with "cause" as an intelligible expression. But since we understand by God the absolutely perfect being, we mean the goodness of His creation or governance when we say that He is the "cause" of something (cf. I 46). By his doctrine of attributes Maimonides not only overcomes all possible anthropomorphisms but also answers the question whether the different perfections that God is said to possess in the highest degree are compatible with one another or whether certain perfections known to us as human perfections—for instance, justice—can be understood to constitute in their absolute form divine perfection: God's perfection is an unfathomable abyss. Thus we understand why the doctrine in question, in spite of its philosophic origin, can be regarded as the indeed unbiblical but nevertheless appropriate expression of the biblical principle, namely, of the biblical teaching regarding the hidden God who created the world out of nothing, not in order to increase the good—for since He is the complete good, the good cannot be increased by His actions—but without any ground, in absolute freedom, and whose essence is therefore indicated by "Will," rather than by "Wisdom" (III 13).

From the speculative discussion of the divine attributes, which as positive predications about God Himself proved to be mere names, Maimonides turns in the second of the three subsections dealing with unity to the purely exegetic discussion of the divine names; the exegetic discussion still deals with "the denial of attributes" (I 62 and 65 beginning). It seems that the audible holy names have taken the place of the visible holy images, and it is certain that "name" is connected with "honor" and everything related to honor. The difficulty is caused less by the multiplicity of divine names—for, as the prophet says, in the day of the Lord "the Lord shall be one and his name shall be one" (Zech. 14:9)—than by the fact that this most sacred name, the only divine name antedating creation (I 61), is communicated to men by God (Exod. 6:2–3) and not coined or created by human beings. Since God does not speak, Maimonides must therefore open the whole question of God's speaking, writing, and ceasing to speak or to act (I 65–67). Furthermore, the most sacred name, which is the only name indicating God's essence and which thus might be thought to lead us beyond the confines of human speculation, is certainly no longer intelligible, since we know very little of Hebrew today (I 61–62). Therefore in the last subsection devoted to unity (I 68–70), which is the last subsection of the first section, Maimonides returns to speculation. It would be more accurate to say that he now turns to philosophy. In the three chapters in question he refers to philosophy, I believe, more frequently than in the whole discussion of incorporeality (I 1–49) and certainly more frequently than in the speculative discussion of the attributes (I 50–60); in the exegetic discussion of the divine names (I 61–67), if I am not mistaken, he does not refer to philosophy at all. He now with the support of the philosophers takes up the subject that we cannot help calling the divine attribute of intellect as distinguished from the divine attribute of speech in particular (cf. I 65 beginning). We learn that in God the triad "intellect, intellecting, and the intellected" are one and the same thing in which there is no multiplicity, just as they are one in us when we actually think (I 68). Maimonides does not even allude here to the possibility that "intellect" when applied to God has only the name in common with "intellect" when applied to us. It may be true that God thinks only Himself so that His intellection is only self-intellection and is therefore one and simple in a way in which our intellection cannot be one and simple, but this does not contradict the univocity of "intellect" in its application to God and to us. Self-intellection is what we mean when we speak of God as "living" (cf. I 53). It follows that even "life" is not merely homonymous when applied to God and to us. It likewise follows that what is true of the intellect is not true of the will: the act of willing and the thing willed as willed are not the same as the act of thinking and the thing thought as thought are the same. The reader of the next chapter (I 69) may find this observation useful for understanding Maimonides' acceptance of the philosophic view according to which God is not only the efficient or moving and the final cause of the world but also the form of the world or, in the expression of the Jewish tradition, "the life of the worlds," which he says means "the life of the world."

This must suffice toward making clear the perplexing and upsetting character of Maimonides' teaching regarding unity. The true state of things is somewhat obscured, to say nothing of other matters, by a certain kind of learning that some readers of the *Guide* can at all times be presumed to possess: the doctrine of attributes restates the Neoplatonic teaching, and Neoplatonism had affected Jewish thinkers long before Maimonides; those thinkers had already succeeded somehow in reconciling Neoplatonism with Judaism. But when different men do the same thing, it is not necessarily the same thing, and Maimonides surely did not do exactly the same thing as the pagan, Islamic, or Jewish Neoplatonists who preceded him. Every open-minded and discerning reader must be struck by the difference between the hidden God of Maimonides' doctrine of attributes and the hidden God who spoke to the Patriarchs and to Moses or, to employ Maimonides' manner of expression, by the difference between the true understanding of God as it was possessed by the Patriarchs and by Moses and the understanding of God on the part of the uninitiated Jews. The result of his doctrine of the divine attributes is that the notion of God that gives life and light to the ordinary believers not only is inadequate or misleading but is the notion of something that simply does not exist—of a merely imaginary being, the theme of deceived and deceiving men (I 60). What is true of the ordinary believer is true at least to some extent of the addressee of the *Guide*. The destruction of the old foundation forces him to seek for a new foundation: he is now compelled to be passionately concerned with demonstration, with the demonstration not only of God's unity but of His very being in a sense of "being" that cannot be entirely homonymous. For now he knows that the being of God is doubtful as long as it is not established by demonstration (I 71). Now he has been brought to the point where he must make up his mind whether or not he will turn altogether to the way of demonstration. Maimonides shows him three ways of demonstrating God's being, unity, and incorporeality: the way of the Kalām, the way of the philosophers, and Maimonides' own way (I 71 end, 76 end, II 1 end). While Maimonides cannot simply accept the philosophers' way, he prefers it to that of the Kalām for the following reason. The Kalām begins, not from the world as we know it through our senses or from the fact that things have determinate natures, but from asserting that what the philosophers call the nature, say, of air is only custom and hence of no inherent necessity: everything could be entirely different from what it is. The Kalām cannot live without reference to what we know through our senses, for in contradistinction to simple belief whose first premise is the absolute will of God, it attempts to demonstrate that God is, and hence it must start from the given and at the same time it must deny the authoritative character of the given. The philosophers on the other hand start from what is given or manifest to the senses (I 71, 73).

Maimonides turns first to the analysis and critique of the Kalām demonstrations. He presents the premises of the Kalām (I 73) and then the Kalām demonstrations that are based on those premises (I 74–76). Maimonides' critique does not limit itself to the technical Kalām reasoning. For instance, the first proof of the createdness of the world and therewith of the being of the Creator assumes that the bodies that we see around us have come into being through an artificer and infers from this that the world as a whole is the work of an artificer. This proof, which does not make any use of the premises peculiar to the Kalām, is based on inability, or at any rate failure, to distinguish between the artificial and the natural. The second proof is based on the premise that no infinite whatever is possible; it therefore first traces men to a first man, Adam, who came out of dust, which in turn came out of water, and then traces water itself to unqualified nothing out of which water could not have been brought into being except by the act of the Creator (I 74; cf. *Logic* chaps. 7, 8, 11). It is not difficult to recognize in this proof elements of biblical origin. Since the Kalām premises as stated by Maimonides are necessary for the Kalām proofs (I 73 beginning and toward the end) and the

Kalām proofs do not in all cases follow from those premises, those premises while necessary are not sufficient. After all, the Kalām selected its premises with a view to proving the roots of the Law: the premise of its premises is those roots. While the First Part ends with the critique of the Kalām, the Second Part opens with "The premises required for establishing the being of God and for demonstrating that He is not a body nor a force in a body and that He is one," that is, with the premises established by the philosophers. Maimonides thus indicates that the seventy-six chapters of the First Part, which lead up to philosophy through a critique of the popular notions of God as well as of theology, are negative and prephilosophic, whereas the one hundred and two chapters of the Second and Third Parts are positive or edifying. In other words, the First Part is chiefly devoted to biblical exegesis and to the Kalām, that is, to the two translogical and transmathematical subjects mentioned even in the very Epistle Dedicatory.

The Kalām proves that God as the Creator is, is one, and is incorporeal by proving first that the world has been created; but it proves that premise only by dialectical or sophistical arguments. The philosophers prove that God is, is one, and is incorporeal by assuming that the world is eternal, but they cannot demonstrate that assumption. Hence both ways are defective. Maimonides' way consists in a combination of these two defective ways. For, he argues, "the world is eternal—the world is created" is a complete disjunction; since God's being, unity, and incorporeality necessarily follow from either of the only two possible assumptions, the basic verities have been demonstrated by this very fact (I 71, II 2). Yet the results from opposed premises cannot be simply identical. For instance, someone might have said prior to World War II that Germany would be prosperous regardless of whether she won or lost the war; if she won, her prosperity would follow immediately; if she lost, her prosperity would be assured by the United States of America who would need her as an ally against Soviet Russia; but the predictor would have abstracted from the difference between Germany as the greatest power which ruled tyrannically and was ruled tyrannically, and Germany as a second-rank power ruled democratically. The God whose being is proved on the assumption of eternity is the unmoved mover, thought that thinks only itself and that as such is the form or the life of the world. The God whose being is proved on the assumption of creation is the biblical God who is characterized by Will and whose knowledge has only the name in common with our knowledge. If we consider the situation as outlined by Maimonides, we see that what is demonstrated by his way is only what is common to the two different notions of God or what is neutral to the difference between God as pure Intellect and God as Will or what is beyond that difference or what has only the name in common with either Intellect or Will. But God thus understood is precisely God as presented in the doctrine of attributes: Maimonides' demonstration of God's being illumines retroactively his merely as-sertoric doctrine of attributes. God thus understood can be said to be more extramundane not only than the philosophers' God but even than the bib-lical God; this understanding of God lays the foundation for the most radical asceticism both theoretical and practical (III 51). In other words, both opposite assumptions lead indeed to God as the most perfect being; yet even the Sabians regard their god, that is, the sphere and its stars, as the most perfect being (III 45); generally stated, everyone understands by God the most perfect being in the sense of the most perfect possible being; the doctrine of attributes understood in the light of its subsequent demon-stration leads to God as the most perfect being whose perfection is charac-terized by the fact that in Him Intelligence and Will are indistinguishable because they are both identical with His essence (cf. I 69). Yet, since the world is of necessity either created or eternal, it becomes necessary to re-store the distinction between Intellect and Will. Generally speaking, the *Guide* moves between the view that Intellect and Will are indistinguish-able and the view that they must be distinguished (and hence that one must understand God as Intelligence rather than as Will) in accordance with the requirements of the different subjects under discussion (cf. II 25 and III 25). For instance, in his discussion of Omniscience—in the same context in which he reopens the question regarding the relative rank of imagination and intellect—Maimonides solves the difficulty caused by the apparent incompatibility of Omniscience and human freedom (III 17) by appealing to the identity of Intellect and Will, whereas in his discussion of the reasons for the biblical commandments he prefers the view that the commandments stem from God's intellect to the view that they stem from His will.

The reader of the *Guide* must consider with the proper care not only the outline of Maimonides' way but also all its windings. In doing this he must never forget that the demonstration of the basic verities and the discussion of that demonstration are immediately preceded by the discussion of unity or that the discussion of unity constitutes the transition from exegesis to speculation. If the world, or more precisely the sphere, is created, it is indeed self-evident that it was created by some agent, but it does not nec-essarily follow that the creator is one, let alone absolutely simple, and that he is incorporeal. On the other hand, if the sphere is eternal, it follows, as Aristotle has shown, that God is and is incorporeal; but on this assumption the angels or separate intelligences, each of which is the mover of one of the many spheres, are as eternal as God (cf. I 71, II 2 and 6). It is there-fore a question whether monotheism strictly understood is demonstrable. Maimonides does say that unity and also incorporeality follow from certain philosophic proofs that do not presuppose either the eternity of the world or its creation, but it is, to say the least, not quite clear whether the proofs in question do not in fact presuppose the eternity of the world (cf. II 2 with II 1). Besides, if there were such proofs, one is tempted to say that there is no need whatever for provisionally granting the eternity of the world in order to demonstrate God's being, unity, and incorporeality; yet Maimonides asserts most emphatically that there is such a need. None of these or similar difficulties is, however, by any means the most serious difficulty. For while the belief in God's unity, being, and incorporeality is required by the Law, that belief, being compatible with the belief in the eternity of the world, is compatible with the unqualified rejection of the Law: the Law stands or falls by the belief in the creation of the world. It is therefore incumbent on Maimonides to show that Aristotle or Aristotelianism is wrong in holding that the eternity of the world has been demonstrated: the eternity of the world which was the basis of the demonstration of God's being, unity, and incorporeality is a dubious assumption. Yet it is not sufficient to refute the claims of Aristotelianism in order to establish the possibility of creation as the Law understands creation, for if the world is not necessarily eternal it may still have been created out of eternal matter. Maimonides is then compelled to abandon or at any rate to refine the disjunction on which his original argument was based. The original disjunction (the world is either eternal or created) is incomplete at least to the extent that it blurs the difference between creation out of matter and creation out of nothing. It brings out the opposition between Aristotle and the Law, but it conceals the intermediate possibility presented in Plato's *Timaeus*. Plato's version of the doctrine of eternity is not inimical to the Law, for while Aristotle's version excludes the possibility of any miracle, the Platonic version does not exclude all miracles as necessarily impossible.

Maimonides does not say which miracles are excluded by the Platonic teaching. Two possible answers suggest themselves immediately. It is according to nature that what has come into being will perish; but according to the Law both Israel and the souls of the virtuous have come into being and will not perish; hence their eternity *a parte post* is a miracle—a miracle that is more in accordance with creation out of nothing than with creation out of eternal matter. Second, God's special providence for Israel, according to which Israel prospers if it obeys and is miserable if it disobeys, is a miracle not likely to be admitted by Plato, whose teaching on providence seems to have been identical with that presented in the Book of Job: providence follows naturally the intelligence of the individual human being. In accordance with his judgment on the relation between the Aristotelian doctrine and the doctrine of the Law, Maimonides proves by an extensive argument that the Aristotelian doctrine is not demonstrated and is in addition not probable. As for the Platonic doctrine, he explicitly refuses to pay any attention to it on the additional ground that it has not been demonstrated (II 13, 25–27, 29, III 18; *Yemen* 24, 7–10; *Resurrection* 33, 16–36, 17; *Letter on Astrology* §§ 19 ff. Marx). That ground is somewhat strange because according to Maimonides the Aristotelian and the biblical alternatives have not been demonstrated either. In his critique of the Aristotelian doctrine he makes use of the Kalām argument based on a premise that so defines the possible that it might be either the imaginable or the nonself-contradictory or that regarding which we cannot make any definite assertions because of our lack of knowledge; the premise in question excludes the view according to which the possible is what is capable of being or what is in accordance with the nature of the thing in question or with what possesses an available specific substratum (cf. I 75, II 14, III 15). The reader must find out what the premises of the preferred premise are, how Maimonides judges of those premises, and whether the argument based on the premise in question renders improbable not only the eternity of the visible universe but the eternity of matter as well.

At any rate, being compelled to question the Aristotelian doctrine, Maimonides is compelled to question the adequacy of Aristotle's account of heaven. That questioning culminates in the assertions that Aristotle had indeed perfect knowledge of the sublunar things, but hardly any knowledge of the things of heaven, and ultimately that man as man has no such knowledge: man has knowledge only of the earth and the earthly things, that is, of beings that are bodies or in bodies. In the words of the Psalmist (115:16): "The heavens, even the heavens, are the Lord's; but the earth hath he given to the children of Man." Accordingly, Maimonides suggests that the truth regarding providence, that is, that theological truth which is of vital importance to human life, comes to sight by the observation of the sublunar phenomena alone. Even the proof of the First Mover of heaven, that is, the philosophic proof of God's being, unity, and incorporeality, to say nothing of the being of the other separate intelligences, becomes a subject of perplexity (II 22, 24; cf. II 3, 19, III 23). And yet it was knowledge of heaven that was said to supply the best proof, not to say the only proof, of the being of God (II 18). Maimonides has said earlier that very little demonstration is possible regarding divine matters and much of it regarding natural matters (I 31). Now he seems to suggest that the only genuine science of beings is natural science or a part of it. It is obvious that one cannot leave it at this apparent suggestion. The least that one would have to add is that the strange remarks referred to occur within the context in which Maimonides questions Aristotle's account of heaven in the name of astronomy or, more precisely, in which he sets forth the conflict between philosophic cosmology and mathematical astronomy—that conflict which he calls "the true perplexity": the hypotheses on which astronomy rests cannot be true, and yet they alone enable one to give an account of the heavenly phenomena in terms of circular and uniform motions. Astronomy shows the necessity of recurring for the purpose of calculation and prediction to what is possible in a philosophically inadmissible sense (II 24).

We have been compelled to put a greater emphasis on Maimonides' perplexities than on his certainties, and in particular on his vigorous and skillful defense of the Law, because the latter are more easily accessible than the former. Besides, what at first glance seems to be merely negative is negative only in the sense in which every liberation, being a liberation not only to something but also from something, contains a negative ingredient. So we may conclude with the words of Maimonides with which we began: The *Guide* is "a key permitting one to enter places the gates to which were locked. When those gates are opened and those places are entered, the souls will find rest therein, the bodies will be eased of their toil, and the eyes will be delighted."

7 / Marsilius of Padua

Marsilius, whose chief work is entitled *Defender of the Peace* (1324), was a Christian Aristotelian. But both his Christianity and his Aristotelianism differ profoundly from the beliefs of the most celebrated Christian Aristotelian, Thomas Aquinas. Marsilius lives as it were in another world than Thomas. In the whole *Defender* he refers to Thomas only once, but even then, when he claims to quote Thomas, he in fact quotes only the statement of another authoritative Christian writer which Thomas had inserted (with that writer's name) [1] in a compilation he had made. Thomas had accepted the traditional ecclesiastical polity of the Roman Church. Marsilius admits that the Christian priesthood is divinely established as distinct from the Christian laity, both being part of the Christian order; but he denies that the ecclesiastical hierarchy is divinely established. According to him all Christian priests are essentially equal in all respects as far as divine right is concerned. He also denies that any priest, even if he be bishop or pope, has by divine right any of the following powers: the power to command or to coerce; the power to decide whether and how coercion is to be exercised against apostates and heretics, be they subjects or princes; and the power to determine in a legally binding way what is orthodox and what is heretical. But we cannot go into Marsilius' doctrine of the Church, although it was of the greatest political importance, especially during the Reformation, for that doctrine belongs to political theology rather than to political philosophy. By following this distinction, we do not distort Marsilius' teaching, for he himself distinguishes throughout his work the political teaching which is "demonstrated" by "human demonstration" from the political teaching which is revealed by God immediately or mediately and is therefore accepted by simple faith as distinguished from reason.[2] This is not to deny that the principle of his doctrine regarding the Christian priesthood supplies the key to almost all the difficulties in which his work abounds, for that principle explains his only explicit deviation from the teaching of Aristotle.

As regards the principles of political philosophy, Marsilius presents himself as a strict follower of Aristotle, "the divine philosopher" or "the pagan sage." [3] He explicitly agrees with Aristotle regarding the purpose of the commonwealth: the commonwealth exists for the sake of the good life, and the good life consists in being engaged in the activity becoming a free man, that is, in the exercise of the virtues of the practical as well as of the speculative soul. While practical or civic felicity "seems to be" the end of human acts, in fact the activity of the metaphysician is more perfect than the activity of the prince who is the active or political man par excellence.[4] Marsilius explicitly agrees with Aristotle in regarding the purpose of the commonwealth as the ground for the other kinds of causes (material, formal, and moving) of the commonwealth and of its parts. He explicitly agrees with him in very many other points. He has only one reservation against Aristotle: Aristotle did not know one very grave disease of civil society, an "evil thing, the common enemy of the human race" which must be eradicated. This ignorance does not derogate from Aristotle's supreme wisdom. Aristotle did not know the "pestilence" in question because he could not know it, for it was the accidental consequence of a miracle, and it could have been even less foreseen by the wisest man than the miracle itself. The miracle was the Christian revelation, and the grave disease arose from the claims, in no way supported by Scripture, of the Christian hierarchy—claims which culminate in the notion of papal plenitude of power. Marsilius declares that this is the only political disease with which he will deal, since the others have been properly dealt with by Aristotle.[5] One ought therefore not even to expect to find a complete presentation of political philosophy in the *Defender*. The work comes to sight as a kind of appendix to that part of Aristotle's *Politics* which may be said to deal with the diseases of civil society.

Yet Aristotle's unawareness of a single, if unusually grave, disease of civil society is only the reverse side of his fundamental error: he was a pagan. That error affects his political philosophy immediately only in one point, however: in the teaching regarding the priesthood. He did not know the true Christian priesthood, but only the false pagan priesthoods. This does not mean that his teaching regarding the priesthood is entirely wrong. On the contrary, within political philosophy that teaching is in the main correct. He saw clearly that the priesthood forms a necessary part of the commonwealth, even a noble part, but cannot be the ruling part: priests cannot have the power to rule or to judge. He also saw clearly that it cannot be left entirely to the individuals whether they become priests or not; the number as well as the qualifications of the priests, and in particular the admission of foreigners to priesthood in the commonwealth, is subject to the decision of the government of the commonwealth. The Christian revelation does not contradict this demonstrated teaching,[6] since revelation is indeed above reason, but not against reason. Nor is this all. Aristotle did not indeed know the true ground of the priesthood, which can only be divine revelation. But if not Aristotle, at any rate other philosophers (who, as philosophers, did not believe in another life) devised or accepted allegedly divine laws accompanied with sanctions in another life, because they held that such sanctions would induce the nonphilosophers to avoid the vices and to cultivate the virtues in this life. Christianity is a truly divine law, and the Christian faith in punishments and rewards after death is the true faith; on the basis of the Christian faith one may then indeed say that the commonwealth is directed toward both this-worldly felicity and otherworldly bliss. But since the otherworldly end cannot be known or demonstrated, political philosophy must conceive of that end as a postulated means for promoting the this-worldly end. Besides, while Christianity is exclusively or chiefly concerned with the other life, it too makes men's fate in the other world dependent on how they lived in this world, and it too contends that the belief in punishments and rewards after death is also politically salutary.[7] The reasoning of the pagan philosophers is then true and therefore may be said to form a part of the demonstrated political teaching. At any rate, that reasoning leads to the philosophic concept, accepted by Marsilius, of the "sect" as a society constituted by belief in a peculiar divine law or by a peculiar religion; that concept embraces equally all allegedly and all truly divine laws, for the truth of the true religion escapes philosophy as philosophy. This religiously neutral concept of the sect is an essential part of Marsilian political science, just as it had been of al-Farabi's political science.[8] It leads to the rational concept of the priesthood according to which the priests are essentially teachers and not rulers or judges: the essential function of the priests in any divine law is to teach a salutary doctrine concerning the afterlife or, more generally, to teach the divine law in which their society happens to believe. The priests are the only teachers who as teachers form a part of the commonwealth.[9] According to Aristotle's *Politics*, the priests form indeed one of the six parts of the commonwealth, but their function does not consist in teaching. Marsilius' deviation from Aristotle in this point is, however, not based on a misunderstanding; he deviates from the letter rather than from the spirit of his master. By asserting that the priesthood is the only part of the commonwealth which is essentially dedicated to teaching, Marsilius draws our attention to the most important fact that, according to Aristotle, the philosophers, so far from being the ruling part of the best commonwealth, as they are according to Plato, are not even as such a part of any commonwealth, for the end of the commonwealth as commonwealth is not speculative perfection: cities and nations do not philosophize.

The fact that the pagan philosophers in general and Aristotle in particular elaborated the rational teaching regarding the priesthood does not mean that Aristotle's whole teaching on this subject is true. According to Aristotle, the action of the priest is less noble or perfect than the action of the ruler, but in "the law of the Christians," and only in that law, the action of the priest is the most perfect of all. According to Aristotle, only old men of the upper class ought to be priests, another point which is denied by Christianity. Finally, according to Aristotle, the priests are simply citizens, but, since the Christian priests ought to imitate Christ and hence to live in evangelical poverty and humility, it would appear that they must not have anything to do with the things that are Caesar's.[10]

The diseases of the commonwealth which Aristotle had discussed endanger this or that kind of government or render good government impossible. But in Marsilius' opinion the disease with which the *Defender* is concerned renders any government impossible, for it destroys the unity of the government and of the legal order, or it brings about permanent anarchy since it consists in the belief that the Christian is subject in this world to two governments (the spiritual and the temporal) which are bound to conflict. That disease endangers not only the good life or the fruits of peace, for the sake of which the commonwealth exists, but mere life or mere peace which is merely the condition—although the necessary condition—for the realization of the true end of the commonwealth. From this we see how appropriate the title of Marsilius' work is: the work is a defender, not of faith, but of peace, and of nothing but peace—not, to repeat, because peace is the highest good or the only political good, but because, being a tract for the time, the work is chiefly concerned with the disease of the time. This is the reason why Marsilius apparently lowers his sights. Thus he abstracts from the question concerning the best regime without in any way denying its importance: any regime is better than anarchy. Thus he is more concerned with mere law, with law as law, than with good laws or the best laws, and with mere government than with the best government. Thus he is satisfied with mere consent as the criterion of legitimacy as distinguished from the level of consent. Aristotle had as it were provided against Marsilius' predicament. When Marsilius in effect says that the law as law need not be good or just whereas the perfect law must be just, he is in entire agreement with Aristotle's remark that a ruler is no less a ruler because he rules unjustly, or with the usage of Aristotle and indeed of common sense which entitles us to speak of bad or unjust laws; to say nothing of the fact that when Aristotle opposes slavery by nature to slavery by law, he certainly does not mean by law a just law. When Marsilius frequently or mostly abstracts from the fact that the commonwealth is ordered toward virtue, he acts in entire agreement with Aristotle's observation that almost all cities are not concerned with virtue—an observation which does not prevent Aristotle from calling those bad cities "cities." [11]

Marsilius' sole reservation against Aristotle was the immediate consequence of the fact that Aristotle was a pagan. It concerned political philosophy or the rational political teaching only accidentally. Still, according to Aristotle, the best polity is the rule of gentlemen who rule their city, a fairly small society, and are enabled to do so because they are men of wealth. How can such men be thought to be rulers in a Christian society where they would have to rule Christian priests and hence the Church? For in a Christian society the activity of the priest is more noble than that of the ruler. Furthermore, the Church is universal. Finally, the best men in Christendom, that is, the best Christians, must live in evangelical poverty. This was the problem which Marsilius believed he had to solve and that he had solved.

The problem of how to reconcile the Aristotelian principle (the men dedicated to the most noble practical activity ought to rule in their own right) with the Christian principle (the activity of the priest is more noble than that of the gentleman) could seem to have been solved in the clearest and simplest manner by the doctrine of papal plenitude of power. Marsilius avoids that conclusion within the confines of political philosophy by teaching that in every commonwealth the fundamental political authority is not the government or the ruling part, but the human legislator, and that the human legislator is the people, the whole body of the citizens. To express this in the language of Rousseau, Marsilius asserts that the only legitimate sovereign is the people, but that the sovereign is to be distinguished from the government. He thus succeeds in subordinating the Christian priests to the Christian laity, the Christian aristocracy to the Christian *populus* or *demos*. But in taking these steps he seems to deviate flagrantly from the teaching of his revered master, who may be said to have identified the sovereign with the government and, above all, to have preferred the sovereignty or government of the gentlemen (aristocracy) to the sovereignty or government of the people (democracy).

Marsilius does not dispose of the difficulty by accepting Aristotle's assertions according to which democracy or the rule of the vulgar is a bad regime and the farmers, artisans, and money-makers, who constitute the vulgar, are not in the strictest sense parts of the commonwealth. He rather increases the difficulty by ascribing to Aristotle himself the following teaching: the legislative power must be entirely in the hands of the whole citizen body; the government ought to be elected by the whole citizen body and ought to be responsible to it; the government must rule in strict adherence to the laws, and if it transgresses a law it is liable to punishment by the whole citizen body. This teaching ascribed to Aristotle is much more democratic than Aristotle's authentic teaching: in the whole body of the citizens, as Marsilius understands it, the vulgar must play a very great, not to say a decisive, role. The reasoning in favor of the vulgar by which Marsilius supports his teaching is indeed almost identical with the argument in favor of democracy which Aristotle had reported and considered in the course of his ascent from the defective regimes to aristocracy (or king-ship). And Marsilius does not tire of explicitly quoting Aristotle in this context, although not without strange misinterpretations. Still stranger is his complete silence in this context about Aristotle's antidemocratic argument. He reports the antidemocratic argument, but omits any reference to Aristotle. He quotes only one authority for the antipopulist position: the saying of the wise king Solomon according to which "the number of the fools is infinite." Marsilius has not quoted any biblical passage in his populist reasoning; he thus perplexes us for a moment by making us think that the Bible, or at any rate Solomon, might favor aristocracy. Yet he disposes of this possibility by suggesting that the sage meant perhaps by the fools the infidels who, however wise in the worldly sciences, are nevertheless absolutely foolish, since, according to Paul, the wisdom of this world is foolishness with God. For from this it follows that the faithful man, and hence all the more the faithful multitude, is truly wise and hence perfectly competent to make laws and to elect kings or magistrates.

There is at least one other remark of Marsilius which shows that his belief in the competence of the people at large originated in his concern, not with authority as such, but with authority in Christendom. He says in effect that the necessity of giving the multitude power to legislate and to elect officials is less evident than the necessity of entrusting the multitude with the power to elect priests and remove them from their priestly offices; for error in the election of a priest can lead to eternal death and to very great harm in this life. That harm consists in the seduction of women during the secret conversations in the course of which they confess their sins to a priest. It is obvious that the simplest citizen, and surely therefore the faithful multitude, is as able to judge the trustworthiness of any individual priest in such matters as the most learned men could be; and the simple multitude might even be better informed in such respects than the learned. Marsilius also suggests that the whole body of all the faithful which is guided in its deliberations by the Holy Spirit, as distinguished from the whole body of citizens as mere citizens, is infallible.[12] By far the most important argument for popular government, however, is supplied by the example of the Church in its purest form, in which there were not yet Christian princes, and the Church consisted exclusively of priests and a multitude of such laymen as were subjects. Precisely in that epoch "Church" meant only the whole body of the faithful, and thus all Christians were ecclesiastics. Hence the traditional distinction between the people and the clergy must be radically revised in favor of the people. In accordance with the practice of the early Church, the election to all priestly offices belongs to the whole multitude of the faithful. This reasoning is not weakened but strengthened by the fact that in the very early Church the multitude was uncivilized and inexperienced: if even then the bishops were frequently elected by the multitude, this procedure is all the more appropriate after the faith has taken root in both subjects and princes.[13]

Let us return to the confines of political philosophy and consider Marsilius' doctrine of the human legislator somewhat more closely. He devotes two whole chapters out of fifty-two to the statement, the proofs, and the defense of that doctrine. He advances three proofs to which he adds a fourth, but that fourth proof is, as he says, hardly more than a summary of the first three. (1) The legislative power ought to belong to those from whom alone the best laws can emerge, but this is the whole citizen body; one reason is that no one harms himself knowingly and hence, we may add, when each thinks of his interest, no one's interest will be neglected or the interest of all will be duly provided for. (2) The legislative power ought to belong only to those who can best guaranteee that the laws made will be observed, but this is the whole citizen body, for each citizen observes better a law, even if it is not good, "which he seems to have imposed on himself"; the reason for this is that every citizen not only is a free man, that is, not subject to a master, but desires to be a free man. We may note that this argument causes a difficulty which Marsilius never discusses regarding the God-given and hence not even apparently self-imposed law. (3) What can benefit and harm each, and hence all, ought to be known and heard by all so that all and each can attain the benefit and repel the harm. The defense of the doctrine is stated in three arguments which are in the main taken from the populist reasoning reported by Aristotle. In the second of the latter group of arguments, Marsilius illustrates the danger of entrusting legislative power to a few or to one by referring to the oligarchic or tyrannical character of the canon law.[14] Marsilius' populist thesis thus appears to be derived from his anticlericalism.

Marsilius ascribes the fundamental political power, the power of the human legislator, not simply to the whole citizen body but to "the whole citizen body or its stronger or superior part." By the stronger or superior part he certainly does not mean the unqualified majority. The stronger or superior part, which as it were replaces the whole citizen body, must be understood in terms of both number and quality, so that the vulgar may not be entirely at the mercy of the better people nor the latter entirely at the mercy of the former. The arrangement sketched by Marsilius might be called a "polity"—a mean between oligarchy and democracy—were it not for the fact that "polity" is a form of government, while Marsilius speaks of the sovereign as distinguished from the government. Furthermore, whereas in a democracy, in Aristotle's sense, the common people participate fully in deliberation and jurisdiction, Marsilius reserves these functions for the government or the ruling part as distinguished from the whole citizen body or its stronger superior part.[15] Above all, as Marsilius already discloses in the chapters explicitly devoted to the definition of the human legislator, the human legislator may delegate his legislative power to one or to several men. Marsilius thus allows the sovereignty of the people to remain entirely dormant. In the same breath in which he proclaims the transcendent virtue of everyone's actually participating in legislation, he dismisses that participation as irrelevant. One must go further and say that he retracts the very principle of popular sovereignty. He compares the position of the ruling part in the body politic to that of the heart in the human body: it is that part which molds the other parts of the body politic. But if this is so, the ruling part is not derivative from a pre-existing sovereign, the human legislator, or the people, that is, the whole which consists of all parts of the body politic in their proper proportion, but is rather the cause of the alleged sovereign. In accordance with this Marsilius compares the position of the ruling part in the commonwealth to that of the prime mover in the universe, that is, of the Aristotelian God who surely is not subject to laws made by the other parts of the universe. In a word, Marsilius returns to the Aristotelian view according to which the human legislator (the sovereign) is identical with the ruling part (the government) or according to which the stronger or superior part is identical with the ruling part; for in every stable political order, the ruling part, whether it consists of one man or a few or the many, is as a matter of course the stronger or superior part. Marsilius even explicitly identifies the ruler with the legislator; for example, by calling the Roman emperors legislators. He does not leave it at saying that the human legislator can give the ruler "plenitude of power." He goes so far as to say that the ruler owes his position to "the human legislator or any other human will": the ruler may owe his position to his own will.[16]

If the ruling part is the legislator it cannot be simply subject to the law. Even in a republic, where no individual is the legislator and hence somehow above the law, it is sometimes necessary for an individual magistrate to act illegally in order to save the republic, as Cicero did when quenching the Catilinian conspiracy. When Marsilius suggests that the ruler is subject only to the divine law, we must not forget that according to him the divine law is not as such knowable to human reason nor does it as such have coercive power in this world. Furthermore, if the ruling part (the government) is the legislator (the sovereign), the government is not subject to punishment in case of misconduct for the same reason for which the sovereign people in the populist hypothesis is not subject to punishment.[17] To sum up, in spite of its dogmatic tone, Marsilius' populist teaching proves to be, if in a different way, as provisional or as tentative as the democratic argument in Aristotle's *Politics*.

The characteristic of the *Defender of the Peace* viewed as a treatise of political philosophy is that it very emphatically sets forth and literally at the same time retracts the doctrine of popular sovereignty. What is the meaning of this striking contradiction concerning the very foundation of political society? What is the meaning of Marsilius' vacillation between populism and what one may call monarchic absolutism? One could say that he takes the side of the people when the people is understood in contradistinction to the clergy and to nothing else, and that he takes the side of the Roman emperors, ancient or medieval, against the popes. In other words, the contradiction disappears once one assumes, as some scholars have done, that the *Defender* is inspired by nothing but anticlericalism. He needed for his anticlerical argument a populist basis because he had to appeal from the accepted opinions regarding the Church to the New Testament. The New Testament, while giving strong support to the demand for submission to absolute monarchs or to despots, does not give support to Marsilius' suggestion that the secular Christian rulers alone as distinguished from the priests ought to rule the Church in everything affecting men's fate in this world (punishment of heretics and apostates, excommunication, property, and so on); but the New Testament apparently gives some support to the view that decisions in such matters rest with the whole body of the faithful as distinguished from the priests alone. Marsilius' "whole body of the citizens" is merely the philosophic or rational counterpart of "the whole body of the faithful," and he needs such a counterpart in order to provide his anticlericalism with the broadest possible basis: both reason and revelation speak against the rule of priests. This explanation implies that the fundamental self-contradiction which is characteristic of the *Defender* is the conscious outcome of a conscious strategy. Both the explanation and its implication are defensible; yet they do not account for certain features of Marsilius' populist teaching or for the essential character of strategies like the one justly ascribed to Marsilius. They fail to account for the latter because it is not sufficient to conceive of Marsilius as a perhaps skillful but rather unscrupulous politician or advocate.

To find a way out of the difficulty, let us consider a Marsilian doctrine which is not affected by either political theology or antitheological preoccupations: his doctrine of monarchy or kingship. He says that kingship is "perhaps" the best form of government, but he makes it his business to discuss the question as to whether hereditary or elective monarchy is preferable. He devotes to this subject only one chapter, but that chapter is longer than the two chapters taken together which are apparently meant to establish popular sovereignty. He decides in favor of elective monarchy strictly understood, that is, of a monarchy in which each monarch, and not a monarch and his descendants, is elected. This decision might have recommended him to the pope, but with greater likelihood to the German emperor, who was at that time engaged in a bitter fight with the pope and who soon became Marsilius' protector; it would not have recommended him to the French king, for instance.[18] Yet it was necessary for the success of his venture—the venture aiming at the eradication of papal plenitude of power and everything reminding of it—to obtain the good will of all secular princes. It can therefore be assumed that his preference for elective monarchy over hereditary monarchy belongs to his final or serious political teaching. He certainly never contradicts this preference as he contradicts the doctrine of popular sovereignty. His argument in favor of elective kingship can be reduced to a single consideration. The most important quality of the ruler is prudence, for the infinite variety of human affairs does not permit an adequate regulation by laws, and prudence does not come by inheritance. Prudence, that is, practical wisdom in contradistinction to mere cleverness, is not separable from moral virtue and vice versa. Prudence is also and especially required for the making of good and just laws. While prudence is then of the utmost importance, it is rare; nature generated only a part of the human race apt for prudence, and still fewer men actualize that potentiality. The foregoing consideration does not imply that hereditary kingship is illegitimate; it merely means that hereditary kingship is as such inferior to elective kingship. Hereditary kingship may even be preferable to elective kingship in most countries at all times and in all countries at the beginning of their political life, when all men are still uncivilized. For in most countries at all times and in all countries at the beginning or in their decay, prudence is as it were at best the preserve of a single family, and there are therefore no prudent electors. Elective kingship is superior to hereditary kingship because the former is suitable to a perfect and civilized commonwealth, whereas the latter is suitable to a still imperfect or irremediably uncivilized society.[19]

Now, this very consideration leads to the conclusion that to a perfect or civilized commonwealth the rule of a number of prudent men, that is, aristocracy, is still more suitable than even elective monarchy, for there is no reason why, if there exists in a commonwealth a number of prudent men, as will be the case in a perfect commonwealth, all except one should always be deprived of the highest honor; those unjustly deprived of their fair share in government would justly engage in sedition. Marsilius devotes a whole chapter to the proof that the indispensable unity of government is in no way impaired if the government consists of a number of men instead of one man. Not only hereditary kingship but kingship as such is proper only at times and in places where there is an extreme paucity of men who are fit to rule a commonwealth as, for instance, perhaps in Rome at the end of the republic. Monarchy is the proper kind of government in the household rather than in the perfect civil society. That aristocracy as distinguished from kingship is possible only under the most favorable conditions, and hence very rarely, in no way contradicts the fact that it is the most natural regime. If the priests were as they ought to be, Marsilius argues, the general council of the Church could consist only of priests, for the most important requirement for participation in such an assembly is thorough knowledge of the divine law, which is the highest form of wisdom; but the priests are not as they ought to be. This amounts to saying that in principle aristocracy or the rule of the wise is preferable; only because the Church is no longer an aristocracy, but, as Marsilius never tires of repeating, is now an oligarchy, is it in need of correction by the best part of the laity; and the laity is, in the Church, the popular element. Within his populist argument Marsilius indicates that the devising and examining of the laws is the proper business of the prudent men; the other members of society are of little use in this matter and would only be disturbed in the performance of their necessary work if they were called upon to do more than to act as "formal" ratifiers. Such popular ratification of the laws would indeed seem to be desirable, since it is likely to make the populace more willing to obey the laws.[20]

Marsilius' very vacillation between populism and absolute monarchy may be said to point to aristocracy as the right mean between these two faulty extremes. What speaks in favor of the legislative power of absolute kings redounds also to the benefit of a sovereign government which consists of the prudent men of a city each of whom owes his position to co-optation by his peers rather than to popular election; and what speaks in favor of the legislative power of "the stronger or superior part of the whole citizen body" redounds to the benefit of what is in truth the stronger or superior part in every city which is not either too young or small or else too old or large for political excellence, namely, the most prudent and virtuous citizens. Marsilius abstains from arguing in favor of kingship while he argues emphatically in favor of popular sovereignty: the regime which he favors is somewhat closer, not indeed to democracy, but to the "polity" than to kingship. At the same time his populist argument points, through its glaring defects, for instance, from the "polity" to an aristocracy which is acceptable to the populace not only because of the inherent qualities of a genuine aristocracy as the rule of the most prudent and virtuous citizens but also because it respects the susceptibilities of the populace. Marsilius presented the argument for aristocracy in the most subdued form because that argument did not provide a sufficiently broad basis for the anticlerical policy which he regarded as by far the most urgent task for his age. In addition, the argument in favor of aristocracy would have redounded in the opinion of the majority of his contemporaries to the benefit of the clergy, for if political power is shown to belong by right to the wisest, it would seem to follow that it belongs less to those wise in human wisdom than to those wise in divine wisdom.

The strategy which Marsilius employed can then be explained by the political impossibility which amounted to a physical impossibility of airing the fundamental political issue. He could have an easy conscience in proceeding as he did because he was satisfied that a government of priests was impossible or undesirable. For according to him the New Testament not only does not authorize government by priests, especially in secular matters, but positively forbids it. In the Christian law, and only in the Christian law, the action of the priest as priest is the most perfect of all. But this action requires a spirit and a way of life which are incompatible with rulership, for it requires contempt for the world and the utmost humility. Christ excluded himself and the apostles from worldly rule in every form. Paul forbade every priest to become entangled in any secular matter whatever, since no one can serve two masters. The New Testament recognizes in the strongest terms the duty of obedience to the human government "which beareth not the sword in vain," not so much for the defense of the fatherland as for executing wrath upon the evildoers, and the New Testament traces to sinful pride the view that bad rulers or masters may be disobeyed. Christian slaves are not permitted to demand that they be set free after six years' servitude as the Hebrew slaves are, for the Old Testament law in question acquires in Christianity a purely mystical meaning. Humility and contempt for the world can then go together perfectly with sincere obedience to worldly masters.

Still, within the confines of political philosophy, Marsilius must put the accents somewhat differently than the highest Christian authorities had done. He almost goes so far as to defend the pagan rulers against the saying of Christ that they "lord it over" their subjects. According to Paul, only those that are "contemptible" in the Church, that is, those who possess wisdom in things which are not spiritual, ought to be judges in worldly matters. The demands of the Sermon on the Mount cannot be reconciled with the status and the duties of governors and their lay subjects.[21] The perfect Christian community was the community of Christ and the apostles in which there was community of goods; but that community was imperfect in other respects since it was meant to become universal, and yet no provision was made for its unity in the future when it would have become a large society; it could become perfect only through the acts of Christian princes. One is tempted to express Marsilius' thought by saying that it was nature which perfected grace rather than grace which perfected nature. He even goes so far as to indicate that there is an opposition between human government and divine providence, the former rewarding in this world the just and the doers of good deeds and the latter inflicting suffering on them in this world.[22] Marsilius indicates the peculiarity of the Christian law by saying that belief in God's future judgment—a belief which Christianity shares with all other religions—would induce the Christian priests not to defraud the poor, while belief in the Christian religion would induce the Christian priests to live in poverty. Evangelical poverty is indeed according to him the inevitable concomitant of radical contempt for this world or of radical humility. Within the confines of human reason, however, wealth, just as honor, comes to sight as something good since it is required for the exercise of moral virtue. But according to the Christian teaching, voluntary poverty is so much required for perfection that those who do not live in voluntary poverty are bad Christians. In spite of this,

Marsilius can complain that the popes did not show proper gratitude for having been raised by the Roman emperors from extreme poverty to abundance of temporal goods. He appears to assume that Christian morality and the worldly morality of the gentleman contradict each other or that revelation is not simply above reason but against reason. This may be one reason why he regarded the New Testament law as especially difficult to fulfill.²³

Marsilius has sometimes been celebrated as a defender of religious freedom. Yet he does not go beyond raising the question as to whether it is permitted to coerce heretics or infidels, while stating in the same context that he does not wish to say that such coercion is inappropriate. He does deny that such coercion can be exercised in this world on the basis of divine law. For according to Marsilius, no divine law has as such any coercive power in this world unless by virtue of a human law which makes it a crime to transgress the divine law in question. In addition, according to the Christian divine law, which, of course, condemns heresy and infidelity and buttresses that condemnation by the threat of punishment in the other life, a man who is coerced into belief is not truly a believer; besides, Christian priests have not been given by Christ any coercive power. In spite of this, the Christian human legislator, not as Christian but as human legislator, may use coercion against heretics and infidels in this world. This right can be illustrated by the following parallel. The Christian divine law forbids drunkenness, but does not as such require that coercion be used in this world against drunkards; yet it does not forbid the human legislator to prohibit drunkenness under penalties in this world. Similarly, the human legislator may enforce religious sobriety, that is, orthodoxy. Whether or not he does so will depend on his judgment on heresy, for instance. He may be guided by the biblical comparison of heresy to fornication and hence permit heresy as he permits fornication, although fornication, too, is forbidden by the Christian divine law. Or he may be guided by the biblical comparison of heresy to leprosy and hence take coercive action against heretics in compliance with the advice of experts (the priests), just as he takes coercive action against lepers in compliance with the advice of experts (the physicians). He may also be guided by the facts that the New Testament surely permits excommunication and that excommunication is bound to affect the excommunicated in this life.²⁴

But apart from any theological consideration, that is, from any consideration peculiar to the Christian divine law, it is clear that if belief in divine judgment in the other world is conducive to virtuous conduct in this world, as even pagan philosophers admitted, it is not inappropriate for the human legislator to protect that belief and its corollaries by forbidding speech which may subvert that belief. This conclusion is not contradicted by Marsilius' teaching that human government is concerned only with "transeunt" as distinguished from "immanent" acts. According to that distinction (which may have been suggested to Marsilius by a passage in Isaac Israeli's *Book of Definitions*), those acts of our cognitive and appetitive powers are immanent which, like thoughts and desires, remain within the agent and are not performed by means of any of the locally moved members of the body, while the other acts of those powers are transeunt. In other words, human government is concerned only with acts the commission of which can be proved even if he who committed the act in question denies having committed it. From this it follows that speeches are transeunt acts. Since subversive speeches of the kind indicated may do harm to others and to the community as a whole, their prohibition clearly falls, according to Marsilius, within the jurisdiction of the human legislator.[25] Marsilius surely did not preach freedom from religion.

Any divine law would lose much of its value if everyone subject to it were free to understand its promises and threats as he pleases. The Christian divine law in particular, with its emphasis on faith as the necessary condition for eternal salvation, would have been given in vain, it would have been given for men's eternal perdition, if Christ had not provided that the one true meaning of His divine law is accessible to all Christians. The indispensable unity of faith is provided in a legally binding manner by the universal or catholic Church, that is, by the whole body of the faithful, insofar as it is the faithful human legislator who authorizes the general councils and gives their decisions coercive power. This provision causes no difficulty when there is a single human legislator of Christian faith whose jurisdiction extends over the whole world. Such a legislator was, according to an opinion adopted by Marsilius, the Roman people or derivatively the Roman emperor. Marsilius tries to preserve this dignity for the Roman emperors of his age. But he cannot conceal from himself or from his readers the fact that there existed in his time a number of faithful human legislators who did not recognize a superior or who were independent of one another. There was then no longer a guarantee of the unity of faith except within the borders of individual independent realms or commonwealths. Hence Marsilius regards it as advisable that the various Christian sovereigns should agree in recognizing the bishop of Rome as "the universal pastor," but in his opinion they are not obliged to do so.[26]

Yet, as he points out, a universal pastor or universal bishop is less necessary than a universal prince, for a universal prince is obviously more capable of keeping the faithful in the unity of faith than a universal bishop could be. As a Christian, Marsilius seems then to be compelled, given his premises, to demand that political society be universal strictly speaking— and not only in pretense, or by courtesy, as the Roman empire was even at the peak of its power—so that it can discharge its duties to the Christian faith. He seems to be compelled, that is, to abandon the very last trace of his doctrine of popular sovereignty or of the Aristotelian preference for aristocracy which that doctrine partly represents; for neither democracy nor aristocracy as understood by Marsilius and Aristotle is feasible in any but fairly small societies. Yet in spite or because of all this, Marsilius denies that a universal prince is necessary. For Scripture does not demand a universal secular empire. Still less does reason demand it: peace among men is sufficiently guaranteed—we may understand this to mean that peace is guaranteed in the only possible way—if there exists unity of government within the particular commonwealths or kingdoms. In his only thematic discussion of the question concerning the desirability of a "world state," Marsilius refuses to decide it. He alludes to the difficulties obstructing world government which are caused by distance and by the lack of communication between the various parts of the world, as well as by the differences of languages and the extreme differences of customs. He refers to the view according to which all these things which separate men might be due to a heavenly cause, that is, to nature which incites men, by means of these divisive things, to wars in order to prevent overpopulation. Marsilius makes it clear that, were it not for wars and epidemics, overpopulation would be inevitable if the human kind had no beginning and will have no end, that is, if there is "eternal generation" or if the visible universe is eternal.[27] The Aristotelian doctrine of the eternity of the visible universe is irreconcilable with the biblical doctrine of the creation of the world. The Aristotelian doctrine of eternal generation is irreconcilable with the biblical doctrine that there was "a first man," with the doctrine which is the premise of the biblical doctrines that our first parents fell and that therefore man is in need of redemption. Marsilius does not declare that the Aristotelian doctrine is true. Still less does he declare that it is untrue because it contradicts the most fundamental and the most manifest doctrines of the Bible. The reader can therefore only guess whether Marsilius was a believer or an unbeliever until he considers Marsilius' discussion, presented in the thirty-eighth chapter of the *Defender* (II 19), of the question concerning the ground of the belief in the truth of the Bible.

Within the confines of political philosophy, Marsilius' tacit opposition to Thomas Aquinas shows itself most obviously in his teaching regarding natural law or natural right. Marsilius denies that there is a natural law properly so called. He presupposes that reason knows no other legislator than man and hence that all laws properly so called are human laws: reason is indeed capable of discerning what is honorable, what is just, and what is of advantage to society. But such insights are not as such laws. Besides, they are not accessible to all men and hence not admitted by all nations; for this reason they cannot be called natural. There are indeed certain rules regarding what is honorable or just which are admitted in all regions and are in addition enforced almost everywhere; these rules can therefore metaphorically be called natural rights. In spite of their being universally or generally admitted, they are not strictly speaking natural, for they are not dictated by right reason. What is universally admitted is not rational, and what is rational is not universally admitted. Among the rules which can metaphorically be called "natural rights" Marsilius mentions the rule that human offspring must be reared by the parents up to a certain time; he may have regarded this rule as not unqualifiedly rational since Aristotle had held that no deformed child should be reared. More generally, if wars are by nature necessary in order to prevent overpopulation, the distinction between just and unjust wars loses much of its force, and this grave qualification of the rules of justice cannot but impair the rationality of those rules of justice which are universally or generally admitted to obtain within the commonwealth. In other words, the universally admitted rules of right are not rational since there exists a natural necessity to transgress them or since man does not possess freedom of will to the extent to which both common opinion and the teaching of revelation assert it.[28]

One can understand Marsilius' denial of natural law best if one starts from the fact that he implicitly denies the existence of first principles of practical reason. The cognitive status of the first principles of action in Aristotle's *Ethics* is obscure. One way of removing this obscurity—the way preferred by Averroës and Dante—is to conceive of the first principles of action and therefore also of politics as supplied by theoretical reason or natural science: it is natural science which makes clear what the end of man is. Let the end of man be the perfection of his mind, that is, the actual thought of the metaphysician as metaphysician. The individual human being who is capable of pursuing this end will then deliberate as to how, given his circumstances, he can reach this end. This deliberation—an act of practical reason—will in many points differ from individual to individual, but there are certain universal rules of conduct with which all men must comply who wish to become perfect as men of speculation. Those rules are, however, not universal strictly speaking since only a minority of men is by nature capable of the contemplative life. But there is also an end which all men are able to pursue; this is the perfection of their bodies. This lower or first perfection requires among other things security in and through political society. Here a profound ambiguity enters: political society is required, although in different ways, for the sake of both man's first and his ultimate (theoretical) perfection. However this may be, political society in its turn requires a variety of "parts" (farmers, artisans, moneyed men, soldiers, priests, governors, or judges) and a certain order of these parts. It requires for its well-being that the legislators and the governors or judges possess prudence and if not all at any rate some of the moral virtues, especially justice. In agreement with Aristotle's procedure in the *Politics*, Marsilius deduces the necessity of those virtues from the purpose of civil society, and the necessity of that purpose from the end or ends of man. That is to say, deviating from the procedure which Aristotle had followed in his *Ethics* for educative or practical reasons, Marsilius does not take those virtues as ultimates, as choiceworthy for their own sake. It is because Marsilius treats prudence and the moral virtues less as choiceworthy for their own sake than as subservient to the two natural ends indicated that his political science is more obviously and more emphatically "demonstrative" than Aristotle's political science.[29]

Marsilius says much less than Aristotle even in his *Politics* about the highest end which is natural to man. For the reasons indicated above he lowered his sights. His doctrine of the commonwealth is reminiscent of the suggestion in Plato's *Republic* according to which the city of pigs is the true city. His doctrine of the human law is reminiscent of Maimonides' suggestion according to which the human law serves no higher goal than the perfection of man's body, whereas the divine law brings about the perfection of both the body and the mind.[30] But Maimonides held that the divine law is essentially rational and not, as it is according to Thomas, suprarational. One may say that Marsilius combines Maimonides' view of the human law with Thomas' view of the divine law and thus arrives, within the confines of political philosophy, at the conclusion that the only law properly so called is the human law which is directed toward the well-being of the body. Marsilius was driven to take this view to some extent by his anticlericalism. When antitheological passion induced a thinker to take the extreme step of questioning the supremacy of contemplation, political philosophy broke with the classical tradition, and especially with Aristotle, and took on an entirely new character. The thinker in question was Machiavelli.

NOTES

1. Marsilius of Padua, *The Defender of the Peace*, trans. with an introduction by Alan Gewirth (New York: Columbia University Press, 1956), II 13.24 (= 169th paragraph of Dictio II).
2. *Ibid.*, I 9.2.
3. *Ibid.*, I 11.2 beginning and 16.15 end.
4. *Ibid.*, I 4.1; 1.7; II 30.4 end (cf. I 6.9 first par.).
5. *Ibid.*, I 1.3–5, 7; 19.3 and 8–13.
6. *Ibid.*, I 5.1; 15.10; 19.12 end. II 1.4; 8.9 toward the end; 30.5 (par. 2).
7. *Ibid.*, I 4.3–4; 5.11; 10.3.
8. *Ibid.*, I 5.2, 3, 13; 10.3. II 8.4 end. (But cf. the derogatory meaning of "sect" in II 16.17.)
9. *Ibid.*, I 5.12; 19.4 (102, 22, ed. Previté-Orton) and 5 beginning. II 6.10 end; 10.6; 20.13. Note that Marsilius does not quote Deut. 33:10.
10. *Ibid.*, I 5.1, 13. II 13–14; 24.1 end; 30.4 (par. 1 end).
11. *Ibid.*, I 1.1; 8.4; 10.4–5; 15.1; 17. II 4.5; 8.9; 28 end. *Politics* 1255ᵇ 13–15; 1276ᵃ 1–3; 1282ᵇ 7–13; 1324ᵇ 7–9; 1333ᵇ 5 ff. *EN* 1180ᵃ 24–35.
12. *Defender*, I 5.1, 13; 8.3; 11 (esp. 11.6); 12.3, 4; 13.1, 3, 4. II 17.10–12; 21.3 and 9 end. *Politics* 1281ᵃ 40 ff. (esp. 1281ᵇ 23–25).

13. *Defender*, II 2.3; 15.8; 16.1 and 9 beginning; 17.5, 7–8, 10; 28.3, 17.

14. *Ibid.*, I 12–13. II 23.9, 13 beginning; 24.11; 26.19; 28.29.

15. *Ibid.*, I 5.1, 7; 8.1; 12.4. II 2.8; 4.8; 8.7.

16. *Ibid.*, I 4.4 (13, 20); 8.5; 10.2; 12.3; 13 end; 14 heading and end; 15.5–6; 16.21; 17.9. II 5.4 (149 bottom); 8.6; 21.2; 30.4 (485, 19–21—one of the two central parts of the chapter). III 2.13. *Defensor Minor*, chap. 3 beginning. *Politics* 1296^b 14–16.

17. *Defender*, I 14.3; 15.4; 26.13. Cf. II 3.15 and 30.6.

18. *Ibid.*, I 9.5–7; 15.3 end; 16. II 24.2.

19. *Ibid.*, I 7.1; 9.4–7, 10; 11.3 (42, 14–15); 14.2–7, 10; 15.1; 16. 11–24 (esp. 16.17).

20. *Ibid.*, I 2.2; 3.4; 9.10; 11.5 end; 12.2; 13.8; 14.9; 16.19, 21, 23; 17. II 20.2 end and 13–14; cf. II 3.15 with 30.6. Alan Gewirth, *Marsilius of Padua*, trans. with an introduction (New York: 1956), I 254. The use of *regnum* suggested in I 2 makes one expect a more monarchistic tendency than Marsilius actually has.

21. *Ibid.*, I 10.3; 12.2. II 4.13; 5.1–2, 4–5, 8 (par. 1); 9.10, 12; 11.2, 7; 28.24 (462, 9); 30.4 par. 1 end.

22. *Ibid.*, II 4.6; 13.28; 17.7–8; 22.1 beginning, 15–16; 24.4; 27.2 (426 par. 2). Gewirth, *op. cit.*, I 81.

23. *Ibid.*, I 6.3, 6; 15.21; 16. II 11.4; 13.16, 23 end–24; 26.12 beginning.

24. *Ibid.*, I 10.3–7. II 5.6, 7 (154, 23–26 and 157, 28); 6.11–13; 8.8; 9.2–5; 10.3, 7, 9; 13.2 end.

25. *Ibid.*, I 5.4, 7. II 2.4 (3); 8.5; 9.11; 10.4, 9; 17.8 toward the end. Gewirth, *op. cit.*, I 284.

26. I 19.10. II 13.28; 17.2; 18.8 (pars. 1–2 and end); 19.1–3; 20.1–2; 21.11, 13; 22.6, 8, 10; 24.9, 12; 25.4–6, 9, 15–18; 28.27; 30.8. *Defensor Minor*, chaps. 7 and 12.

27. *Defender*, I 17.10. II 28.15.

28. *Ibid.*, I 10.3–7; 12.2–3; 14.4; 15.6 end; 19.13. II 8.3; 12.7–8.

29. *Ibid.*, I 6–9; 11.3; 14.2, 6–7. Dante, *De Monarchia*, I 14.

30. *Republic*, 372^e 6–7; *Guide of the Perplexed*, II 40 and III 27.

8 / An Epilogue

What one may call the new science of politics emerged shortly before World War I; it became preponderant and at the same time reached its mature or final form before, during, and after World War II. It need not be a product or a symptom of the crisis of the modern Western world—of a world which could boast of being distinguished by ever broadening freedom and humanitarianism; it is surely contemporary with that crisis.

The new political science shares with the most familiar ingredients of our world in its crisis the quality of being a mass phenomenon. That it is a mass phenomenon is compatible with the fact that it possesses its heights and its depths, the handful of opinion leaders, the men responsible for the breakthroughs on the top, and the many who drive on the highways projected by the former at the bottom. It wields very great authority in the West, above all in this country. It controls whole departments of political science in great and in large universities. It is supported by foundations of immense wealth with unbounded faith and unbelievably large grants. In spite of this one runs little risk in taking issue with it. For its devotees are fettered by something like a Hippocratic oath to subordinate all considerations of safety, income, and deference to concern with the truth. The difficulty lies elsewhere. It is not easy to free one's mind from the impact of any apparently beneficent authority, for such freeing requires that one step outside of the circle warmed and charmed by the authority to be questioned.

Yet it is necessary to make the effort. The new political science itself must demand it. One might say that precisely because it is an authority operating within a democracy it owes an account of itself to those who are subjected, or are to be subjected, to it. However sound it may be, it is a novelty. That it emerged so late is probably no accident: deep-seated resistances had to be overcome step by step in a process of long duration.

Precisely if the new political science constitutes the mature approach to political things, it presupposes the experience of the failure of earlier approaches. We ourselves no longer have that experience: "George" has had it for us. Yet to leave it at that is unbecoming for men of science; men of science cannot leave it at hearsay or at vague remembrances. To this one might reply that the resistances to the new political science have not entirely vanished: the old Adam is still alive. But precisely because this is so, the new political science, being a rational enterprise, must be able to lead the old Adam by a perfectly lucid, coherent, and sound argument from his desert which he mistakes for a paradise to its own green pastures. It must cease to demand from us, in the posture of a noncommissioned officer, a clean and unmediated break with our previous habits, that is, with common sense; it must supply us with a ladder by which we can ascend, in full clarity as to what we are doing, from common sense to science. It must begin to learn to look with sympathy at the obstacles to it if it wishes to win the sympathy of the best men of the coming generation—those youths who possess the intellectual and the moral qualities which prevent men from simply following authorities, to say nothing of fashions.

The fairly recent change within political science has its parallels in the other social sciences. Yet the change within political science appears to be both more pronounced and more limited. The reason is that political science is the oldest of the social sciences and therefore willy-nilly a carrier of old traditions which resist innovation. Political science as we find it now consists of more heterogeneous parts than any other social science. "Public law" and "international law" were established themes centuries before "politics and parties" and "international relations," nay, sociology, emerged. If we look around us, we may observe that the political science profession contains a strong minority of the right, consisting of the strict adherents of the new political science or the "behavioralists," a small minority of the left, consisting of those who reject the new political science root and branch, and a center consisting of the old-fashioned political scientists, men who are concerned with understanding political things without being much concerned with "methodological" questions but many of whom seem to have given custody of their "methodological" conscience to the strict adherents of the new political science and who thus continue their old-fashioned practice with a somewhat uneasy conscience. It may seem strange that I called the strict adherents of the new political science the right wing and their intransigent opponents the left wing, seeing that the former are liberals almost to a man and the latter are in the odor of conservatism. Yet since I have heard the intransigent opponents of the new political science described as unorthodox I inferred that the new political science is the orthodoxy in the profession, and the natural place of an orthodoxy is on the right.

A rigorous adherent of the new political science will dismiss the preceding remarks as quasi-statistical or sociological irrelevancies which have no bearing whatever on the only important issue, that issue being the soundness of the new political science. To state that issue means to bring out the fundamental difference between the new political science and the old. To avoid ambiguities, irrelevancies, and beatings around the bush, it is best to contrast the new political science directly with the "original" of the old, that is, with Aristotelian political science.

For Aristotle, political science is identical with political philosophy because science is identical with philosophy. Science or philosophy consists of two kinds, theoretical and practical or political; theoretical science is subdivided into mathematics, physics (natural science), and metaphysics; practical science is subdivided into ethics, economics (management of the household), and political science in the narrower sense; logic does not belong to philosophy or science proper, but is as it were the prelude to philosophy or science. The distinction between philosophy and science or the separation of science from philosophy was a consequence of the revolution which occurred in the seventeenth century. This revolution was primarily not the victory of science over metaphysics, but what one may call the victory of the new philosophy or science over Aristotelian philosophy or science. Yet the new philosophy or science was not equally successful in all its parts. Its most successful part was physics (and mathematics). Prior to the victory of the new physics, there was not the science of physics simply: there were Aristotelian physics, Platonic physics, Epicurean physics, Stoic physics; to speak colloquially, there was no metaphysically neutral physics. The victory of the new physics led to the emergence of a physics which seemed to be as metaphysically neutral as, say, mathematics, medicine, or the art of shoemaking. The emergence of a metaphysically neutral physics made it possible for "science" to become independent of "philosophy" and in fact an authority for the latter. It paved the way for an economic science which is independent of ethics, for sociology as the study of nonpolitical associations as not inferior in dignity to the political association, and, last but not least, for the separation of political science from political philosophy as well as the separation of economics and sociology from political science.

Second, the Aristotelian distinction between theoretical and practical sciences implies that human action has principles of its own which are known independently of theoretical science (physics and metaphysics) and therefore that the practical sciences do not depend on the theoretical sciences or are not derivative from them. The principles of action are the natural ends toward which man is by nature inclined and of which he has by nature some awareness. This awareness is the necessary condition for his seeking and finding appropriate means for his ends, or for his becoming practically wise or prudent. Practical science in contradistinction to practical wisdom itself sets forth coherently the principles of action and the general rules of prudence ("proverbial wisdom"). Practical science raises questions which within practical or political experience, or at any rate on the basis of such experience, reveal themselves to be the most important questions and which are not stated, let alone answered, with sufficient clarity by practical wisdom itself. The sphere governed by prudence is then in principle self-sufficient or closed. Yet prudence is always endangered by false doctrines about the whole of which man is a part, by false theoretical opinions; prudence is therefore always in need of defense against such opinions, and that defense is necessarily theoretical. The theory defending prudence is, however, misunderstood if it is taken to be the basis of prudence. This complication—the fact that the sphere of prudence is as it were only *de jure* but not *de facto* wholly independent of theoretical science—makes understandable, although it does not by itself justify, the view underlying the new political science according to which no awareness inherent in practice, and in general no natural awareness is genuine knowledge, or, in other words, only "scientific" knowledge is genuine knowledge. This view implies that there cannot be practical sciences proper or that the distinction between practical and theoretical sciences must be replaced by the distinction between theoretical and applied sciences, applied sciences being sciences which are based on theoretical sciences that precede the applied sciences in time and in order. It implies above all that the sciences dealing with human affairs are essentially dependent on the theoretical sciences—especially on psychology which in the Aristotelian scheme is the highest theme of physics, not to say that it constitutes the transition from physics to metaphysics—or become themselves theoretical sciences to be supplemented by such applied sciences as the policy sciences or the sciences of social engineering. The new political science is then no longer based on political experience, but on what is called scientific psychology.

Third, according to the Aristotelian view, the awareness of the principles of action shows itself primarily to a higher degree in public or authoritative speech, particularly in law and legislation, rather than in merely private speech. Hence Aristotelian political science views political things in the perspective of the citizen. Since there is of necessity a variety of citizen perspectives, the political scientist or political philosopher must become the umpire, the impartial judge; his perspective encompasses the partisan perspectives because he possesses a more comprehensive and a clearer grasp of man's natural ends and their natural order than do the partisans. The new political science on the other hand looks at political things from without, in the perspective of the neutral observer, in the same perspective in which one would look at triangles or fish, although or because it may wish to become "manipulative"; it views human beings as an engineer would view materials for building bridges. It follows that the language of Aristotelian political science is identical with the language of political man; it hardly uses a term which did not originate in the market place and is not in common use there; but the new political science cannot begin to speak without having elaborated an extensive technical vocabulary.

Fourth, Aristotelian political science necessarily evaluates political things; the knowledge in which it culminates has the character of categoric advice and of exhortation. The new political science on the other hand conceives of the principles of action as "values" which are merely "subjective"; the knowledge which it conveys has the character of prediction and only secondarily that of hypothetical advice.

Fifth, according to the Aristotelian view, man is a being *sui generis*, with a dignity of its own: man is the rational and political animal. Man is the only being which can be concerned with self-respect; man can respect himself because he can despise himself; he is "the beast with red cheeks," the only being possessing a sense of shame. His dignity is then based on his awareness of what he ought to be or how he should live. Since there is a necessary connection between morality (how man should live) and law, there is a necessary connection between the dignity of man and the dignity of the public order: the political is *sui generis* and cannot be understood as derivative from the subpolitical. The presupposition of all this is that man is radically distinguished from nonman, from brutes as well as from gods, and this presupposition is ratified by common sense, by the citizen's understanding of things; when the citizen demands or rejects, say, "freedom from want for all," he does not mean freedom from want for tigers, rats, or lice. This presupposition points to a more fundamental presupposition according to which the whole consists of essentially different parts. The new political science on the other hand is based on the fundamental premise that there are no essential or irreducible differences: there are only differences of degree; in particular there is only a difference of degree between men and brutes or between men and robots. In other words, according to the new political science, or the universal science of which the new political science is a part, to understand a thing means to understand it in terms of its genesis or its conditions and hence, humanly speaking, to understand the higher in terms of the lower: the human in terms of the subhuman, the rational in terms of the subrational, the political in terms of the subpolitical. In particular the new political science cannot admit that the common good is something that is.

Prior to the emergence of the new political science, political science had already moved very far from Aristotelian political science in the general direction of the new political science. Nevertheless it was accused of paying too great attention to the law or to the Ought and of paying too little attention to the Is or to the actual behavior of men. For instance, it seemed to be exclusively concerned with the legal arrangements regarding universal suffrage and its justification and not to consider at all how the universal right to vote is exercised; yet democracy, as it is, is characterized by the manner in which that right is exercised. We may grant that not so long ago there was a political science which was narrowly legalistic—which, for example, took the written constitution of the U.S.S.R. very seriously—but we must add immediately that that error had been corrected, as it were in advance, by an older political science, the political science of Montesquieu, of Machiavelli, or of Aristotle himself. Besides, the new political science, in its justified protest against a merely legalistic political science, is in danger of disregarding the important things known to those legalists: "voting behavior" as it is now studied would be impossible if there were not in the first place the universal right to vote, and this right, even if not exercised by a large minority for very long periods, must be taken into consideration in any long-range prediction since it may be exercised by all in future elections taking place in unprecedented and therefore particularly interesting circumstances. That right is an essential ingredient of democratic "behavior," for it partly explains "behavior" in democracies (for instance, the prevention by force or fraud of certain people from voting). The new political science does not simply deny these things, but it literally relegates them to the background, to "the habit background"; in so doing it puts the cart before the horse. Similar considerations apply, for instance, to the alleged discovery by the new political science of the importance of "propaganda"; that discovery is in fact only a partial rediscovery of the need for vulgar rhetoric, a need that had become somewhat obscured from a few generations which were comforted by faith in universal enlightenment as the inevitable by-product of the diffusion of science, which in its turn was thought to be the inevitable by-product of science. Generally speaking, one may wonder whether the new political science has brought to light anything of political importance which intelligent political practitioners with a deep knowledge of history, nay, intelligent and educated journalists, to say nothing of the old political science at its best, did not know at least as well beforehand.

The main substantive reason, however, for the revolt against the old political science would seem to be the consideration that our political situation is entirely unprecedented and that it is unreasonable to expect earlier political thought to be of any help in coping with our situation; the unprecedented political situation calls for an unprecedented political science, perhaps for a judicious mating of dialectical materialism and psychoanalysis to be consummated on a bed supplied by logical positivism. Just as classical physics had to be superseded by nuclear physics so that the atomic age could come in via the atomic bomb, the old political science has to be superseded by a sort of nuclear political science so that we may be enabled to cope with the extreme dangers threatening atomic man; the equivalent in political science of the nuclei is probably the most minute events in the smallest groups of humans if not in the life of infants; the small groups in question are certainly not of the kind exemplified by the small group which

Lenin gathered around himself in Switzerland during World War I. In making this comparison we are not oblivious of the fact that the nuclear physicists show a greater respect for classical physics than the nuclear political scientists show for classical politics. Nor do we forget that, while the nuclei proper are simply prior to macrophysical phenomena, the "political" nuclei which are meant to supply explanations for the political things proper are already molded, nay, constituted, by the political order or the regime within which they occur: an American small group is not a Russian small group.

We may grant that our political situation has nothing in common with any earlier political situation except that it is a political situation. The human race is still divided into a number of the kind of societies which we have come to call states and which are separated from one another by unmistakable and sometimes formidable frontiers. Those states still differ from one another not only in all conceivable other respects but above all in their regimes and hence in the things to which the preponderant part of those societies is dedicated or in the spirit which more or less effectively pervades those societies. They have very different images of the future so that for all of them to live together, in contradistinction to uneasily coexisting, is altogether impossible. Each of them, receiving its character from its regime, is still in need of specific measures for preserving itself and its regime and hence is uncertain of its future. Acting willy-nilly through their governments (which may be governments in exile), those societies still move as if on an uncharted sea and surely without the benefit of tracks toward a future which is veiled from everyone and which is pregnant with surprises. Their governments still try to determine the future of their societies with the help partly of knowledge, partly of guesses, the recourse to guesses still being partly necessitated by the secrecy in which their most important opponents shroud their most important plans or projects. The new political science which is so eager to predict is, as it admits, as unable to predict the outcome of the unprecedented conflict peculiar to our age as the crudest soothsayer of the most benighted tribe. In former times people thought that the outcome of serious conflicts is unpredictable because one cannot know how long this or that outstanding leader in war or counsel will live, or how the opposed armies will act in the test of battle, or similar things. We have been brought to believe that chance can be controlled or does not seriously affect the fate of societies. Yet the science which is said to have rendered possible the control of chance has itself become the refuge of chance: man's fate depends now more than ever on science or technology, hence on discoveries or inventions, hence on events whose precise occurrence is by their very nature not predictable. A simply unprecedented political situation would be a situation of no political interest, that is, not a political situation. Now, if the essential character of all political situations was grasped by the old political science, there seems to be no reason why it must be superseded by a new political science. In case the new political science should tend to understand political things in nonpolitical terms, the old political science, wise to many ages, would even be superior to the new political science in helping us to find our bearings in our unprecedented situation in spite or rather because of the fact that only the new political science can boast of being the child of the atomic age.

But one will never understand the new political science if one does not start from that reason advanced on its behalf which has nothing whatever to do with any true or alleged blindness of the old political science to any political things as such. That reason is a general notion of science. According to that notion, only scientific knowledge is genuine knowledge. From this it follows immediately that all awareness of political things which is not scientific is cognitively worthless. Serious criticism of the old political science is a waste of time; for we know in advance that it could only have been a pseudo science, although perhaps including a few remarkably shrewd hunches. This is not to deny that the adherents of the new political science sometimes engage in apparent criticism of the old, but that criticism is characterized by a constitutional inability to understand the criticized doctrines on their own terms. What science is, is supposed to be known from the practice of the other sciences, of sciences which are admittedly in existence, and not mere desiderata, and the clearest examples of such sciences are the natural sciences. What science is, is supposed to be known, above all, from the science of science, that is, logic.

The basis of the new political science is then logic—a particular kind of logic; the logic in question is not, for instance, Aristotelian or Kantian or Hegelian logic. This means, however, that the new political science rests on what for the political scientists as such is a mere assumption which he is not competent to judge on its own terms—namely, as a logical theory—for that theory is controversial among the people who must be supposed to be competent in such matters, the professors of philosophy. He is, however, competent to judge it by its fruits; he is competent to judge whether his understanding of political things as political things is helped or hindered by the new political science which derives from the logic in question. He is perfectly justified in regarding as an imposition the demand that he comply with "logical positivism" or else plead guilty to being a "metaphysician." He is perfectly justified in regarding this epithet as not "objective," because it is terrifying and unintelligible, like the war cries of savages.

What strikes a sympathetic chord in every political scientist is less the demand that he proceed "scientifically"—for mathematics also proceeds scientifically, and political science surely is not a mathematical discipline —than the demand that he proceed "empirically." This is a demand of common sense. No one in his senses ever dreamt that he could know anything, say, of American government as such or of the present political situation as such except by looking at American government or at the present political situation. The incarnation of the empirical spirit is the man from Missouri, who has to be shown. For he knows that he, as well as everyone else who is of sound mind and whose sight is not defective, can see things and people as they are with his eyes and that he is capable of knowing how his neighbors feel; he takes it for granted that he lives with other human beings of all descriptions in the same world and that because they are all human beings, they all understand one another somehow; he knows that if this were not so, political life would be altogether impossible. If someone would offer him speculations based on extrasensory perception, he would turn his back on him more or less politely. The old political science would not quarrel in these respects with the man from Missouri. It did not claim to know better or differently than he such things as that the Democratic and Republican parties are now, and have been for some time, the preponderant parties in this country and that there are presidential elections every fourth year. By admitting that facts of this kind are known independently of political science, it admitted that empirical knowledge is not necessarily scientific knowledge or that a statement can be true and known to be true without being scientific, and, above all, that political science stands or falls by the truth of the prescientific awareness of political things.

Yet one may raise the question as to how one can be certain of the truth of empirical statements which are prescientific. If we call an elaborate answer to this question an epistemology, we may say that an empiricist, in contradistinction to an empirical, statement is based on the explicit assumption of a specific epistemology. Yet every epistemology presupposes the truth of empirical statements. Our perceiving things and people is more manifest and more reliable than any "theory of knowledge"—any explanation of how our perceiving things and people is possible—can be; the truth of any "theory of knowledge" depends on its ability to give an adequate account of this fundamental reliance. If a logical positivist tries to give an account of "a thing" or a formula for "a thing" in terms of mere sense data and their composition, he is looking, and bids us to look, at the previously grasped "thing"; the previously grasped "thing" is the standard by which we judge of his formula. If an epistemology—for example, solipsism—manifestly fails to give an account of how empirical statements as meant can be true, it fails to carry conviction. To be aware of the necessity of the fundamental reliance which underlies or pervades all empirical statements means to recognize the fundamental riddle, not to have solved it. But no man needs to be ashamed to admit that he does not possess a solution to the fundamental riddle. Surely no man ought to let himself be bullied into the acceptance of an alleged solution—for the denial of the existence of a riddle is a kind of solution of the riddle—by the threat that if he fails to do so he is a "metaphysician." To sustain our weaker brethren against that threat one might tell them that the belief accepted by the empiricists, according to which science is in principle susceptible of infinite progress, is itself tantamount to the belief that being is irretrievably mysterious.

Let us try to restate the issue by returning first to our man from Missouri. A simple observation seems to be sufficient to show that the man from Missouri is "naïve": he does not see things with his eyes; what he sees with his eyes is only colors, shapes, and the like; he would perceive "things," in contradistinction to "sense data," only if he possessed "extrasensory perception"; his claim—the claim of common sense—implies that there is "extrasensory perception." What is true of "things" is true of "patterns," at any rate of those patterns which students of politics from time to time claim to "perceive." We must leave the man from Missouri scratching his head; by being silent, he remains in his way a philosopher. But others do not leave it at scratching their heads. Transforming themselves from devotees of *empeiria* into empiricists, they contend that what is perceived or "given" is only sense data; the "thing" emerges by virtue of unconscious or conscious "construction": the "things" which to common sense present themselves as "given" are in truth constructs. Common-sense understanding is understanding by means of unconscious construction; scientific understanding is understanding by means of conscious construction. Somewhat more precisely, common-sense understanding is understanding in terms of "things possessing qualities"; scientific understanding is understanding in terms of "functional relations between different series of events." Unconscious constructs are ill made, for their making is affected by all sorts of purely "subjective" influences; only conscious constructs can be well made, perfectly lucid, in every respect the same for everyone, or "objective." Still, one says with greater right that we perceive things than that we perceive human beings as human beings, for at least some of the properties which we ascribe to things are sensually perceived, whereas the soul's actions, passions, or states can never become sense data.

Now, that understanding of things and human beings which is rejected by empiricism is the understanding by which political life, political understanding, political experience, stands or falls. Hence, the new political science, based as it is on empiricism, must reject the results of political understanding and political experience as such, and since the political things are given to us in political understanding and political experience, the new political science cannot be helpful for the deeper understanding of political things: it must reduce the political things to nonpolitical data. The new political science comes into being through an attempted break with common sense. But that break cannot be consistently carried out, as can be seen in a general way from the following consideration. Empiricism cannot be established empiricistically: it is not known through sense data that the only possible objects of perception are sense data. If one tries therefore to establish empiricism empirically, one must make use of that understanding of things which empiricism renders doubtful: the relation of eyes to colors or shapes is established through the same kind of perception through which we perceive things as things rather than sense data or constructs. In other words, sense data as sense data become known only through an act of abstraction or disregard which presupposes the legitimacy of our primary awareness of things as things and of people as people. Hence the only way of overcoming the naïveté of the man from Missouri is in the first place to admit that that naïveté cannot be avoided in any way or that there is no possible human thought which is not in the last analysis dependent on the legitimacy of that naïveté and the awareness or the knowledge going with it.

We must not disregard the most massive or the crudest reason to which empiricism owes much of its attractiveness. Some adherents of the new political science would argue as follows: One can indeed not reasonably deny that prescientific thought about political things contains genuine knowledge; but the trouble is that within prescientific political thought, genuine knowledge of political things is inseparable from prejudices or superstitions; hence one cannot get rid of the spurious elements in prescientific political thought except by breaking altogether with prescientific thought or by acting on the assumption that prescientific thought does not have the character of knowledge at all. Common sense contains indeed genuine knowledge of broomsticks; but the trouble is that this knowledge has in common sense the same status as the alleged knowledge concerning witches; by trusting common sense one is in danger of bringing back the whole kingdom of darkness with Thomas Aquinas at its head. The old political science was not unaware of the imperfections of political opinion, but it did not believe that the remedy lies in the total rejection of common-sense understanding as such. It was critical in the original sense, that is, discerning, regarding political opinion. It was aware that the errors regarding witches were found out without the benefit of empiricism. It was aware that judgments or maxims which were justified by the uncontested experience of decades, and even of centuries or millenniums, may have to be revised because of unforeseen changes; it knew in the words of Burke "that the generality of people are fifty years, at least, behind hand in their politics." Accordingly, the old political science was concerned with political improvement by political means as distinguished from social engineering; it knew that those political means include revolutions and wars since there may be foreign regimes (Hitler Germany is the orthodox example) which are dangerous to the survival in freedom of this country and of which it would be criminally foolish to assume that they will transform themselves gradually into good neighbors.

Acceptance of the distinctive premises of the new political science leads to the consequences which have been sufficiently illustrated in the four preceding essays. In the first place, the new political science is constantly compelled to borrow from common-sense knowledge, thus unwittingly testifying to the truth that there is genuine prescientific knowledge of political things which is the basis of all scientific knowledge of them. Second, the logic on which the new political science is based may provide sufficient criteria of exactness; it does not provide objective criteria of relevance. Criteria of relevance are inherent in the prescientific understanding of political things; intelligent and informed citizens distinguish soundly between important and unimportant political matters. Political men are concerned with what is to be done politically here and now in accordance with principles of preference of which they are aware, although not necessarily in an adequate manner; it is those principles of preference which supply the criteria of relevance in regard to political things. Ordinarily a political man must at least pretend to "look up" to something to which at least the preponderant part of his society looks up. That to which at least everyone who counts politically is supposed to look up, that which is politically the highest, gives a society its character; it constitutes and justifies the regime of the society in question. The "highest" is that through which a society is "a whole," a distinct whole with a character of its own, just as for common sense "the world" is a whole by being overarched by heaven of which one cannot be aware except by "looking up." There is obviously, and for cause, a variety of regimes and hence of what is regarded as the politically highest, that is, of the purposes to which the various regimes are dedicated.

The qualitatively different regimes, or kinds of regimes, and the qualitatively different purposes constituting and legitimating them by revealing themselves as the most important political things, supply the key to the understanding of all political things and the basis for the reasoned distinction between important and unimportant political things. The regimes and their principles pervade the societies throughout, in the sense that there are no recesses of privacy which are simply impervious to that pervasion, as is indicated by such expressions, coined by the new political science, as "the democratic personality." Nevertheless, there are political things which are not affected by the difference of regimes. In a society which cannot survive without an irrigation system, every regime will have to preserve that system intact. Every regime must try to preserve itself against subversion by means of force. There are both technical things and politically neutral things (things which are common to all regimes) which necessarily are the concern of political deliberation without ever being as such politically controversial. The preceding remarks are a very rough sketch of the view of political things that was characteristic of the old political science. According to that view, what is most important for political science is identical with what is most important politically. To illustrate this by the present-day example, for the old-fashioned political scientists today, the most important concern is the Cold War, or the qualitative difference which amounts to a conflict, between liberal democracy and Communism.

The break with the common-sense understanding of political things compels the new political science to abandon the criteria of relevance which are inherent in political understanding. Hence, the new political science lacks orientation regarding political things; it has no protection whatever except by surreptitious recourse to common sense against losing itself in the study of irrelevancies. It is confronted by a chaotic mass of data into which it must bring an order alien to those data and originating in the demands of political science as a science anxious to comply with the demands of logical positivism. The universals in the light of which the old political science viewed the political phenomena (the various regimes and their purposes) must be replaced by a different kind of universals. The first step toward the finding of the new kind of universals may be said to take this form: what is equally present in all regimes (the politically neutral) must be the key to the different regimes (the political proper, the essentially controversial); what is equally present in all regimes is, say, coercion and freedom; the scientific analysis of a given regime will then indicate exactly—in terms of percentages—the amount of coercion and the amount of freedom peculiar to it. That is to say, as political scientists we must express the political phenomena par excellence, the essential differences or the heterogeneity of regimes, in terms of the homogeneous elements which pervade all regimes. What is important for us as political scientists is not the politically important. Yet we cannot forever remain blind to the fact that what claims to be a purely scientific or theoretical enterprise has grave political consequences—consequences which are so little accidental that they appeal for their own sake to the new political scientists: everyone knows what follows from the demonstration, which presupposes the begging of all important questions, that there is only a difference of degree between liberal democracy and Communism in regard to coercion and freedom. The Is necessarily leads to an Ought, all sincere protestations to the contrary notwithstanding.

The second step toward the finding of the new kind of universals consists in the following reasoning: all political societies, whatever their regimes, surely are groups of some kind; hence, the key to the understanding of political things must be a theory of groups in general. Groups must have some cohesion, and groups change; we are then in need of a universal theory which tells us why or how groups cohere and why or how they change. Seeking for those why's or how's we shall discover n factors and m modes of their interaction. The result of this reduction of the political to the sociological—of a reduction for which it is claimed that it will make our understanding of political things more "realistic"—is in fact a formalism unrivaled in any scholasticism of the past. All peculiarities of political societies, and still more of the political societies with which we are concerned as citizens, become unrecognizable if restated in terms of the vague generalities which hold of every conceivable group; at the end of the dreary and boring process we understand what we are interested in not more but less than we understood it at the beginning. What in political language is called the rulers and the ruled (to say nothing of oppressors and oppressed) becomes through this process nothing but different parts of a social system, of a mechanism, each part acting on the other and being acted upon by it; there may be a stronger part, but there cannot be a ruling part; the relation of parts of a mechanism supersedes the political relation.

We need not dwell on the next, but not necessarily last, step of the reasoning which we are trying to sketch, namely, the requirement that the researches regarding groups must be underpinned, nay, guided, by "a general theory of personality" or the like: we know nothing of the political wisdom or the folly of a statesman's actions until we know everything about the degree of affection which he received from each of his parents, if any. The last step might be thought to be the use by the new political science of observations regarding rats: can we not observe human beings as we observe rats, are decisions which rats make not much simpler than the decisions which humans frequently make, and is not the simpler always the key to the more complex? We do not doubt that we can observe, if we try hard enough, the overt behavior of humans as we observe the overt behavior of rats. But we ought not to forget that in the case of rats we are limited to observing overt behavior because they do not talk, and they do not talk because they have nothing to say or because they have no inwardness. Yet to return from these depths to the surface, an important example of the formalism in question is supplied by the well-known theory regarding the principles of legitimacy which substitutes formal characteristics (traditional, rational, charismatic) for the substantive principles which are precisely the purposes to which the various regimes are dedicated and by which they are legitimated. The universals for which the new political science seeks are "laws of human behavior"; those laws are to be discovered by means of "empirical" research. There is an amazing disproportion between the apparent breadth of the goal (say, a general theory of social change) and the true pettiness of the researches undertaken in order to achieve that goal (say, a change in a hospital when one head nurse is replaced by another). This is no accident. Since we lack objective criteria of relevance, we have no reason to be more interested in a world-shaking revolution which affects directly or indirectly all men than in the most trifling "social changes." Moreover, if the laws sought are to be "laws of human behavior" they cannot be restricted to human behavior as it is affected by this or that regime. But human behavior as studied by "empirical" research always occurs within a peculiar regime. More precisely, the most cherished techniques of "empirical" research in the social sciences can be applied only to human beings living now in countries in which the government tolerates research of this kind. The new political science is therefore constantly tempted (and as a rule it does not resist the temptation) to absolutize the relative or peculiar, that is, to be parochial. We have read statements about "the revolutionary" or "the conservative" which did not even claim to have any basis other than observations made in the United States at the present moment; if those statements had any relations to facts at all, they might have some degree of truth regarding revolutionaries or conservatives in certain parts of the United States today, but they reveal themselves immediately as patently wrong if taken as they were meant—namely, as descriptions of the revolutionary or the conservative as such; the error in question was due to the parochialism inevitably fostered by the new political science.

At the risk of some repetition we must say a few words about the language of the new political science. The break with the political understanding of political things necessitates the making of a language different from the language used by political men. The new political science rejects the latter language as ambiguous and imprecise and claims that its own language is unambiguous and precise. Yet this claim is not warranted. The language of the new political science is not less vague, but more vague, than the language used in political life. Political life would be altogether impossible if its language were unqualifiedly vague; that language is capable of the utmost unambiguity and precision as in a declaration of war or in an order given to a firing squad. If available distinctions like that between war, peace, and armistice prove to be insufficient, political life finds, without the benefit of political science, the right new expression (Cold War as distinguished from Hot or Shooting War) which designates the new phenomenon with unfailing precision. The alleged vagueness of political language is primarily due to the fact that it corresponds to the complexity of political life or that it is nourished by long experience with political things in a great variety of circumstances. By simply condemning pre-scientific language, instead of deviating from usage in particular cases because of the proved inadequacy of usage in the cases in question, one simply condemns oneself to irredeemable vagueness. No thoughtful citizen would dream of equating politics with something as vague and empty as "power" or "power relations." The thinking men who are regarded as the classic interpreters of power—Thucydides and Machiavelli—did not need these expressions; these expressions as now used originate, not in political life, but in the academic reaction to the understanding of political life in terms of law alone: these expressions signify nothing but that academic reaction.

Political language does not claim to be perfectly clear and distinct; it does not claim that it is based on a full understanding of the things which it designates unambiguously enough; it is suggestive: it leaves those things in the penumbra in which they come to sight. The purge effected by "scientific" definitions of those things has the character of sterilization. The language of the new political science claims to be perfectly clear and distinct and at the same time entirely provisional; its terms are meant to imply hypotheses about political life. But this claim to undogmatic open-ness is a mere ceremonial gesture. When one speaks of "conscience" one does not claim that one has fathomed the phenomenon indicated by that term. But when the new political scientist speaks of the "Super-Ego," he is certain that anything meant by "conscience" which is not covered by the "Super-Ego" is a superstition. As a consequence he cannot distinguish be-tween a bad conscience, which may induce a man to devote the rest of his life to compensating another man to the best of his powers for an irrepara-ble damage, and "guilt feelings" which one ought to get rid of as fast and as cheaply as possible. Similarly he is certain to have understood the trust which induces people to vote for a candidate for high office by speaking of the "father image"; he does not have to inquire whether and to what ex-tent the candidate in question deserves that trust—a trust different from the trust which children have in their father. The allegedly provisional or hypothetical terms are never questioned in the process of research, for their implications channel the research in such directions that the "data" which might reveal the inadequacy of the hypotheses never turn up. We con-clude that to the extent to which the new political science is not formalis-tic, it is vulgarian. This vulgarianism shows itself particularly in the "value-free" manner in which it uses and thus debases terms that originally were meant only for indicating things of a noble character—terms like "cul-ture," "personality," "values," "charismatic," and "civilization."

The most important example of the dogmatism to which we have alluded is supplied by the treatment of religion in the new political or so-cial science. The new science uses sociological or psychological theories re-garding religion which exclude, without considering it, the possibility that religion rests ultimately on God's revealing Himself to man; hence those theories are mere hypotheses which can never be confirmed. Those theories are in fact the hidden basis of the new science. The new science rests on a dogmatic atheism which presents itself as merely methodological or hypo-thetical. For a few years, logical positivism tried with much noise and little thought to dispose of religion by asserting that religious assertions are "meaningless statements." This trick seems to have been abandoned with-out noise. Some adherents of the new political science might rejoin with some liveliness that their posture toward religion is imposed on them by intellectual honesty: not being able to believe, they cannot accept belief as the basis of their science. We gladly grant that, other things being equal, a frank atheist is a better man than an alleged theist who conceives of God as a symbol. But we must add that intellectual honesty is not enough. In-tellectual honesty is not love of truth. Intellectual honesty, a kind of self-denial, has taken the place of love of truth because truth has come to be believed to be repulsive, and one cannot love the repulsive. Yet just as our opponents refuse respect to unreasoned belief, we on our part, with at least equal right, must refuse respect to unreasoned unbelief; honesty with one-self regarding one's unbelief is in itself not more than unreasoned unbelief, probably accompanied by a vague confidence that the issue of unbelief versus belief has long since been settled once and for all. It is hardly necessary to add that the dogmatic exclusion of religious awareness proper renders questionable all long-range predictions concerning the future of societies.

The reduction of the political to the subpolitical is the reduction of primarily given wholes to elements which are relatively simple, that is, sufficiently simple for the research purpose at hand, yet necessarily susceptible of being analyzed into still simpler elements *in infinitum*. It implies that there cannot be genuine wholes. Hence it implies that there cannot be a common good. According to the old political science, there is necessarily a common good, and the common good in its fullness is the good society and what is required for the good society. The consistent denial of the common good is as impossible as every other consistent manifestation of the break with common sense. The empiricists who reject the notion of wholes are compelled to speak sooner or later of such things as "the open society," which is their definition of the good society. The alternative (if it is an alternative) is to deny the possibility of a substantive public interest, but to admit the possibility of substantive group interests; yet it is not difficult to see that what is granted to the goose "group" cannot be consistently denied to the gander "country." In accordance with this, the new political science surreptitiously reintroduces the common good in the form of "the rules of the game" with which all conflicting groups are supposed to comply because those rules reasonably fair to every group can reasonably be admitted by every group. The "group politics" approach is a relic of Marxism, which more reasonably denied that there can be a common good in a society consisting of classes that are locked in a life-and-death struggle, overt or hidden, and therefore found the common good in a classless and hence stateless society comprising the whole human race or the surviving part of it. The consistent denial of the common good requires a radical "individualism." In fact, the new political science appears to teach that there cannot be a substantive public interest because there is not, and cannot be, a single objective which is approved by all members of society: murderers show by their action that not even the prohibition against murder is strictly speaking to the public interest. We are not so sure whether the murderer wishes that murder cease to be a punishable action and not rather that he himself get away with murder. Be this as it may, this denial of the common good is based on the premise that even if an objective is to the interest of the overwhelming majority, it is not to the interest of all: no minority, however small, no individual, however perverse, must be left out. More precisely, even if an objective is to the interest of all, but not believed by all to be to the interest of all, it is not to the public inter-

est: everyone is by nature the sole judge of what is to his interest; his judgment regarding his interest is not subject to anybody else's examination on
the issue whether his judgment is sound.

This premise is not the discovery or invention of the new political science; it was stated with the greatest vigor by Hobbes, who opposed it to
the opposite premise which had been the basis of the old political science
proper. But Hobbes still saw that his premise entails the war of everybody
against everybody and hence drew the conclusion that everyone must cease
to be the sole judge of what is to his interest if there is to be human life;
the individual's reason must give way to the public reason. The new political science denies in a way that there is a public reason: government may
be a broker, if a broker possessing "the monopoly of violence," but it surely
is not the public reason. The true public reason is the new political science
which judges in a universally valid, or objective, manner of what is to the
interest of each, for it shows to everyone what means he must choose in
order to attain his attainable ends, whatever those ends may be. It has been
shown earlier in this volume what becomes of the new political science, or
of the only kind of rationality which the new political science still admits,
if its Hobbesian premise is not conveniently forgotten: the new form of
public reason goes the way of the old.

The denial of the common good presents itself today as a direct consequence of the distinction between facts and values according to which only
factual judgments, not value judgments, can be true or objective. The new
political science leaves the justification of values or of preferences to "political philosophy" or more precisely to ideology on the ground that any justification of preferences would have to derive values from facts, and such
derivation is not legitimately possible. Preferences are not strictly speaking
opinions and hence cannot be true or false, whereas ideologies are opinions
and, for the reason given, false opinions. Whereas acting man has necessarily chosen values, the new political scientist as pure spectator is not
committed to any value; in particular, he is neutral in the conflict between
liberal democracy and its enemies. The traditional value systems antedate
the awareness of the difference between facts and values; they claimed to
be derived from facts—from Divine Revelation or from similar sources—in
general from superior or perfect beings which as such unite in themselves
fact and value; the discovery of the difference between facts and values
amounts therefore to a refutation of the traditional value systems as originally meant. It is at least doubtful whether those value systems can be
divorced from what present themselves as their factual bases. At any rate, it
follows from the difference between facts and values that men can live
without ideology: they can adopt, posit, or proclaim values without making
the illegitimate attempt to derive their values from facts or without relying
on false or at least unevident assertions regarding what is. One thus arrives
at the notion of the rational society or of the nonideological regime: a soci-

ety which is based on the understanding of the character of values. Since this understanding implies that before the tribunal of reason all values are equal, the rational society will be egalitarian or democratic and permissive or liberal: the rational doctrine regarding the difference between facts and values rationally justifies the preference for liberal democracy—contrary to what is intended by that distinction itself. In other words, whereas the new political science ought to deny the proposition that there can be no society without an ideology, it asserts that proposition.

One is thus led to wonder whether the distinction between facts and values, or the assertion that no Ought can be derived from an Is, is well founded. Let us assume that a man's "values" (that is, what he values) are fully determined by his heredity and environment (that is, by his Is), or that there is a one-to-one relation between value *a* and Is A. In this case the Ought would be determined by the Is or derivative from it. But the very issue as commonly understood presupposes that this assumption is wrong: man possesses a certain latitude; he can choose not only from among various ways of overt behavior (like jumping or not jumping into a river in order to escape death at the hands of a stronger enemy who may or may not be able to swim) but from among various values; this latitude, this possibility, has the character of a fact. A man lacking this latitude—for example, a man for whom every stimulus is a value or who cannot help giving in to every desire—is a defective man, a man with whom something is wrong. The fact that someone desires something does not yet make that something his value; he may successfully fight his desire, or if his desire overpowers him, he may blame himself for this as for a failure on his part; only choice, in contradistinction to mere desire, makes something a man's value. The distinction between desire and choice is a distinction among facts. Choice does not mean here the choice of means to pregiven ends; choice here means the choice of ends, the positing of ends, or rather of values.

Man is then understood as a being which differs from all other known beings because it posits values; this positing is taken to be a fact. In accordance with this, the new political science denies that man has natural ends—ends toward which he is by nature inclined; it denies more specifically the premise of modern natural right according to which self-preservation is the most important natural end: man can choose death in preference to life, not in a given situation, out of despair, but simply: he can posit death as his value. The view that the pertinent Is is our positing of values in contradistinction to the yielding to mere desires necessarily leads to Oughts of a radically different character from the so-called Oughts corresponding to mere desires. We conclude that the "relativism" accepted by the new political science according to which values are nothing but objects of desire is based on an insufficient analysis of the Is, that is, of the pertinent Is, and furthermore that one's opinion regarding the character of the

Is settles one's opinion regarding the character of the Ought. We must leave it open here whether a more adequate analysis of the pertinent Is, that is, of the nature of man, does not lead to a more adequate determination of the Ought or beyond a merely formal characterization of the Ought. At any rate, if a man is of the opinion that as a matter of fact all desires are of equal dignity, since we know of no factual consideration which would entitle us to assign different dignities to different desires, he cannot but be of the opinion, unless he is prepared to become guilty of gross arbitrariness, that all desires ought to be treated as equal within the limits of the possible, and this opinion is what is meant by permissive egalitarianism.

There is then more than a mysterious pre-established harmony between the new political science and a certain version of liberal democracy. The alleged value-free analysis of political phenomena is controlled by an un-avowed commitment built into the new political science to that version of liberal democracy. That version of liberal democracy is not discussed openly and impartially, with full consideration of all relevant pros and cons. We call this characteristic of the new political science its democratism. The new political science looks for laws of human behavior to be discovered by means of data supplied through certain techniques of research which are believed to guarantee the maximum of objectivity; it therefore puts a premium on the study of things which occur frequently now in democratic societies: neither those in their graves nor those behind the Curtains can respond to questionnaires or interviews. Democracy is then the tacit presupposition of the data; it does not have to become a theme; it can easily be forgotten: the wood is forgotten for the trees; the laws of human behavior are in fact laws of the behavior of human beings more or less molded by democracy; man is tacitly identified with democratic man. The new political science puts a premium on observations which can be made with the utmost frequency, and therefore by people of the meanest capacities. It therefore frequently culminates in observations made by people who are not intelligent about people who are not intelligent. While the new political science becomes ever less able to see democracy or to hold a mirror to democracy, it ever more reflects the most dangerous proclivities of democracy. It even strengthens those proclivities. By teaching in effect the equality of literally all desires, it teaches in effect that there is nothing of which a man ought to be ashamed; by destroying the possibility of self-contempt, it destroys with the best of intentions the possibility of self-respect. By teaching the equality of all values, by denying that there are things which are intrinsically high and others which are intrinsically low as well as by denying that there is an essential difference between men and brutes, it unwittingly contributes to the victory of the gutter.

Yet the same new political science came into being through the revolt against what one may call the democratic orthodoxy of the immediate past. It had learned certain lessons which were hard for that orthodoxy to swallow regarding the irrationality of the masses and the necessity of elites; if it had been wise, it would have learned those lessons from the galaxy of antidemocratic thinkers of the remote past. It believed, in other words, it had learned that contrary to the belief of the orthodox democrats, no compelling case can be made for liberalism (for example, for the unqualified freedom of such speech as does not constitute a clear and present danger) nor for democracy (free elections based on universal suffrage). But it succeeded in reconciling those doubts with the unfaltering commitment to liberal democracy by the simple device of declaring that no value judgments, including those supporting liberal democracy, are rational and hence that an ironclad argument in favor of liberal democracy ought in reason not even to be expected. The very complex pros and cons regarding liberal democracy have thus become entirely obliterated by the poorest formalism. The crisis of liberal democracy has become concealed by a ritual which calls itself methodology or logic. This almost willful blindness to the crisis of liberal democracy is part of that crisis. No wonder then that the new political science has nothing to say against those who unhesitatingly prefer surrender, that is, the abandonment of liberal democracy, to war.

Only a great fool would call the new political science diabolic: it has no attributes peculiar to fallen angels. It is not even Machiavellian, for Machiavelli's teaching was graceful, subtle, and colorful. Nor is it Neronian. Nevertheless one may say of it that it fiddles while Rome burns. It is excused by two facts: it does not know that it fiddles, and it does not know that Rome burns.

9/ Preface to Spinoza's Critique of Religion

The study on Spinoza's *Theologico-political Treatise* to which this was a preface was written during the years 1925–1928 in Germany. The author was a young Jew born and raised in Germany who found himself in the grips of the theologico-political predicament.

At that time Germany was a liberal democracy. The regime was known as the Weimar Republic. In the light of the most authoritative political document of recent Germany, Bismarck's *Thoughts and Recollections*, the option for Weimar reveals itself as an option against Bismarck. In the eyes of Bismarck, Weimar stood for leanings to the West, if not for the inner dependence of the Germans on the French and above all on the English, and a corresponding aversion to everything Russian. But Weimar was, above all, the residence of Goethe, that contemporary of the collapse of the Holy Roman Empire of the German nation and of the victory of the French Revolution and Napoleon, whose sympathetic understanding was open to both antagonists and who identified himself in this thought with neither. By linking itself to Weimar the German liberal democracy proclaimed its moderate, nonradical character: its resolve to keep a balance between the dedication to the principles of 1789 and the dedication to the highest German tradition.

The Weimar Republic was weak. It had a single moment of strength, if not of greatness: its strong reaction to the murder of the Jewish Minister of Foreign Affairs Rathenau in 1922. On the whole it presented the sorry spectacle of justice without a sword or of justice unable to use the sword. The election of Field Marshal von Hindenburg to the presidency of the German Reich in 1925 showed everyone who had eyes to see that the Weimar Republic had only a short time to live: the old Germany was stronger—stronger in will—than the new Germany. What was still lacking then for the destruction of the Weimar Republic was the opportune moment; that moment was to come within a few years. The weakness of the Weimar Republic made certain its speedy destruction. It did not make certain the victory of National Socialism. The victory of National Socialism became necessary in Germany for the same reason for which the victory of Communism had become necessary in Russia: the man who had by far the strongest will or single-mindedness, the greatest ruthlessness, daring, and power over his following, and the best judgment about the strength of the various forces in the immediately relevant political field was the leader of the revolution.[1]

Half-Marxists trace the weakness of the Weimar Republic to the power of monopoly capitalism and the economic crisis of 1929, but there were other liberal democracies which were and remained strong although they had to contend with the same difficulties. It is more reasonable to refer to the fact that the Weimar Republic had come into being through the defeat of Germany in World War I, although this answer merely leads to the further question as to why Germany had not succeeded in becoming a liberal democracy under more auspicious circumstances (for instance, in 1848), that is, why liberal democracy had always been weak in Germany. It is true that the Bismarckian regime as managed by William II had become discredited already prior to World War I and still more through that war and its outcome, and correspondingly liberal democracy had become ever more attractive; but at the crucial moment the victorious liberal democracies discredited liberal democracy in the eyes of Germany by the betrayal of their principles through the Treaty of Versailles.

It is safer to try to understand the low in the light of the high than the high in the light of the low. In doing the latter one necessarily distorts the high, whereas in doing the former one does not deprive the low of the freedom to reveal itself fully as what it is. By its name the Weimar Republic refers one to the greatest epoch of German thought and letters, to the epoch extending from the last third of the eighteenth century to the first third of the nineteenth century. No one can say that classical Germany spoke clearly and distinctly in favor of liberal democracy. This is true despite the fact that classical Germany had been initiated by Rousseau. In the first place Rousseau was the first modern critic of the fundamental modern project (man's conquest of nature for the sake of the relief of man's estate) who therewith laid the foundation for the distinction, so fateful for German thought, between civilization and culture. Above all, the radicalization and deepening of Rousseau's thought by classical German philosophy culminated in Hegel's *Philosophy of Right*, the legitimation of that kind of constitutional monarchy which is based on the recognition of the rights of man and in which government is in the hands of highly educated civil servants appointed by a hereditary king. It has been said, not without reason, that Hegel's rule over Germany came to an end only on the day that Hitler came to power. But Rousseau prepared not only the French Revolution and classical German philosophy but also that extreme reaction to the French Revolution which is German romanticism. To speak politically and crudely, "the romantic school in Germany . . . was nothing other than the resurrection of medieval poetry as it had manifested itself . . . in art and in life." [2] The longing for the Middle Ages began in Germany in the same moment in which the actual Middle Ages—the Holy Roman Empire ruled by a German—ended, in what was then thought to be the moment of Germany's deepest humiliation. In Germany, and only there, did the end of the Middle Ages coincide with the beginning of the longing for the Middle Ages. Compared with the medieval Reich, which had lasted for almost a millennium until 1806, Bismarck's Reich (to say nothing of Hegel's Prussia) revealed itself as a little Germany not only in size. All profound German longings—for those for the Middle Ages were not the only ones nor even the most profound ones—all these longings for the origins or, negatively expressed, all German dissatisfactions with modernity pointed toward a third Reich, for Germany was to be the core even of Nietzsche's Europe ruling the planet.[3]

The weakness of liberal democracy in Germany explains why the situation of the indigenous Jews was more precarious in Germany than in any other Western country. Liberal democracy had originally defined itself in theologico-political treatises as the opposite, less of the more or less enlightened despotism of the seventeenth and eighteenth centuries, than of "the kingdom of darkness," that is, of medieval society. According to liberal democracy, the bond of society is universal human morality, whereas religion (positive religion) is a private affair; in the Middle Ages religion, that is, Catholic Christianity, was the bond of society. The action most characteristic of the Middle Ages is the Crusades; it may be said to have culminated not accidentally in the murder of whole Jewish communities. The German Jews owed their emancipation to the French Revolution or its effects. They were given full political rights for the first time by the Weimar Republic. The Weimar Republic was succeeded by the only German regime—by the only regime that ever was anywhere—which had no other clear principle except murderous hatred of the Jews, for "Aryan" had no clear meaning other than "non-Jewish." One must keep in mind the fact that Hitler did not come from Prussia, nor even from Bismarck's Reich.

While the German Jews were politically in a more precarious situation than the Jews in any other Western country, they originated "the science of Judaism," the historical-critical study by Jews of the Jewish heritage. The emancipation of the Jews in Germany coincided with the greatest epoch of German thought and poetry, with the epoch in which Germany was the foremost country in thought and poetry. One cannot help comparing the period of German Jewry with the period of Spanish Jewry. The greatest achievements of Jews during the Spanish period were partly rendered possible by the fact that Jews became open to the influx of Greek thought which was understood to be Greek only accidentally. During the German period, however, the Jews became open to the influx of German thought, of the thought of the particular nation in the midst of which they lived—of a thought which was understood to be German essentially: the political dependence was also spiritual dependence. This was the core of the predicament of German Jewry.

Three quotations may serve to illustrate the precarious situation of the Jews in Germany. Goethe, the greatest among the cosmopolitan Germans, a "decided non-Christian," summarizes the results of a conversation about a new society to be founded, between his Wilhelm Meister and "the gay Friedrich," without providing his summary with quotation marks, as follows:

> To this religion [the Christian religion] we hold on, but in a particular manner; we instruct our children from their youth on in the great advantages which [that religion] has brought to us; but of its author, of its course we speak to them only at the end. Then only does the author become dear and cherished, and all reports regarding him become sacred. Drawing a conclusion which one may perhaps call pedantic, but of which one must at any rate admit that it follows from the premise, we do not tolerate any Jew among us; for how could we grant him a share in the highest culture, the origin and tradition of which he denies? [4]

Two generations later Nietzsche could say: "I have not yet met a German who was favorably disposed toward the Jews." [5] One might try to trace Nietzsche's judgment to the narrowness of his circle of acquaintances: no one would expect to find people favorably disposed toward Jews among the German Lutheran pastors among whom Nietzsche grew up, to say nothing of Jakob Burckhardt in Basel. Nietzsche has chosen his words carefully; he surely excluded himself when making the judgment quoted, as appears, in addition, from the context. But he does not say something trivial. While his circle of acquaintances was limited—perhaps unusually limited—he was of unusual perspicacity. Besides, being favorably disposed toward this or that man or woman of Jewish origin does not mean being favorably disposed toward Jews. Two generations later, in 1953, Heidegger could speak of "the inner truth and greatness of National Socialism." [6]

In the course of the nineteenth century many Western men had come to conceive of many, if not all, sufferings as problems which as such were held to be soluble as a matter of course. Thus they had come to speak also of the Jewish problem. The German-Jewish problem was never solved. It was annihilated by the annihilation of the German Jews. Prior to Hitler's rise to power most German Jews believed that their problem had been solved in principle by liberalism: the German Jews were Germans of the Jewish faith, that is, they were no less German than the Germans of the

Christian faith or of no faith. They assumed that the German state (to say nothing of German society or culture) was or ought to be neutral to the difference between Christians and Jews or between non-Jews and Jews. This assumption was not accepted by the strongest part of Germany and hence by Germany. In the words of Herzl: "Who belongs and who does not belong, is decided by the majority; it is a question of power." At any rate it could seem that in the absence of a superior recognized equally by both parties the natural judge on the Germanness of the German Jews was the non-Jewish Germans. As a consequence a small minority of the German Jews, but a considerable minority of the German-Jewish youth studying at the universities, had turned to Zionism. Zionism was almost never wholly divorced from the traditional Jewish hopes. On the; other hand, Zionism never intended to bring about a restoration like the one achieved in the days of Ezra and Nehemiah: the return to the land of Israel was not thought to culminate in the building of the third temple and in the restoration of the sacrificial service.

The peculiarity of Zionism as a modern movement comes out most clearly in the strictly political Zionism as presented in the first place by Leon Pinsker in his *Autoemancipation* and then by Theodor Herzl in *The Jews' State*. Pinsker and Herzl started from the failure of the liberal solution but continued to see the problem to be solved as it had begun to be seen by liberalism, that is, as a merely human problem. They radicalized this purely human understanding. The terrible fate of the Jews was in no sense to be understood any longer as connected with divine punishment for the sins of our fathers or with the providential mission of the chosen people and hence to be borne with the meek fortitude of martyrs. It was to be understood in merely human terms: as constituting a purely political problem which as such cannot be solved by appealing to the justice or generosity of other nations, to say nothing of a league of all nations. Accordingly, political Zionism was concerned primarily with nothing but the cleansing of the Jews from millennial degradation or with the recovery of Jewish dignity, honor, or pride. The failure of the liberal solution meant that the Jews could not regain their honor by assimilating themselves as individuals to the nations among which they lived or by becoming citizens like all other citizens of the liberal states: the liberal solution brought at best legal equality, but not social equality; as a demand of reason it had no effect on the feelings of the non-Jews. To quote Herzl again: "We are a nation—the enemy makes us a nation whether we like it or not." In the last analysis this is nothing to be deplored, for "the enemy is necessary for the highest effort of the personality." Only through securing the honor of the Jewish nation could the individual Jew's honor be secured. The true solution of the Jewish problem requires that the Jews become "like all the nations" (I Sam. 8), that the Jewish nation assimilate itself to the nations of the world or that it establish a modern, liberal, secular (but not necessarily democratic) state. Political Zionism strictly understood was then the movement of an elite on behalf of a community constituted by common descent and common degradation for the restoration of their honor through the acquisition of statehood and therefore of a country—of any country: the land which the strictly political Zionism promised to the Jews was not necessarily the land of Israel.

This project implied a profound modification of the traditional Jewish hopes—a modification arrived at through a break with these hopes. For the motto of his pamphlet Pinsker chose these words of Hillel: "If I am not for myself, who will be for me? And if not now, when?" He omitted the sentence which forms the center of Hillel's statement: "And if I am only for myself, what am I?" He saw the Jewish people as a herd without a shepherd who protects and gathers it; he did not long for a shepherd, but for the transformation of the herd into a nation which can take care of itself. He regarded the Jewish situation as a natural sickness which can be cured only by natural means. What the change effected by strictly political Zionism means, one sees most clearly when, returning to the origin, one ponders over this sentence of Spinoza: "If the foundations of their religion did not effeminate the minds of the Jews, I would absolutely believe that they will at some time, given the occasion (for human things are mutable), establish their state again."

Strictly political Zionism became effective only through becoming an ingredient, not to say the backbone, of Zionism at large, that is, by making its peace with traditional Jewish thought. Through this alliance or fusion it brought about the establishment of the state of Israel and therewith that cleansing which it had primarily intended; it thus procured a blessing for all Jews everywhere regardless of whether they admit it or not.[7] It did not, however, solve the Jewish problem. It could not solve the Jewish problem because of the narrowness of its original conception, however noble. This narrowness was pointed out most effectively by cultural Zionism: strictly political Zionism, concerned only with the present emergency and resolve, lacks historical perspective; the community of descent, of the blood, must also be a community of the mind, of the national mind; the Jewish state will be an empty shell without a Jewish culture which has its roots in the Jewish heritage. One could not have taken this step unless one had previously interpreted the Jewish heritage itself as a culture, that is, as a product of the national mind, of the national genius.[8] Yet the foundation, the authoritative layer, of the Jewish heritage presents itself, not as a product of the human mind, but as a divine gift, as divine revelation. Did one not completely distort the meaning of the heritage to which one claimed to be loyal by interpreting it as a culture like any other high culture? Cultural Zionism believed to have found a safe middle ground between politics (power politics) and divine revelation, between the subcultural and the supracultural, but it lacked the sternness of the two extremes. When cultural Zionism understands itself, it turns into religious Zionism. But when religious Zionism understands itself, it is in the first place Jewish faith and only secondarily Zionism. It must regard as blasphemous the notion of a human solution to the Jewish problem. It may go so far as to regard the establishment of the state of Israel as the most important event in Jewish history since the completion of the Talmud, but it cannot regard it as the arrival of the Messianic age, of the redemption of Israel and all men. The establishment of the state of Israel is the most profound modification of the Galuth which has occurred, but it is not the end of the Galuth: in the religious sense, and perhaps not only in the religious sense, the state of Israel is a part of the Galuth. Finite, relative problems can be solved; infinite, absolute problems cannot be solved. In other words, human beings will never create a society which is free from contradictions. From every point of view it looks as if the Jewish people were the chosen people, at least in the sense that the Jewish problem is the most manifest symbol of the human problem insofar as it is a social or political problem.

To realize that the Jewish problem is insoluble means never to forget the truth proclaimed by Zionism regarding the limitations of liberalism. Liberalism stands and falls by the distinction between state and society or by the recognition of a private sphere, protected by the law but impervious to the law, with the understanding that, above all, religion as particular religion belongs to the private sphere. As certainly as the liberal state will not "discriminate" against its Jewish citizens, as certainly is it constitutionally unable and even unwilling to prevent "discrimination" against Jews on the part of individuals or groups. To recognize a private sphere in the sense indicated means to permit private "discrimination," to protect it, and thus in fact to foster it. The liberal state cannot provide a solution to the Jewish problem, for such a solution would require the legal prohibition against every kind of "discrimination," that is, the abolition of the private sphere, the denial of the difference between state and society, the destruction of the liberal state. Such a destruction would not by any means solve the Jewish problem, as is shown in our days by the anti-Jewish policy of the U.S.S.R. It is foolish to say that that policy contradicts the principles of Communism, for it contradicts the principles of Communism to separate the principles of Communism from the Communist movement. The U.S.S.R. owes its survival to Stalin's decision not to wait for the revolution of the Western proletariat, that is, for what others would do for the U.S.S.R., but to build up socialism in a single country where his word was the law, by the use of any means, however bestial, and these means could include, as a matter of course, means successfully used before, not to say invented, by Hitler: the large-scale murder of party members and anti-Jewish measures. This is not to deny that Communism has not become what National Socialism always was, the prisoner of an anti-Jewish ideology, but makes use of anti-Jewish measures in an unprincipled manner, when and where they seem to be expedient. It is merely to confirm our contention that the uneasy "solution of the Jewish problem" offered by the liberal state is superior to the Communist "solution."

There is a Jewish problem which is humanly soluble: [9] the problem of the Western Jewish individual who or whose parents severed his connection with the Jewish community in the expectation that he would thus become a normal member of a purely liberal or of a universal human society and who is naturally perplexed when he finds no such society. The solution to his problem is return to the Jewish community, the community established by the Jewish faith and the Jewish way of life—*teshubah* (ordinarily rendered by "repentance") in the most comprehensive sense. Some of our contemporaries believe that such a return is altogether impossible because they believe that the Jewish faith has been overthrown once and for all, not by blind rebellion, but by evident refutation. While admitting that their deepest problem would be solved by that return, they assert that intellectual probity forbids them to bring the sacrifice of the intellect for the sake of satisfying even the most vital need. Yet they can hardly deny that a vital need legitimately induces a man to probe whether what seems to be an impossibility is in fact only a very great difficulty.

The founder of cultural Zionism could still deny that the Jewish people have a providential mission on the ground that Darwin had destroyed the most solid basis of teleology.[10] At the time and in the country in which the present study was written, it was granted by everyone except backward people that the Jewish faith had not been refuted by science or by history. The storms stirred up by Darwin and to a lesser degree by Wellhausen had been weathered; one could grant to science and history everything they seem to teach regarding the age of the world, the origin of man, the impossibility of miracles, the impossibility of the immortality of the soul and of the resurrection of the body, the Jahvist, the Elohist, the third Isaiah, and so on, without abandoning one iota of the substance of the Jewish faith. Some haggling regarding particular items which issued sometimes in grudging concessions was still going on in outlying districts, but the battle for the capital had been decided by the wholesale surrender to science and history of the whole sphere in which science and history claim to be or to become competent and by the simultaneous depreciation of that whole sphere as religiously irrelevant. It had become religiously relevant, it was affirmed, only through a self-misunderstanding of religion, if of a self-misunderstanding which was inevitable in earlier times and which on the whole was even harmless in earlier times. That self-misunderstanding consisted in understanding revelation as a body of teachings and rules which includes such teachings and rules as could never become known to the unassisted human mind as true and binding, such as the human mind would reject as subrational were they not proved to be suprarational by the certainty that they are the word of God; men who were not earwitnesses of

God's declaring these teachings and rules could have that certainty only through a reliable tradition which also vouches for the reliable transmission of the very words of God, and through miracles. The self-misunderstanding is removed when the content of revelation is seen to be rational, which does not necessarily mean that everything hitherto thought to be revealed is rational. The need for external credentials of revelation (tradition and miracles) disappears as its internal credentials come to abound. The truth of traditional Judaism is the religion of reason, or the religion of reason is secularized Judaism. But the same claim could be made for Christianity, and however close secularized Judaism and secularized Christianity might come to each other, they are not identical, and as purely rational they ought to be identical. Above all, if the truth of Judaism is the religion of reason, then what was formerly believed to be revelation by the transcendent God must now be understood as the work of the human imagination in which human reason was effective to some extent; what has now become a clear and distant idea was originally a confused idea.[11] What, except demonstrations of the existence of God by theoretical reason or postulations of His existence by practical reason which were becoming ever more incredible, could prevent one from taking the last step, that is, to assert that God Himself is a product of the human mind, at best "an idea of reason"?

These and similar denials or interpretations suddenly lost all their force by the simple observation that they contradict not merely inherited opinions but present experience. At first hearing one may be reminded of what Leibniz had said when overcoming Bayle's doubt regarding revelation: "Toutes ces difficultés invincibles, ces combats prétendus de la raison contre la foi s'évanouissent.

> Hi motus animorum atque haec discrimina tanta
> Pulveris exigui jactu compressa quiescunt.[12]

God's revealing Himself to man, His addressing man, is not merely known through traditions going back to the remote past and is therefore now "merely believed" but is genuinely known through present experience which every human being can have if he does not refuse himself to it. This experience is not a kind of self-experience, of the actualization of a human potentiality, of the human mind coming into its own, into what it desires or is naturally inclined to, but of something undesired, coming from the outside, going against man's grain; it is the only awareness of something absolute which cannot be relativized in any way as everything else, rational or nonrational, can; it is the experience of God as the Thou, the father and king of all men; it is the experience of an unequivocal command addressed to me here and now as distinguished from general laws or ideas which are always disputable and permitting of exceptions; only by surrendering to God's experienced call which calls for one's loving Him with all one's heart, with all one's soul, and with all one's might can one come to see the other human being as his brother and love him as himself. The absolute experience will not lead back to Judaism—for instance, to the details of what the Christians call the ceremonial law—if it does not recognize itself in the Bible and clarify itself through the Bible and if it is not linked up with considerations of how traditional Judaism understands itself and with meditations about the mysterious fate of the Jewish people. The return to Judaism also requires today the overcoming of what one may call the perennial obstacle to the Jewish faith: of traditional philosophy, which is of Greek, pagan origin. For the respectable, impressive, or specious alternatives to the acceptance of revelation, to the surrender to God's will, have always presented themselves and still present themselves as based on what man knows by himself, by his reason. Reason has reached its perfection in Hegel's system; the essential limitations of Hegel's system show the essential limitations of reason and therewith the radical inadequacy of all rational objections to revelation. With the final collapse of rationalism the perennial battle between reason and revelation, between unbelief and belief, has been decided in principle, even on the plane of human thought, in favor of revelation. Reason knows only of subjects and objects, but surely the living and loving God is infinitely more than a subject and can never be an object, something at which one can look in detachment or indifference. Philosophy as hitherto known, the old thinking, so far from starting from the experience of God, abstracted from such experience or excluded it; hence, if it was theistic, it was compelled to have recourse to demonstrations of the existence of God as a thinking or a thinking and willing being. The new thinking as unqualified empiricism speaks of God, man, and the world as actually experienced, as realities irreducible to one another, whereas all traditional philosophy was reductionist. For if it did not assert that the world and man are eternal, that is, deny the creator-God, it sought for the reality preceding world and man as it precedes world and man and as it succeeds world and man, that is, for what cannot be experienced by man, by the whole man, but only be inferred or thought by him. Unqualified empiricism does not recognize any such Without or Beyond as a reality, but only as unreal forms, essences, or concepts which can never be more than objects, that is, objects of mere thought.[13]

The new thinking had been originated, above all, by Franz Rosenzweig, who is thought to be the greatest Jewish thinker whom German Jewry has brought forth. It was counteracted by another form of the new thinking, the form originated by Heidegger.[14] It was obvious that Heidegger's new thinking led far away from any charity as well as from any humanity. On the other hand, it could not be denied that he had a deeper understanding than Rosenzweig of what was implied in the insight or demand that the traditional philosophy which rested on Greek foundations must be superseded by a new thinking. He would never have said as Rosenzweig did that "we know in the most precise manner, we know it with the intuitional knowledge of experience, what God taken by Himself, what man taken by himself, what the world taken by itself 'is.' " Nor did he assume, as Rosenzweig assumed, that we possess without further ado an adequate understanding of Greek philosophy, of the basic stratum of that old thinking which has to be overcome: with the questioning of traditional philosophy the traditional understanding of the tradition becomes questionable. For this reason alone he could not have said as Rosenzweig did that most Platonic dialogues are "boring." [15] This difference between Rosenzweig and Heidegger, about which much more could be said, was not unconnected with their difference regarding revelation. At that time Heidegger expressed his thought about revelation by silence or deed rather than by speech. Rosenzweig's friend Martin Buber quotes a much later utterance of Heidegger which gives one, I believe, an inkling of Heidegger's argument—especially if it is taken in conjunction with well-known utterances of Nietzsche whom Heidegger evidently follows in this matter.

"The 'prophets' of these religions [sc. Judaism and Christianity]," says Heidegger according to Buber, "do not begin by foretelling the word of the Holy. They announce immediately the God upon whom the certainty of salvation is a supernatural blessedness reckons." [16] Buber comments on this statement as follows:

> Incidentally, I have never in our time encountered on a high philosophical plane such a far-reaching misunderstanding of the prophets of Israel. The prophets of Israel have never announced a God upon whom their hearers' striving for security reckoned. They have always aimed to shatter all security and to proclaim in the opened abyss of the final insecurity the unwished for God who demands that His human creatures become real, they become human, and confounds all who imagine that they can take refuge in the certainty that the temple of God is in their midst.

Heidegger does not speak of the prophets' "hearers," but he clearly means that the prophets themselves were concerned with security.[17] This assertion is not refuted by the well-known facts which Buber points out—by the fact, in a word, that for the prophets there is no refuge and fortress except God: the security afforded by the temple of God is nothing, but the security afforded by God is everything. As Buber says seventeen pages earlier in the same publication, "He who loves God only as a moral ideal, can easily arrive at despairing of the guidance of a world the appearance of which contradicts, hour after hour, all principles of his moral ideality." [18] Surely the Bible teaches that in spite of all appearances to the contrary the world is guided by God or, to use the traditional term, that there is particular providence, that man is protected by God if he does not put his trust in flesh and blood but in God alone, that he is not completely exposed or forsaken, that he is not alone, that he has been created by a being which is, to use Buber's expression, a Thou. Buber's protest would be justified if the biblical prophets were only, as Wellhausen may seem to have hoped, prophets of insecurity, not to say of an evil end,[19] and not also predictors of the Messianic future, of the ultimate victory of truth and justice, of the final salvation and security, although not necessarily of the final salvation and security of all men. In other words, the biblical experience is not simply undesired or against man's grain: grace perfects nature; it does not destroy nature. Not every man but every noble man is concerned with justice or righteousness and therefore with any possible extrahuman, suprahuman support of justice or with the security of justice. The insecurity of man and everything human is not an absolutely terrifying abyss if the highest of which a man knows is absolutely secure. Plato's Athenian Stranger does not indeed experience that support, that refuge and fortress as the biblical prophets experienced it, but he does the second best: he tries to demonstrate its existence. But for Heidegger there is no security, no happy ending, no divine shepherd; hope is replaced by thinking; the longing for eternity, belief in anything eternal is understood as stemming from "the spirit of revenge," from the desire to escape from all passing away into something which never passes away.[20]

The controversy can easily degenerate into a race in which he wins who offers the smallest security and the greatest terror and regarding which it would not be difficult to guess who will be the winner. But just as an assertion does not become true because it is shown to be comforting, it does not become true because it is shown to be terrifying. The serious question concerns man's certainty or knowledge of the divine promises or covenants. They are known through what God Himself says in the Scriptures. According to Buber, whose belief in revelation is admittedly "not mixed up with any 'orthodoxy,'" what we read in the Bible is in all cases, even when God is said to have said something (as for example and above all in the case of the Ten Commandments), what the biblical authors say, and what the biblical authors say is never more than a human expression of God's speechless call or a human response to that call or a man-made "image," a human interpretation—an experienced human interpretation, to be sure—of what God "said." Such "images" constitute not only Judaism and Christianity but all religions. All such "images" are "distorting and yet correct, perishable like an image in a dream and yet verified in eternity."[21] The experience of God is surely not specifically Jewish. Besides, can one say that one experiences God as the creator of heaven and earth, that is, that one knows from the experience taken by itself of God that He is the creator of heaven and earth, or that men who are not prophets experience God as a thinking, willing, and speaking being? Is the absolute experience necessarily the experience of a Thou?[22] Every assertion about the absolute experience which says more than that what is experienced is the Presence or the Call, is not the experiencer, is not flesh and

blood, is the wholly other, is death or nothingness, is an "image" or interpretation; that any one interpretation is the simply true interpretation is
not known, but "merely believed." One cannot establish that any particular interpretation of the absolute experience is the most adequate interpretation on the ground that it alone agrees with all other experiences, for
instance, with the experienced mystery of the Jewish fate, for the Jewish
fate is a mystery only on the basis of a particular interpretation of the absolute experience, or rather the Jewish fate is the outcome of one particular
interpretation of the absolute experience. The very emphasis on the absolute experience as experience compels one to demand that it be made as
clear as possible what the experience by itself conveys, that it not be
tampered with, that it be carefully distinguished from every interpretation
of the experience, for the interpretations may be suspected of being
attempts to render bearable and harmless the experienced which admittedly comes from without down upon man and is undesired, or to cover
over man's radical unprotectedness, loneliness, and exposedness.[23]

Yet—Buber could well have retorted—does not precisely this objection
mean that the atheistic suspicion is as much a possibility, an interpretation,
and hence as much "merely believed" as the theistic one? And is not being
based on belief, which is the pride of religion, a calamity for philosophy?
Can the new thinking consistently reject or (what is the same thing) pass
by revelation? Through judging others, Nietzsche himself had established
the criterion by which his doctrine is to be judged. In attacking the "optimistic" as well as the "pessimistic" atheism of his age, he had made clear
that the denial of the biblical God demands the denial of biblical morality,
however secularized, which, so far from being self-evident or rational, has
no other support than the biblical God; mercy, compassion, egalitarianism,
brotherly love, or altruism must give way to cruelty and its kin.[24] But
Nietzsche did not leave things at "the blond beast." He proclaimed "the
overman," and the overman transcends man as hitherto known at his
highest. What distinguishes Nietzsche in his view from all earlier philosophers is the fact that he possesses "the historical sense," [25] that is, the
awareness that the human soul has no unchangeable essence or limits, but
is essentially historical. The most profound change which the human soul
has hitherto undergone, the most important enlargement and deepening
which it has hitherto experienced, is due, according to Nietzsche, to the
Bible. "These Greeks have much on their conscience—falsification was
their particular craft, the whole European psychology suffers from the
Greek superficialities; and without that little bit of Judaism etc. etc."
Hence the overman is "the Roman Caesar with Christ's soul." [26] Not
only was biblical morality as veracity or intellectual probity at work in
the destruction of biblical theology and biblical morality; not only is it
at work in the questioning of that very probity, of "our virtue, which
alone has remained to us"; [27] biblical morality will remain at work in the

morality of the overman. The overman is inseparable from "the philosophy of the future." The philosophy of the future is distinguished from traditional philosophy, which pretended to be purely theoretical, by the fact that it is consciously the outcome of a will: the fundamental awareness is not purely theoretical, but theoretical and practical, inseparable from an act of the will or a decision. The fundamental awareness characteristic of the new thinking is a secularized version of the biblical faith as interpreted by Christian theology.[28] What is true of Nietzsche is no less true of the author of *Sein und Zeit*. Heidegger wishes to expel from philosophy the last relics of Christian theology like the notions of "eternal truths" and "the idealized absolute subject." But the understanding of man which he opposes to the Greek understanding of man as the rational animal is, as he emphasizes, primarily the biblical understanding of man as created in the image of God. Accordingly, he interprets human life in the light of "being towards death," "anguish," "conscience," and "guilt"; in this most important respect he is much more Christian than Nietzsche.[29] The efforts of the new thinking to escape from the evidence of the biblical understanding of man, that is, from biblical morality, have failed. And, as we have learned from Nietzsche, biblical morality demands the biblical God.

Considerations of this kind seemed to decide the issue in favor of Rosenzweig's understanding of the new thinking or in favor of the unqualified return to biblical revelation. In fact, Rosenzweig's return was not unqualified. The Judaism to which he returned was not identical with the Judaism of the age prior to Moses Mendelssohn. The old thinking had brought about since the days of Mendelssohn, to say nothing of the Middle Ages, some more or less important modifications of native Jewish thought. While opposing the old thinking, the new thinking was nevertheless its heir. Whereas the classic work of what is called Jewish medieval philosophy, the *Guide of the Perplexed*, is primarily not a philosophic book, but a Jewish book, Rosenzweig's *Star of Redemption* is primarily not a Jewish book, but "a system of philosophy." The new thinking is "experiencing philosophy." As such it is passionately concerned with the difference between what is experienced, or at least capable of being experienced, by the present-day believer and what is merely known by tradition; that difference was of no concern to traditional Judaism. As experiencing philosophy it starts in each case from the experienced, and not from the nonexperienced "presuppositions" of experience. For instance, we experience things "here" or "there," in given "places"; we do not experience the homogeneous infinite "space" which may be the condition of the possibility of "places." I experience a tree; in doing so, I am not necessarily aware of my "Ego" which is the condition of possibility of my experiencing anything.

Accordingly, when speaking of the Jewish experience, one must start from what is primary or authoritative for the Jewish consciousness, and not from what is the primary condition of possibility of the Jewish experience: one must start from God's Law, the Torah, and not from the Jewish nation. But in this decisive case Rosenzweig proceeds in the opposite manner; he proceeds, as he puts it, "sociologically." He notes that the Jewish dogmaticists of the Middle Ages, especially Maimonides, proceeded in the first manner: traditional Jewish dogmatics understood the Jewish nation in the light of the Torah; it was silent about the "presupposition" of the Law, viz. the Jewish nation and its chosenness. One begins to wonder whether our medieval philosophy, and the old thinking of Aristotle of which it made use, was not more "empirical," more in harmony with the "given," than an unqualified empiricism which came into being through opposition to modern constructionist philosophy as well as to modern scientific empiricism: if the Jewish nation did not originate the Torah, but is manifestly constituted by the Torah, it is necessarily preceded by the Torah, which was created prior to the world and for the sake of which the world was created. The dogma of Israel's chosenness becomes for Rosenzweig "the truly central thought of Judaism" because, as he makes clear, he approaches Judaism from the point of view of Christianity, because he looks for a Jewish analogon to the Christian doctrine of the Christ.[30] It is not necessary to emphasize that the same change would have been effected if the starting point had been mere secularist nationalism.

Rosenzweig never believed that his return to the biblical faith could be a return to the form in which that faith had expressed or understood itself in the past. What the author of a biblical saying or a biblical story or the compilers of the canon meant is one thing; how the text affects the present-day believer, and hence what the latter truly understands, that is, appropriates and believes, is another. The former is the concern of history as history which, if it regards itself as self-sufficient, is one of the decayed forms of the old thinking; the latter, if it is practiced with full consciousness, calls for the new thinking. Since the new thinking is the right kind of thinking, it would seem that the understanding of the Bible of which it is capable is in principle superior to all other forms. At any rate, Rosenzweig agrees with religious liberalism as to the necessity of making a selection from among the traditional beliefs and rules. Yet his principle of selection differs radically from the liberal principle.

The liberals made a distinction between the essential and the unessential, that is, they made a distinction which claimed to be objective. Rosenzweig's principle is not a principle strictly speaking, but "a force": the whole "reality of Jewish life," even those parts of it which never acquired formal authority (like "mere" stories and "mere" customs), must be approached as the "matter" out of which only a part can be transformed into "force"; only experience can tell which part will be so transformed; the selection cannot but be "wholly individual." [31] The sacred law, as it were the public temple, which was a reality thus becomes a potential, a quarry, or a storehouse out of which each individual takes the materials for building up his private shelter. The community of the holy people is henceforth guaranteed by the common descent of its members and the common origin of the materials which they transform by selecting them. This conscious and radical historicization of the Torah—the necessary consequence of the assumed primacy of the Jewish people under the conditions of modern "individualism" [32]—is in Rosenzweig's view perfectly compatible with the fact that the Jewish people is the ahistorical people.

Rosenzweig could not believe everything which his orthodox Jewish contemporaries in Germany believed. His system of philosophy supplies the reasons why he thought that in spite of their piety they were mistaken. He has discussed by themselves two points regarding which he disagreed with them and which are of utmost importance. He opposed to their inclination to understand the Law in terms of prohibition, denial, refusal, and rejection, rather than in terms of command, liberation, granting, and transformation, the opposite inclination. It is not immediately clear, however, whether the orthodox austerity or sternness does not rest on a deeper understanding of the power of evil in man than Rosenzweig's at first glance more attractive view which resembles one of "the favorite topics" of Mittler in Goethe's *Elective Affinities*.[33] Second, Rosenzweig was unable simply to believe all biblical miracles. All biblical miracles were indeed susceptible of becoming credible to him. For instance, when the story of Balaam's speaking she-ass was read from the Torah, it was not a fairy tale for him, whereas on all other occasions he might doubt this miracle.[34] The orthodox Jew would reproach himself for his doubts as for failings on his part, for he would not determine what he is obliged to believe by his individual and temporary capacity or incapacity to believe; he would argue with Maimonides' *Treatise on the Resurrection of the Dead* that if God has created the world out of nothing and hence is omnipotent, there is no reason whatever for denying at any time any miracle vouched for by the word of God.

Considerations like those sketched in the preceding paragraphs made one wonder whether an unqualified return to Jewish orthodoxy was not both possible and necessary—was not at the same time the solution to the problem of the Jew lost in the non-Jewish modern world and the only course compatible with sheer consistency or intellectual probity. Vague difficulties remained like small faraway clouds on a beautiful summer sky. They soon took the shape of Spinoza—the greatest man of Jewish origin who had openly denied the truth of Judaism and had ceased to belong to the Jewish people without becoming a Christian. It was not the "God-intoxicated" philosopher, but the hardheaded, not to say hardhearted, pupil of Machiavelli and philologic-historical critic of the Bible. Orthodoxy could be returned to only if Spinoza was wrong in every respect.

That Spinoza was wrong in the decisive respect had been asserted about a decade earlier by the most authoritative German Jew who symbolized more than anyone else the union of Jewish faith and German culture: Hermann Cohen, the founder of the Neo-Kantian school of Marburg. Cohen was a Jew of rare dedication, the faithful guide, defender, and warner of the German Jewry, and at the same time, to say the least, the one who by far surpassed in spiritual power all the other German professors of philosophy of his generation. It became necessary to examine Cohen's attack on Spinoza. That attack had been occasioned by a particularly striking act of celebration of Spinoza on the part of German Jews.

There were two reasons why contemporary Jews were inclined to celebrate Spinoza. The first is Spinoza's assumed merit about mankind and only secondarily about the Jews; the second is his assumed merit about the Jewish people and only secondarily about mankind. Both reasons had induced contemporary Jews, not only informally to rescind the excommunication which the Jewish community in Amsterdam had pronounced against Spinoza, but even, as Cohen put it, to canonize him.

The great revolt against traditional thought or the emergence of modern philosophy or natural science was completed prior to Spinoza. One may go further and say that, so far from being a revolutionary thinker, Spinoza is only the heir of the modern revolt and the medieval tradition as well. At first glance he might well appear to be much more medieval than Descartes, to say nothing of Bacon and Hobbes. The modern project as understood by Bacon, Descartes, and Hobbes demands that man should become the master and owner of nature or that philosophy or science should cease to be essentially theoretical. Spinoza, however, attempts to restore the traditional conception of contemplation: one cannot think of conquering nature if nature is the same as God. Yet Spinoza restored the dignity of speculation on the basis of modern philosophy or science, of a new understanding of "nature." He thus was the first great thinker who attempted a synthesis of premodern (classical-medieval) and of modern philosophy. His speculation resembles Neoplatonism; he understands all things as proceeding from, not made or created by, a single being or origin; the One is the sole ground of the Many. Yet he no longer regards this process as a descent or decay, but as an ascent or unfolding: the end is higher than the origin. According to his last word on the subject, the highest form of knowledge, which he calls intuitive knowledge, is knowledge, not of the one substance or God, but of individual things or events: God is fully God, not qua substance or even in His eternal attributes, but in His noneternal modes understood *sub specie aeternitatis*. The knowledge of God as presented in the First Part of the *Ethics* is only universal or abstract; only the knowledge of individual things or rather events qua caused by God is concrete.[35]

Spinoza thus appears to originate the kind of philosophic system which views the fundamental *processus* as a progress: God in Himself is not the *ens perfectissimum.* In this most important respect he prepares German idealism. Furthermore, just as he returns to the classical conception of *theoria,* he returns in his political philosophy to classical republicanism. The title of the crowning chapter of the *Theologico-political Treatise* is taken as literally as possible from Tacitus. But just as his theoretical philosophy is more than a restatement of classical doctrines and in fact a synthesis of classical and modern speculation, his political philosophy is more than a restatement of classical republicanism. The republic which he favors is a liberal democracy. He was the first philosopher who was both a democrat and a liberal. He was the philosopher who founded liberal democracy, a specifically modern regime. Directly and through his influence on Rousseau, who gave the decisive impulse to Kant, Spinoza became responsible for that version of modern republicanism which takes its bearings by the dignity of every man rather than by the interest narrowly conceived of every man. Spinoza's political teaching starts from a natural right of every human being as the source of all possible duties. Hence it is free from that sternness and austerity which classical political philosophy shares with ancient law—a sternness which Aristotle expressed classically by saying that what the law does not command it forbids. Hence Spinoza is free from the classical aversion to commercialism; he rejects the traditional demand for sumptuary laws. Generally speaking his polity gives the passions much greater freedom and correspondingly counts much less on the power of reason than the polity of the classics. For whereas for the classics the life of passion is a life against nature, for Spinoza everything that is, is natural. For Spinoza there are no natural ends, and hence in particular there is no end natural to man. He is therefore compelled to give a novel account of man's end (the life devoted to contemplation): man's end is not natural, but rational, the result of man's figuring it out, of man's "forming an idea of man, as of a model of human nature." He thus decisively prepares the modern notion of the "ideal" as a work of the human mind or as a human project, as distinguished from an end imposed on man by nature.

The formal reception of Spinoza took place in 1785 when F. H. Jacobi published his book *On the Doctrine of Spinoza, in Letters to Herr Moses Mendelssohn.* Jacobi made public the fact that in Lessing's view there was no philosophy but the philosophy of Spinoza. The philosophy of Kant's great successors was consciously a synthesis of Spinoza's and Kant's philosophies. Spinoza's characteristic contribution to this synthesis was a novel conception of God. He thus showed the way toward a new religion or religiousness which was to inspire a wholly new kind of society, a new kind of Church. He became the sole father of that new Church which was to be universal in fact, and not merely in claim as other churches, because its foundation was no longer any positive revelation—a Church whose rulers were not priests or pastors, but philosophers and artists and whose flock were the circles of culture and property. It was of the utmost importance to that Church that its father was not a Christian, but a Jew who had informally embraced a Christianity without dogmas and sacraments. The millennial antagonism between Judaism and Christianity was about to disappear. The new Church would transform Jews and Christians into human beings—into human beings of a certain kind: cultured human beings, human beings who, because they possessed science and art, did not need religion in addition. The new society, constituted by the aspiration common to all its members toward the True, the Good, and the Beautiful, emancipated the Jews in Germany. Spinoza became the symbol of that emancipation which was to be not only emancipation but secular redemption. In Spinoza, a thinker and a saint who was both a Jew and a Christian and hence neither, all cultured families of the earth, it was hoped, would be blessed. In a word, the non-Jewish world, having been molded to a considerable extent by Spinoza, had become receptive to Jews who were willing to assimilate themselves to it.

The celebration of Spinoza had become equally necessary on purely Jewish grounds. As we have seen, the emphasis had shifted from the Torah to the Jewish nation, and the Jewish nation could not be considered the source of the Torah if it was not understood as an organism with a soul of its own; that soul had expressed itself originally and classically in the Bible, although not in all parts of the Bible equally. From the days of the Bible on, there was always the conflict between prophet and priest, between the inspired and the uninspired, between profound subterranean Judaism and official Judaism. Official Judaism was legalistic and hence rationalistic. Its rationalism had received most powerful support from the philosophic rationalism of alien origin which had found its perfect expression in the Platonic conception of God as an artificer who makes the universe by looking up to the unchangeable, lifeless ideas. In accordance with this, official Judaism asserted that God has created the world and governs it *sub ratione boni*. Precisely because he believed in the profoundly understood divinity of the Bible, Spinoza revolted against this official assertion in the name of the absolutely free or sovereign God of the Bible—of the God who will be what He will be, who will be gracious to whom He will be gracious and will show mercy to whom He will show mercy. Moved by the same spirit, he embraced with enthusiasm Paul's doctrine of predestination. The biblical God has created man in His image: male and female did He create them. The male and the female, form and matter, cogitation and extension, are then equally attributes of God; Spinoza rejects both Greek idealism and Christian spiritualism. The biblical God forms light and creates darkness, makes peace and creates evil; Spinoza's God is simply beyond good and evil. God's might is His right, and therefore the power of every being is as such its right; Spinoza lifts Machiavellianism to theological heights. Good and evil differ only from a merely human point of view; theologically the distinction is meaningless. The evil passions are evil only with a view to human utility; in themselves they show forth the might and the right of God no less than other things which we admire and by the contemplation of which we are delighted. In the state of nature, that is, independently of human convention, there is nothing just and unjust, no duty and no guilt, and the state of nature does not simply vanish when civil society is established: pangs of conscience are nothing but feelings of displeasure which arise when a plan has gone wrong. Hence there are no vestiges of divine justice to be found except where just men reign. All human acts are modes of the one God who possesses infinitely many attributes each of which is infinite and only two of which are known to us, who is therefore a mysterious God, whose mysterious love reveals itself in eternally and necessarily bringing forth love and hatred, nobility and baseness, saintliness and depravity, and who is infinitely lovable not in spite but because of His infinite power beyond good and evil.

Compared with the fantastic flights of the Spinoza enthusiasts in the two camps, of the moralists and the immoralists, Cohen's understanding of Spinoza is sobriety itself. All the more impressive is his severe indictment of Spinoza.[36] He shows first that in his *Theologico-political Treatise* Spinoza speaks from a Christian point of view and accordingly accepts the entire Christian critique of Judaism, but goes much even beyond that Christian critique in his own critique. He accepts against his better knowledge the assertion of Jesus that Judaism commands the hatred of the enemy. He opposes spiritual and universalistic Christianity to carnal and particularistic Judaism: the core of Judaism is the Mosaic law as a particularistic, not to say tribal, law which serves no other end than the earthly or political felicity of the Jewish nation; the Torah does not teach morality, that is, universal morality; the Mosaic religion is merely national; Moses' God is a tribal and in addition a corporeal God. By denying that the God of Israel is the God of all mankind Spinoza has blasphemed the God of Israel. He reduces Jewish religion to a doctrine of the Jewish state. For him, the Torah is of merely human origin.

Cohen shows next that the Christianity in the light of which Spinoza condemns Judaism is not historical or actual Christianity, but an idealized Christianity and hence that while he idealizes Christianity, he denigrates Judaism. He shows then that Spinoza admits the universalistic character of the Old Testament prophecy, thus contradicting himself grossly. This contradiction clearly proves his lack of good faith.[37] Nor is this all. While taking the side of spiritual and transpolitical Christianity against carnal and political Judaism, Spinoza contradicts this whole argument by taking the side of the state not only against all churches but against all religion as well. "He put religion altogether," that is, not merely Judaism, "outside the sphere of truth." Starting like all other sophists from the equation of right and might, he conceives of the state entirely in terms of power politics, that is, as divorced from religion and morality, and he puts the state thus conceived above religion. This does not mean that he deifies the state. On the contrary, he is concerned above everything else with what he calls philosophy, which he assumes to be wholly inaccessible directly or indirectly to the large majority of men. He has no compunction whatever about affirming the radical and unmodifiable inequality of men without ever wondering "how can nature, how can God answer for this difference among men?" Hence his sympathy for democracy is suspect. He is compelled to erect an eternal barrier between popular education and science or philosophy and therewith between the state and reason. There is no place in his thought for the enlightenment of the people. He has no heart for the people, no compassion. He cannot admit a Messianic future of mankind when all men will be united in genuine knowledge of God. This is the reason why he is altogether blind to biblical prophecy and hence to the core of Judaism.[38]

On the basis of all these facts Cohen reached the conclusion that so far from deserving celebration, Spinoza fully deserved the excommunication. So far from rescinding the excommunication, Cohen confirmed it, acting as a judge in the highest court of appeal. The grounds of his verdict were not the same as the grounds of the lower court. He was not concerned with Spinoza's transgression of the ceremonial law and his denial of the Mosaic authorship of the Pentateuch. He condemned Spinoza because of his infidelity in the simple human sense, of his complete lack of loyalty to his own people, of his acting like an enemy of the Jews and thus giving aid and comfort to the many enemies of the Jews, of his behaving like a base traitor. Spinoza remains up to the present day the accuser par excellence of Judaism before an anti-Jewish world; the disposition of his mind and heart toward Jews and Judaism was "unnatural," he committed a "humanly incomprehensible act of treason," he was possessed by "an evil demon." [39]

Our case against Spinoza is in some respects even stronger than Cohen thought. One may doubt whether Spinoza's action is humanly incomprehensible or demoniac, but one must grant that it is amazingly unscrupulous. Cohen is justly perplexed by the fact that "the center of the whole [theologico-political] treatise" is the disparagement of Moses and the idealization of Jesus, although the purpose of the work is to secure the freedom of philosophizing. He explains this anomaly by Spinoza's belief that the suppression of philosophy goes back to the Mosaic law. Cohen does not assert that Moses championed the freedom of philosophy, but he raises the pertinent question whether Jesus championed it.[40] Why then does Spinoza treat Judaism and Christianity differently? Why does he take the side of Christianity in the conflict between Judaism and Christianity, in a conflict of no concern to him as a philosopher? Cohen believes that Spinoza had a genuine reverence for Jesus' teachings. According to Spinoza's own statements he preferred spiritual Christianity to carnal Judaism.[41] But is Spinoza a spiritualist? Cohen says that spirit or mind, if applied to God, is no less a metaphor than hand, voice, or mouth. He thus merely repeats what Spinoza himself asserts; Spinoza may be said to have denied that God has a spirit or mind. The question returns: why does Spinoza treat Christianity differently from Judaism? Cohen comes closest to the truth in saying that Spinoza's motive was fear,[42] surely a "humanly comprehensible" motive. Or, to start again from the beginning, Spinoza, attempting to achieve the liberation of philosophy in a book addressed to Christians, cannot but appeal to the Christian prejudices which include anti-Jewish prejudices; he fights Christian prejudices by appealing to Christian prejudices; appealing to the Christian prejudice against Judaism, he exhorts the Christians to free essentially spiritual Christianity from all carnal Jewish relics (for example, the belief in the resurrection of the body). Generally speaking, he makes the Old Testament against his better knowledge the scapegoat for everything he finds objectionable in actual Christianity. In spite of all this he asserts that the prophets were as universalistic as Jesus and the apostles or, more precisely, that both Testaments teach with equal clarity everywhere the universal divine law or the universal religion of justice and charity. Why this strange reversal, this flagrant contradiction?

At this point Cohen fails to follow Spinoza's thought. The purpose of the *Treatise* is to show the way toward a liberal society which is based on the recognition of the authority of the Bible, that is, of the Old Testament taken by itself and of the two Testaments taken together. The argument culminates in the fourteenth chapter in which he enumerates seven dogmas which are the indispensable fundamentals of faith, of biblical faith—the seven "roots," as the Jewish medieval thinkers would say. They are essential to "the catholic or universal faith," to the religion which will be the established religion in the well-ordered republic; belief in these seven dogmas is the only belief necessary and sufficient for salvation. They derive equally from the Old Testament taken by itself and from the New Testament taken by itself.[43] They do not contain anything specifically Christian nor anything specifically Jewish. They are equally acceptable to Jews and to Christians. The liberal society with a view to which Spinoza has composed the *Treatise* is then a society of which Jews and Christians can be equally members, of which Jews and Christians can be equal members. For such a society he wished to provide. The establishment of such a society required in his opinion the abrogation of the Mosaic law insofar as it is a particularistic and political law and especially of the ceremonial laws: since Moses' religion is a political law, to adhere to his religion as he proclaimed it is incompatible with being the citizen of any other state, whereas Jesus was not a legislator, but only a teacher.[44] It is for this reason that he is so anxious to prove that Moses' law lost its obligatory power, and that the Jews ceased to be the chosen people, with the loss of the Jewish state: the Jews cannot be at the same time the members of two nations and subject to two comprehensive legal codes. Spinoza stresses the

abrogation of the ceremonial law, however, not only because that abrogation is in his opinion a necessary condition of civic equality of the Jews but
also as desirable for its own sake: the ceremonial law is infinitely burden-
some, nay, a curse.[45]

In providing for the liberal state, Spinoza provides for a Judaism which
is liberal in the extreme. The "assimilationist" "solution to the Jewish
problem" which Spinoza may be said to have suggested was more important from his point of view than the "Zionist" one which he likewise suggested. The latter as he understood it could seem to require the preservation of the ceremonial law although the abandonment of the spirit which
has animated it hitherto.[46] The former suggestion and the general purpose
of the *Theologico-political Treatise* are obviously connected: freedom of
philosophy requires, or seems to require, a liberal state, and a liberal state is
a state which is not as such either Christian or Jewish. Even Cohen sensed
for a moment that Spinoza was not entirely free from sympathy with his
people.[47] Spinoza may have hated Judaism; he did not hate the Jewish
people. However bad a Jew he may have been in all other respects, he
thought of the liberation of the Jews in the only way in which he could
think of it, given his philosophy. But precisely if this is so, we must stress
all the more the fact that the manner in which he sets forth his proposal—to say nothing of the proposal itself—is Machiavellian: the humani-
tarian end seems to justify every means; he plays a most dangerous
game; [48] his procedure is as much beyond good and evil as his God.

All this does not mean, however, that Cohen's critique of Spinoza's
Theologico-political Treatise is altogether convincing. His political thought
claims to be inspired by biblical prophecy and hence is Messianic. In opposition to Spinoza, it starts from the radical difference between nature and
morality, the Is and the Ought, egoism and pure will. The state is essentially moral, and morality cannot be actual except in and through the state.
The difficulty presented by the fact that morality is universal and the state
is always particular is overcome by the consideration that the state is part
of a universal moral order, as is shown by the existence of international
law and by the intrinsic possibility, which is at the same time a moral necessity, of a universal league of states. The radical difference between
nature and morality does not amount to a contradiction between nature
and morality: nature does not render impossible the fulfillment of the
moral demands. The morally demanded infinite progress of morality, and
in particular the "eternal progress" toward "eternal peace," nay, every
single step of morality, requires for its "ultimate security" the infinite duration *a parte post* of the human race and hence of nature; this infinite
duration or eternity is secured by the idea of God "who signifies the harmony of the knowledge of nature and of moral knowledge," who is not a
person, nor living, nor existing, nor a spirit or mind, but an idea, "our"
idea, that is, our *hypothesis* in what Cohen regards as the Platonic meaning

of the term. This is the Cohenian equivalent of Creation and Providence. Without "the idea of God" as Cohen understands it morality as he understands it becomes baseless. That idea is the basis of his trust in infinite progress or of his belief in history, of his "optimism," of his certainty of the ultimate victory of the good: "there is no evil."

But eternal progress also requires eternal tension between the actual state and the state as it ought to be: [49] immorality is coeval with morality. Here Cohen seems to join Spinoza, whose political thought is based on the truth, allegedly proved by experience, that there will be vices as long as there will be human beings and who takes it therefore for granted that the state is necessarily repressive or coercive. Cohen too cannot well deny that the state must use coercion, but, opposing the Kantian distinction between morality and legality, he denies that coercion is the principle of law: coercion means nothing other than law and needs therefore not to be mentioned. He is as uneasy about coercion as he is about power: the state is law, for the state is essentially rational, and coercion begins where reason ends. All this follows from the premise that morality is self-legislation and that it can be actual only in and through the state. A further consequence is that Cohen must understand punishment, not in terms of the protection of society or other considerations which may be thought to regard the criminal not as "an end in himself" and only as a means, but in terms of the self-betterment of the criminal alone.[50] Cohen obscures the fact that while the self-betterment is necessarily a free act of the criminal, his forcible seclusion for the purpose of that self-betterment, in which he may or may not engage, is not. In other words, all men are under a moral obligation to better themselves, but the specific difference of the condemned criminal is that he is put behind bars. For it goes without saying that Cohen denies the justice of capital punishment. However justly Spinoza may deserve condemnation for his Machiavelli-inspired hardheartedness, it is to be feared that Cohen has not remained innocent of the opposite extreme. Since he attacks Spinoza in the name of Judaism, it may suffice here to quote a Jewish saying: "But for the fear of the government, men would swallow each other alive." [51]

One may doubt whether Cohen's political teaching is unqualifiedly superior to Spinoza's from the moral point of view. Cohen "rejects war." On the other hand he does not reject revolution, although, as he emphasizes, Kant had "coordinated wars to revolutions." Revolutions are political but not legal acts, and hence the state is not simply law; revolutions "suspend" positive law, but are justified by natural law. They do not necessarily occur without the killing of human beings; Cohen, the sworn enemy of capital punishment, reflects only on the death of "the revolutionary martyrs" who voluntarily sacrifice their lives, but not on the death of their victims. Kant had questioned the legitimacy of revolution on the ground that its maxim does not stand the test of publicity, which in his view every honest maxim stands: the preparation of every revolution is necessarily conspiratorial or secret. To counter this argument Cohen observes that the moral basis of revolutions is the original contract which, "being only an idea, is always only an interior, hence secret presupposition." The same reasoning would lead to the further conclusion that the original contract, nay, Cohen's theology, must never be publicly mentioned, let alone be taught. It is altogether fitting that Cohen, who was no friend of the "irrational" or of "mysticism," should be driven in his defense of the revolutionary principle to become friendly to the "irrational" and to "mysticism." [52] To say nothing of other things, he would never have been driven to this surrender of reason if he had taken seriously the law of reason or the natural law which may be said to indicate the right mean between hardheartedness and softheartedness.

While admitting "the deep injustice" of Cohen's judgment on Spinoza, Rosenzweig asserts that Cohen has honestly complied in his critique of the *Theologico-political Treatise* with the duty of scholarly objectivity.[53] This assertion must be qualified. Since Cohen accuses Spinoza of having been unfair in his treatment of the universalism of the prophets, one must consider in fairness to Spinoza whether the Jewish tradition with which Spinoza was directly confronted had preserved intact that universalism. Cohen failed to make this investigation. Once one makes it, one observes that Spinoza recognized the universalism of the prophets in some respects more clearly than some of the greatest traditional Jewish authorities. In his critique of Spinoza, Cohen is silent about the fact, which he mentions elsewhere, that prophetic universalism had become obscured in later times for easily understandable reasons.[54] Cohen is particularly indignant about Spinoza's using a remark of Maimonides in order to prove that according to Judaism non-Jews cannot be saved unless they believe in the Mosaic revelation,[55] that is, unless, as one is tempted to say, they are Christians or Muslims. More precisely, Spinoza quotes a passage from Maimonides' Code in which it is said that a Gentile is pious and has a share in the world to come if he performs the seven commandments given to Noah qua commanded by God in the Torah, but that if he performs them because of a decision of reason, he does not belong to the pious Gentiles nor to the wise ones. Cohen accuses Spinoza of having used a false reading of a single passage of the Code—of a passage which expresses only Maimonides' private opinion and which in addition is contradicted by two other passages of the Code—in order to deny the universalism of postbiblical Judaism. He (or the authority to which he defers) notes that according to the most authoritative commentator on the Code, Joseph Caro, the qualification stated by Maimonides (viz. that piety requires recognition of the Mosaic revelation) is his private opinion, but he fails to add that Caro adds that the opinion is correct. Caro would not have said this if Maimonides' opinion contradicted the consensus of Judaism.

Cohen (or his authority) also notes that according to the most authentic text of the Code, the Gentile who performs the seven Noahidic commandments because of a decision of reason does not indeed belong to the pious Gentiles, but to the wise ones.[56] But he does not show that Spinoza knew that reading to be the most authentic reading. The reading used by Spinoza is still the common reading, which it would not be if it were in shocking contrast to the consensus of Judaism as Cohen asserts and hence would have shocked every Jewish reader.[57] In addition, the allegedly best reading does not necessarily improve the fate of the wise Gentiles unless one proves first that the fate of the wise Gentiles is as good as that of the pious Gentiles. Cohen finally asserts that the passage in question contradicts two other passages of the Code which in his opinion do not demand that the pious Gentile believe in the revealed character of the Torah. It suffices to say that the two passages are silent on what precisely constitutes the piety of the Gentiles and are therefore irrelevant to the issue.[58] Cohen also refers to a different treatment of the subject in Maimonides' commentary on the Mishna; but this merely leads to the further question whether that commentary, composed much earlier than the Code, is equal in authority to the Code.

But, to return to the main issue, that is, to the question whether the ordinary reading, used by Spinoza, of the passage under consideration makes sense as a Maimonidean utterance: can Maimonides have taught, as Spinoza asserts he did, that Gentiles who perform the seven Noahidic commandments because reason decides so are not wise men? The answer is simple: Maimonides must have taught it because he denied that there are any rational commandments. Cohen might have objected to this argument on the ground that if Maimonides' denial of the rationality of any commandments or laws were his last word, he could not well have attempted to show that all or almost all commandments of the Torah have "reasons." [59] The reply is obvious: according to Maimonides all or almost all commandments of the Torah serve the purpose of eradicating idolatry, an irrational practice, and are in this sense "rational"; they are rational in the sense in which, not a healthy body, but a medicine, is "healthy." [60] One could say that Maimonides' denial of the rationality of any law is implied in the incriminated passage itself regardless of which of the two readings one prefers; for the term which Cohen renders by "reason" (*da'at*) does not necessarily mean reason in particular, but may mean thought or opinion in general: [61] it makes sense both to assert and to deny that opinion justifies the seven Noahidic commandments.

These and similar considerations do not affect the main issue, namely, the fact that Cohen may well be right in asserting that Spinoza acted ignobly in basing his denial of the universalism of traditional, postprophetic Judaism on a single Maimonidean utterance. In the words of Rosenzweig, beneath the deep injustice of Cohen's judgment lies its still much deeper justification. What Rosenzweig meant may be stated as follows. Cohen was a more profound thinker than Spinoza because unlike Spinoza he did not take for granted the philosophic detachment or freedom from the tradition of his own people; that detachment is "unnatural," not primary, but the outcome of a liberation from the primary attachment, of an alienation, a break, a betrayal; the primary is fidelity, and the sympathy and love which go with fidelity. Genuine fidelity to a tradition is not the same as literalist traditionalism and is in fact incompatible with it. It consists in preserving not simply the tradition but the continuity of the tradition. As fidelity to a living and hence changing tradition, it requires that one distinguish between the living and the dead, the flame and the ashes, the gold and the dross: the loveless Spinoza sees only the ashes, not the flame; only the letter, not the spirit. He is not excusable on the ground that Jewish thought may have declined in the centuries preceding him from its greatest height; for he "on whose extraction, whose gifts, whose learning the Jews had put the greatest hope" was under an obligation to understand contemporary Judaism, and still more Maimonides, to say nothing of Scripture itself, in the light of the highest or, if necessary, better than they understood themselves. Within a living tradition, the new is not the opposite of the old, but its deepening: one does not understand the old in its depth unless one understands it in the light of such deepening; the new does not emerge through the rejection or annihilation of the old, but through its metamorphosis of reshaping. "And it is a question whether such reshaping is not the best form of annihilation." [62] This is indeed the question: whether the loyal and loving reshaping or reinterpretation of the inherited or the pitiless burning of the hitherto worshiped is the best form of annihilation of the antiquated, that is, of the untrue or bad. On the answer to this question the ultimate judgment on Spinoza as well as on Cohen will depend: is the right interpretation "idealizing" interpretation—the interpretation of a teaching in the light of its highest possibility regardless of whether or not that highest possibility was known to the originator—or is it historical interpretation proper which understands a teaching as meant by its originator? Is the conservatism which is generally speaking the wise maxim of practice the sacred law of theory?

It would not be reasonable to demand from Cohen that he should give the benefit of idealizing interpretation to Spinoza, who had become an ingredient of the modern tradition on which Cohen's philosophy as a philosophy of culture is based. For the kind of interpretation which Spinoza calls for is not idealizing since his own doctrine is not idealistic. As was shown before, Cohen's political philosophy did not pay sufficient attention to the harsh political verities which Spinoza has stated so forcefully. Accordingly, he does not pay sufficient attention to the harsh necessity to which Spinoza bowed by writing in the manner in which he wrote. He did not understand Spinoza's style, which was indeed entirely different from his own. Cohen sometimes writes like a commentator on a commentary on an already highly technical text and hence like a man whose thought is derivative and traditional in the extreme; and yet he surprises time and again with strikingly expressed original and weighty thoughts. Be this as it may, he goes so far as to deny that in Spinoza's time the freest minds were compelled to withhold and to deny the truth; "Think only of Jean Bodin who in his Heptaplomeres not only directed the strongest attacks against Christianity but also celebrated Judaism most highly. It must appear strange that this writing, which was known to Leibniz and Thomasius, which was at that time widely distributed, should have remained unknown to Spinoza." He forgets here to say what he says elsewhere: "Leibniz had seen the manuscript of the Heptaplomeres and had advised against its being printed"; [63] it was not printed before the nineteenth century. Once one takes into consideration the consequences of persecution, Spinoza's conduct in the *Theologico-political Treatise* ceases to be that "psychological riddle" which Cohen saw in it. He wondered whether that conduct could not be traced to the fact that the Spanish Jews' feelings of anxiety caused by the terrors of the Inquisition had eventually turned into hatred for that for the sake of which they had been so cruelly persecuted. A different explanation was suggested by Nietzsche in his verses addressed to Spinoza. After having paid homage to Spinoza's *amor dei* and to his being "blissful through intelligence," he goes on to say that beneath the love of the "One in all" there was eating a secret desire for revenge: *am Judengott frass Judenhass*. Nietzsche understood Spinoza in his own image. He traced his own revolt against the Christian God to his Christian conscience. The premise of this explanation is Hegelian dialectics: every form of the mind perishes through its antithesis which it necessarily produces. Spinoza's break with the Torah is the consequence of the *Sithrei Torah* in the double sense of the expression: the secrets of the Torah and the contradictions of the Torah. Spinoza was not swayed by Hegelian dialectics, but by the Aristotelian principle of contradiction.

Cohen read Spinoza on the one hand not literally enough and on the other hand much too literally; he understood him too literally because he did not read him literally enough. Hence he did not find his way among the contradictions in which the *Theologico-political Treatise* abounds. As he exclaims on one occasion, "No reason of reasonable men can understand, let alone overcome, these difficulties." A single example must here suffice. He wonders whether Spinoza does not contradict himself by admitting that the Mosaic law is a divine law although he understands by a divine law a law which aims only at the highest good, viz. true knowledge of God and love of God, or intellectual love of God, and he denies that the Mosaic law aims at that highest good. The contradiction disappears once one considers the fact, which Cohen observes, that according to Spinoza a law may also be called divine with a view to its origin: the Mosaic law is human as regards its end, since it aims only at political felicity, but it is divine qua divinely revealed. Cohen quotes Spinoza's explanation: the Mosaic law "may be called the law of God or divine law since we believe that it is sanctioned by the prophetic light." He remarks: "But why do we believe this? This question is not answered by the anonymous author." But does not the community consisting of the anonymous author who speaks as a Christian and his Christian readers believe it as a matter of course, so that the question as to why "we believe it" does not have to arise? Spinoza had originally said that the divine law aims only at the highest good; immediately before saying that the Mosaic law can be called divine with a view to its origin as distinguished from its aim, he says according to Cohen that the divine law "consists chiefly in the highest good": hence, Cohen infers, Spinoza admits now a secondary content of the divine law without stating immediately what that secondary content is, namely, the sensual means which sensual men need. But Spinoza did not say that the divine law consists in the highest good; he says that it consists in the prescriptions regarding the means required for achieving the highest good: the divine law consists chiefly of the prescriptions regarding the proximate means and secondarily of the prescriptions regarding the remote means; since "sensual man" is incapable of intellectual love of God, his needs fall wholly outside of the divine law as here considered by Spinoza. It must be added that according to Spinoza even the divine law in the strictest sense is of human origin; every law is prescribed by human beings to themselves or to other human beings. Cohen throws some light on Spinoza's teaching regarding the divine law by making this remark on Spinoza's assertion that "the highest reward of the divine law is the law itself": "here he has literally taken over a sentence of the Mishna from the well-known Sayings of the Fathers, only adding the word 'highest.' " Cohen underestimates the importance of Spinoza's addition: Spinoza's egoistic morality demands for the fulfillment of the commandments rewards other than the commandments or perhaps additional commandments; it does not leave room for martyrdom.[64]

Rosenzweig finds Cohen guilty of injustice to Spinoza, not because of defective objectivity, but rather because of defective "subjectivity," that is, of "insufficient reflection about the conditions and foundations of his own person. He ought to have made his attack with a clearer consciousness of the fact that, not indeed he himself, but the times which had borne and raised him, Cohen himself, would not have been possible without Spinoza." The distinction between Cohen himself and his time, which is due to idealizing or apologetic interpretation, is immaterial here, for if Cohen's thought had nothing to do with the thought of his time, he would not have met Spinoza by reflecting about the presuppositions of "his own person." Cohen accuses Spinoza of blindness to biblical prophetism, but this phenomenon as Cohen understood it was brought to light by what he calls "the historical understanding of the Bible," and this understanding is not possible without higher criticism of the Bible, that is, without a public effort which was originated with the necessary comprehensiveness by Spinoza. Cohen blames Spinoza for disregarding the difference between mythical and historical elements of the Bible, a distinction which, as Cohen states, was alien to our traditional exegesis; and as regards the doctrinal elements of the Bible, he blames him for not distinguishing between the less and the more mature biblical statements; he blames him for the immaturity or incompetence of his biblical criticism, not at all for his biblical criticism itself: for Cohen, biblical criticism is a matter of course.

Similarly, he states that Spinoza opposed rabbinical Judaism, especially its great concern with the ceremonial law, and that his sharp opposition had a certain salutary effect on the liberation of opinion; he notes without any disapproval that "modern Judaism" has freed itself from part of the ceremonial law; he fails to admit that modern Judaism is a synthesis between rabbinical Judaism and Spinoza. As for Spinoza's denial of the possibility of miracles, Cohen gives an extremely brief summary of the chapter which Spinoza devotes to the subject of miracles without saying a word in defense of miracles.[65] In brief, Cohen does not discuss at all the issue between Spinoza and Jewish orthodoxy, that is, the only issue with which Spinoza could have been concerned, since there was no modern or liberal Judaism in his time. One may say that in his critique of Spinoza, Cohen commits the typical mistake of the conservative, which consists in concealing the fact that the continuous and changing tradition which he cherishes so greatly would never have come into being through conservativism or without discontinuities, revolutions, and sacrileges committed at the beginning of the cherished tradition and at least silently repeated in its course.

This much is certain: Cohen's critique of Spinoza does not come to grips with the fact that Spinoza's critique is directed against the whole body of authoritative teachings and rules known in Spinoza's time as Judaism and still maintained in Cohen's time by Jewish orthodoxy. Cohen took it for granted that Spinoza had refuted orthodoxy as such. Owing to the collapse of "the old thinking" it became then necessary to examine the *Theologico-political Treatise* with a view to the question of whether Spinoza had in fact refuted orthodoxy. Cohen's critique remained helpful for this purpose almost only insofar as it had destroyed the prejudice in favor of Spinoza, or the canonization of Spinoza by German or Jewish romanticism, to say nothing of the canonization by liberalism. Cohen's critique had the additional merit that it was directed chiefly against the *Theologico-political Treatise*. The seeming neglect of the *Ethics* proved to be sound, and thus to be obligatory for the re-examination of Spinoza's critique of orthodoxy, for the following reason. The *Ethics* starts from explicit premises by the granting of which one has already implicitly granted the absurdity of orthodoxy and even of Judaism as understood by Cohen or Rosenzweig; at first glance these premises seem to be arbitrary and hence to beg the whole question. They are not evident in themselves, but they are thought to become evident through their alleged result: they and only they are held to make possible the clear and distinct account of everything; in the light of the clear and distinct account, the biblical account appears to be confused. The *Ethics* thus begs the decisive question—the question as to whether the clear and distinct account is as such true and not merely a plausible hypothesis. In the *Theologico-political Treatise*, however, Spinoza starts from premises which are granted to him by the believers in revelation; he attempts to refute them on the bases of Scripture, of theologoumena formulated by traditional authorities, and of what one may call common sense. For in the *Treatise* Spinoza addresses men who are still believers and whom he intends to liberate from their "prejudices" so that they can begin to philosophize; the *Treatise* is Spinoza's introduction to philosophy.

The results of this examination of Spinoza's critique may be summarized as follows. If orthodoxy claims to know that the Bible is divinely revealed, that every word of the Bible is divinely inspired, that Moses was the writer of the Pentateuch, that the miracles recorded in the Bible have happened and similar things, Spinoza has refuted orthodoxy. But the case is entirely different if orthodoxy limits itself to asserting that it believes the aforementioned things, that is, that they cannot claim to possess the binding power peculiar to the known. For all assertions of orthodoxy rest on the irrefutable premise that the omnipotent God, whose will is unfathomable, whose ways are not our ways, who has decided to dwell in the thick darkness, may exist. Given this premise, miracles and revelations in general, and hence all biblical miracles and revelations in particular, are possible. Spinoza has not succeeded in showing that this premise is contradicted by anything we know. For what we are said to know, for example, regarding the age of the solar system, has been established on the basis of the assumption that the solar system has come into being naturally; miraculously it could have come into being in the way described by the Bible. It is only naturally or humanly impossible that the "first" Isaiah should have known the name of the founder of the Persian empire; it was not impossible for the omnipotent God to reveal to him that name. The orthodox premise cannot be refuted by experience nor by recourse to the principle of contradiction. An indirect proof of this is the fact that Spinoza and his like owed such success as they had in their fight against orthodoxy to laughter and mockery. By means of mockery they attempted to laugh orthodoxy out of its position from which it could not be dislodged by any proofs supplied by Scripture or by reason. One is tempted to say that mockery does not succeed the refutation of the orthodox tenets, but is itself the refutation. The genuine refutation of orthodoxy would require the proof that the world and human life are perfectly intelligible without the assumption of a mysterious God; it would require at least the success of the philosophic system: man has to show himself theoretically and practically as the master of the world and the master of his life; the merely given world must be replaced by the world created by man theoretically and practically. Spinoza's *Ethics* attempts to be the system, but it does not succeed; the clear and distinct account of everything which it presents remains fundamentally hypothetical. As a consequence, its cognitive status is not different from that of the orthodox account. Certain it is that Spinoza cannot legitimately deny the possibility of revelation. But to grant that revelation is possible means to grant that the philosophic account and the philosophic way of life are not necessarily, not evidently, the true account and the right way of life: philosophy, the quest for evident and necessary knowledge, rests itself on an unevident decision, on an act of the will, just as faith. Hence the antagonism between Spinoza and Judaism, between unbelief and belief, is ultimately not theoretical, but moral.

For the understanding of that moral antagonism the Jewish designation of the unbeliever as Epicurean seemed to be helpful, especially since from every point of view Epicureanism may be said to be the classic form of the critique of religion and the basic stratum of the tradition of the critique of religion. Epicureanism is hedonism, and traditional Judaism always suspects that all theoretical and practical revolts against the Torah are inspired by the desire to throw off the yoke of the stern and exacting duties so that one can indulge in a life of pleasure. Epicureanism can lead only to a mercenary morality, whereas traditional Jewish morality is not mercenary: "the reward for [the fulfillment of] the commandment is the commandment." Epicureanism is so radically mercenary that it conceives of its theoretical doctrines as the means for liberating the mind from the terrors of religious fear, of the fear of death, and of natural necessity. Characteristically modern unbelief is indeed no longer Epicurean. It is no longer cautious or retiring, not to say cowardly, but bold and active. Whereas Epicureanism fights the religious "delusion" because of its terrible character, modern unbelief fights it because it is a delusion: regardless of whether religion is terrible or comforting, qua delusion it makes men oblivious of the real goods, of the enjoyment of the real goods, and thus seduces them into being cheated of the real, "this-worldly" goods by their spiritual or temporal rulers who "live" from that delusion. Liberated from the religious delusion, awakened to sober awareness of his real situation, taught by bad experiences that he is threatened by a stingy, hostile nature, man recognizes as his sole salvation and duty not so much "to cultivate his garden" as in the first place to plant a garden by making himself the master and owner of nature. But this whole enterprise requires, above all, political action, revolution, a life-and-death struggle: the Epicurean who wishes to live securely and retiredly must transform himself into an "idealist" who has learned to fight and to die for honor and truth. But in proportion as the systematic effort to liberate man completely from all nonhuman bonds seems to succeed, the doubt increases of whether the goal is not fantastic—whether man has not become smaller and more miserable in proportion as the systematic civilization progresses.

Eventually the belief that by pushing ever farther back the "natural limits" man will advance to ever greater freedom, that he can subjugate nature and prescribe to it his laws, begins to wither away. In this stage the religious "delusion" is rejected, not because it is terrible, but because it is comforting: religion is not a tool which man has forged for dark reasons in order to torment himself, to make life unnecessarily difficult, but a way out chosen for obvious reasons in order to escape from the terror, the exposedness, and the hopelessness of life which cannot be eradicated by any progress of civilization. A new kind of fortitude which forbids itself every flight from the horror of life into comforting delusion, which accepts the eloquent descriptions of "the misery of man without God" as an additional proof of the goodness of its cause, reveals itself eventually as the ultimate and purest ground for the rebellion against revelation. This new fortitude, being the willingness to look man's forsakenness in its face, being the courage to welcome the most terrible truth, is "probity," "intellectual probity." This final atheism with a good conscience, or with a bad conscience, is distinguished from the atheism at which the past shuddered by its conscientiousness. Compared not only with Epicureanism but with the unbelief of the age of Spinoza, it reveals itself as a descendant of biblical morality. This atheism, the heir and the judge of the belief in revelation, of the secular struggle between belief and unbelief, and finally of the short-lived but by no means therefore inconsequential romantic longing for the lost belief, confronting orthodoxy in complex sophistication formed out of gratitude, rebellion, longing, and indifference, and in simple probity, is according to its claim as capable of an original understanding of the human roots of the belief in God as no earlier, no less complex-simple philosophy ever was. The last word and the ultimate justification of Spinoza's critique is the atheism from intellectual probity which overcomes orthodoxy radically by understanding it radically, that is, without the polemical bitterness of the Enlightenment and the equivocal reverence of romanticism. Yet this claim, however eloquently raised, cannot deceive one about the fact that its basis is an act of will, of belief, and that being based on belief is fatal to any philosophy.

The victory of orthodoxy through the self-destruction of rational philosophy was not an unmitigated blessing, for it was a victory, not of Jewish orthodoxy, but of any orthodoxy, and Jewish orthodoxy based its claim to superiority to other religions from the beginning on its superior rationality (Deut. 4:6). Apart from this, the hierarchy of moralities and wills to which the final atheism referred could not but be claimed to be intrinsically true, theoretically true: "the will to power" of the strong or of the weak may be the ground of every other doctrine; it is not the ground of the doctrine of the will to power: the will to power was said to be a fact. Other observations and experiences confirmed the suspicion that it would be unwise to say farewell to reason. I began therefore to wonder whether the self-destruction of reason was not the inevitable outcome of modern rationalism as distinguished from premodern rationalism, especially Jewish-medieval rationalism and its classical (Aristotelian and Platonic) foundation. The present study was based on the premise, sanctioned by powerful prejudice, that a return to premodern philosophy is impossible. The change of orientation which found its first expression, not entirely by accident, in the article published at the end of this volume [66] compelled me to engage in a number of studies in the course of which I became ever more attentive to the manner in which heterodox thinkers of earlier ages wrote their books. As a consequence of this, I now read the *Theologico-political Treatise* differently than I read it when I was young. I understood Spinoza too literally because I did not read him literally enough.

NOTES

1. Consider Leon Trotsky, *The History of the Russian Revolution*, translated by Max Eastman (Ann Arbor: University of Michigan Press), I 329–331, III 154–155.
2. Heinrich Heine, "Die romantische Schule," in *Sämtliche Werke* (Elster), V 217. Cf. the discussion of romanticism in Hegel's *Aesthetik*.
3. Consider *Jenseits von Gut und Böse*, chap. 8.
4. *Wilhelm Meisters Wanderjahre*, 3. Buch, 11. Kapitel.
5. *Jenseits von Gut und Böse*, No. 251; cf. *Morgenröte*, No. 205.
6. *Einführung in die Metaphysik* (Tübingen: 1953), p. 152. This book consists of a course of lectures given in 1935, but as stated in the Preface, "Errors have been removed." Cf. also the allusion on p. 36 to a recent "cleansing" of the German universities.
7. Cf. Gerhard Scholem, "Politik der Mystik. Zu Isaac Breuer's 'Neuem Kusari,'" *Juedische Rundschau*, No. 57 (1934).
8. Cf. Yehezkel Kaufmann, *The Religion of Israel*, translated and abridged by Moshe Greenberg (Chicago: University of Chicago Press, 1960), pp. 2, 233–234.
9. Maimonides, *Mishneh Torah*, H. teshubah VI 3.
10. Achad ha-Am in his essay "External Freedom and Internal Servitude."
11. Cf. Spinoza, *Theologico-political Treatise*, praef. (sect. 7 Bruder).
12. *Théodicée*, Discours de la Conformité de la foi avec la raison, sect. 3, and Vergil, *Georgica*, IV 86–87. The poet speaks of the battle between two rival queens for the rule of a single beehive. The philosopher seems to think of the question whether philosophy or revelation ought to be the queen.
13. Cf. Franz Rosenzweig, *Kleinere Schriften* (Berlin: Schocken, 1937), pp. 354–398.
14. On the relation between Rosenzweig's and Heidegger's thought, see Karl Löwith, *Gesammelte Abhandlungen* (Stuttgart: 1960), pp. 68–92.
15. Rosenzweig, *op. cit.*, pp. 380, 387.
16. *Eclipse of God* (New York: 1952), p. 97; cf. the German original, *Gottesfinsternis*

(Zürich: 1953), pp. 87–88. I did not attempt to bring the translation somewhat closer to Heidegger's German statement which, incidentally, is not quite literally quoted by Buber. Cf. Heidegger, *Nietzsche*, II 320.

17. Hermann Cohen, *Ethik des reinen Willens*, 4th ed., p. 422: "Der Prophet hat gut reden: Himmel und Erde mögen vergehen; er denkt sie in seinem Felsen, den ihm Gott bildet, wohlgegründet."

18. *Eclipse of God*, p. 81; *Gottesfinsternis*, p. 71. I believe that the translator made a mistake in rendering "Führung einer Welt" by "Conduct of the world," and I changed his translation accordingly, but I do not know whether I am right; it does not appear from the Preface that Buber has approved the translation.

19. Cf. the reasoning with which Wellhausen justifies his athetesis of Amos 9:13–15: "Roses and lavender instead of blood and iron." *Skizzen und Vorarbeiten* (Berlin: 1893), V 94.

20. *Der Satz vom Grund*, p. 142; *Was heisst Denken?* pp. 32 ff.

21. *Gottesfinsternis*, pp. 143, 159–161; *Eclipse of God*, pp. 154, 173–175. Cf. Rosenzweig, *op. cit.*, pp. 192, 530. Cf. above all the thorough discussion of this theme by Gershom Scholem, *Zur Kabbala und ihrer Symbolik* (Zürich: 1960), chaps. 1, 2.

22. Cf. *Gottesfinsternis*, p. 34 with pp. 96–97 and 117 or *Eclipse of God*, pp. 39–40 with pp. 106 and 127.

23. Heidegger, *Sein und Zeit*, sect. 57. Consider C. F. Meyer's *Die Versuchung des Pescara*.

24. Cf. *Fröhliche Wissenschaft*, No. 343.

25. *Jenseits*, Nos. 45, 224; *Götzen-Dämmerung*, "Die 'Vernunft' in der Philosophie," Nos. 1–2.

26. Letter to Overbeck of February 23, 1887. Cf. *Jenseits*, No. 60; *Genealogie der Moral*, I No. 7, III Nos. 23, 28 beginning; Nietzsche, *Werke* (Schlechta), III 422.

27. *Fröhliche Wissenschaft*, No. 344; *Jenseits*, No. 227; *Genealogie der Moral* III No. 27.

28. *Jenseits* I; *Fröhliche Wissenschaft*, Nos. 347, 377. Thomas Aquinas *S.th.* 1 q. 1. a. 4. and 2 2 q. 1. a. 1.

29. *Sein und Zeit*, pp. 48–49, 190 n. 1, 229–230, 249 n. 1.

30. *Kleinere Schriften*, pp. 31–32, 111, 281–282, 374, 379, 382, 391, 392.

31. *Op. cit.*, pp. 108–109, 114, 116–117, 119, 155–156.

32. Nietzsche, *Also Sprach Zarathustra*, "Of Thousand Goals and One."

33. Cf. also Kant, *Die Religion innerhalb der Grenzen* (Kehrbach), p. 43.

34. *Kleinere Schriften*, p. 154; *Briefe* (Berlin: Schocken, 1935), p. 520.

35. *Ethics*, V prop. 25 and prop. 36 schol.; cf. *Tr. theol.-pol.* VI sect. 23. Cf. Goethe's letter to F. H. Jacobi of May 5, 1786.

36. "Spinoza über Staat und Religion, Judentum und Christentum," in *Hermann Cohens Jüdische Schriften* (Bruno Strauss), III 290–372; "Ein ungedruckter Vortrag Hermann Cohens über Spinozas Verhältnis zum Judentum," eingeleitet von Franz Rosenzweig, *Festgabe zum zehnjährigen Bestehen der Akademie für die Wissenschaft des Judentums, 1919–1929*, pp. 42–68. Cf. Ernst Simon, "Zu Hermann Cohens Spinoza-Auffassung," *Monatsschrift für Geschichte und Wissenschaft des Judentums* (1935), pp. 181–194.

37. *Jüdische Schriften*, pp. 293, 320, 325–326, 329–331, 343, 358, 360; *Festgabe*, pp. 47–50, 57, 61–64.

38. *Jüdische Schriften*, pp. 299, 306–309, 329, 360–362.

39. *Ibid.*, pp. 333, 361, 363–364, 368, 371; *Festgabe*, p. 59.

40. *Ibid.*, pp. 46, 47, 49–50; *Jüdische Schriften*, p. 344.

41. *Ibid.*, pp. 317–321, 323, 337–338.

42. *Ibid.*, p. 367; *Festgabe*, p. 56. Cf. *Tr. theol.-pol.* I sect. 35 and 37 with the titles of *Ethics* I and II (cf. *Cogitata Metaphysica* II 12) and V 36 cor.

43. *Tr.* XII 19, 24, 37; XIII 23; XIV 6, 22–29, 34–36; XX 22, 40; *Tr. pol.* VIII 46. Cf. especially *Tr.* XII 3 where Spinoza takes the side of the Pharisees against the Sadducees. The contrast of *Tr.* XIV with Hobbes's *Leviathan*, chap. 43, is most revealing.

44. *Tr.* V 7–9.

45. *Ibid.*, V 13, 15, 30–31; XVII 95–102; XIX 13–17.

46. Cohen, *Jüdische Schriften*, III 333.

47. *Ibid.*

48. Cohen, *Kants Begründung der Ethik*, 2d ed., p. 490, speaks of the "gewagte Spiel" of Kant in his *Die Religion innerhalb der Grenzen der blossen Vernunft*, a work according to Cohen rich in "ambiguities and inner contradictions."

49. *Ethik*, pp. 61, 64, 94, 439–458, 468–470, 606. Cf. *Kants Begründung der Ethik*, 2d ed., pp. 356–357.

50. Spinoza, *Tr. pol.* I 2. Cohen, *Ethik*, pp. 64, 269, 272, 285–286, 378, 384–386; *Kants Begründung der Ethik*, pp. 394–406, 454. Cf., however, Hegel, *Rechtsphilosophie*, sect. 94 ff.

51. *Pirke Abot*, III 2.

52. *Kants Begründung der Ethik*, pp. 309, 430, 431, 439, 446, 452, 511, 544–545, 554.

53. *Festgabe*, p. 44 (*Kleinere Schriften*, p. 355).

54. *Jüdische Schriften*, II 265–267. Cf. *Tr.* III 25, 33, 34, for example, with Rashi on Isaiah 19:25, Jeremiah 1:5, and Malachi 1:10–11 and Kimhi on Isaiah 48:17.

55. *Festgabe*, pp. 64–67; *Jüdische Schriften*, III 345–351. Cf. *Tr.* V 47–48.

56. Misreading his authority or Caro, Cohen erroneously asserts that Caro declares the reading "but to the wise ones" to be the correct reading.

57. Cf. also Manasse ben Israel, *Conciliator* (Frankfort: 1633), *ad* Deut. q. 2. (p. 221).

58. In one of the passages (Edut XI 10) Maimonides says that the pious idolators have a share in the world to come; but how do we know that he does not mean by a pious idolator an idolator who has forsworn idolatry (cf. Issure Biah XIV 7) on the ground that idolatry is forbidden to all men by divine revelation? In the other passage (Teshubah III 5) he merely says that the pious Gentiles have a share in the world to come; the sequel (III 6 ff., see especially 14) could seem to show that the pious Gentile is supposed to believe in the revealed character of the Torah.

59. *Jüdische Schriften*, III 240.

60. *Guide*, III 29 end; Aristotle, *Metaphysics*, 1003a33 ff.

61. Cf. M. T. H. Yesodei ha-Torah I 1.

62. Cohen, *Die Religion der Vernunft aus den Quellen des Judentums*, p. 205.

63. *Festgabe*, p. 53; *Jüdische Schriften*, III 365; cf. II 257.

64. *Ibid.*, pp. 335–336; *Tr.* IV 17 (cf. 9–16) and 21.

65. *Jüdische Schriften*, III 351; *Festgabe* 50–54.

66. Comments on *Der Begriff des Politischen* by Carl Schmitt.

10 / Perspectives on the Good Society

At the request of Professor Rylaarsdam I attended a Jewish-Protestant Colloquium sponsored by the Divinity School of the University of Chicago and the Anti-Defamation League of B'nai B'rith. I attended the Colloquium as an observer with the understanding that I would write a report about it. I am a Jew, but I was not meant to write the report as a Jew, but as an observer, an impartial and friendly observer, or as a social scientist, for the social scientist is supposed to be particularly concerned with every effort directed toward the good society. This concern was the common ground of the participants and the observer, for the Colloquium was based on the premise that in spite of their profound disagreements Jews and Protestants can be united in their concern for the good society and in their effort to bring it about or to secure it.

The Colloquium consisted of two parts: of three discussion sessions and two meal sessions. The discussion sessions dealt with (1) "Common Ground and Difference," (2) "Faith and Action," (3) "Needs and Justice"; they descended from the question regarding the highest principles to the question regarding the most important social action here and now; at each of these sessions a Protestant and a Jew spoke. The speaker at the luncheon session was a Protestant, and the speaker at the dinner session was a Jew; the meal sessions may be said to have been devoted to the situation which has rendered possible a Jewish-Protestant Colloquium about the perspectives on the good society. Since not indeed the highest principles by themselves, but the manner in which they are approached or come to light, depends decisively on the given situation, it will be best to speak first of the meal sessions.

At the luncheon session Professor Nathan A. Scott, Jr. (Professor of Theology in Literature, Divinity School, University of Chicago), spoke of "Society and the Self in Recent American Literature." He concentrated on the American novel of the time following World War II since the novel enjoys a particularly high prestige in present-day America. Above all, the contemporary American novel—especially if contrasted with the contemporary British novel—shows how much Judaism and Christianity are embattled in present-day America. According to Mr. Scott, this kind of literature preaches up the radical divorce of the self from contemporary society or the existence without roots. By confining itself "to the narrow enclave of the self," recent American fiction has compelled itself to produce—apart from very few exceptions—nothing but "pale and bloodless ghosts." Since it does not see human beings in the light of the biblical faith in creation, it does not see them with humility and charity: the individual without history and hence authenticity creates beings without history and hence authenticity. Of this literature it has been claimed that it corresponds to the "post-Christian" character of our world. Mr. Scott rejected this claim with contempt. If I understood him correctly, in his view it is not the non-Christian character of our world, but the non-Christian or non-Jewish character of the writers concerned, which is responsible for their sterility. I cannot comment on the literature in question since I do not know it. Yet living in this country at this time in constant contact with young Americans who are compelled to face and to resist that literature, I cannot help having some familiarity with the moral phenomenon of which the contemporary American novel as characterized by Mr. Scott seems to be an expression if not a cause.

Not a few people who have come to despair of the possibility of a decent secularist society, without having been induced by their despair to question secularism as such, escape into the self and into art. The "self" is obviously a descendant of the soul; that is, it is not the soul. The soul may be responsible for its being good or bad, but it is not responsible for its being a soul; of the self, on the other hand, it is not certain whether it is not a self by virtue of its own effort. The soul is a part of an order which does not originate in the soul; of the self it is not certain whether it is a part of an order which does not originate in the self. Surely the self as understood by the people in question is sovereign or does not defer to anything higher than itself; yet it is no longer exhilarated by the sense of its sovereignty, but rather oppressed by it, not to say in a state of despair. One may say that the self putting its trust in itself and therefore in man is cursed (Jer. 17:5–8). It is an unwilling witness to the biblical faith. Mr. Scott was right in rejecting the view that our world is "irredeemably post-Christian" on the ground that "the Holy Spirit bloweth where it listeth," but I believe that one should admit the fact that the unbelief in question is in no sense pagan, but shows at every point that it is the unbelief of men who or whose parents were Christians or Jews. They are haunted men. Deferring to nothing higher than their selves, they lack guidance. They lack thought and discipline. Instead they have what they call sincerity. Whether sincerity as they understand it is necessary must be left open until one knows whether sincerity is inseparable from shamelessness; sincerity is surely not sufficient; it fulfills itself completely in shrill and ugly screams, and such screams are not works of art. "Life is a tale told by an idiot" is a part of a work of art, for life is such a tale only for him who has violated the law of life, the law to which life is subject. It is true that the message of the writers in question is not that of Macbeth. They scream that life is gutter. But one cannot sense that life is gutter if one has not sensed purity in the first place, and of this which is by nature sensed first, they say nothing, they convey nothing. The self which is not deferential is an absurdity. Their screams are accusations hurled against "society"; they are not appeals to human beings uttered in a spirit of fraternal correction; these accusers believe themselves to be beyond the reach of accusation; their selves constitute themselves by the accusation; the self as they understand it is nothing but the accusation or the scream. Every accusation presupposes a law; accusations of the kind voiced by them would require a holy law; but of this they appear to be wholly unconscious. Their screams remind one of the utterances of the damned in hell; they themselves belong to hell. But hell is for them not society as such, but "life in the United States in 1963." Their despair is due to their having believed in the first place that life in the United States in 1963 is heaven or could be heaven or ought to be heaven. They condemn contemporary American society; their selves constitute themselves by this condemnation; they are nothing but this condemnation or rejection—a condemnation not based on any law; they belong to this society as completely as their twin, the organization man; their only difference from the latter is, or seems to be, that they are miserable and obsessed.

The speaker at the dinner session, Mr. Dore Schary (Anti-Defamation League of B'nai B'rith), agreed with Mr. Scott in implicitly suggesting that contemporary America is fundamentally healthy, that is, possesses within itself the remedies for the ills from which it suffers, and that this fundamental health is connected with its being not purely secularist and its not meaning to be it. The society attacked by the literary avant-gardists is held together, or is what it is, by the dedication to freedom in the sense that the freedom and dignity of anyone is supposed to require the freedom and dignity of everyone. According to Mr. Schary, democracy is not primarily the rule of the majority, but recognition of the dignity of the individual, that is, of every individual in his individuality. Only a society in which everyone can be what he is or can develop his unique potentialities is truly free and truly great or excellent. What is true of the individual is true also of the groups of which society consists and in particular of the religious groups; the freedom and excellence of this country require, above all, that its citizenry belong to a variety of faiths. Why this is so appears from a consideration of the ills from which American society suffers. Those ills can be reduced to one head: the tendency toward homogeneity or conformism, that is, toward the suppression by nonpolitical means of individuality and diversity; all Americans are to be remolded in the likeness of "the typical American." American society is in danger of becoming ever more a mass society which is "informed" in the common and in the metaphysical meaning of the term by mass communication, by the mass communication industry, the most visible and audible part of which is the advertising industry. Everyone can see that the youngest girl and the oldest great-grandmother tend ever more to look alike; the natural differences of age and beauty are overlaid by the conventional identity of the ideal, formed not without the support of the cosmetics industry. It is not merely amusing to observe that whereas there is a single model of womanhood —say, the attractive young woman of twenty-one—there is a dual model of manhood which one may describe as that of the good-looking and successful junior executive on the one hand and that of the good-looking and successful senior executive on the other; in this sphere cosmetics cannot help respecting the most important natural difference: "the body is at its peak from thirty to thirty-five years of age, the soul at about forty-nine" (Aristotle, *Rhetoric*, II 14). On the whole, however, mass society succeeds amazingly well in rendering irrelevant all natural differences and therefore in particular also the racial differences: one can easily visualize a society consisting of racially different men and women each of whom dresses, has "fun," mourns, talks, feels, thinks, and is buried exactly like everyone else. It is for this reason, I suppose, that Mr. Schary found religious diversity most annoying to the lovers of homogeneity. The difference in religious faith—in dedication to what simply transcends humanity—is the obstacle par excellence to conformism.

One may well find it paradoxical that a society dedicated to the free development of each individual in his individuality should be threatened by a particularly petty kind of conformism, but the paradox disappears on reflection. It is merely a shallow hope to expect that the uninhibited "growth" of each individual to its greatest height will not lead to serious and bloody conflict. The growth must be kept within certain limits: everyone may grow to any height and in any direction provided his growth does not prevent the growth of anybody else to any height and in any direction. The limits, the right limits, are to be set by the law. But in order to fulfill this function, the lawmakers and ultimately the sovereign must possess both knowledge and good will. The sovereign must be enlightened, free from prejudice; such freedom can be expected to come from exposure to science (both natural and social) and its consequences (technology, facility of traveling, and so on). "People and ideas all over the world are increasingly accessible, and the sense of what is 'alien' grows dimmer"; the "more remarkable differences [among the races of men] tend to dissipate." Mr. Schary was, to say the least, not quite certain whether this is a pure gain. One must be grateful to science and its concomitants for the liberation from prejudice which it achieves; but, as was indicated, the same power also endangers diversity or fosters homogeneity. As for good will, democracy was originally said to be the form of government the principle of which is virtue. But it is obviously impossible to restrict the suffrage to virtuous men, men of good will, conscientious men, responsible men, or whichever expression one prefers. While in a democracy the government is made responsible to the governed in the highest degree possible—ideally the government will not have any secrets from the governed—the governed cannot be held responsible in a comparable manner: the place par excellence of sacred secrecy or privacy is not the home, which may be entered with a search warrant, but the voting booth. In the voting booth the prejudices can assert themselves without any hindrance whatever. Voting is meant to determine the character of the legal majority. The legal majority is not simply the majority, but it is not irrelevant to the legal majority how the simple majority feels. There may be a stable or permanent majority; in the United States the stable majority is "white Protestant." As a consequence there is a social hierarchy at the bottom of which are the Negroes (or colored people in general), and barely above them are the Jews. There is then a prejudice which is both constitutional and unconstitutional against Negroes and Jews. If I understood Mr. Schary correctly, the conformism against which he directed his attack has the unavowed intention either to transform all Americans into white Protestants or else to deny those Americans who are not white Protestants full equality of opportunity. Yet would not one have to say that this pressure toward conformism is not the same as that which is exerted by the communications and cosmetics industries?

Recognition of religious diversity, as Mr. Schary understood it, is not merely toleration of religions other than one's own but respect for them. The question arises as to how far that respect can be extended. "We who are religiously oriented state that there *is* God; clearer identification than that is denied us." Who are the "we"? If the "we" are Jews or Christians, Mr. Schary admits too little; if they are religious human beings as such, he admits too much. The singular "God" would seem to exclude the possibility of respect for Greek polytheism and still more of the polytheism of the Egyptians who had "a bizarre pantheon of their own . . . they invented monsters to worship." Can one respect a religion which worships monsters or, to use the biblical expression, abominations? Mr. Schary concluded the paragraph from which these quotations are taken with the remark that "all men of decency, self-respect and good will are joined in a common brotherhood." I take it that he does not deny that men who are not "religiously oriented" may be "men of decency, self-respect and good will" and that men who lack decency, self-respect, and good will and therefore refuse to join the common brotherhood do not for this reason cease to be our brothers. But under no circumstances can we be obliged to respect abominations, although it may be necessary to tolerate them.

Mr. Schary, I thought, in contradistinction to Mr. Scott, was less concerned with the truth common to Judaism and Christianity than with the virtues of diversity. But this very concern made him a defender of the religious point of view since religion rather than science is the bulwark of genuine diversity. As is shown in our age especially by the U.S.S.R., the secularist state is inclined to enforce irreligious conformism, just as in the past the religious state was inclined to enforce religious conformism. It seems that only a qualifiedly secularist, that is, a qualifiedly religious, state which respects equally religious and nonreligious people can be counted upon to contain within itself the remedy against the ill of conformism. However this may be, it is the danger caused by radical secularism in its Communist or non-Communist form which provides the incentive for such undertakings as a Protestant-Jewish Colloquium.

This is perfectly compatible with the fact that the condition of the Colloquium is the secular state. This fact was pointed out by the chairman of the session devoted to "Common Ground and Difference," Professor J. T. Petuchowski (Hebrew Union College), in his comment on the papers read by Professor J. Coert Rylaarsdam (Professor of Old Testament, Divinity School, University of Chicago) and Mr. Arthur A. Cohen (Director of Religious Publishing for Holt, Rinehart and Winston, Inc.). The secular state may be said to derive from the view that the basis of the civil order must be reason alone, and not revelation, for if revelation, that is, a particular revelation, were made that basis, one would use compulsion open or disguised in the service of faith to the detriment of the purity of faith. In other words, a Protestant-Jewish Colloquium as an *amica collatio* presupposes friendship, and friendship presupposes equality, at least civic equality of Jews and Christians; without civic equality not even the necessary civility is likely to be forthcoming. On the other hand, as Mr. Petuchowski indicated, if the secular state were self-sufficient, there would be no secure place within it for transsecular Judaism and Christianity: Judaism and Christianity must have something to say to the secular state which secularism is unable to say, and in order to be effective, the message of Judaism and the message of Christianity must be to some extent identical. It was taken for granted by all participants in the Colloquium that that message could not be the natural religion or the religion of reason which was in the past sometimes regarded as the basis of the secular state, for the religion of reason (assuming that it is possible) would tempt one to believe in the self-sufficiency of reason or to regard the specifically Jewish or Christian message as an unnecessary and peace-disturbing addition to the one thing needful, and it tends to lead toward the euthanasia of religious belief or toward "ethical culture." The common ground on which Jews and

Christians can make a friendly *collatio* to the secular state cannot be the belief in the God of the philosophers, but only the belief in the God of Abraham, Isaac, and Jacob—the God who revealed the Ten Command-ments or at any rate such commandments as are valid under all circum-stances regardless of the circumstances. That common ground was indeed not articulated in the meeting devoted to the common ground. The reason was not that that ground is trivial—in an age in which both Judaism and Christianity have been affected by existentialist ethics, it is surely not trivial—but because, as is shown by the whole history of Christian-Jewish relations, recognition of that common ground is not in any way sufficient for mutual recognition of the two faiths.

What can such recognition mean? This much: that Church and Syna-gogue recognize each the noble features of its antagonist. Such recognition was possible even during the Christian Middle Ages: while the Synagogue was presented as lowering its head in shame, its features were presented as noble. However far the mutual recognition may go in our age, it cannot but be accompanied by the certainty on the part of each of the two antag-onists that in the end the other will lower its head. Recognition of the other must remain subordinate to recognition of the truth. Even the pagan philosophers Plato and Aristotle remained friends, although each held the truth to be his greatest friend, or rather because each held the truth to be his greatest friend. The Jew may recognize that the Christian error is a blessing, a divine blessing, and the Christian may recognize that the Jewish error is a blessing, a divine blessing. Beyond this they cannot go without ceasing to be Jew or Christian.

To say the least, it was always easier for Christians to recognize the di-vine origin of Judaism than for Jews to recognize the divine origin of Christianity. On the other hand, it was easier for Jews to recognize that Christians may have a "share in the world to come" than it was for Chris-tians to recognize that Jews may be "saved." This is due to the Jewish union of the "carnal" and the "spiritual," of the "secular" and the "eternal," of the "tribal" and the "universal": the Torah which contains the promise of the eventual redemption of all children of Adam (cf. Maimonides, *Mishneh Torah* H. Melakhim XI–XII) was given to, or accepted by, Israel alone. As a consequence, it was easier for Jews to admit the divine mission of Christianity (cf. Yehuda Halevi, *Cuzari* IV 23) than it was for Christians to admit the abiding divine mission of Judaism. It is therefore not surprising that, as Mr. Rylaarsdam pointed out, the first genuine meeting of Jews and Christians should have been initiated by a Jew, Franz Rosenzweig, and that a comparable Christian response to this Jewish call should not yet have been forthcoming. Such a response, includ-ing above all the recognition of the abiding mission of Judaism, is urgently demanded in the opinion of Mr. Rylaarsdam because of what happened to the Jewish people in our lifetime: the butchery of six million Jews by

Hitler-led Germany and the establishment of the state of Israel; Jewish agony and Jewish rebirth are not adequately understandable on the basis of the traditional Christian view of Judaism. In addition, the traditional Christian judgment on the Jew is at least partly responsible for the persecution of the Jews in the Christian world and therefore, if indirectly, for Hitler Germany's action. The Christian must begin to ask himself whether he can "acknowledge that the mission of Israel did not end when his own mission began." One cannot leave matters at asserting the undeniable fact that the Jew denies and the Christian maintains that the Messiah, that Redemption, has come. Judaism says that "there is no redemption yet God has redeemed his people"; Christianity says that there is no redemption yet God has redeemed mankind in the death and resurrection of Jesus Christ. Judaism, in contradistinction to Christianity, "is concerned with the redemption of history," with redemption on this side of death, with redemption on earth: according to Judaism, the Elect One is Israel which never dies; according to Christianity, the Elect One is Jesus the Christ who died on the cross. Yet "the Christian must agree with the Jew that the world [*this* world] is unredeemed" and that "this world matters to God." The agony of the Jew and the agony of the Cross belong together; "they are aspects of the same agony." Judaism and Christianity need each other.

One may say that Mr. Rylaarsdam stated what Christianity has to learn from Judaism; he did not presume to tell the Jews what they have to learn from Christianity; he left the performance of that task to his Jewish partner. But Mr. Cohen did not perform this task. I do not think that he can be blamed for this. He did not, of course, mistake learning from Christianity for assimilation to Christianity. For instance, to move the day of rest from the seventh day of the week to the first day is an act of assimilation to Christianity which does not involve learning from Christianity. Nor did he deny, he even asserted, that Judaism and Christianity need each other; in fact, in this respect he agreed entirely with Mr. Rylaarsdam. But in the main he limited himself to reasserting vigorously the traditional Jewish position toward Christianity: there is an irreconcilable disagreement between Judaism and Christianity; Christianity depends on Judaism, and not vice versa; Christianity has to learn from Judaism; there is no Judaeo-Christian tradition; at least from Paul on, Christianity has never understood Judaism. And yet he stressed the fact that the contemporary Jew and Christian are not, and can never become again, the Jew and the Christian of old: they confront each other "no longer as dogmatic enemies, but as common seekers of the truth." He admitted, in other words, that the misunderstanding has been mutual. But he did not explain what the Jewish misunderstanding of Christianity was. He did not go beyond alluding to certain defects of Jewish Messianism at the time of Jesus and to the deplorable if excusable alliance of Judaism with secularist, anti-Christian movements. Why did he fail to make clear what Judaism may have to learn from Christianity? Are Jews still in greater danger to abandon Judaism in favor of Christianity than Christians are to abandon Christianity in favor of Judaism? Is there still a greater worldly premium on being a Christian than on being a Jew? Or is it obvious to everyone what the Jews have learned from Christianity since it is obvious what the Jews have learned from modernity and it is obvious that modernity is secularized Christianity? But is modernity in fact secularized Christianity? Mr. Cohen seemed to doubt this. However this may be, he surely referred to the Jew's "pain of his historical encounter with Christendom."

Which Jew can indeed forget that pain? But confronted by the fact that the most noble Christians of our age have shown sincere repentance and sincerely offer us peace, we Jews must not regard Christendom as if it were Amalek; we must even cease to regard it as Edom. Above all, *noblesse oblige*. Mr. Cohen rightly rejected the common Christian notion of Jewish "pharisaism": no Jew who ever took the Torah seriously could be self-righteous, or believe that he could redeem himself from sin by the fulfillment of the Law, or underestimate the power of sin over him. The true "Pharisee" in the Christian sense is not the Pharisee proper, but Aristotle's perfect gentleman who is not ashamed of anything or does not regret or repent anything he has done because he always does what is right or proper. Mr. Cohen went beyond this. He demanded that the Christian view of the power and the depth of sin be mitigated in the light of "a realistic humanism," and he asserted that that humanism is found in the Jewish Bible. Isaiah's words in 6:5–7 and David's prayer in Psalm 51:12 sound "realistic" enough; they are, however, hardly "humanistic." Similar considerations apply to Mr. Cohen's remark about Pauline theology as "a theology for disappointment." I had thought that the days of historicist "debunking" had gone. Yet I cannot but agree with his concluding sentence: "What more has Israel to offer the world than eternal patience?" This sentence calls indeed for a long commentary. One sentence must here suffice: what is called here "eternal patience" is that fortitude in suffering, now despised as "ghetto mentality" by shallow people who have surrendered wholeheartedly to the modern world or who lack the intelligence to consider that a secession from this world might again become necessary for Jews and even for Christians.

If I understood him correctly, Mr. John Wild (Professor of Philosophy, Northwestern University) introduced the meeting devoted to "Faith and Action" with the observation that while Judaism and Christianity agree in believing that faith must issue in action, Christianity has sometimes succumbed to the Greek, intellectualist understanding of faith and accordingly severed or almost severed the connection between faith and action. M. Paul Ricœur (Professor of Philosophy, Sorbonne), presenting "a Christian view" of faith and action, started from the facts that the opposition between the contemplative life and the active life stems from Greek philosophy and is wholly alien to Judaism and that in this respect Christianity is simply the heir to Judaism. One may agree with M. Ricœur while admitting that there is some evidence supporting the view that Greek philosophy did not as such assert that opposition. It suffices to mention the name of the citizen-philosopher Socrates. But perhaps one will be compelled eventually to say that his being a citizen culminated in his transcending the city, not only the city of Athens but even the best city, in speech, as well as that the only comprehensive and effective reply to the claim of contemplation to supremacy is supplied by the Bible. Be this as it may, M. Ricœur was chiefly concerned with the question as to whether the doctrines distinguishing Christianity from Judaism do not lead again to the depreciation of action. His answer was in the negative. He conveyed to me the impression that the doctrine of original sin, for instance, is "the speculative expression" alien to Judaism of an experience which is not alien to Judaism. Differently stated, the Christian doctrine of justification by faith was perhaps "present from the beginning in the Bible"; the Jewish saying that everything is in the hands of God except fear of God would contradict the doctrine of justification by faith only if it were meant, as it surely is not meant, to arouse or confirm "any desire to draw glory" over against God from one's fearing God. M. Ricœur asserted that Christianity sometimes succumbed to "Hellenistic" ways of understanding the relation of faith and action by divorcing faith from action, especially from social action, or by denying that there is any connection between the salvation of the individual and "historical redemption," or by being unconcerned with the evil embodied in "impersonal institutions" (the state, property, and culture) as distinguished from sin proper; yet in his view this is simply a "reactionary conception," incompatible with original Christianity. At any rate, there is no serious difference in this respect between Christianity and Judaism: "it is always its Jewish memory that guards (Christianity) against its own deviations."

Mr. Nahum N. Glatzer (Professor of Jewish History, Brandeis University) presented "a Jewish view of faith and action." He gave a comprehensive survey of Jewish thought on this subject from the days of the Bible down to the present. According to what one may call the classic Jewish view, "knowledge of God," study, faith, learning, or wisdom both presupposes and issues in righteous action or active piety or "fear of heaven," but in such a way that what counts is action. The basis of this view appeared to be the talmudic theologoumenon that by his right or pious action man becomes "a participant with God in the work of creation": whereas regarding revelation and redemption, man is merely a recipient; regarding creation, or rather regarding the continuity of creation, "man is an active partner" of God. The Jewish view of faith and action was obscured in different ways and for different reasons in the Middle Ages on the one hand and in modern times on the other. Owing to their subjugation many

medieval Jews came to believe that "the world matters little; the rectifica-
tion of its ills and, finally, its redemption, would come in God's good
time." As a consequence of the emancipation of the Jews in the nineteenth
century, an important part of Jewish opinion came to identify social and
other progress with the process of redemption; that which transcends progress and action, that with which faith is concerned, tended to be forgotten.
Modern secularism believed that it would put an end to the Jewish-
Christian antagonism by depriving Judaism and Christianity of their
raisons d'être; its manifest failure which affects equally Jews, Christians,
and nonbelievers calls for a community of seeking and acting of both Jews
and Christians—a community which has originally been rendered possible
by secularism. The failure of secularism shows itself, for instance, in the
ever increasing cleavage between science and humanism. In Mr. Glatzer's
view that gulf cannot be bridged by a "synthesis" of science and humanism because science is "neutralist" and humanism is "traditionalist":
the required "redefinition of the image of man" is beyond the competence of either or both, not in spite but because of the fact that it
must be a redefinition of man as created in the image of God. "The
hybris of scientism" cannot be overcome with the help of a humanism
which is inspired by the belief in man as a creator. Over against scientism and humanism Judaism and Christianity are at one.

The greatest divisive power in the past was revealed religion. Even today,
as we have been led to see by reflecting on one of the papers read at the
Colloquium, religious diversity is the obstacle par excellence to conformism
in this country. The differences at any rate between Judaism and Christianity do not preclude the availability of a common ground. What divides the
human race today in the most effective manner is, however, the antagonism between the liberal West and the Communist East. Even in this case
there exists, as Mr. Gibson Winter (Divinity School, University of Chicago) pointed out in his paper on "National Identity and National Purpose," a "common ground": "their common ground is the limit set upon
their opposition by [their] nuclear power." Thermonuclear war being
manifestly an act of madness, the common ground must become the basis
of a dialogue—a dialogue to be conducted, not in ideological terms, but
with a view to the duties of this country faced by the world-wide "struggle
against hunger and the aspiration for human dignity"; this country must
cease to "endorse a status quo position in a hungry world." The dialogue
required is then in the first place a dialogue, not with Soviet Russia, but
with the "have-nots" within the U.S.A. and without. As for the dialogue
with the U.S.S.R., it requires that the "purpose and interest" of "our enemies" be respected and, above all, that the "apocalyptic framework" for
the dialogue be recognized: in the spirit of Deuteronomy 30:19, we must
choose life—"a future in justice and community"—in the certainty that
the alternative choice leads to thermonuclear annihilation as God's judg-

ment. What will enable us to continue the dialogue with the U.S.S.R. in spite of all its hazards is faith, not, of course, in the good will of the Soviet rulers, but in God. It goes without saying that no such faith can be expected from the Soviet rulers: unilateral disarmament is out of the question. Faith equally forbids preventive war. On the other hand one cannot simply assert that this country must not under any circumstances initiate the use of nuclear weapons. "The most difficult problem in the use of nuclear power," however, concerns retaliation. "Retaliation after a destructive attack becomes simply vengeance" and seems therefore to be incompatible with Christian ethics: "to choose the life of others over our own— this is the message of the Cross." Yet "the possibility of retaliation is the power which restrains aggression."

Two comments on this proposal seem to be appropriate. The possibility of retaliation would lose much of its restraining power if the enemy knew that a second strike force which survived his successful attack would never be used against him; hence a decision allegedly demanded by faith must remain the most closely guarded secret; in other words, the tongue must pronounce the opposite of what the heart thinks. Second, by saving the lives of the Soviet people in the contingency under consideration, one would surrender all the have-not nations to Soviet rule and thus deprive them for all the foreseeable future of the possibility to be nonatheistic nations or, more generally stated, to have a future of their own, neither Russian nor American; in other words, Mr. Winter's proposal is based on a tacit claim to know what God alone can know. Considerations like these may explain the fact deplored by him that "the institutional weight of our religious traditions [viz. Christian and Jewish] falls . . . on the conservative side in the struggle which separates the world." At any rate there seems to be a tension between his plea for universal prosperity and freedom and his remark that "the grave danger for Judaism at this moment is the prosperity which distracts her from [her] vocation. . . . External oppression can fortify the [chosen] people."

The Jewish partner of Mr. Winter, Mr. Nathan Glazer (Housing and Financing Agency, Washington, D.C.), spoke on "The Shape of the Good Society." He did not speak from a distinctly Jewish point of view. He dealt with the most successful revolution of our age, "the organizational revolution, or the scientific revolution," and its implications. Through this revolution the gap between "the intellectuals," "the radical and liberal critics," on the one hand and the organizations "representing the status quo" has been closed or at least very much narrowed. The reason was that the intellectuals proved to possess "new techniques for making organizations more efficient." One might say that in proportion as the scientists drew all conclusions from their basic premise, which is the assertion that science is limited to "factual" assertions as distinguished from "value" assertions, they lost the right to be radical critics of institutions and became willing servants of any institutions. Yet, strangely, the co-operation of scientists and men of affairs has affected the "values" of the latter: could there be a pre-established harmony between the allegedly value-free science and the liberal values? Be this as it may, the question which troubled Mr. Glazer was whether the society rendered possible by the co-operation of the scientists and the managers—the society guaranteeing to everyone "simple justice and simple freedom"—can be regarded as the good society: "both conservatives or reactionaries, on the one hand, and intellectuals and radicals and anarchists on the other, often come together in opposition to what we might call establishment Liberalism." Both the reactionary and the intellectual question the claim of the welfare state—"the whole organization, the machine for doing good"—to be the good society. Mr. Glazer sees only one way out: "to improve the organizations" by setting up "the great organization" or "the big organization" or "the determining center of allocation" which is enabled to direct all other organizations because it "will have far more information and will make much better diagnoses" than anyone else can. Hence it will be "the good big society." Alongside it, Mr. Glazer predicted "there will be developing . . . good small societies," composed "of reactionaries and anarchists and radical intellectuals." But he was not sure whether "the organization will be tolerant enough to let them be" nor whether "they will be clever enough to evade it." Faced with the grim prospect of universal philistinism, we are forced to wonder whether, according to Mr. Glazer, Judaism and Christianity belong on the side of the big organization or on that of the anarchists. I believe that Jews and Christians would have to choose anarchism or secession—a kind of secession radically different from that castigated by Mr. Scott. The reason why I believe this is Exodus 13:17: "And it came to pass, when Pharaoh had let the people go, that God led them not through the way of the land of the Philistines, although that was near." The land of the Philistines is perhaps nearer today than it ever was. The meaning which we ascribe to the scriptural verse may not be its literal meaning; it may nevertheless be its true meaning. For, as Jews and Christians agree, the literal meaning isolated from everything else "killeth." Pharisaic rabbinical Judaism always held that the written Torah must be understood in the light of the oral or unwritten Torah, and the most profound reason for this is that the most profound truth cannot be written and not even said: what Israel heard at Sinai from God Himself "was nothing but that [inaudible] *Aleph* with which in the Hebrew text of the Bible the First Commandment begins" (Gershom Scholem, *Zur Kabbala und ihrer Symbolik* [Zürich: 1960], 47).

Acknowledgments

"What Is Liberal Education?" was an address delivered at the tenth annual graduation exercises of the Basic Program of Liberal Education for Adults, University College, the University of Chicago, on June 6, 1959; it was printed by the University of Chicago Press and reprinted in C. Scott Fletcher, ed., *Education for Social Responsibility* (New York: Norton, 1961), pp. 43–51.

"Liberal Education and Responsibility" is reprinted from C. Scott Fletcher, ed., *Education: The Challenge Ahead* (New York: Norton, 1962), pp. 49–70. Copyright 1962 by the American Foundation for Continuing Education.

"The Liberalism of Classical Political Philosophy" is reprinted from *Review of Metaphysics*, XII, No. 3 (March 1959), 390–439.

"How To Begin To Study *The Guide of the Perplexed*" is reprinted from the introductory essay to Moses Maimonides, *The Guide of the Perplexed* (Chicago: University of Chicago Press, 1963), pp. xi–lvi.

"Marsilius of Padua" is reprinted from Leo Strauss and Joseph Cropsey, eds., *History of Political Philosophy* (Chicago: Rand McNally, 1963), pp. 227–246.

"An Epilogue" is reprinted from Herbert J. Storing, ed., *Essays on the Scientific Study of Politics* (New York: Holt, Rinehart and Winston, 1962), pp. 305–327. Copyright © 1962 by Holt, Rinehart and Winston, Inc. Reprinted by permission of Holt, Rinehart and Winston, Inc.

"Preface to *Spinoza's Critique of Religion*" is reprinted from Leo Strauss, *Spinoza's Critique of Religion* (New York: Schocken Books, 1965). Copyright 1965 by Schocken Books, Inc.

"Perspectives on the Good Society" is reprinted from *Criterion: A Publication of the Divinity School of the University of Chicago*, II, No. 3 (Summer 1963), 2–9.

273

Index of Names